A STOVALL MUSEUM PUBLICATION

Reptiles of Oklahoma

GEORGE
MIKSCH
SUTTON

Crotaphytus collaris collaris, the Eastern Collared Lizard, also known as the "Mountain Boomer," is the official reptile of the state of Oklahoma.

Reptiles of Oklahoma
by Robert G. Webb

NORMAN

UNIVERSITY OF OKLAHOMA PRESS

Reptiles of Oklahoma is published by the University of Oklahoma Press for the Stovall Museum, University of Oklahoma, Norman. Other Stovall Museum Publications are:

1 *Oklahoma Archaeology: An Annotated Bibliography*, by Robert E. Bell, available in cloth and paper.

INTERNATIONAL STANDARD BOOK NUMBER: 0–8061–0892–4 (cloth), 0–8061–0896–7 (paper)

LIBRARY OF CONGRESS CATALOG CARD NUMBER: 69–16716

Dedicated to
ARTHUR IRVING ORTENBURGER

Born in Detroit, Michigan, June 8, 1898, Arthur Ortenburger received his B.S. and M.S. from the University of Michigan and his Ph.D. from the same school in 1925. During 1922 and 1923, he was associated with Gladwyn Kingsley Noble as assistant curator of herpetology at The American Museum of Natural History; in July and August of 1923 he headed a museum-sponsored field expedition to Arizona, principally to study the Gila monster (*Heloderma*). In 1924 he came to the University of Oklahoma, where he remained until his retirement in 1958; he was chairman of the zoology department from 1942 to 1945. In 1956 he took a year's sabbatical leave to observe whales and study whale embryology in British Columbia. His postretirement years were spent on Galiano Island off the coast of British Columbia, where he built a home near the edge of a thirty-foot cliff above the sea and continued his observations on whales. Dr. Ortenburger died on Galiano Island, after a brief illness, on November 18, 1961.

Dr. Ortenburger is best known for his Ph.D. dissertation, published in 1928—a monographic treatment of the American whip snakes and racers (genera *Masticophis* and *Coluber*). He was especially mindful of the importance of the hemipenes as an aid in classification, and he devised a method of injecting them with wax so that they could be stored for permanent study. Dr. Ortenburger's most active period of research was from 1923 to 1930, his principal interest being herpetology, but he was almost equally interested in ichthyology. During this period, his efforts in establishing the herpetological collections at the University of Oklahoma marked him as the state's leading figure in herpetology—he may well be regarded as the Father of Oklahoma Herpetology.

Preface

This book had its beginning in 1952, when a survey of Oklahoma reptiles served as my dissertation for the degree of Master of Science at the University of Oklahoma. Because Dr. Ortenburger's illustrated keys to lizards and snakes (1927b; 1930b) had been so successful, he suggested that we prepare for use by the layman an up-to-date key to the turtles, lizards, and snakes, and include maps showing the distribution of each species. The finished work, entitled *A Guide to the Reptiles of Oklahoma*, was submitted for publication and its production was anticipated by Conant (1958:312), in whose work the above title appears in a bibliography with the notation "In press." Unfortunately, however, fiscal problems prevented publication, and the manuscript was returned to me in early 1962. Meanwhile, Dr. Ortenburger had died in late 1961. Since I had been working in the intervening years on a more informative study, intended as a supplement to the above-mentioned guide, I decided to combine the contents of both projects: the result is *Reptiles of Oklahoma*.

I am most grateful to Dr. Harold A. Dundee, who first aroused my interest in herpetology during our association at the University of Oklahoma. For many years he has been preparing a report on the snakes of the state, and he has unselfishly relinquished many of his observations for inclusion in this book. Dr. Hobart M. Smith and the late Mr. C. B. Perkins offered helpful suggestions when I was preparing the "Keys to Reptiles of Oklahoma." Gratitude is also expressed to Mr. Thomas J. Jones of the Jones Oil Company, Duncan, Oklahoma, who provided a scholarship fund, administered by the University of Oklahoma Foundation, for study at the University of Oklahoma

Biological Station in the summer of 1951; to Dr. William T. Penfound for helpful suggestions about the section on "Faunal Regions of Reptiles in Oklahoma"; to Drs. Carl D. Riggs and Charles C. Carpenter for numerous courtesies and information and for special interest in this work; and to the following authors for the use of illustrations from their publications: W. J. Breckenridge (1944), L. M. Klauber (1940), Hobart Smith (1950), and Philip Smith (1961). Many of the illustrations that appeared in Ortenburger's keys to lizards and snakes (1930b) are still available, and I have used some of them to illustrate the "Keys to Reptiles of Oklahoma" (pp. 63–94).

In addition, others that aided me in field work, permitted me to examine specimens in their care, provided information about specimens or localities, criticized parts of the manuscript, or helped in other capacities include Kraig K. Adler, Neil D. Richmond, Edmond V. Malnate, Roger Conant, Ernest E. Williams, Charles F. Walker, Robert F. Inger, Donald W. Tinkle, James R. Dixon, Ralph W. Axtell, Clarence J. McCoy, Jr., Morgan Sisk, Bryan P. Glass, William A. Carter, Milton Curd, John R. Preston, Richard L. Lardie, Harold E. Laughlin, Dwight R. Platt, Frank B. McMurray, Walter W. Dalquest, W. Howard McCarley, Doris M. Cochran, Richard G. Zweifel, and Thomas Swearingen.

Finally, I am grateful to Rosa V. Dominguez for the final typing of the manuscript, to Dr. George M. Sutton for his painting of *Crotaphytus collaris collaris*, the Oklahoma state reptile, the frontispiece of this book, and to Dr. J. Keever Greer, Director of the Stovall Museum of Science and History at the University of Oklahoma, for his interest in this work and his initiative in providing for its publication.

Contents

Reptiles of Oklahoma

Introduction

The living reptiles of Oklahoma, about 95 different kinds, include turtles, lizards, snakes, and the American alligator, which is only occasionally seen in extreme southeastern Oklahoma. Unfortunately, many snakes are needlessly killed because of man's exaggerated fear of them, because they are thought to be poisonous, or because their food (both fish and fowl) is of benefit to man. Although some snakes are poisonous, most snakes in Oklahoma are harmless; of the nonpoisonous kinds, some are vicious and bite when provoked, whereas others are gentle and never attempt to bite. Some snakes do eat fish and small birds and their eggs occasionally, and would be harmful in fish hatcheries or crowded poultry farms. Under natural conditions, however, snakes are decidedly beneficial. Countless studies have stressed their economic importance in destroying rats, mice, gophers, and other harmful rodents, as well as injurious insects. In the long run, snakes certainly do more good than harm.

Aquatic turtles are quite unpopular among fishermen, who kill them because of the mistaken belief that they are harmful to fish or waterfowl populations. The common snapping turtle normally eats small, predominantly nongame fish, and occasionally waterfowl, but even in crowded waterfowl refuges during breeding seasons those foods never constitute much of their diet, the bulk of which is plant food (Coulter, 1957). Soft-shelled turtles, and especially red-eared turtles, are abundant and are often condemned as detrimental to fish populations. They probably would be if they could catch healthy fish; instead, these turtles tend to promote better fishing by removing the slow-moving, sickly, and decrepit fish. They have probably earned their bad reputation among fishermen because they eat fish enmeshed in gill nets, caught on hooks, or confined in fyke nets, which are therefore easy prey. In general, the food of turtles consists mostly of vegetation, insects, crawfish, and snails. Some aquatic turtles may compete with game fishes for food; others eat carrion and are useful as scavengers. In crowded ponds of fish hatcheries, it is desirable to remove turtles, but under natural conditions no kind of turtle poses any special threat to fish management (Lagler, 1943; 1945:147; Moss, 1955). Turtle eradication programs (Anon. 1950a, 1955c) are impractical, involving wasted time, effort, and expense. Furthermore, the destruction of predators on fish tends to promote overpopulation, resulting in large numbers of stunted fish.

The only poisonous reptiles recorded in Oklahoma are eight snakes—five kinds of rattlesnakes, two kinds of copperheads, and the cottonmouth, or water moccasin. One or another kind of poisonous snake may be found any place in Oklahoma. The coral snake, also poisonous, has not been recorded in the state but is expected to occur in southeastern Oklahoma. None of the lizards in Oklahoma is poisonous; in fact, the only poisonous lizards in the world are the Gila monsters and the related Mexican beaded lizards of the southwestern United States and the west coast of Mexico. Many harmless snakes are considered poisonous, especially the large, unfriendly water snakes (genus *Natrix*), which are commonly called "moccasins," and certain smaller snakes that are marked with red and consequently mistaken for coral snakes. Unfortunately, the characters that distinguish harmless and poisonous snakes are not of much help unless the snake is dead and can be examined closely.

This book is intended for use by advanced students of herpetology (the study of amphibians and reptiles), as well as by persons with little technical knowledge of the field. Emphasis is on the identification and distribution of each species. My main purpose in writing this book has been to provide a basis for

4

future studies of Oklahoma reptiles. It is designed to have four functions—to provide an up-to-date account of the kinds of reptiles living in Oklahoma, to indicate what is known of their distribution and their relation to the faunal regions in the state, to provide methods for identifying reptiles from Oklahoma, and to disclose some taxonomic problems that require further study.

The information fills a geographical gap in that it supplements corresponding data in the herpetological accounts of the adjacent states of Missouri (Anderson, 1965), Kansas (Smith, 1950; revised, 1956), Arkansas (Dowling, 1957), Texas (Brown, 1950), and Colorado (Maslin, 1959; Smith, Maslin, and Brown, 1965).

Two recent books that are indispensable for the interested student are Roger Conant's *A Field Guide to Reptiles and Amphibians of Eastern North America* (1958) and Robert Stebbins' *A Field Guide to Western Reptiles and Amphibians* (1966), both published by Houghton Mifflin Company, Boston.

The annotated accounts of species are arranged alphabetically by scientific name under each group of reptiles—turtles, the alligator, lizards, then snakes. Unfortunately perhaps, a synonymy for each species is omitted; the name combinations employed are those most recently proposed in the literature when such proposals are accompanied by substantial commentary. The vernacular names used are those recommended by the Committee on Herpetological Common Names of the American Society of Ichthyologists and Herpetologists (1956).

Each account of species includes a brief subsection on *Recognition*, in which are described the combinations of characteristics that most readily serve to distinguish the particular species from related species. The descriptions are based on Oklahoma specimens so far as possible. Unqualified terms such as "size" or "length," or statements pertaining to size, refer to the total length of the species. A subsection on *Distribution* gives the species' general range in the state in terms of counties. A subsection on *Remarks* may contain comments on distribution, variation, habits and habitat, subspecies and intergradation, and problems that require further study. Circumstances have prevented detailed examination of every specimen and accumulation of data on morphological variation for every species, and I have not summarized published information pertaining to the life history of each species. Only unpublished information is included, but a final paragraph under *Remarks* lists all citations to references that provide information pertaining to Oklahoma specimens, three of which include only the briefest of comments (Force, 1925a, 1925b; Carpenter, 1956). References previously mentioned in the account, and those that refer only to locality, are not cited. Unfamiliar technical terms used in the keys and accounts are explained in the Glossary.

The University of Oklahoma, Norman, has by far the largest collection of specimens of Oklahoma reptiles. Other institutions in the state, as well as most of the major museums in the country, have been canvassed for Oklahoma reptiles. Not all specimens in the collections at these institutions were examined, and some specimens may be misidentified. Records of occurrence have been assembled from each of the collections named below, and these are indicated in the text by the following abbreviations:

AMNH   American Museum of Natural History
ANSP   Academy of Natural Sciences, Philadelphia
CCC   Charles C. Carpenter, personal records
CM   Carnegie Museum, Pittsburgh
ECSC   East Central State College, Ada, Oklahoma
FMNH   Field Museum of Natural History, Chicago
FWCM   Fort Worth Children's Museum
HAD   Harold A. Dundee, personal records
INHS   Illinois Natural History Survey, University of Illinois
KKA   Kraig K. Adler, personal records
KU   Museum of Natural History, The University of Kansas
MCZ   Museum of Comparative Zoology, Harvard University

MU Midwestern University, Wichita Falls, Texas
NWSC Northwestern State College, Alva, Oklahoma
OSU Oklahoma State University
OU University of Oklahoma Museum, Division of Zoology (including uncataloged specimens at the University of Oklahoma Biological Station [UOBS]).
RGW Specimens examined by the author in the field, but not collected
RWA Specimens in private collection of Ralph W. Axtell
SESC Southeastern State College, Durant, Oklahoma
SWSC Southwestern State College, Weatherford, Oklahoma
TCWC Texas Cooperative Wildlife Collection, Texas A&M University
TNHC Texas Natural History Collection, The University of Texas
TTC Texas Technological University, Lubbock
TU Tulane University
UA University of Arkansas
UI Museum of Natural History, The University of Illinois
UMMZ Museum of Zoology, The University of Michigan
USNM United States National Museum

The geographic ranges of most forms are shown on distribution maps. The ranges of species obtained just once, and of those otherwise confined to one county, are not shown on maps. The names of the 77 counties in Oklahoma are indicated in Figure 4. Each distribution map shows the outlines of the counties; the heavy black lines on these maps mark the approximate boundaries of the faunal regions, which are based primarily on the Game Type Map prepared by Duck and Fletcher (1943b) and are discussed in the section on faunal regions. Localities of specimens examined by me are shown by solid circles (including those no more precise than county, which are placed in the center of the county). Additional records of occurrence (published records or specimens otherwise not examined by me) are shown by open circles. Localities a short distance apart share the

7

same circle. Shaded areas indicate approximate areas of inter-gradation between subspecies.

In the subsections on *Specimens examined* and *Additional records*, localities are arranged alphabetically by county. Abbreviations in parentheses refer to the collections previously listed, and indicate that the collection contains one or more specimens. Records of occurrence are excluded if they refer either to the same locality from which at least one specimen has been examined or to a less restricted locality that includes the area from which at least one specimen has been examined. Published records have precedence over those indicating specimens in museum collections. Bracketed insertions of locality data are not stated either in the published reports cited or in the data available in the museum catalogs. The bracketed comments attempt to clarify the locality data as stated, or provide more precise locality data.

Previous Collections
and Reports

The earliest collections of reptiles in Oklahoma known to me were acquired in the course of exploratory surveys sponsored by the United States government. The first collection was made by Major Stephen H. Long's expedition from Pittsburgh to the Rocky Mountains in 1819 and 1820. That expedition, during which observations on reptiles were recorded by Thomas Say (published by James, 1823), traveled in two detachments through Oklahoma on the return trip from the Rocky Mountains. One party, commanded by Long, entered western Oklahoma in the area that is now Roger Mills County and followed the Canadian River (mistaken for the Red River) eastward to Fort Smith, Arkansas (arriving September 13, 1820). The other party, under Captain John R. Bell, followed the Arkansas River southeastward through northeastern Oklahoma to Fort Smith (arriving September 9, 1820). The type specimen of *Crotaphytus collaris collaris* was obtained in Oklahoma by Bell's detachment, and the type specimen of *Sistrurus catenatus tergeminus* may have been found in Oklahoma either by Bell's or Long's detachment (see Gloyd, 1940:39). Specimens collected by Long's expedition were deposited in the Peale Museum at Philadelphia (later known as The Philadelphia Museum). Half of the specimens in the Peale Museum subsequently were acquired by the AMNH, where they were destroyed by fire in 1865. The other half of the Peale Museum collection was first acquired by the Boston Museum but was later moved to the Boston Society of Natural History. The specimens unfortunately received no curatorial attention, and most were either destroyed or damaged;

9

in 1914 most of the remaining items were transferred to the MCZ (see Faxon, 1915:119, 121, 125).

Some reptiles in the USNM, collected some time after 1831 and before 1854 from the vicinity of Fort Towson, are credited to Dr. L. A. Edwards, and some to Major Stephen W. Kearney. Although Kearney's specimens are labeled simply "Arkansas" (see account of *Micrurus fulvius*, p. 62), he re-established Fort Towson in 1831 (initially established in 1824, but abandoned in 1829) and was stationed there for some time; perhaps Kearney's specimens are from near Fort Towson.

Dr. Samuel W. Woodhouse served as physician-naturalist with parties under the command of Captain Lorenzo Sitgreaves in 1849 and Lieutenant J. C. Woodruff in 1850 that were surveying the northern border of the Creek Nation (which at that time extended west to the hundredth meridian; see Fig. 1). Woodhouse collected several reptiles, including the type specimens of *Natrix rhombifera rhombifera*, *Natrix erythrogaster transversa*, *Psammophis flavi-gularis* (= *Masticophis flagellum testaceus*), and *Caudisona lecontei* (= *Crotalus viridis*). The last two species were obtained farther west than the two *Natrix* and were designated as from the "Cross Timbers." Most of Woodhouse's specimens were deposited in the ANSP, but some are in the USNM. The novelties were first described by Hallowell (1852), and these and other reptiles were mentioned in his subsequent papers (1854, 1857).

The next collection of any consequence was obtained by the expedition of Captains Randolph B. Marcy and George B. McClellan which explored the Red River in 1852 (route traveled in southwestern Oklahoma and adjacent parts of Texas depicted by Dowling, 1951:40, Map). Reptiles collected by that expedition, which included the type specimens of *Thamnophis marcianus marcianus* and *Sceloporus undulatus consobrinus*, were deposited in the museum of the Smithsonian Institution (USNM), and bore the indefinite locality of Red River, Arkansas. Baird and Girard (1853) first described the snakes obtained, and later the same year (reprinted in 1854) they discussed all the reptiles collected on the Marcy and McClellan expedition.[1]

Other reptiles obtained in the 1800's and deposited in the USNM are recorded from Fort Supply (established in 1868 as Camp Supply, but designated a fort in 1878), Fort Cobb, and several places along the route traveled by Lieutenant Amiel W. Whipple. The only known dates of collection for reptiles from Fort Supply are 1870 (by Dr. J. E. Wilcox) and 1880 (by Dr. A. W. Taylor). Most of the reptiles from Fort Cobb, which was established in 1859, are credited to the naturalist-explorer Dr. Edward Palmer (only known dates of collection are 1868, 1879, and 1880). Lieutenant Whipple, in charge of one of the several Pacific Railroad Survey field parties, traveled west from Fort Smith on July 14, 1853, his route through Oklahoma to Tucumcari and Albuquerque generally following the south bank of the Canadian River. Whipple's party included the German artist-topographer Heinrich Baldwin Möllhausen, who is credited as the collector of some reptiles.[2] Oklahoma reptiles in the USNM are listed by Yarrow (1882) and Cope (1900), and the types therein by Cochran (1961).

Jenness Richardson and Charles P. Rowley made a small col-

[1] Different aspects of scutellation of many of the snakes obtained (six of ten species) were subsequently illustrated by Baird (1859, Reptiles, in Reports of explorations and surveys, to ascertain the most practicable and economical route for a railroad from the Mississippi River to the Pacific Ocean, 33rd Congress, 2nd Session, Senate Exec. Doc. No. 78, Vol. X, Part III, Pls. XXIV–XXXVI [plates only, no text published]). Further indication of this reference in the text was not possible; included are the seemingly little-known illustrations of the types of *Scotophis laetus*, *Tropidonotus transversus*, *T. rhombifer*, and *Eutaenia marciana*.

[2] Baird (1859, Report upon the reptiles of the route, in *ibid.*, Report of Lieut. A. W. Whipple, Vol. X, Part VI, No. 4, pp. 37–45, Pls. XXV–XXVII) mentioned the reptiles obtained by Whipple's survey. Inclusion of the few localities that are mentioned in this paper in the text was not possible.

lection of reptiles around 1889 in the Neutral Strip for the AMNH. Reptiles in the ANSP, mostly from western Oklahoma, were reported by Cope (1894), and some collected by Henry A. Pilsbry in eastern Oklahoma were reported by Stone (1903). Some reptiles collected in 1899 by Thaddeus S. Surber from the vicinity of Alva and Whitehorse Springs in Woods County were deposited in the FMNH. A small collection from the vicinity of Sapulpa, Creek County, was deposited in the AMNH and discussed by Schmidt (1919). Blair (1939:85) noted that some of the above-mentioned collectors obtained mammals, and he mentioned other collecting forays in Oklahoma on which reptiles also were probably obtained. Principal observations in succeeding years, other than those by students headquartered in Oklahoma, were published by Burt and his colleagues (1929–1935, most specimens deposited in AMNH and USNM) and Smith and Leonard (1934, most specimens at KU).

The earliest attempt to summarize a part of the herpetofauna of Oklahoma was an annotated list of snakes by Van Vleet (1902). The efforts of Arthur I. Ortenburger, however, provided the foundation and bulk of the herpetological collections at the University of Oklahoma. When he came to that institution in January, 1924, Oklahoma was almost a virgin field so far as knowledge of its herpetology was concerned. For six summers, beginning in 1925, he was in the field in charge of the Museum of Zoology expeditions and later the Biological Survey expeditions; collecting efforts were concentrated mostly at the periphery of the state. In addition to several short papers, Ortenburger published a list of snakes (1925), and later (1927a) a list of all reptiles and amphibians known to occur in Oklahoma. He also devised a key to the snakes (1927b) and included it in a subsequent key to the lizards and snakes (1930b). In this same period, Edith R. Force also studied the herpetofauna of northeastern Oklahoma, especially in Tulsa and Okmulgee counties (many specimens deposited at FMNH, UMMZ, AMNH, UI, and OU).

Although some published reports (e.g., Webster, 1936; Trowbridge, 1937; Smith and Acker, 1940; and Moore and Rigney, 1942, specimens at OSU and UMMZ) appeared in the years immediately following the Force-Ortenburger era, herpetological interest intensified in subsequent years. The efforts of Harold A. Dundee, W. Leslie Burger, Jr., Frank B. McMurray, Arthur N. Bragg, and Charles C. Carpenter, University of Oklahoma; Bryan P. Glass and Clarence J. McCoy, Jr., Oklahoma State University; William A. Carter, East Central State College; and Albert P. Blair, University of Tulsa, to mention a few, have increased the collections at those institutions and most of them have published their findings (see Literature Cited). The largest collections of Oklahoma reptiles within the state are housed at the University of Oklahoma, Norman, and at Oklahoma State University, Stillwater. Other sizable collections of Oklahoma reptiles are in the AMNH, FMNH, TNHC, UI, UMMZ, and USNM.

Bragg and others (1950) summarized our knowledge of the amphibian fauna in Oklahoma, but aside from an uncritical list of Oklahoma snakes published by Wright and Wright (1952:596), no comprehensive, up-to-date account of all the reptiles living in Oklahoma has been published.

Localities of Reptiles
in Oklahoma

Because the localities from which many reptile specimens were taken in the early days are indefinite—for example, Oklahoma Territory, Indian Territory, Cherokee Nation, Neutral Strip—it seems worthwhile to comment briefly on the history of those and other place names that are now included within the present boundaries of the state of Oklahoma. The following paragraphs are based largely upon the works of Snider (1917:23–24, 143–152), Wyatt and Rainey (1919), and Morris and McReynolds (1965). Indispensable for further detail are Thoburn's two volumes on the history of Oklahoma (1916).

The region that is now Oklahoma was claimed at various times by Spain, France, and England during the period of colonial struggle and territorial dispute that marked the 1600's and 1700's. Most of the region was acquired by the United States under the terms of the Louisiana Purchase in 1803, but the exact boundaries between the Purchase and Spanish territory to the southwest were not definitely established until the Adams-Onís Treaty of 1819. Those boundaries included the Red River and the hundredth meridian and formed the southern and western limits, respectively, of Arkansas Territory, which was created in 1819. The creation of Kansas Territory fixed the northern border of Arkansas Territory as the thirty-seventh parallel.

The western part of Arkansas Territory, which included most of what is now Oklahoma, was designated Indian Territory by the United States under an act passed on June 30, 1834, for the possession of the Five Civilized Tribes (Choctaws, Cherokees, Chickasaws, Creeks, and Seminoles), which were removed from their homelands east of the Mississippi River. Removal began with the Choctaws and ended with the Seminoles, and lasted some twenty years. The residence of the Choctaws in Arkansas Territory caused concern among white settlers and resulted in the establishment of a new western boundary for Arkansas. In 1824 it was defined as a straight, north-south line from a point forty miles west of the present southwest corner of Missouri to the Red River. In 1825 the Choctaw-Arkansas line was moved eastward and fixed at the present Oklahoma-Arkansas border.

By terms of treaties beginning in 1816 and ending in 1830, the Choctaws agreed to occupy the land bounded by the hundredth meridian, the Red River, and the Canadian-Arkansas rivers, and in 1837 the Choctaws agreed to share that land with the Chickasaws. The Creeks officially ceded all their lands east of the Mississippi in 1832, and in the same year a tentative treaty, which later became binding, forced the reluctant Seminoles to share the Creek lands west of Arkansas; most of the Seminoles moved west between 1836 and 1842. The boundaries of the Creek lands were established in 1833, with the northern border beginning twenty-five miles north of the Arkansas River and extending due west to the hundredth meridian, the southern boundary as the Canadian River, and the eastern limit as an irregular boundary negotiated with the Cherokees. The first contingent of Cherokees occupied lands that are now part of Oklahoma in 1828, and others followed in accordance with a treaty of 1835 (also in 1828, other Indian tribes had begun to occupy small areas in the northeastern part of the Cherokee Nation). Other tracts of land ceded to the Cherokees were the Cherokee Outlet, which extended westward from the Cherokee Nation to the hundredth meridian (the common boundary was definitely fixed at the ninety-sixth meridian in 1866), and two areas in Kansas—the Cherokee Strip, a strip approximately two and one-half miles wide bordering the Cherokee lands along the thirty-seventh parallel, and the Neutral Lands, a twenty-five by

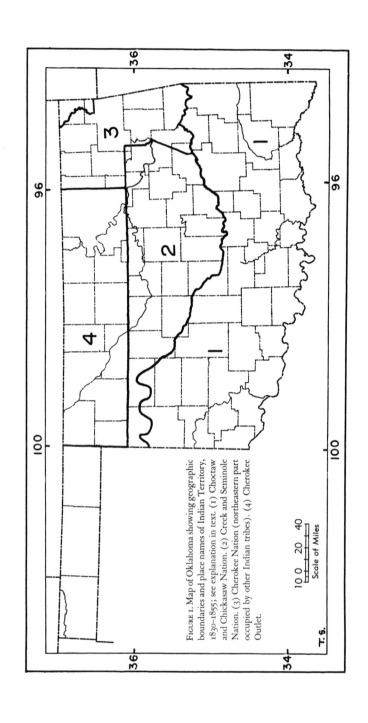

FIGURE 1. Map of Oklahoma showing geographic boundaries and place names of Indian Territory, 1830–1855; see explanation in text. (1) Choctaw and Chickasaw Nation. (2) Creek and Seminole Nation. (3) Cherokee Nation (northeastern part occupied by other Indian tribes). (4) Cherokee Outlet.

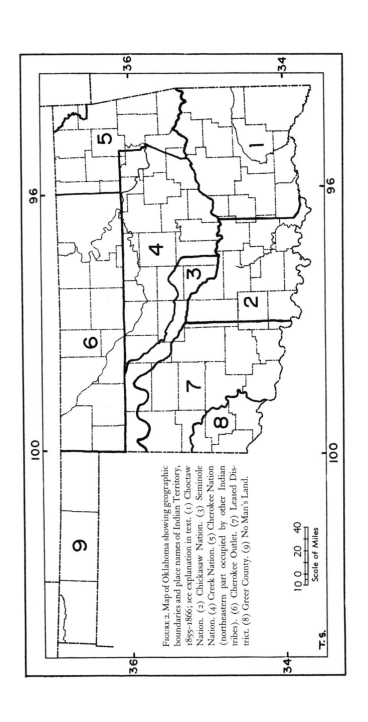

FIGURE 2. Map of Oklahoma showing geographic boundaries and place names of Indian Territory, 1855–1866; see explanation in text. (1) Choctaw Nation. (2) Chickasaw Nation. (3) Seminole Nation. (4) Creek Nation. (5) Cherokee Nation (northeastern part occupied by other Indian tribes). (6) Cherokee Outlet. (7) Leased District. (8) Greer County. (9) No Man's Land.

fifty mile rectangular area along the western border of Missouri. The two areas in Kansas are mentioned in order to avoid confusion with the geographically distinct Cherokee Outlet and Neutral Strip in Oklahoma. The initial geographic boundaries of the lands ceded to the Five Civilized Tribes in Indian Territory are shown in Figure 1.

Tribal segregation subdivided the Creek-Seminole and Choctaw-Chickasaw nations in 1855 and 1856 and resulted in the boundaries between each nation as shown in Figure 2; in addition, the Choctaw-Chickasaw land west of the ninety-eighth meridian was leased to the United States for settlement of other Indian tribes. After the Civil War, a series of treaties (the first of which was signed in 1866) compelled the Five Civilized Tribes, who had sided with the Confederacy, to cede the western parts of their respective lands to the United States for settlement of other Indian tribes. Negotiations were completed in 1874, but some tracts of land remained unassigned to any Indian tribe; these were the western part of the Cherokee Outlet—known as The Neutral Strip (Ortenburger, 1927a:89 and Blair, 1939:106) but considered the same as No Man's Land by Wyatt and Rainey (1919:49) and Gould (1933:121)—and a tract of land in the center of Indian Territory known as the Unassigned Lands or Unassigned District, and since 1879 as the Oklahoma Country (Fig. 3).

The place names No Man's Land, The Public Land Strip, Beaver Country or Territory, and Cimarron Territory (and Neutral Strip according to some authors) have been applied to the present-day panhandle of Oklahoma, which includes Cimarron, Texas, and Beaver counties. This region was not acquired by the United States by terms of the Adams-Onís Treaty, but was controlled by Spain until 1821, by Mexico until 1836, and then by Texas. Texas, which was annexed to the United States as a slave state in 1845, was forced to relinquish claims to all land north of latitude 36°30' in 1850 according to the terms of the

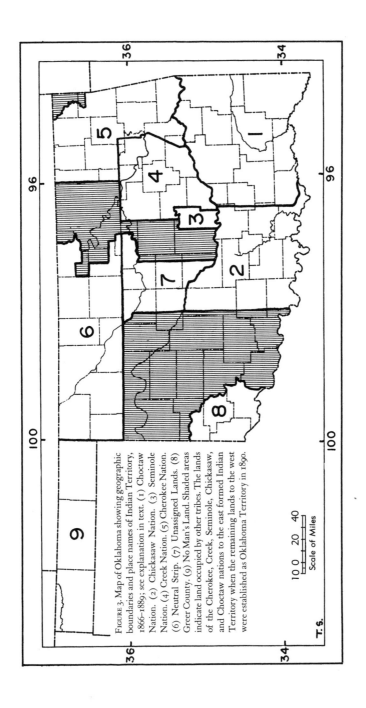

FIGURE 3. Map of Oklahoma showing geographic boundaries and place names of Indian Territory, 1866–1889; see explanation in text. (1) Choctaw Nation. (2) Chickasaw Nation. (3) Seminole Nation. (4) Creek Nation. (5) Cherokee Nation. (6) Neutral Strip. (7) Unassigned Lands. (8) Greer County. (9) No Man's Land. Shaded areas indicate land occupied by other tribes. The lands of the Cherokee, Creek, Seminole, Chickasaw, and Choctaw nations to the east formed Indian Territory when the remaining lands to the west were established as Oklahoma Territory in 1890.

Scale of Miles

Missouri Compromise of 1820. This action, coupled with the previous establishment of other boundaries, left the rectangular piece of land between the 100th and 103rd meridians and between latitude 36° 30' north and the 37th parallel unattached to any territory, and it henceforth became commonly known as No Man's Land.

Another tract of land in southwestern Oklahoma (including Harmon, Greer, Jackson, and southern Beckham counties) was named Greer County in 1860 by the Texas Legislature and claimed by that state. Greer County was bounded by the North Fork of the Red River, the hundredth meridian, and the Red River (South Fork). However, there was indecision whether the North or South Fork of the Red River was the boundary between the Louisiana Purchase (Indian Territory) and the Spanish possessions (Texas).

The tract called the Unassigned Lands, the first region opened to white settlement, was occupied by the "Run of 1889," and other tracts of land were opened soon afterward. This action prompted Congress to organize the western half of Indian Territory, including No Man's Land, as Oklahoma Territory in 1890. The Cherokee Outlet was relinquished by the Cherokee Nation in 1892 and added to Oklahoma Territory. A decision rendered by the United States Supreme Court in 1896 added Greer County to Oklahoma Territory. By 1904 the entire Oklahoma Territory was opened for white settlement. Oklahoma and Indian territories were admitted to the Union as the state of Oklahoma (from the Choctaw, *okla*, "people"; *humma*, or *homma*, "red") in 1907.

Some reptiles collected in the 1800's bear the indefinite locality of "Cross Timbers." In a broad sense, the name refers to the north-south trending timber belts that posed barriers to east-west travel. In general, the Cross Timbers correspond to the blackjack–post-oak region of Duck and Fletcher (see discussion in Foreman, 1947). Gould (1933:125–126) noted that the Okla-

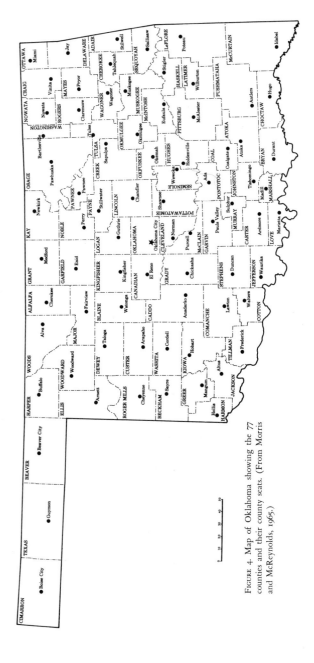

FIGURE 4. Map of Oklahoma showing the 77 counties and their county seats. (From Morris and McReynolds, 1965.)

homa Cross Timbers may refer to parts of Stephens, Grady, and Caddo counties, as well as certain timbered areas in east central Oklahoma, extending from the Arbuckle Mountains north to the Arkansas River. The itinerary of the Marcy and McClellan expedition (see Baird and Girard, 1854:87–88; area also depicted on folded map included with another map as separate volume accompanying text) suggests that they entered the Cross Timbers in eastern Stephens County and left them in western Carter County. Stejneger (in Amaral, 1929:87) placed the Cross Timbers along the northern boundary of the Creek Nation in Blaine County.

Most place names cited in the text are readily located on recent service station highway maps. Unfortunately, localities may not be permanent. Names (post offices) may be changed (for example, the locality in the OU catalog for a copperhead from Carter County is Berwyn, which was changed to Gene Autry in 1942); sites may be inundated by impoundments, which are "blooming" in the state (see Keystone below); and place names may no longer be in existence (see Togo below). Most of the past and present place names in Oklahoma are mentioned by either Gould (1933) or Shirk (1965).

For various reasons, it has been tempting to alter localities, but in order to avoid possible confusion on the part of future investigators, who examine museum or card catalogs, this has not been done except in rare instances. Many localities as listed are cumbersome; one locality in LeFlore County, frequently mentioned in the text and referred to by Ortenburger (1928b) as "Kiamichi River, 8 miles west Oklahoma-Arkansas state line," is herein shortened to 5 miles east Big Cedar. Localities that refer to highway numbers are undesirable, since the numbers may change; for example, the north-south trending U.S. Highway 177 in central Oklahoma was formerly State Highway 40 and 18, and the east-west trending State Highway 6 and 152 in western Oklahoma was formerly State Highway 72. In one instance, and perhaps in others, it is known that a frequently visited collecting site in McCurtain County—Little River bridge on U.S. Highway 70, 6 miles northeast of Idabel—is recorded differently in some of the species accounts (as 7 miles N Idabel, 6–7 miles N Idabel, and usually as 6 miles N Idabel).

Localities that are frequently mentioned in the text and are either vague or shown on few maps are identified below.

Black Bear Creek: In Noble County at intersection with U.S. Highway 177, 14 miles north Stillwater, Payne County.

Caddo Canyon: Caddo, Devils, and Kiwanis canyons, in northern Caddo County, known collectively as the Caddo Canyons; generalized locality is 4 miles southeast Hinton; largest canyon is Devils, which extends into adjacent southwestern Canadian County.

Camp Classen: Recreation area, including Turner Falls and Price's Falls in Arbuckle Mountains; these areas from 7 to 9 miles south Davis, Murray County.

Camp Egan: In Cherokee County, 11 miles east Tahlequah.

Camp Muskogee: Specimens bearing this locality were collected in Cherokee County from 2 to 4 miles south Welling along Barren Fork River.

Devils Canyon: See Caddo Canyon.

Dripping Springs: In Delaware County, about 2.5 miles east Flint; some specimens recorded from as far east of Flint as 7 miles.

Dwight Mission: Established in 1829, but now abandoned; in Sequoyah County at Marble City (Shirk, 1965:68); recent collections bearing this locality are from about 3 miles south Marble City.

Garnett: In Tulsa County about 6.5 miles south and 1.5 miles east Owasso, close to Rogers County line (see map in Blair, 1938:474); many specimens bearing this locality were probably taken in Rogers County, as indicated in UMMZ catalog.

Hanging Rock: Fishing camp in Cherokee County, 2 miles north Ellerville.

Keystone: In extreme southeastern Pawnee County close to Tulsa County line; site now inundated by Keystone Reservoir.

Kiwanis Canyon: See Caddo Canyon.

Limestone: In Tulsa County about 1 mile south and 5 miles west Tulsa.

Lost City: In Tulsa County about 6 miles west of Tulsa near Arkansas River.

McSpadden Falls: In Cherokee County, 8 miles northeast Tahlequah.

Mohawk Park: In Tulsa County about 6 miles northeast Tulsa (see map in Blair, 1938:474).

Oakhurst: About 4 miles southwest Tulsa, Tulsa County (Shirk, 1965:152), close to Creek County line.

Parthenia Park: In Tulsa County near Oakhurst.

Price's Falls: See Camp Classen.

Red Fork: In Tulsa County, adjoining Tulsa on the southwest and now within the city limits (Shirk, 1965:176).

Red River Fisheries: Fisheries experimental station about 1 mile from Red River and 10 miles south Hugo, Choctaw County.

Reservoir Hill: Northwest edge of city of Tulsa; mostly in Osage County, but some specimens are probably from Tulsa County.

Rich Mountain: East-west trending range of some 20 miles, extending from just southwest of Page, LeFlore County, to near Mena, Arkansas; the name generally refers to the vicinity of the highest peak just south of Page.

Ripley Bluffs: Along Cimarron River about 1 mile north and 3 miles west Ripley, Payne County.

Salt Creek Canyon: In northern Blaine County; KU specimens of mammals bearing this locality were recorded as 4 miles southeast Southard by Blair (1939:99).

Sugarloaf Mountain: In LeFlore County, 4 miles east and 1 mile south Gilmore, near Arkansas state line.

Tishomingo Fish Hatchery: Federal fish hatchery at Reagan, Johnston County.

Togo: Post office in northwestern Major County, where State Highway 15 intersects Griever Creek, 14 miles southeast Waynoka, Woods County; abandoned in 1921 and no longer in existence (Shirk, 1965:207).

Tulsa Fin and Feather Club: In Rogers County about 20 miles east of Tulsa.

Turner Falls: See Camp Classen.

UOBS: University of Oklahoma Biological Station, Lake Texoma, 2 miles east Willis, Marshall County.

Whitehorse Springs: Same as Tegarden in Woods County.

Faunal Regions
of
Reptiles in Oklahoma

Eastern Oklahoma includes the most mountainous region of the state and is well forested. Westward, the forests become dwarfed in stature, and areas of grassland become more abundant. The change in vegetation corresponds with an east-west change in climatic conditions, the extremes of which are in the warm, humid southeast and in the cold, arid panhandle of northwestern Oklahoma.

Most of Oklahoma receives between twenty-six and forty inches of rain each year. The average annual rainfall of about forty-two to fifty-six inches in eastern Oklahoma contrasts sharply with an average of about sixteen to twenty inches in the west. The Ouachita Mountains receive the most rain, usually more than fifty inches, whereas the westernmost part of the panhandle receives only about ten inches per year. Spring is the wettest season of the year, and winter the driest. Snowfall averages less than three inches in the southeast, but more than twenty inches in the panhandle. The western part of the state is characterized by torrential rains and the greatest extremes in temperature. The average annual temperature is 60.5° F, with a slight north-south gradient varying from about 60° in the north to about 65° in the south; the highest average annual temperature (64° F) is in the southeast corner of Oklahoma, whereas the lowest (54° F) is in the westernmost part of the panhandle. There is a corresponding change in the annual number of frost-free days from 240 in the southeast to about 180 days in the panhandle. The elevation increases slowly from approximately three hundred feet in southeastern Oklahoma to almost five thousand feet in the extreme northwestern corner of the panhandle. Tornadoes are frequent; in the period 1953 through 1962, Oklahoma had the highest annual tornado frequency (forty to fifty) in the United States (Kessler, 1966:15).

Bruner (1931) discussed the vegetation of Oklahoma, and Rice and Penfound (1959) treated the forest cover. The obvious east-west zonation of types of vegetation is reflected in corresponding patterns of distribution of much of the fauna in Oklahoma. The floral and faunal assemblages of the various biotic districts of Oklahoma were discussed in some detail by Blair and Hubbell (1938). Snider (1917) and Duck and Fletcher (1943a, ch. 2) provided useful supplementary information. Duck and Fletcher also published photographs of the principal habitats in Oklahoma. Ortenburger published photographs of localities from which reptiles were collected in western Oklahoma (1928a) and eastern Oklahoma (1928b). Included here are photographs of some places in each of the faunal regions where reptiles were collected. The distribution of reptiles in Oklahoma generally coincides with the geographic extent of established physiographic regions (Fig. 5).

Coastal Plain.—The mesic, lowland habitats of the Gulf Coast extend northwestward and occur principally in the southern half of McCurtain County, Oklahoma, along the broad floodplain of the Red River and some of its larger tributaries (Figs. 6, 7). The elevation is the lowest (324 feet) and the climate the warmest and most humid in the state. Bald cypress (*Taxodium distichum*) and water elm (*Planera aquatica*) grow only in permanently swampy areas and at the water's edge along stable stream banks. The poorly drained, silty floodplains support forests dominated by water oak (*Quercus nigra*) and willow oak (*Q. phellos*); other common species are white oak (*Q. alba*), sugar maple (*Acer saccharum*), American holly (*Ilex opaca*), black gum (*Nyssa sylvatica*), American elm (*Ulmus americana*), slippery elm (*U. rubra*), and often bamboo (*Arundinaria gigantea*).

27

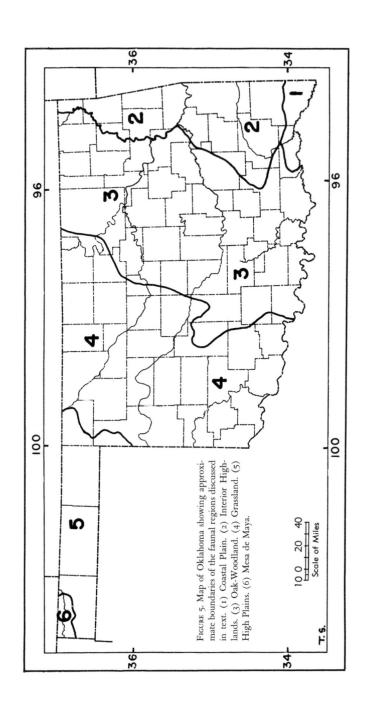

FIGURE 5. Map of Oklahoma showing approximate boundaries of the faunal regions discussed in text. (1) Coastal Plain. (2) Interior Highlands. (3) Oak-Woodland. (4) Grassland. (5) High Plains. (6) Mesa de Maya.

Scale of Miles

10 0 20 40

The undisturbed climatic climax of the uplands of this region is an oak-hickory forest, the most important species of which are white oak (*Quercus alba*), post oak (*Q. stellata*), spotted oak (*Q. shumardi*), northern red oak (*Q. rubra*), and mockernut hickory (*Carya tomentosa*). Shortleaf pine (*Pinus echinata*) and loblolly pine (*P. taeda*) grow on cut-over or burned-over sites on the higher, better-drained, sandy soils and sometimes form pure stands. Sweet gum (*Liquidambar styraciflua*) is characteristic of the transition to the water oak-floodplain habitat.

Interior Highlands.—The eastern quarter of Oklahoma is the most wooded and mountainous part of the state. The Interior Highlands include parts of the Ozark Plateau in the north and the Ouachita Mountains in the south. The two regions are separated by the valley of the Arkansas River. Each region was uplifted in late Paleozoic times and was not covered by the encroaching seas in succeeding geologic periods. Most of the forest is deciduous, but pine is common in the Ouachitas. Dowling (1956) commented on the geographic relationships of the herpetofauna of the Interior Highlands in Oklahoma.

The Ouachita uplift, formed by extensive thrust faulting, extends westward from west-central Arkansas to Atoka County, Oklahoma. The Ouachitas, the most rugged mountains in the state, are formed by a series of curved ridges that include the Kiamichi, Winding Stair, and San Bois mountains (Fig. 8). The elevation gradually decreases westward from the Arkansas border; the highest peak is Rich Mountain, about twenty-eight hundred feet high. The northern part of the uplift is drained by the Fourche Maline–Poteau River of the Arkansas River drainage, and the southern part is drained by the Kiamichi River of the Red River drainage. Near their sources, the rivers are clear and swift. On the more elevated parts of the sandstone uplift to

FIGURE 6. Coastal Plain. Water oak–floodplain of Red River with palmettos (*Sabal minor*) in foreground, 2 miles southeast of Harris, McCurtain County. Photograph taken in early April, 1950, by Jackson Hill.

the east, the forests are generally more dense and support taller trees than those farther west. The slopes, having thin soils and an abundant cover of leaves, are strewn with boulders; the vegetation on the summits of the higher peaks, however, is stunted. The Ozarks, which are of late Mississippian age, extend southwestward into northeastern Oklahoma from Arkansas and Missouri. The Ozark Plateau has several large, level areas in the northern part, whereas the rugged southern part is formed by the Cookson Hills and Boston Mountains. The drainage is southward into the Arkansas River via the Illinois and Grand rivers, the tributaries of which are clear and cold. The western boundary of the region is formed by the Grand River. Forests grow on a dissected plateau of limestone hills, valleys, and bluffs.

Figure 7. Coastal Plain. Abandoned stock pond at Red River Fisheries with aquatic buttercup (*Ranunculus*) on surface, 10 miles south of Hugo, Choctaw County. Habitat for *Deirochelys reticularia, Pseudemys scripta, Natrix fasciata* and *Natrix rhombifera*. Photograph taken on September 8, 1953.

There are many sinks and caves, and much of the drainage is underground.

The Interior Highlands are covered essentially by an oak-hickory forest with oak-hickory-pine forest extensive in the south. Rice and Penfound (1959:603, Table VI) noted the dominant trees for sections of Oklahoma; in the eastern oak-hickory forest, the most abundant were post oak (*Quercus stellata*), blackjack oak (*Q. marilandica*), black oak (*Q. velutina*), black hickory (*Carya texana*), and, in the south, shortleaf pine (*Pinus echinata*). Interesting mesophytic species in the oak-hickory forest include sugar maple (*Acer saccharum*), linden (*Tilia floridana*), pawpaw (*Asimina triloba*), and sassafras (*Sassafras variifolium*). Loblolly pine (*Pinus taeda*),

31

FIGURE 8. Interior Highlands. Wooded knoll in Ouachita Mountains, 0.5 mile south of Clayton, Pushmataha County. The species *Terrapene carolina, Cnemidophorus sexlineatus, Sceloporus undulatus, Eumeces fasciatus, Lygosoma laterale, Tantilla gracilis,* and *Virginia striatula* were collected here on April 18, 1959.

magnolia (*Magnolia acuminata*), and southern witchhazel (*Hamamelis macrophylla*), grow only in the Ouachita Mountains, where a few beech trees (*Fagus grandifolia* var. *carolina*) can also be found in valleys along streams.

Central Lowland Plains.—This physiographic region crosses the central and western part of the state in a generally north-south direction, and extends from the Interior Highlands to the east-facing, eroded escarpment of the High Plains in northwestern Oklahoma. Actually, this region (most of Oklahoma) is a broad ecotone between forest in the east and grassland in the west. Grassy landscapes become increasingly more extensive

FIGURE 9. Oak-Woodland. Overturning small limestone rocks atop bluff just east of Briar Creek, 1 mile east of Powell, Marshall County. Habitat for *Leptotyphlops dulcis*, *Sonora episcopa*, and *Tantilla gracilis*. Photograph taken on April 18, 1954.

westward; the forests, which form a vegetational continuum with the oak-hickory forest of the Interior Highlands (Rice and Penfound, 1959:598), become correspondingly more open and scrubby, with the average stature of the cover decreasing from fifty feet in the east, to thirty-five feet in the central part of the state, to twenty feet in western Oklahoma (Penfound, 1962).

Most of the reptiles in Oklahoma reach their eastern or western limits of distribution in this transitional area. On the basis of east-west distributional patterns, it seems practical to subdivide the Central Lowland Plains into an eastern, predominantly forested Oak-Woodland and a western Grassland.

Oak-Woodland: The western border of the oak-hickory forest of the Interior Highlands merges into an open woodland that becomes progressively more open westward. The western

33

limit of the Oak-Woodland is a rather arbitrary line bounding the most extensive timbered areas on the west and extending southwesterly from Osage County to Jefferson County.

The flat to gently rolling topography has undergone differential erosion and is interrupted by numerous escarpments and outcrops (Fig. 9). Areas underlaid with porous soils derived from sandstones or granites are dry, and support post oak (*Quercus stellata*), blackjack oak (*Q. marilandica*), and, to a lesser extent, black oak (*Q. velutina*) and black hickory (*Carya texana*); the last two species are scarce in the rather extensive westernmost timber belts in Stephens, Grady, and Caddo counties. The understory consists principally of grasses, smooth sumac (*Rhus glabra*), coral berry (*Symphoricarpus orbicularis*), and green briar (*Smilax*). Soils derived from limestones or shales are interspersed throughout the region and are covered mostly by tall grasses—chiefly big bluestem (*Andropogon gerardi*), little bluestem (*A. scoparius*), Indian grass (*Sorghastrum nutans*), and switch grass (*Panicum virgatum*). An extensive grassland with little forest cover occurs in the northeastern part of the Oak-Woodland (see Buck and Kelting, 1962).

The Arbuckle Mountains in Murray, Carter, Johnston, and Pontotoc counties are a conspicuous physiographic feature in south central Oklahoma. Uplifted in late Pennsylvanian time, these mountains form a low, dissected plateau composed mostly of Paleozoic limestones. The western part of the range (mostly in Murray County) is the most elevated (about 700 feet above the surrounding country), and shows the mountainous aspect. Cool, clear springs, streams with waterfalls (Fig. 10), and caves are common. In addition to forested areas of oak and hickory, the limestone soils support extensive stands of cedar (*Juniperus ashei* and *J. virginiana*). Many species of plants in the Arbuckles (some endemic to Oklahoma) show a relationship to the flora of the Edwards Plateau in Texas, and to a lesser extent that of the Ozarks.

34

Figure 10. Oak-Woodland. Honey Creek below Turner Falls, Arbuckle Mountains, Murray County. Habitat for *Sternotherus odoratus*. Photograph taken on March 17, 1951.

Grassland: This flat to gently rolling plain is developed on the Permian Redbeds (red shales and sandstones with intercalated layers of gypsum). A product of differential erosion, the Gypsum Hills are characterized by extensive outcrops and numerous gorges and canyons (principally in the northern part of the region, in Blaine and Major counties); solution channels account for many caves. The Grassland consists of mixed grasses, which are transitional from the tall grasses in the east to the short-grass plains in the west. The tall-grass species are essentially those found in the tall-grass prairie, although the medium grass, little bluestem (*Andropogon scoparius*), is the most abundant. The short grasses, principally smooth grama (*Bouteloua gracilis*), hairy grama (*B. hirsuta*), and buffalo grass (*Buchloë dactyloides*), are abundant farther west.

Post oak (*Quercus stellata*) and blackjack oak (*Q. mari-*

FIGURE 11. Grassland. Mesquite–short-grass plains showing gypsum outcrops, 2 miles west of Reed, Greer County, in Harmon County. Habitat for *Cnemidophorus gularis gularis*. Photograph taken on July 11, 1951.

landica) grow on scattered outcrops of sandstone. Extensive stands of timber are found in the Wichita and Quartz mountains (Comanche and Kiowa counties). In parts of some of the westernmost counties (mostly Woodward, Ellis, Roger Mills, and Beckham) there is a shrubland, or shinnery, composed of shin oak (*Quercus havardi*). Most stands of shinnery are two to four feet high, but some oaks may be as much as forty feet high (Wiedeman and Penfound, 1960). Mesquite (*Prosopis glandulosa*) grows mostly in the southwestern part of the Grassland (Fig. 11), but does extend north to Major County. Scattered throughout the region are sand sage (*Artemisia filifolia*), yucca (*Yucca glauca*), and wild plum thickets (*Prunus angustifolia*). Cottonwood (*Populus deltoides*), salt cedar (*Tamarix gallica*), and black willow (*Salix nigra*) predominate on the sandy floodplains of rivers and streams. Along the north banks of the Salt

FIGURE 12. Grassland. Headwaters of West Cache Creek just below Lost Lake Dam, Wichita Mountains Wildlife Refuge, Comanche County. Habitat for *Crotaphytus collaris, Sceloporus undulatus, Crotalus atrox,* and *Sistrurus catenatus.* Photograph taken on April 8, 1951.

Fork of the Arkansas, Cimarron, North Canadian, and South Canadian rivers in northwestern Oklahoma, areas of sand hills or stabilized dunes support stands of American elm (*Ulmus americana*), western hackberry (*Celtis reticulata*), and chittamwood (*Bumelia lanuginosa* var. *oblongifolia*), which may be superseded by post and blackjack oak (Rice and Penfound, 1959:596–597).

In some places, there are low, level, sandy tracts with salt springs at or under the surface; these are known as salt plains (see discussion by Ortenburger and Bird, 1933). The largest of them, the Great Salt Plain in Alfalfa County, covers an area of approximately forty square miles (about nine miles long and six miles across).

A series of canyons, collectively called the Caddo Canyons

37

(largest are Caddo, Devils, and Kiwanis), occur in northeastern Caddo County and extreme southwestern Canadian County. The largest canyons support an eastern deciduous forest, in which sugar maple (*Acer sacharrum*) is dominant and disjunct. The vegetation of these canyons is discussed by Little (1939).

The Wichita Mountains are the most divergent physiographic feature in the Grassland (Fig. 12). The main mountain mass is mostly in northwestern Comanche County, but isolated outliers extend west to Greer County. The uplift, formed in early Pennsylvanian times, consists of a Pre-Cambrian, crystalline, igneous core surrounded by outcrops of Paleozoic sediments, mainly limestone and sandstone. The summits of the higher peaks may rise eleven hundred feet above the surrounding mixed-grass plains. Geologically related to the Arbuckle uplift, the Wichitas present a somewhat different aspect owing to their loss of much of the limestone mantle which is still a conspicuous feature of the Arbuckles. Their streams are relatively clear and cool, and some have been dammed to form artificial lakes. Forests grow in the protected valleys and canyons.

The Antelope Hills comprise a series of eroded hills in northwestern Roger Mills County near the Canadian River. In the days of the early exploratory expeditions that often followed the Canadian River westward into New Mexico, the Antelope Hills, which lie near the hundredth meridian, served as a topographic landmark and were known as the Boundary Buttes. The series of buttes, or hills, were formerly a continuous tableland, and presumably were once part of the Llano Estacado of the High Plains to the west.

High Plains.—This region includes the panhandle. It is higher than the mixed prairie, and a dissected escarpment forms its eastern edge, the crest of which is commonly referred to as the caprock. The escarpment is pronounced in the Texas panhandle, but is indistinct in Oklahoma because of the leveling

FIGURE 13. Mesa de Maya. Butte covered mostly with short grass and scattered junipers, 2 miles west of Kenton, Cimarron County. The species *Cnemidophorus tesselatus, Eumeces obsoletus, Sceloporus undulatus, Crotalus viridis*, and *Thamnophis elegans* were taken here on May 31, 1958.

action of rivers and streams. The High Plains is relatively flat, having short grasses, and, in sandy areas, much sand sage and some tall grasses. Although overgrazed by cattle and now relatively unproductive, the High Plains was covered with thick grass in the 1870's and 1880's. The High Plains is underlaid by the porous Ogallala formation, the many limestone beds of which vary in resistance to erosion.

Mesa de Maya: The Mesa de Maya, a prominent topographic feature on the High Plains, is actually an outlier of the Rocky Mountains and consists of a group of several large mesas (Fig. 13). Most of the region lies in northern New Mexico and

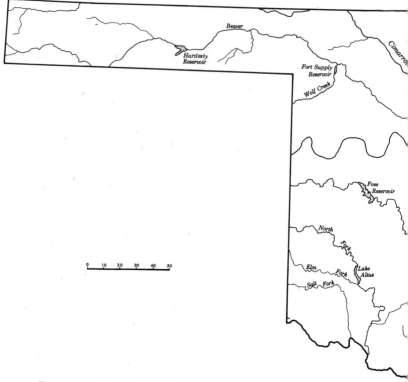

FIGURE 14. Map of Oklahoma showing principal rivers and impoundments. (From Morris and McReynolds, 1965.)

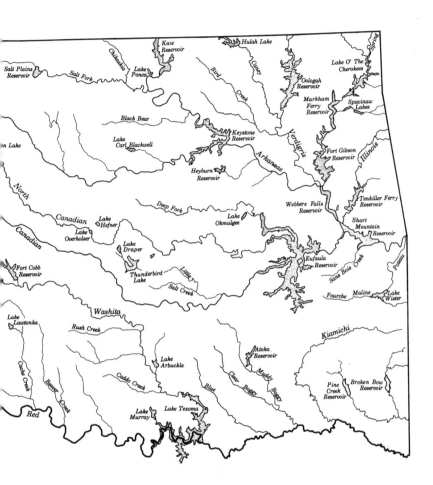

Salt Plains
Reservoir

Salt Fork

Chikaskia

Kaw
Reservoir

Lake
Ponca

Hulah Lake

Bird

Caney

Creek

Spring

Lake O' The
Cherokees

Oologah
Reservoir

Markham
Ferry
Reservoir

Spavinaw
Lakes

Black Bear

Lake
Carl Blackwell

Keystone
Reservoir

Arkansas

Verdigris

Fort Gibson
Reservoir

Illinois

n Lake

Heyburn
Reservoir

North

Canadian

Deep Fork

Lake
Hefner

Lake
Okmulgee

Webbers Falls
Reservoir

Tenkiller Ferry
Reservoir

Short
Mountain
Reservoir

Canadian

Lake
Overholser

Lake
Draper

Fort Cobb
Reservoir

Thunderbird
Lake

Little

Salt Creek

Eufaula
Reservoir

Sans Bois Creek

Poteau

Fourche

Maline

Lake
Wister

Washita

Kiamichi

Lake
Lawtonka

Rush Creek

Atoka
Reservoir

Cache Creek

Beaver

Creek

Lake
Arbuckle

Caddo Creek

Blue

Clear Boggy

Muddy

Boggy

Pine
Creek
Reservoir

Broken Bow
Reservoir

Red

Lake
Murray

Lake Texoma

southern Colorado, and extends into Oklahoma only in the extreme northwestern corner of the panhandle in Cimarron County. It is the highest topographic feature in the state (4,978 feet). The underlying sandstone has been eroded to form many deep, rocky canyons between numerous flat-topped buttes and mesas which are capped with a black, basaltic lava (as suggested by the Spanish name Mesa de Maya, meaning "armored table"); the steep slopes are often littered with boulders. The largest butte, known as Black Mesa, extends without interruption for about five miles in an east-west direction. The vegetation consists mostly of grama grasses (*Bouteloua*) and buffalo grass (*Buchloë dactyloides*), western hackberry (*Celtis reticulata*), piñon pine (*Pinus edulis*), and Rocky Mountain cedar (*Juniperus monosperma*); but cholla (*Opuntia*), scrub oak (*Quercus undulata*), and some yellow pine (*Pinus ponderosa*) are of occasional occurrence. The biota is allied to that of the foothills of the southern Rocky Mountains.

River Systems.—Oklahoma has two large drainage systems. Approximately the northern two-thirds of the state is drained by tributaries of the Arkansas River system, whereas the southern third of the state is drained by the Red River and its tributaries. Both the Arkansas and Red rivers empty into the Mississippi River. The principal east–west-trending tributaries of the Arkansas River that drain the panhandle and northwestern and central Oklahoma are the Salt Fork of the Arkansas, Cimarron, North Canadian, and South Canadian rivers. Northeastern Oklahoma is drained by the Verdigris, Grand, and Illinois rivers of the Arkansas drainage system. The Red River forms the southern boundary of Oklahoma; the principal tributaries of the Red River are the North and Salt Forks in the southwest, the Washita, Blue, and Muddy Boggy rivers in south central Oklahoma, and the Kiamichi, Little, and Mountain Fork rivers in the southeastern part of the state (Fig. 14).

42

Some of the above-mentioned rivers are known, or have been known, by different names. The Cimarron was known previously as the Red Fork of the Arkansas, and the North Canadian as the North Fork of the Canadian. The name Beaver River is now commonly applied in the panhandle to the North Canadian River upstream from its confluence with Wolf Creek, and the South Canadian River is usually referred to simply as the Canadian.

Rivers and streams in western Oklahoma are usually shallow, sluggish, sand-choked, and often intermittent, whereas those in eastern Oklahoma are deep and have moderate to rapid currents. Headwater streams having clear, cold water and rock or gravel bottoms occur in the Ozark, Ouachita, Arbuckle, and Wichita mountains. In some counties (e.g., LeFlore, see Trowbridge, 1937:289; and Pontotoc) tributaries of the Red and Arkansas drainage systems are so close to one another that stream piracy may, in time, alter existing patterns of distribution for some aquatic and riparian species of reptiles.

There are no natural lakes in Oklahoma other than a few oxbows of the Red River in extreme southeastern McCurtain County. Several large permanent impoundments are scattered throughout the state. The largest are Grand Lake or Lake o' the Cherokees (Delaware County), Oologah Reservoir (Nowata and Rogers counties), Fort Gibson Reservoir (Muskogee and Wagoner counties), Tenkiller Reservoir (Cherokee and Sequoyah counties), Keystone Reservoir (Osage and Pawnee counties), Eufaula Reservoir (McIntosh and Pittsburg counties), and Lake Texoma (Fig. 14). Cattle tanks or farm ponds occur throughout the state. These small impoundments are formed by rainwater which backs up behind earthen dams constructed across areas of natural drainage, and they may be permanent or temporary depending on size, depth, rate of evaporation, and frequency and amount of rainfall.

Faunal Relationships
of
Reptiles in Oklahoma

The distribution of most reptiles generally coincides with the geographic extent of the faunal regions discussed in the preceding section. Some reptiles, however, occur throughout the state, and the distribution of others is either incompletely known or not correlated with faunal regions.

Coastal Plain.—Seven reptiles that have eastern faunal affinities and which occur only in southeastern Oklahoma are considered to be associates of the Coastal Plain; these are:

Sternotherus carinatus
Alligator mississippiensis
Anolis carolinensis carolinensis
Farancia abacura reinwardti
Lampropeltis triangulum amaura
Natrix fasciata confluens
Regina rigida sinicola

Seven forms of uncertain status that have suggested affinities with the Coastal Plain are:

Chrysemys picta dorsalis
Ophisaurus ventralis
Agkistrodon contortrix contortrix
Coluber constrictor priapus
Crotalus horridus atricaudatus
Diadophis punctatus stictogenys
Micrurus fulvius tenere

Interior Highlands.—Five reptiles that have eastern faunal affinities are largely restricted to this faunal region, and thus

44

reach their western extent of geographic range in Oklahoma; they are:

Graptemys kohni
Sceloporus undulatus hyacinthinus
Agkistrodon contortrix mokasen
Lampropeltis triangulum syspila
Storeria occipitomaculata occipitomaculata

The status of four species, *Graptemys geographica*, *Pseudemys concinna hieroglyphica*,[1] *Natrix erythrogaster flavigaster*, and *Storeria dekayi wrightorum*, is uncertain, but evidence suggests that they are limited to the Interior Highlands.

Oak-Woodland.—Twenty-one species and subspecies of eastern faunal affinities that reach their westernmost limits of distribution in the Oak-Woodland and are limited westward by the Grassland include:

Deirochelys reticularia miaria
Graptemys pseudogeographica ouachitensis
Kinosternon subrubrum hippocrepis
Macroclemys temmincki
Pseudemys floridana hoyi
Sternotherus odoratus
Terrapene carolina triunguis
Eumeces anthracinus pluvialis
Eumeces fasciatus
Eumeces laticeps
Agkistrodon piscivorous leucostoma
Carphophis amoenus vermis
Cemophora coccinea copei

[1] Recent studies (see Weaver and Rose, 1967) have suggested that the genus *Pseudemys* should be synonymized with the genus *Chrysemys*. However, in this book I have retained *Pseudemys* as a genus distinct from *Chrysemys* pending a contemplated publication expressing this opinion by Dr. John M. Legler (personal conversation).

Crotalus horridus horridus
Masticophis flagellum flagellum
Natrix sipedon pleuralis
Opheodrys aestivus majalis
Sistrurus miliarius streckeri
Tantilla gracilis
Virginia striatula
Virginia valeriae elegans

Twelve forms of western faunal affinities reach their eastern extent of geographic range in the Oak-Woodland and are limited eastward by the Interior Highlands; these are:

Terrapene ornata ornata
Cnemidophorus gularis gularis
Eumeces obsoletus
Eumeces septentrionalis obtusirostris
Phrynosoma cornutum
Sceloporus undulatus garmani
Agkistrodon contortrix laticinctus
Heterodon nasicus gloydi
Lampropeltis triangulum gentilis
Leptotyphlops dulcis
Pituophis melanoleucus sayi
Tropidoclonion lineatum annectens

Of these, *Heterodon n. gloydi* and *Tropidoclonion l. annectens* are largely restricted to the Oak-Woodland. Parts of the Oak-Woodland that blend into either the Interior Highlands to the east or the Grassland to the west serve as areas of intergradation between five pairs of subspecies, and perhaps between *Storeria dekayi texana* and *S. d. wrightorum*; the five are:

Sceloporus undulatus hyacinthinus, S. u. garmani
Agkistrodon contortrix mokasen, A. c. laticinctus
Heterodon nasicus gloydi, H. n. nasicus
Lampropeltis triangulum syspila, L. t. gentilis
Masticophis flagellum flagellum, M. f. testaceus

Grassland.—Twelve reptiles of western faunal affinities, whose distributions eastward largely terminate in the Grassland and are limited by the Oak-Woodland, are these:

Kinosternon flavescens flavescens
Holbrookia maculata perspicua
Sceloporus undulatus consobrinus
Arizona elegans blanchardi
Crotalus viridis viridis
Heterodon nasicus nasicus
Hypsiglena ochrorhyncha texana
Masticophis flagellum testaceus
Rhinocheilus lecontei tesselatus
Tantilla nigriceps
Thamnophis marcianus
Sistrurus catenatus tergeminus

Of these, *Holbrookia m. perspicua* and *Sistrurus c. tergeminus* are confined mostly to the Grassland.

Seven forms that have eastern faunal affinities reach their western extent of geographic range in the Grassland and are limited by the High Plains; they are:

Lygosoma laterale
Ophisaurus attenuatus attenuatus
Elaphe obsoleta obsoleta
Natrix rhombifera rhombifera
Regina grahami
Storeria dekayi
Thamnophis sirtalis parietalis

The Grassland, with its many wooded areas, is a transitional region between the Oak-Woodland to the east and the High Plains to the west and serves as an area of intergradation between *Holbrookia maculata perspicua* and *H. m. maculata,* and perhaps between the subspecies of two other species, *Sistrurus catenatus tergeminus–S. c. edwardsi* and *Thamnophis proximus proximus–T. p. diabolicus.*

47

In Oklahoma, *Eumeces septentrionalis obtusirostris* and *Agkistrodon contortrix laticinctus* are restricted mostly to the Grassland and Oak-Woodland of the Central Lowland Plains.

High Plains.—Two reptiles having western faunal affinities occur principally in northwestern Oklahoma and seem to be largely confined to the High Plains; these are:

Holbrookia maculata maculata
Thamnophis radix haydeni

Three other reptiles of uncertain status that may be largely restricted to the High Plains are:

Chrysemys picta belli
Sistrurus catenatus edwardsi
Thamnophis proximus diabolicus

Mesa de Maya.—Three species of western faunal affinities are confined to this faunal region:

Cnemidophorus tesselatus
Sceloporus undulatus erythrocheilus
Thamnophis elegans vagrans

Two species of uncertain status, *Phrynosoma modestum* and *Tropidoclonion lineatum* subsp., have been captured just once in the Mesa de Maya area.

Species of Statewide Distribution.—Fourteen reptiles are considered to occur throughout the state. Five of them having western faunal affinities are these:

Trionyx muticus muticus
Cnemidophorus sexlineatus viridis
Crotaphytus collaris collaris
Elaphe guttata emoryi
Sonora episcopa episcopa

Nine statewide species of eastern faunal affinities are:

Chelydra serpentina
Pseudemys scripta elegans
Coluber constrictor flaviventris
Diadophis punctatus arnyi
Heterodon platyrhinos
Lampropeltis calligaster calligaster
Lampropeltis getulus holbrooki
Natrix erythrogaster transversa
Thamnophis proximus proximus

Filter Barriers.—Aside from the boundaries of the physiographic-vegetational faunal regions mentioned above, which are variously traversed by different reptiles, the Red River and an ill-defined faunal divide in southwestern Oklahoma also serve as filter barriers.

The Red River is a barrier to the north-south dispersal of some reptiles. *Natrix sipedon* is abundant in southeastern Oklahoma but is unrecorded in northeastern Texas, whereas *Micrurus fulvius* occurs in northeast Texas but not in southeast Oklahoma. The distribution of *Sceloporus olivaceus, Cophosaurus texanus,* and perhaps *Salvadora lineata* northward into Oklahoma from Texas is checked by the Red River. *Elaphe obsoleta obsoleta, Lampropeltis getulus holbrooki, Tropidoclonion lineatum annectens,* and *Thamnophis sirtalis parietalis* occur in Oklahoma, whereas subspecies of those species across the Red River in Texas are *E. o. lindheimeri, L. g. splendida, T. l. texanum,* and *T. s. annectens.*

Another east-west trending filter barrier in southwestern Oklahoma also limits the north-south dispersal of some reptiles. Forms that are confined mostly to southwestern Oklahoma (some extending eastward into eastern Oklahoma) include *Cnemidophorus gularis gularis, Sceloporus undulatus consobrinus* (subspecies *garmani* to the north), *Leptotyphlops dulcis*

dulcis (subspecies *dissectus* to the north), *Tantilla nigriceps fumiceps* (subspecies *nigriceps* to the north), and perhaps *Thamnophis marcianus marcianus* (subspecies *nigrolateris* to the north). The features defining this southwestern filter barrier are obscure. Of possible significance is the Mesquite Plains of Blair and Hubbell (1938:439)—a part of the Grassland in southwestern Oklahoma—or, perhaps in combination with the Mesquite Plains, the Arkansas-Red River divide, which separates the two subspecies of *Trionyx spiniferus*.

Faunal analysis.—Of the ninety-five reptiles listed under Taxonomic List of Reptiles of Oklahoma (p. 54), eight are not amenable to discussion of faunal relationships. Four of these are known only from one or from too few specimens and have uncertain distributions; they are *Chrysemys picta belli*, *Chrysemys picta dorsalis*, *Graptemys geographica*, and *Phrynosoma modestum*. Another species, *Uta stansburiana stejnegeri*, is presumably well established only in sandy habitats of the floodplain of the Red River in extreme southwestern Harmon County. The distributions of *Trionyx spiniferus hartwegi* and *Trionyx spiniferus pallidus* bear no relation to faunal boundaries, but are correlated with the drainage systems of the Arkansas and Red rivers, respectively. The distribution of *Crotalus atrox* in Oklahoma seems to be determined mostly by the presence of rocky habitats; the species occurs in rocky parts of several faunal regions.

Of the remaining eighty-seven forms, the two subspecies of each of four species are not amenable to an analysis of faunal relationships. The relationships of the subspecies of *Storeria dekayi* are uncertain, whereas the subspecies of *Leptotyphlops dulcis*, *Tantilla nigriceps*, and perhaps *Thamnophis marcianus* are affected by the southwestern filter barrier (see p. 49). Only the four species are considered, thus leaving eighty-three forms.

The bulk of the reptiles in Oklahoma have eastern faunal

affinities. Most of the turtles (eleven of fourteen, 79%) and snakes (thirty of forty-nine, 61%) have eastern faunal affinities, but most of the lizards (twelve of nineteen, 63%) have western faunal affinities. Of eighty-three species and subspecies of reptiles in Oklahoma, forty-nine (59.0%) are eastern forms of which nine (18.4%) are statewide and forty (81.6%) reach their western limits of range in Oklahoma. Twelve (30.0%) are confined to the eastern quarter of Oklahoma in the Interior Highlands (five, 12.5%) and Coastal Plain (seven, 17.5%), whereas twenty-one (52.5%) extend westward into the Oak-Woodland but are limited by the Grassland, and seven (17.5%) extend westward into the Grassland but are limited by the High Plains.

Of the eighty-three Oklahoma reptiles, thirty-four (41.0%) are western forms of which five (14.7%) are statewide, and twenty-nine (85.3%) reach their eastern limits of range in the state. Of the limited forms, five (17.2%) are confined mostly to the High Plains of the panhandle, in which three (10.3%) occur only in the Mesa de Maya, and twelve (41.4%) range eastward into the Grassland but are limited by the Oak-Woodland; another twelve (41.4%) range into the Oak-Woodland and are checked by the Interior Highlands and Coastal Plain.

Of the eighty-three, then, fourteen (16.8%, nine eastern and five western) are statewide, whereas sixty-nine (83.2%) reach their eastern or western limits of distribution in Oklahoma. The principal barriers to east-west dispersal of this last group are the ecotones, or transitions, between: (1) the Interior Highlands–Coastal Plain and Oak-Woodland, which limit twenty-four forms (34.8%, twelve eastern and twelve western), (2) the Oak-Woodland and Grassland, which limit thirty-three (47.8%, twenty-one eastern and twelve western), and (3) the Grassland and High Plains, which limit twelve (17.4%, seven eastern and five western). Almost half the reptiles reach their eastern or western extent of range at the faunal boundary of the Grassland

and Oak-Woodland. Excluding statewide species, western forms seem to be more successful in penetrating eastward into the Oak-Woodland (41.4%, twelve of twenty-nine) than the eastern forms in extending their range westward into the Grassland (17.5%, seven of forty).

The Oak-Woodland and Grassland merge and interfinger over such a large area that their mutual boundary is irregular and ill-defined, and the judgment as to whether a species or subspecies is associated with the Oak-Woodland or with the Grassland is sometimes arbitrary. For example, *Sceloporus undulatus garmani* and *Lampropeltis triangulum gentilis*, both seemingly characteristic of the Grassland, are considered in the faunal analyses as western forms that extend eastward into the Oak-Woodland. But *Hypsiglena ochrorhyncha* and *Kinosternon flavescens*, for which there are few records of occurrence in the Oak-Woodland, are considered in the faunal analyses as Grassland species. Moreover, the maximum eastward or westward extent in each of the two habitats varies from species to species. For example, in the Grassland, *Thamnophis marcianus* occurs farther eastward than *Crotalus viridis*, and in the Oak-Woodland, *Eumeces fasciatus* extends farther westward than *Eumeces anthracinus*. Nevertheless, notwithstanding a few possible changes with reference to the faunal affinities of some reptiles, the percentages given above are probably representative of the over-all faunal relationships of reptiles in Oklahoma.

The above discussion implies that species are extending their geographic ranges eastward or westward, but the peripheral records of some species may indicate relict populations or the attenuations of receding ranges. The known present distribution of reptiles in Oklahoma, plus the records of occurrence for species in places where they are not now known, and the distribution of fossils all suggest an east-west shift in the vegetational cover of Oklahoma. When a mesic, probably subtropical environment prevailed, some eastern species no doubt occurred farther west than they do now (e.g., *Macroclemys temmincki, Alligator mississippiensis,* and *Ophisaurus attenuatus*). In Pliocene times there was a general shift to a semi-arid, then arid, climate in the western part of Oklahoma (Hibbard, 1960:14, 24) and a corresponding vegetational change to a presumably grassy landscape with scattered woodland. This shift from a mesic to a more arid climate stranded eastern species in moist habitats within arid regions to the west. Four eastern species, which are not statewide and seem to have relict populations westward in the Texas panhandle, are *Storeria dekayi, Tantilla gracilis, Thamnophis sirtalis,* and *Tropidoclonion lineatum.*

The increase of human population and the resulting destruction or alteration of habitat by the clearing of land for agriculture, the grazing of livestock, or industrialization causes a decline in the numbers of reptiles or influences their distribution. In eastern Oklahoma, such practices could favor the eastward extension of range of western species (e.g., *Terrapene ornata* and *Holbrookia maculata*). In western Oklahoma, factors that seem to be resulting in an increase of forest cover in areas that were previously savanna or grassland, and thus favoring the westward spread of eastern species of reptiles, are the combination of heavy grazing and the low frequency of grass fires, the formation of ravines by erosion, and the planting of trees (Rice and Penfound, 1959:596–597). The construction of dams and formation of impoundments for recreation, flood control, or hydroelectric power affects the distribution of aquatic and riparian species by altering previously existing aquatic habitats, or by preventing movement upstream or downstream, or, especially in western Oklahoma, by providing oases for eastern species.

Taxonomic List
of
Reptiles of Oklahoma

The following ninety-five species and subspecies of living reptiles in Oklahoma (listed phylogenetically by family and alphabetically by species under each group of reptiles—turtles, lizards, snakes, and alligator) are discussed in the accounts of species.

CLASS REPTILIA

ORDER TESTUDINES—TURTLES (19)

The influence or occurrence of perhaps fourteen other kinds of reptiles in Oklahoma is suggested, but their status is uncertain because of insufficient study. These forms, which are mentioned in the account of the appropriate species, are:

Pseudemys concinna hieroglyphica
Cnemidophorus sexlineatus sexlineatus
Eumeces septentrionalis septentrionalis
Agkistrodon contortrix phaeogaster
Agkistrodon contortrix contortrix
Coluber constrictor priapus
Diadophis punctatus stictogenys
Crotalus horridus atricaudatus
Lampropeltis getulus splendida
Natrix erythrogaster flavigaster
Natrix sipedon sipedon
Sistrurus catenatus edwardsi
Thamnophis proximus diabolicus
Thamnophis sirtalis annectens

UNVERIFIED, PROBLEMATICAL, AND PROBABLE SPECIES

Of the species discussed below, only *Salvadora* and *Tantilla* are excluded from the keys to identification. Obvious waifs reported from Oklahoma include the loggerhead turtle, *Caretta caretta* (Carr, 1952:385) and the boa, *Boa constrictor* (Anon., 1959c).

Ophisaurus ventralis (Linnaeus).—The only known Oklahoma specimen (UMMZ 86538), mentioned by McConkey (1954:143) and somewhat isolated from records of the species to the east, was obtained one-quarter mile west of Glover, McCurtain County, by W. Frank Blair on June 16, 1938. The specimen seems to be *ventralis* in that it lacks a distinct, dark middorsal stripe (uppermost six scale rows of dorsum with narrowly connected dark spots arranged in six dark longitudinal stripes) and lacks dark longitudinal striping below the lateral groove.

Another specimen from McCurtain County, in the Coastal Plain (OU 11890), is referred to *Ophisaurus attenuatus* because it has a distinct middorsal stripe but only faint dark striping below the lateral body fold. A specimen of *attenuatus* from Muskogee County (OU 30324), however, resembles *ventralis* in that it lacks dark striping below the lateral groove. Further study of glass lizards in Oklahoma is needed to clarify the status of *Ophisaurus ventralis*.

Cophosaurus texanus texanus Troschel.—The Texas earless lizard occurs in north central Texas and is expected to occur in southwestern Oklahoma. The nearest record of occurrence is about ten miles south of the Oklahoma state line near Vernon, Wilbarger County, Texas (Brown, 1950:95), and probably is the same locality that Peters (1951:8) recorded as Hilltop Oil Field. Individuals of this species also have been taken twelve miles west of Quanah, Hardeman County, in Cottle County, Texas (TTC 2030).

Sceloporus olivaceus Smith.—Smith and Leonard (1934:192)

reported the Texas Spiny Lizard (as *Sceloporus spinosus flori-danus*) in Oklahoma from "Love county, Near Marietta." The record is based on three males (KU 15024–26) collected by Dr. Edward H. Taylor on June 17, 1930. Data include: body lengths, 69, 80, and 85 mm; tail lengths, 113, 127, and 142 mm; femoral pores, 11–12, 14–14, and 12–13; longitudinal middorsal scales, 29, 29, and 28; and transverse middorsal scales, 37, 37, and 35, respectively.

Field work in Love and adjacent Marshall counties, mostly resulting from the yearly summer activities at the University of Oklahoma Biological Station in Marshall County, has failed to yield additional specimens of this mostly arboreal species, and prompted Carpenter (1956:41) to consider *Sceloporus oli-vaceus* as "Rare." Taylor traveled south from Marietta and crossed the Red River into Texas, but he has no recollection of having collected the lizards (personal conversation), and perti-nent field notes could not be found. If *Sceloporus olivaceus* oc-curs in south central Love County, it is not common. Brown (1950:104) lists *olivaceus* from only one of the Texas counties (Cooke, adjacent to Love) that border Oklahoma to the south (Howard McCarley informs me that *olivaceus* has been taken in Montague County). It is possible that the three lizards were captured south of the Red River in Texas. The Red River is a filter barrier that affects the north-south distribution of other reptiles (see p. 49).

Salvadora lineata Schmidt.—The occurrence of the genus *Salvadora* in Oklahoma is indicated by the maps in Bogert (1939:215, Map 2) and Wright and Wright (1957:646, Map 49, 649). To my knowledge, there are no specimens that verify the occurrence of the patch-nosed snake in Oklahoma. The north-ernmost records in Texas seem to be from Palo Pinto (Ander-son, 1942:127; Conant, 1942:196), Tarrant (Ramsey, 1951:176), and Young (Brown, 1950:179) counties.

Opheodrys vernalis blanchardi Grobman.—Branson (1904: 409) recorded the western smooth green snake as statewide in

Kansas, listing the species from some of the southern counties bordering Oklahoma. Branson's report probably motivated Ortenburger to include *vernalis* (with some doubt indicated) in his keys to the snakes of Oklahoma (1927b:208, 1930b:220). Smith and Leonard (1934:194) reported the species from "Southern Oklahoma" on the basis of KU 2357 (a soft, dark-colored male having 129 ventrals), which was obtained by a Dr. Miller in 1916. Grobman (1941:14–15) pointed out that Branson's records of *vernalis* in southern and western Kansas probably were based on the rough green snake, *Opheodrys aestivus*, and he also preferred to delete *vernalis* from the Oklahoma faunal list. Smith (1956:234), however, considered *vernalis* statewide in Kansas, whereas Conant (1958:332, Map 120) agreed with Grobman (1941:38, Map) in restricting the species to northeastern Kansas. Aside from KU 2357, no other smooth green snakes have been discovered in Oklahoma. Records of occurrence of *vernalis* that are nearest to Oklahoma seem to be from Pittsburg, Crawford County, Kansas (Smith, 1956:234), and Colfax County, New Mexico (Grobman, 1941:17).

Regina septemvittata (Say).—Ortenburger (1925:86) and Force (1925a:25, 27; 1925b:81, 83) reported the queen snake from Okmulgee County. Conant (1960:26–27) observed that their reports were based on two specimens of *Regina grahami*, but that *Regina septemvittata* is expected in northeastern Oklahoma.

Tantilla atriceps (Günther).—This species has been included in the herpetofauna of Oklahoma on the basis of two specimens, KU 16144–45 (these numbers appear as 16414 and 16415 in Taylor, 1937:340), collected by Mildred Parker at Drumright, Creek County, Oklahoma, in April, 1931. Smith and Leonard (1934:195) referred the two snakes to *Tantilla nigriceps*, whereas Taylor (1937:339–340) regarded the two snakes as representative of the species *atriceps*. It is peculiar that one of the specimens Taylor referred to *atriceps*, KU 16145, is illustrated as representative of *nigriceps* (1937:342, Fig. 3). The lateral view of the head of one specimen is reproduced by Smith (1950:206, Fig. 148B; 1956:214, Fig. 158B) and referred to *atriceps*.

Other authors (Blanchard, 1938:372; Schmidt, 1953:220) have regarded *atriceps* as occurring in Oklahoma on the basis of Taylor's report. It is not known why the distributional map of *atriceps* given by Wright and Wright (1957:722, Map 55, 725) includes southern Oklahoma but excludes Creek County, from which the only specimens known to me have been reported. Stebbins (1954:502, Pl. 100) did not include Oklahoma within the range of *atriceps*, and Conant (1958:182) suggested that confirmation of the presence of the species in the state is required.

The dark head cap of KU 16144 and 16145 is truncate posteriorly, extending about one scale-length behind the parietals, and is bordered posteriorly by a pale band about one scale-length wide (indistinct in 16144). Both specimens are females having, respectively, 148 and 143 ventrals and 60 and 55 caudals, and the mental touching the anterior pair of genials. The two specimens are referable to *Tantilla atriceps*. I have not seen any specimen of *Tantilla nigriceps* from Oklahoma that can match the combination of characters of KU 16144–45. None have the truncate posterior end of the head cap or the adjacent pale band of *atriceps*, although the configuration of the posterior edge of the head cap is variable. The largest number of caudals in females of *nigriceps* from Oklahoma is 45, and most specimens (nineteen of twenty-two) have the mental separated from the first pair of genials.

The nearest records of occurrence of *atriceps* are some three hundred miles southwest of Oklahoma in Terrell County (Conant, 1958:182) and Sutton County (Raun, 1965:66), Texas, and Eddy County, New Mexico (Taylor, 1937:339). Possibly the locality data of KU 16144–45 are in error. Until the presence of *atriceps* in Oklahoma is confirmed, it seems best to delete that species from the faunal list.

Micrurus fulvius tenere (Baird and Girard).—Some reptiles in the USNM collected by Major Stephen W. Kearney are labeled "Arkansas." One of these is a Texas coral snake, USNM 4391 (Yarrow, 1882:81; Cope, 1900:1122). The late Dr. Asa O. Weese, University of Oklahoma, told me that Kearney was stationed at Fort Towson (see also p. 10) and that his collecting was done west of the present Oklahoma-Arkansas border. Possibly USNM 4391 came from the vicinity of Fort Towson, Choctaw County (Dellinger and Black, 1938:37).

Cross (in Snider, 1917:211) listed the coral snake from Oklahoma, and Ortenburger's keys to the snakes of Oklahoma (1927b:209; 1930b:220) include *Micrurus* as being of possible occurrence in extreme southeastern Oklahoma. The nearest records to Oklahoma are from Miller and Hempstead counties, Arkansas (Dowling, 1957:32), and Morris County, Texas (Werler, 1964:49, Map, 51).

Keys
to
Reptiles of Oklahoma

The following keys serve to identify the species of Oklahoma reptiles (subspecies are distinguished in the accounts of species). The keys include all species listed previously under "Taxonomic List of Reptiles of Oklahoma," as well as some others of uncertain status or of probable occurrence.

For those not familiar with using keys, they are usually dichotomous; that is, they consist of a series of couplets, each offering two choices, or alternatives, of contrasting characters. Beginning with the first couplet, choose the alternative of characters that most closely matches the characters possessed by the reptile to be identified, and then proceed as directed by the key—that is, to the next couplet indicated. Be sure to use *all* characters of one choice as a basis for identification, as one character may not be sufficient, and then compare those characters with the ones given in the alternative choice. Persons not familiar with the technical terms employed should refer to the glossary (p. 334) and the accompanying diagrams. If a specimen does not exactly fit the sets of characters given in the key, its identification may be clarified by referring to the distribution map and the subsection *Recognition* under the account of the appropriate species.

CLASS REPTILIA

KEY TO ORDERS AND SUBORDERS

1 Body short and broad, enclosed between two (upper and lower)
   shells (Fig. 15). Turtles . . . Order Testudines (p. 66)
   Body elongate, covered with scales, not enclosed between two
   shells; fingers and toes with claws 2

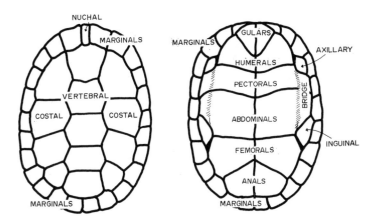

FIGURE 15. Left, carapace of turtle with names of scutes; right, plastron of turtle with names of scutes. (Redrawn from Breckenridge, 1944.)

2 Legs present 3
  Legs absent 4
3 Only the three inner fingers and toes with claws; four toes;
  nostrils elevated at tip of, and on top of, elongate snout;
  tail markedly compressed; anal opening longitudinal; copulatory organ single. Alligator . . . .
  . . . . Order Crocodilia (p. 138)
  All fingers and toes with claws; five toes; nostrils not elevated
  on top of elongate snout; tail roundish; anal opening transverse; copulatory organ double. Lizards . . . . . .
  . . . . . . Order Squamata, Suborder Sauria (p. 72)
4 External ear opening present; eye with eyelid. Lizards (Glass
  lizards) . . . . Genus *Ophisaurus* (p. 73)
  External ear opening absent; no eyelids. Snakes . . . . .
  . . . . . Order Squamata, Suborder Serpentes (p. 81)

ORDER TESTUDINES—TURTLES

KEY TO SPECIES

1 Shell flattened, edges flexible; carapace covered with skin
  (no scutes); snout pointed, fleshy, tubate (Fig. 16); three
  claws. Family Trionychidae, genus *Trionyx*, Soft shelled
  turtles 2
  Shell not much flattened, edges not flexible; carapace covered
  with horny shields or scutes (Fig. 15, left; if horny shields
  not evident, carapace roughened—juveniles of *Chelydra* and
  Macroclemys); snout not pointed, fleshy or tubate; more
  than three claws 3
2 Each nostril having ridge (resembling papilla in front view)
  projecting from nasal septum; anterior margin of carapace
  with projecting tubercles (Fig. 16, left); if tubercles absent
  or inconspicuous as in small turtles, carapace pattern uniformly pale tan or having white dots or black spots. Spiny
  Softshell Turtles (two subspecies) . . . .
  . . . . *Trionyx spiniferus* (p. 134)
  Each nostril lacking ridge projecting from nasal septum; anterior margin of carapace smooth (Fig. 16, right); carapace

66

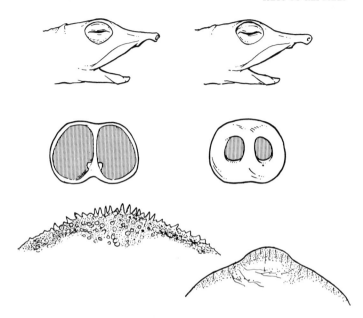

FIGURE 16. Side of head (top row), front view of tip of snout (middle row), and anterior edge of carapace (bottom row) of *Trionyx spiniferus* (left) and *Trionyx muticus* (right; from Webb, 1962).

pattern in small turtles consisting of dusky spots and streaks. Midland Smooth Softshell Turtle . . . .
. . . . *Trionyx muticus muticus* (p. 133)
3. Plastron composed of nine shields (Fig. 17, left), carapace notched or jagged posteriorly; tail long, more than half length of carapace. Family Chelydridae. Snapping turtles 4
Plastron composed of 10, 11, or 12 shields; tail short, less than half length of carapace 5

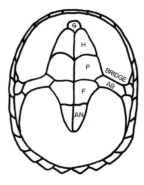 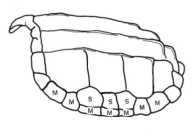

FIGURE 17. Left, plastron of *Chelydra serpentina*; AB, abdominal; AN, anal; F, femoral; G, gular; H, humeral; P, pectoral (redrawn from Smith, 1950). Right, lateral view of carapace of *Macroclemys*; M, marginals; S, supramarginals.

4 Three or four supramarginals above bridge between marginals and costals (Fig. 17, right); shields on top of head. Alligator Snapping Turtle . . . *Macroclemys temmincki* (p. 112)
No supramarginals above bridge; no shields on top of head. Common Snapping Turtle . . *Chelydra serpentina* (p. 95)

5 Plastron composed of 10 (gular absent) or 11 (gular single, unpaired) shields; pectorals not contacting marginals (Fig. 18); 22 marginals. Family Kinosternidae 6
Plastron composed of 12 (gular paired) shields; pectorals contacting marginals; 24 marginals (Fig. 15, right). Family Testudinidae 9

6 Pectorals mostly 3-sided with interpectoral suture very short, much shorter than interhumeral suture (Fig. 18, right); tail having horny, clawlike tip. Genus *Kinosternon*. Mud turtles 7
Pectorals 4-sided with interpectoral suture equal to or greater than length of interhumeral suture (Fig. 18, left); tail lacking horny, clawlike tip. Genus *Sternotherus* 8

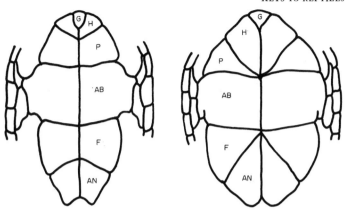

FIGURE 18. Left, plastron of *Sternotherus odoratus*; right, plastron of *Kinosternon* (redrawn from Smith, 1950); labels as in legend of Figure 17.

7 Ninth and tenth marginals enlarged, higher than eighth (not evident in juveniles); side of head yellowish or greenish; lacking distinct pale spots or stripes. Yellow Mud Turtle . . . . *Kinosternon flavescens flavescens* (p. 106)
   Only tenth marginal enlarged, higher than ninth (not evident in juveniles); side of head having two distinct, continuous or interrupted, pale stripes. Mississippi Mud Turtle . . . . *Kinosternon subrubrum hippocrepis* (p. 108)
8 Gular absent; carapace highly arched with sharp middorsal keel (three keels in juveniles); head pale brown with dark spots. Razor-backed Musk Turtle . . . . *Sternotherus carinatus* (p. 122)
   Gular present; carapace not conspicuously keeled (three keels in juveniles); head blackish with two pale stripes on sides. Stinkpot . . . . . . *Sternotherus odoratus* (p. 124)
9 Anterior lobe of plastron movable (not discernible in juveniles); head, neck, and limbs spotted but lacking distinct pale stripes; feet stumpy or clublike. Genus *Terrapene*. Box

turtles 10
Anterior lobe of plastron immovable; distinct striped pattern on
soft parts of body; feet paddlelike 11
10 Carapace having middorsal raised ridge posteriorly; plastron
unmarked, widest across femorals; interfemoral suture less
than half length of interabdominal suture; hind foot with
three toes, sometimes four. Three-toed Box Turtle . . .
. . . . *Terrapene carolina triunguis* (p. 125)
Carapace lacking middorsal raised ridge; plastron streaked with
black and yellow, usually widest across abdominals; interfemoral suture usually more than half length of interabdominal suture; hind foot with four toes. Ornate Box
Turtle . . . . . . *Terrapene ornata ornata* (p. 128)
11 Posterior surface of thighs having conspicuous, closely set, vertical, black and yellow stripes; large black mark or marks on
bridge; neck long, about two-thirds length of carapace.
Western Chicken Turtle . . . .
. . . . *Deirochelys reticularia miaria* (p. 99)
Posterior surface of thighs lacking vertical striped pattern;
markings on bridge variable; neck short, less than one-half
length of carapace 12
12 Carapace having pale, narrow or broad, middorsal stripe; hind
edge of carapace mostly smooth (edges of scutes even); tip
of upper jaw flanked on either side by short projection (Fig.
19, left, absent in young turtles). Painted Turtles (two subspecies) . . . . *Chrysemys picta* (p. 98)
Carapace lacking middorsal stripe; hind edge of carapace un-
even or jagged; tip of upper jaw not flanked on either side
by short projection 13
13 Crushing surface of upper jaw having raised "toothed" ridge
parallel to edge of jaw (Fig. 19, middle); carapace without
middorsal series of blackened knobs; plastron mostly black,
or having dark splotches, or black mostly concentrated along
sutures (large males), or, if mostly pale yellow, cutting edge
of lower jaw finely "toothed" (Fig. 19, right). Genus
Pseudemys 14

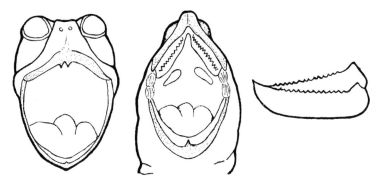

Figure 19. Left, front view of head of *Chrysemys picta* (redrawn from Smith, 1961); middle, front view of head of *Pseudemys scripta* with mouth open wide (redrawn from Smith, 1961); right, lateral view of lower jaw of *Pseudemys floridana* (redrawn from Smith, 1950).

Crushing surface of upper jaw smooth, without raised ridge; carapace having slightly raised or conspicuous middorsal series of black knobs at rear of vertebrals; plastron lacking separate dark blotches or black concentrated only along sutures; cutting edge of lower jaw smooth. Genus *Graptemys*. Map turtles 15

14 Plastron having black, roundish blotch on each scute, or mostly uniformly black posteriorly (large females), or buff except for black concentrated along sutures (melanistic males); enlarged red (in life) blotch behind eye (yellowish or buff, slightly red-tinged in melanistic males); cutting edge of lower jaw smooth, not finely "toothed." Red-eared Turtle . . . . *Pseudemys scripta elegans* (p. 116)

Plastron mostly pale yellow or having dusky, centrally located, usually interrupted pattern; side of head lacking red blotch, having pale yellow stripes on blackish background; cutting edge of lower jaw finely "toothed" (Fig. 19, right). Missouri Slider . . . . . . *Pseudemys floridana hoyi* (p. 114)

71

15 Carapace having inconspicuous middorsal series of blackened knobs on vertebrals; posterior edge of carapace only slightly notched or jagged; thin yellow line on mandibular symphysis; small yellow spot behind eye, separated from eye by short, vertical yellow line (Fig. 20, left). Map Turtle . . . .
. . . . *Graptemys geographica* (p. 100)
Carapace having conspicuous middorsal series of black knobs on vertebrals; rear margin of carapace strongly notched; thick line or large pale spot on mandibular symphysis 16

FIGURE 20. Patterns on side of head of species of *Graptemys* (black markings represent pale striping); left, *G. geographica*; middle, *G. kohni;* right, *G. pseudogeographica ouachitensis.*

16 Linear mark behind eye continuous with upper longitudinal line and curving under eye; no yellow spot on upper jaw under eye (Fig. 20, middle). Mississippi Map Turtle . . . . *Graptemys kohni* (p. 102)
Roundish blotch behind eye, about same size as eye, continuous with upper longitudinal line in some specimens; yellow spot on upper jaw under eye (Fig. 20, right). Ouachita Map Turtle . . . .
. . . *Graptemys pseudogeographica ouachitensis* (p. 104)

ORDER SQUAMATA, SUBORDER SAURIA—LIZARDS
KEY TO SPECIES

1 Snake-like, legs absent; well defined fold of skin along side

of body. Family Anguidae, genus *Ophisaurus*. Glass
lizards 2
Legs present; no well defined fold or tuck of skin along side
of body 3
2 Dark middorsal stripe; dark longitudinal stripes usually present
below lateral fold of skin. Western Slender Glass Lizard
. . . . . . *Ophisaurus attenuatus attenuatus* (p. 177)
Distinct middorsal stripe lacking; dorsum lacking stripes or
having narrowly connected dark spots arranged to form
several parallel longitudinal lines; no longitudinal dark
stripes below lateral fold of skin. Eastern Glass Lizard
. . . . *Ophisaurus ventralis* (p. 58)

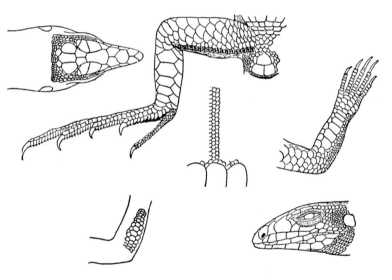

FIGURE 21. Aspects of scutellation in *Cnemidophorus gularis gularis*.
Upper left, dorsal view of head; lower left, posterior surface of
forearm; upper center, ventral surface of leg; center, scales on side
of body and belly; upper right, anterior surface of forearm; lower
right, side of head. (From Ortenburger, 1930b, after Cope.)

73

3 Belly scales large, squarish or rectangular, conspicuously oriented in eight longitudinal rows; belly scales much larger than, and abruptly differentiated from, small granules on sides and back (Fig. 21, center). Family Teiidae, genus *Cnemidophorus* 4
  Belly scales mostly roundish, neither conspicuously oriented in eight longitudinal rows nor abruptly differentiated from scales on sides of body 6
4 Light longitudinal lines on back and sides of body straight and continuous; no wavy middorsal pale stripe; no dark crossbars or checkerboard pattern 5
  Light longitudinal lines on back and sides connected by short crossbars forming checkerboard pattern; pattern conspicuously striped, and middorsal pale stripe slightly wavy in young. Checkered Whiptail . . . .
  . . . . *Cnemidophorus tesselatus* (p. 149)
5 Light spots (ill-defined in some specimens) in dark areas between light stripes, at least posteriorly between lateralmost stripes; no greenish suffusion on body; small patch of enlarged scales on rear surface of forearm (Fig. 21, lower left). Eastern Spotted Whiptail . . . .
  . . . . . . *Cnemidophorus gularis gularis* (p. 140)
  Light spots lacking between light stripes; greenish suffusion often on body; no patch of enlarged scales on rear surface of forearm. Prairie Lined Racerunner . . . .
  . . . . . *Cnemidophorus sexlineatus viridis* (p. 144)
6 Scales on back, sides of body, and belly smooth, flat, and of about uniform size and overlapping (Fig. 24); small beadlike or granular scales absent. Family Scincidae. Skinks 7
  Scales on back keeled, pointed, and overlapping, or small and granular and smaller than scales on belly. Family Iguanidae 12
7 Supranasals absent, frontonasal touching rostral; lower eyelid with transparent spot (Fig. 23, left). Ground Skink
  . . . . *Lygosoma laterale* (p. 173)
  Supranasals present, separating frontonasal and rostral (Fig.

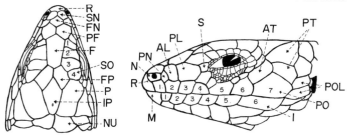

FIGURE 22. Scutellation of top of head (left) and side of head (right) of *Eumeces*. AL, anterior loreal; AT, anterior temporal; FN, fronto-nasal; FP, frontoparietal; F, frontal; I, infralabial; IP, interparietal; M, mental; N, nasal; NU, nuchal; P, parietal; PF, prefrontal; PL, posterior loreal; PN, postnasal; PO, preocular; POL, postlabial; PT, posterior temporal; R, rostral; S, supralabial; SN, supranasal; SO, supraocular. (Redrawn from Smith, 1950.)

22, left); lower eyelid covered with small scales (Fig. 23, right). Genus *Eumeces* 8

8 Most of scales on back and sides white to tan with dark borders; dark areas usually arranged to form lateral band and often longitudinal rows on back, or body black with broken white streaks on head (young); scales in diagonal rows on sides of body (Fig. 24, left). Great Plains Skink . . . . *Eumeces obsoletus* (p. 162)
Adult and young coloration and pattern not as just described; scales in parallel rows on sides of body (Fig. 24, right). 9

9 Postnasal present (Fig. 22, right) 10
Postnasal absent 11

10 Supralabials usually eight; postlabials of small size; snout-vent length more than 85 mm (3½ inches). Broad-headed Skink . . . . *Eumeces laticeps* (p. 161)
Supralabials usually seven; two large postlabials (Fig. 22, right); snout-vent length not more than 85 mm. Five-lined Skink . . . . *Eumeces fasciatus* (p. 156)

75

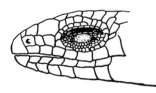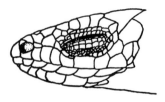

FIGURE 23. Left, side of head of *Lygosoma laterale*; right, side of head of *Eumeces obsoletus*. (From Ortenburger, 1930b.)

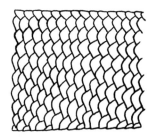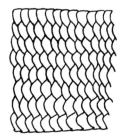

FIGURE 24. Left, side of body (posterior to left) of *Eumeces obsoletus*; right, side of body of *Eumeces fasciatus*. (From Ortenburger, 1930b.)

11 One postmental (Fig. 25, left). Southern Coal Skink . . .
. . . . *Eumeces anthracinus pluvialis* (p. 155)
Two postmentals (Fig. 25, right). Southern Prairie Skink.
. . . . . *Eumeces septentrionalis obtusirostris* (p. 166)
12 Head having bony spines posteriorly (Fig. 26); body conspicuously depressed. Genus *Phrynosoma*. Horned lizards 13
Head lacking bony spines posteriorly; body roundish . . 14
13 Pale middorsal stripe on back; two rows of projecting, spinelike, movable scales on sides. Texas Horned Lizard
. . . . *Phrynosoma cornutum* (p. 178)

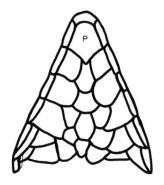

FIGURE 25. Ventral view of head of *Eumeces anthracinus* (left) and *Eumeces septentrionalis* (right); P, postmental. (Redrawn from Smith, 1950.)

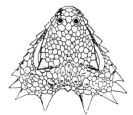

FIGURE 26. Dorsal, ventral, and side views of head of *Phrynosoma cornutum*. (From Ortenburger, 1930b, after Cope.)

    Pale middorsal stripe and projecting, spinelike scales lacking. Round-tailed Horned Lizard . . . .
. . . . *Phrynosoma modestum* (p. 183)
14 Underside of fingers and toes expanded, padlike; femoral pores absent; dorsal scales small and granular (Fig. 27). Carolina Anole . . . .
. . . . *Anolis carolinensis carolinensis* (p. 139)
Underside of fingers and toes not expanded; femoral pores present 15

FIGURE 27. Aspects of scutellation in *Anolis carolinensis*. Left, underside of foot; right, ventral surface of hind leg. (From Ortenburger, 1930b, after Cope.)

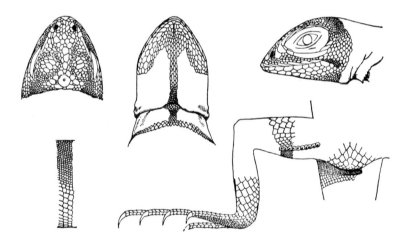

FIGURE 28. Aspects of scutellation in *Holbrookia maculata*. Upper left, top of head; lower left, side of body and belly; upper center, underside of head and neck; upper right, side of head; lower right, ventral surface of leg. (From Ortenburger, 1930b, after Cope.)

15· Ear opening absent; at least two black marks, usually barlike, on sides of body (Fig. 28). Earless lizards 16

Ear opening present; black spots absent on sides of body or one just behind foreleg 17

16 Tail flattened with black bands underneath. Texas Earless Lizard . . . . . *Cophosaurus texanus texanus* (p. 58)

Tail roundish, lacking black bands underneath. Earless Lizards (two subspecies) . . . . *Holbrookia maculata* (p. 169)

17 Scales on back small and granular (Fig. 29, lower right); usually two interrupted black bands on neck. Eastern Collard Lizard . . . *Crotaphytus collaris collaris* (p. 150)

Scales on back small or large, but flat, keeled, and overlapping (Fig. 30, upper right); distinct black bands lacking on neck 18

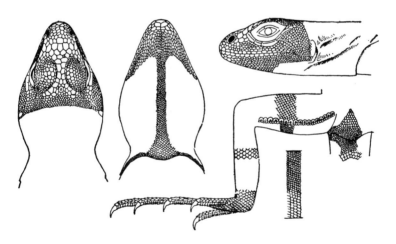

FIGURE 29. Aspects of scutellation in *Crotaphytus collaris*. Left, top of head; center, underside of head and neck; upper right, side of head; right center, ventral surface of leg; lower right, side of body and belly. (From Ortenburger, 1930b, after Cope.)

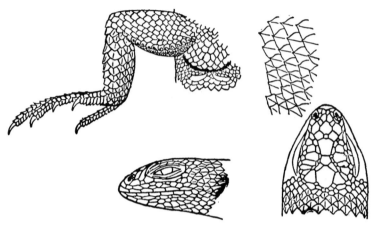

FIGURE 30. Aspects of scutellation in *Sceloporus undulatus*. Upper left, ventral surface of leg; lower left, side view of head; upper right, side of body; lower right, top of head. (From Ortenburger, 1930b, after Cope.)

18   Roundish black spot just behind foreleg on side of body; scales on back small (more than 80 dorsal scales). Desert Side-blotched Lizard . . . .
. . . . *Uta stansburiana stejnegeri* (p. 190)
Black spot behind foreleg absent; scales on back large (less than 60 dorsal scales). Genus *Sceloporus* 19

19   Dorsal scales large, 33 or fewer; posterior surface of thighs whitish, lacking markings or only very few; snout-vent length exceeding 80 mm (3¼ inches). Texas Spiny Lizard . . . . *Sceloporus olivaceus* (p. 58)
Dorsal scales small, more than 33; posterior surface of thighs mottled and streaked; snout-vent length not exceeding 80 mm. Prairie, Plateau, and Fence Lizards (four subspecies) . . . . *Sceloporus undulatus* (p. 184)

Order Squamata, Suborder Serpentes—Snakes

Key to Species

1 Scales on belly same size as those on rest of body (Fig. 32, upper center). Family Leptotyphlopidae. Blind snakes (two subspecies) . . . . . . *Leptotyphlops dulcis* (p. 248)
  Scales on belly larger than those on rest of body (Fig. 31 E) 2

2 Facial pit on side of head between eye and nostril (Fig. 33, upper right). Family Viperidae, poisonous snakes . . 3
  Facial pit absent. Family Colubridae, nonpoisonous snakes
  9

3 Rattle or horny button on tip of tail (Fig. 34) 4
  No rattle or horny button on tail tip. Genus *Agkistrodon*
  8

4 Several small scales on top of head and several between large supraoculars (Fig. 33, left). Genus *Crotalus* 5
  Few large scales on top of head; only one scale between large supraoculars (Fig. 35, left). Genus *Sistrurus* 7

5 Pattern of dark, chevron-shaped or barlike marks across back; tail black; young with ill-defined ringed pattern on tail. Timber Rattlesnake . . . .
  . . . . *Crotalus horridus horridus* (p. 212)
  Pattern of roundish or diamond-shaped blotches on back; tail with ill-defined or contrasting ringed pattern, not all black 6

6 Pattern on back of brownish, white-edged, diamond-shaped blotches that seem to overlap; tail with contrasting black and whitish rings. Western Diamond-back Rattlesnake . .
  . . . . *Crotalus atrox* (p. 209)
  Pattern on back of separate brown, roundish to rectangular blotches; tail with ill-defined ringed pattern. Prairie Rattle-snake . . . . *Crotalus viridis viridis* (p. 215)

7 Dorsal scale rows number 23 or 25 at midbody; upper pre-ocular large, touching nasal (Fig. 35, lower center). Western Massasauga . . . .
  . . . . *Sistrurus catenatus tergeminus* (p. 284)

81

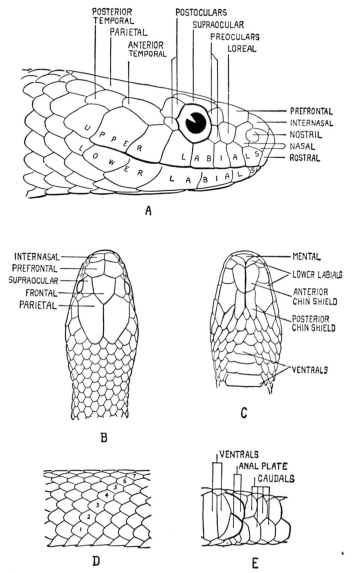

FIGURE 31. Names of scales of snake, *Diadophis punctatus*. A, side of head; B, top of head; C, underside of head; D, side of body, showing method of counting dorsal scale rows; E, ventral view of anal region. (From Ortenburger, 1930b, after Blanchard.)

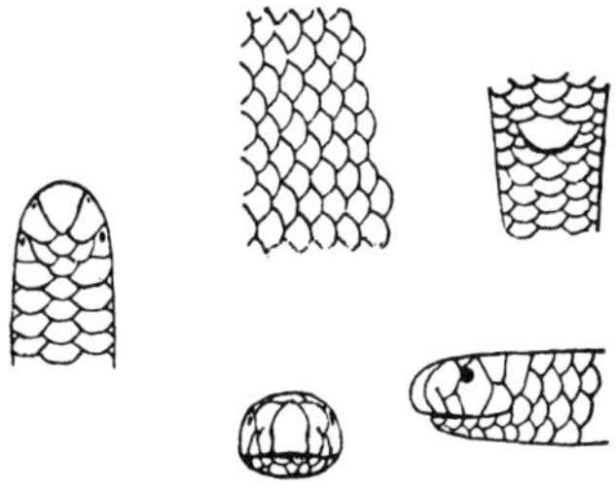

FIGURE 32. Aspects of scutellation in *Leptotyphlops dulcis.* Left, top of head; upper center, ventral scales; lower center, snout view of head; upper right, ventral view of anal region; lower right, side of head. (From Ortenburger, 1930b, after Cope.)

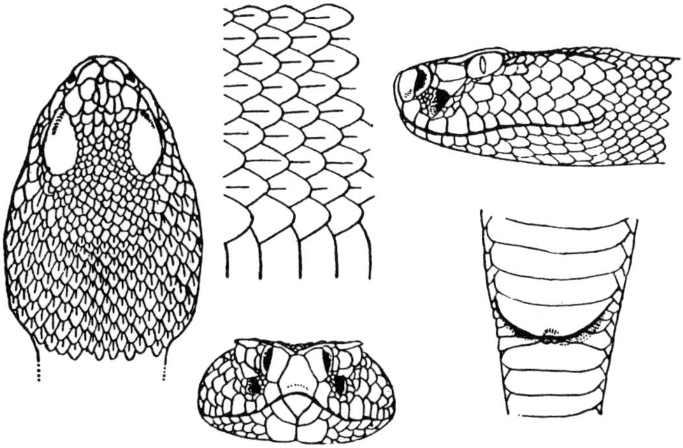

FIGURE 33. Aspects of scutellation in *Crotalus horridus.* Left, top of head; upper center, side of body; lower center, snout view of head; upper right, side of head; lower right, ventral view of anal region. (From Ortenburger, 1930b, after Cope.)

FIGURE 34. Tail tip with rattle of *Crotalus horridus.* (From Ortenburger, 1930b, after Stejneger and Garman.)

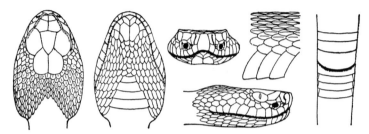

FIGURE 35. Aspects of scutellation in *Sistrurus catenatus*. Left, top and underside of head; upper center, snout view of head and side of body; lower center, side of head; right, ventral view of anal region. (From Ortenburger, 1930b, after Cope.)

       Dorsal scale rows number 21 at midbody; upper preocular small, not touching nasal. Western Pigmy Rattlesnake . . . . *Sistrurus miliarius streckeri* (p. 288)

8 Scale rows number 25 at midbody; suboculars absent, at least one upper labial touching orbit (Fig. 36, right). Western Cottonmouth . . . . *Agkistrodon piscivorous leucostoma* (p. 195)
       Scale rows number 23 at midbody; suboculars present, no upper labial touching orbit (Fig. 36, left). Copperheads (two subspecies) . . . . . *Agkistrodon contortrix* (p. 191)

9 Dorsal scales smooth (Fig. 37, right) 10
       Keels on some or all of dorsal scales (Fig. 37, left) . . . 30

10 Anal plate entire (Fig. 38) 11
       Anal plate divided (Figs. 31E, 39) 16

11 All or most of caudals undivided (Fig. 38); body patterned mostly with black and red. Texas Long-nosed Snake . . . . *Rhinocheilus lecontei tesselatus* (p. 282)
       Caudals divided (Fig. 39) 12

 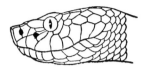

FIGURE 36. Left, side of head of *Agkistrodon contortrix*; right, side of head of *Agkistrodon piscivorous*. (From Ortenburger, 1930b, after Stejneger.)

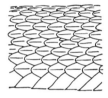 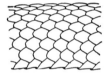

FIGURE 37. Left, side of body having keeled dorsal scales; right, side of body having smooth dorsal scales. (From Ortenburger, 1930b, after Blanchard.)

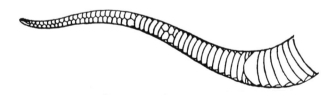

FIGURE 38. Underside of tail of *Agkistrodon piscivorous*, showing entire anal plate and undivided caudals. (From Ortenburger, 1930b, after Stejneger.)

85

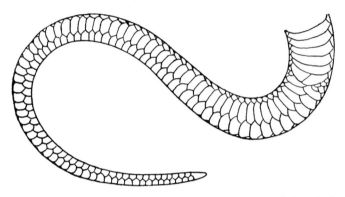

FIGURE 39. Underside of tail of *Natrix*, showing divided anal plate and divided caudals. (From Ortenburger, 1930b, after Stejneger.)

12 Belly whitish, lacking dark markings 13
   Belly having dark markings. Genus *Lampropeltis* . . . 14
13 Dorsal scale rows at midbody number 29 or 31; pattern on
   body of brownish blotches. Kansas Glossy Snake . . .
   . . . . *Arizona elegans blanchardi* (p. 198)
   Dorsal scale rows at midbody number 19; black, red, and yellow
   banded pattern. Scarlet Snake . . . .
   . . . . *Cemophora coccinea copei* (p. 203)
14 Dorsal ringlike pattern of red or orange, black, and yellow or
   whitish. Milk Snakes (three subspecies) . . . . . .
   . . . . *Lampropeltis triangulum* (p. 244)
   Dorsal pattern of brown blotches, or yellow-speckled on
   black 15
15 Dorsal pattern of brown blotches. Prairie Kingsnake . .
   . . . . . . *Lampropeltis calligaster calligaster* (p. 236)
   Dorsal pattern speckled, yellow dots on black background.
   Speckled Kingsnake . . . .
   . . . . *Lampropeltis getulus holbrooki* (p. 240)
16 Dorsum uniform gray black except for pale ring on neck; belly

orange with black spots. Prairie Ringneck Snake . . . .
. . . . *Diadophis punctatus arnyi* (p. 218)
Coloration and pattern not as just described 17

17 Dorsum uniform green or grayish green (bluish in preserva-
tive); belly pale yellow, unmarked. Western Smooth Green
Snake . . . . . *Opheodrys vernalis blanchardi* (p. 59)
Coloration not as just described 18

18 Dorsum of broad black and red rings separated by narrow
yellow rings; loreal absent (Fig. 40). Texas Coral Snake
. . . . *Micrurus fulvius tenere* (p. 62)
Dorsum lacking red, yellow, and black rings; loreal present or
absent 19

FIGURE 40. Side of head of coral
snake, *Micrurus fulvius*. (From
Ortenburger, 1930b, after
Blanchard.)

19 Dorsal scale rows number 25 or more at midbody. Genus
Elaphe. Rat snakes 20
Dorsal scale rows number fewer than 25 at midbody . . 21

20 Large black snakes having faint blotched pattern, white fleck-
ing, and reddish skin between scales in some specimens, or
small snakes, having fewer than 35 conspicuous, squarish,
dorsal blotches on body. Black Rat Snake . . . . . .
. . . . *Elaphe obsoleta obsoleta* (p. 225)
Large or small snakes having more than 35 conspicuous, oblong, and transversely oriented, dorsal blotches on body.
Great Plains Rat Snake . . *Elaphe guttata emoryi* (p. 222)

21 Dorsal scale rows at midbody number 21, rarely 23; dorsal pat-
tern of brownish blotches. Texas Night Snake . . . . .
. . . . . . *Hypsiglena ochrorhyncha texana* (p. 235)
Dorsal scale rows at midbody number fewer than 21 . . 22

Figure 41. Left, top of head of *Farancia abacura*; right, top of head of *Virginia valeriae*. (From Ortenburger, 1930b, after Blanchard.)

22 Dorsal scale rows number 13 at midbody; dorsum uniformly dark gray; belly uniformly salmon pink. Western Worm Snake . . . . . *Carphophis amoenus vermis* (p. 200)

Dorsal scale rows number more than 13 at midbody . . 23

23 Dorsal scale rows number 19 at midbody; dorsum uniformly blue black; belly contrastingly marked with black and orange; internasals fused into single scale (Fig. 41, left). Western Mud Snake . . *Farancia abacura reinwardti* (p. 228)

Dorsal scale rows number fewer than 19 at midbody . . 24

24 Dorsal scale rows number 17 at midbody 25

Dorsal scale rows number 15 at midbody 28

25 Maximal length usually not exceeding one foot; dorsum uniformly brown; five or six supralabials; no preoculars. Genus *Virginia*. Earth snakes 26

Maximal length much more than one foot; if one foot long or less, dorsal pattern of blotches or crossbands; seven or more supralabials; two preoculars, lowermost very small (Fig. 42, lower right) 27

26 Dorsal scales keeled; five upper labials; one postocular (Fig. 43, left); usually one internasal. Rough Earth Snake . . . .
. . . . *Virginia striatula* (p. 320)

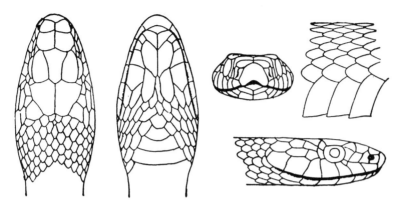

FIGURE 42. Aspects of scutellation in *Coluber constrictor*. Left, dorsal and ventral views of head; upper right, snout view of head and side of body; lower right, side of head. (From Ortenburger, 1930b, after Cope.)

Dorsal scales smooth (keeled faintly posteriorly); six upper labials; two or three postoculars (Fig. 43, right); usually two internasals (Fig. 41, right). Western Earth Snake . . . . *Virginia valeriae elegans* (p. 324)

27 Dorsal scale rows at posterior end of body number 13. Coachwhips (two subspecies) . . *Masticophis flagellum* (p. 252)
Dorsal scale rows at posterior end of body number 15. Yellow-bellied Racer . . *Coluber constrictor flaviventris* (p. 204)

28 Loreal usually present; usually seven, rarely six, supralabials; two or three postoculars; dorsum uniformly pale brown or reddish, or with one or several dark crossbands in some specimens. Great Plains Ground Snake . . . . *Sonora episcopa episcopa* (p. 290)
Loreal absent (Fig. 44); six supralabials; if seven supralabials, head is black; one postocular, if two postoculars, head is black. Genus *Tantilla* 29

29 Head brownish, about same color as rest of body; six supra-

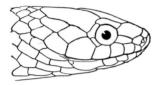

FIGURE 43. Left, side of head of *Virginia striatula*; right, side of head of *Virginia valeriae*. (From Ortenburger, 1930b, after Blanchard.)

        labials; one postocular (Fig. 44). Flat-headed Snake . . .
        . . . . *Tantilla gracilis* (p. 298)
        Head black, sharply contrasting with brownish body; seven
        supralabials; two postoculars. Black-headed Snakes (two sub-
        species) . . . . *Tantilla nigriceps* (p. 302)

30 Anal plate entire (Fig. 38) 31
      Anal plate divided (Fig. 39) 37
31 Pattern of brownish dorsal blotches; four prefrontals. Bull-
      snake . . . . . *Pituophis melanoleucus sayi* (p. 275)
      Pattern of conspicuous longitudinal stripes; if stripes obscure,
      belly partly blackish; two prefrontals 32
32 Double row of black spots midventrally. Central Lined Snake
      . . . . . *Tropidoclonion lineatum annectens* (p. 318)
      Belly lacking midventral double row of discrete black spots, but
      belly having midventral black streak, or blackish marks
      laterally on ends of ventrals in some specimens. Genus
      Thamnophis 33
33 Pale lateral stripe only on third dorsal scale row anteriorly.
      Checkered Garter Snakes (two subspecies) . . . . . .
      . . . . *Thamnophis marcianus* (p. 306)
      Pale lateral stripe on at least two dorsal scale rows anteriorly 34
34 Pale lateral stripe on second and third scale rows anteriorly 35
      Pale lateral stripe on third and fourth scale rows anteriorly 36
35 Dorsal scale rows number 21 at midbody; eight supralabials;

belly with blackish midventral area. Wandering Garter
Snake . . . . . *Thamnophis elegans vagrans* (p. 306)
Dorsal scale rows number 19 at midbody; seven supralabials;
belly lacking markings except for dark marks laterally on
ends of ventrals. Red-sided Garter Snake . . . . . .
. . . . *Thamnophis sirtalis parietalis* (p. 314)

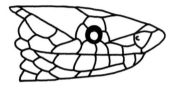

FIGURE 44. Side of head of
Tantilla gracilis. (Redrawn
from Smith, 1950).

36 Supralabials with dark borders; belly having dark marks
laterally on ends of ventrals; black spots evident between
stripes and below lateral stripe. Western Plains Garter
Snake . . . . . *Thamnophis radix haydeni* (p. 313)
Supralabials lacking dark borders; belly lacking dark marks;
dark spots not evident on body. Western Ribbon Snake . .
. . . . . . *Thamnophis proximus proximus* (p. 308)
37 Rostral enlarged and keeled above, projecting forward or
turned up. Genus *Heterodon*. Hognose snakes . . . 38
Rostral normal, not enlarged, keeled, or turned up . . . 39
38 Rostral enlarged, projecting forward, not turned up; one small
azygous scale separating internasals (Fig. 45, lower left);
belly with dusky marks, not mostly blackish; dorsal scale
rows number 25 at midbody. Eastern Hognose Snake . .
. . . . *Heterodon platyrhinos* (p. 232)
Rostral enlarged, turned up; several small scales separating
prefrontals and internasals (Fig. 46, upper left); belly mostly
black; dorsal scale rows number 23, rarely 21, at midbody.
Dusty and Plains Hognose Snakes (two subspecies) . . .
. . . . *Heterodon nasicus* (p. 229)

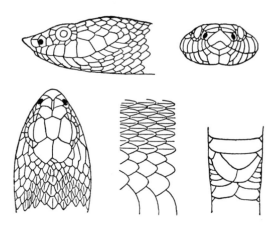

FIGURE 45. Aspects of scutellation in *Heterodon platyrhinos*. Upper left, side of head; lower left, top of head; lower center, side of body; upper right, snout view of head; lower right, ventral view of anal region. (From Ortenburger, 1930b, after Cope.)

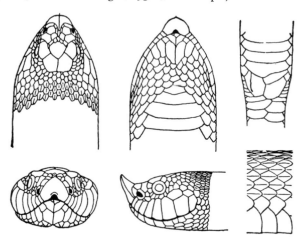

FIGURE 46. Aspects of scutellation in *Heterodon nasicus*. Upper left, top of head; upper center, underside of head; upper right, ventral view of anal region; lower left, snout view of head; lower center, side view of head; lower right, side of body. (From Ortenburger, 1930b, after Cope.)

39 Dorsal scale rows number 17 or fewer at midbody . . . 40
    Dorsal scale rows number 19 or more at midbody . . . 43
40 Dorsum uniform green or gray green (blue in preservative);
    belly pale yellow, unmarked. Western Rough Green Snake.
    . . . . *Opheodrys aestivus majalis* (p. 272)
    Coloration not as just described 41
41 Preocular absent; loreal elongate, entering orbit (Fig. 43).
    Genus *Virginia*. Earth snakes 26
    One or two preoculars; loreal absent (Fig. 47). Genus
    Storeria 42

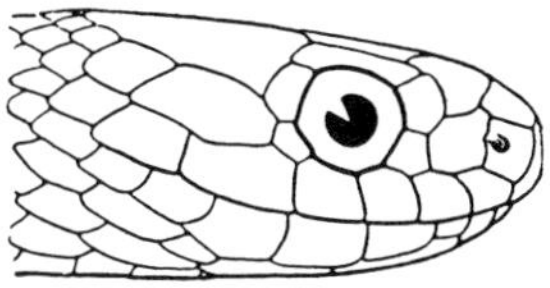

FIGURE 47. Side of head of *Storeria occipitomaculata* (From Ortenburger, 1930b, after Blanchard.)

42 Dorsal scale rows number 15 at midbody; two preoculars.
    Northern Red-bellied Snake . . . .
    . . . *Storeria occipitomaculata occipitomaculata* (p. 297)
    Dorsal scale rows number 17 at midbody; one preocular. Brown
    Snakes (two subspecies) . . . *Storeria dekayi* (p. 293)
43 Internasals fused into single scale (Fig. 41, left); preoculars
    absent; dorsal scales smooth (keeled above anal plate in some
    specimens) in 19 rows at midbody. Western Mud Snake . .
    . . . . *Farancia abacura reinwardti* (p. 228)
    Two internasals; preoculars present; dorsal scales strongly
    keeled if 19 rows at midbody 44
44 Dorsal scales smooth or weakly keeled, in 25 or more rows at
    midbody; two postoculars. Genus *Elaphe*. Rat snakes . . 20
    Dorsal scale rows strongly keeled; three postoculars; if two
    postoculars, dorsal scale rows number 19 or 23 at midbody 45
45 Dorsal scale rows number 19 at midbody. Genus *Regina* 46
    Dorsal scale rows number more than 19 at midbody. Genus
    Natrix. Water snakes 48

46 Belly without markings, or with a single dark line or row of spots, at least posteriorly. Graham's Water Snake . . . . *Regina grahami* (p. 279)
Belly with at least two dark stripes or rows of spots . . . 47

47 Belly with two rows of large black spots. Glossy Water Snake . . . . *Regina rigida sinicola* (p. 280)
Belly with four brownish stripes; two in middle narrow, often series of spots and most distinct anteriorly; two outer stripes wide, on edges of ventrals. Queen Snake . . . . *Regina septemvittata* (p. 60)

48 Dorsal scale rows number 27 (rarely 25) or more at mid-body; dark chainlike pattern enclosing pale diamond-shaped blotches on back. Diamond-backed Water Snake . . . . *Natrix rhombifera rhombifera* (p. 264)
Dorsal scale rows number 23 or 25 (rarely 27) or fewer at midbody; pattern not of diamond-shaped blotches . . 49

49 Belly mostly without markings or with dark marks along edges, and at ends, of ventrals. Blotched Water Snake . . . . *Natrix erythrogaster transversa* (p. 259)
Belly with large dark blotches or extensively mottled . . 50

50 Belly with large, squarish dark markings, mostly at sides; dorsal pattern of fewer than 20, narrowly separated, large blackish blotches. Broad-banded Water Snake . . . . *Natrix fasciata confluens* (p. 263)
Belly extensively mottled and blotched with relatively small markings; dorsal blotches or bands number more than 20. Midland Water Snake . . *Natrix sipedon pleuralis* (p. 269)

Annotated Accounts
of Species

ORDER TESTUDINES—TURTLES

Chelydra serpentina (Linnaeus)

Common Snapping Turtle

Recognition.—Tail long, about as long as carapace; plastron small, having nine shields with abdominals forming part of bridge; carapace ruffled, with three low, blunt, longitudinal keels, and lacking supramarginals; scales lacking on top of head. Young blackish or dark gray to brown, usually with buffy streak on side of head and having white marks on underside of marginals.

Distribution.—Throughout the state (map, Fig. 48).

Remarks.—Individuals of this widespread species have been obtained from large rivers and impoundments, small pasture ponds, and narrow headwater streams and may be expected in almost any kind of relatively permanent, clear or turbid, aquatic habitat. The turtle from the westernmost locality—in the panhandle near the Cimarron River—is represented only by a plastron from a crushed road-kill; the turtle from Texas County is from Coldwater Creek, a tributary of Beaver River. Overland movements have been observed on warm, sunny days on dirt roads and in open fields. A sluggish snapper with reddish clay caked on parts of the carapace and soft parts of the body was found on the bank of a farm pond (McClain County) during a short interval of unseasonably warm weather on January 19, 1952.

95

See Anon. (1955a, presumably *Chelydra* instead of *Macroclemys*; 1960b), Bonn and McCarley (1953:468), Carpenter (1955c; 1956:41; 1959c:34), Force (1925a:27; 1925b:83; 1930:38), Ortenburger and Bird (1933:60), Schmidt (1919:72), Self (1938), Webb (1961:194; 1962:435).

Specimens examined (OU except as indicated).—*Alfalfa*: Salt Plains Reservoir (NWSC); 2–4 mi. E Cherokee. *Beaver*: near Gate. *Bryan*: Durant. *Caddo*: 10 mi. S Anadarko. *Cleveland*: 2–4 mi. S Norman; N Moore. *Coal*: 13 mi. W Coalgate (ECSC). *Comanche*: Wichita Mts. Wildlife Refuge. *Craig*: 10 mi. W Vinita; 7 mi. S Centralia; 6 mi. E Craig-Nowata county line on U.S. Highway 60. *Custer*: Clinton (SWSC); 2 mi. W Custer (RGW); Weatherford. *Delaware*: 6 mi. E Flint. *Garvin*: Maysville. *Grant*: N Pond Creek (TTC). *Hughes*: Long George Creek, 1 mi. E Hughes-Seminole county line. *Johnston*: 4 mi. W Tishomingo. *Kiowa*: Kiowa-Tillman county line. *Latimer*: Wilburton. *LeFlore*: 5 mi. E Big Cedar; 1.5 mi. E Zoe; 6.5 mi. W Heavener. *Major*: Cleo Springs. *Marshall*: UOBS. *McClain*: 6 mi. SW Norman, Cleveland County. *McCurtain*: 14 mi. SE Broken Bow. *Murray*: Dougherty; Platt National Park. *Okmulgee*: no data. *Osage*: 3 mi. N Wynona. *Pawnee*: near Quay. *Payne*: 4 mi. W Cushing. *Pontotoc*: 11 mi. SE Ada. *Pottawatomie*: Shawnee. *Seminole*: Bowlegs. *Texas*: 8 mi. SE Guymon. *Woods*: 2 mi. W Edith; 2.5 mi. W and 1 mi. S Waynoka. *Woodward*: 6 mi. E Woodward.

Additional records.—*Adair*: near Proctor (Carter, 1966:33). *Alfalfa*: 2 mi. W Goltry (Burt, 1935:320). *Atoka*: Potapo Creek near Stringtown (Anon., 1955a). *Beckham*: 4 mi. W Sayre (Burt, 1935:320). *Blaine*: no data (CCC). *Caddo*: Kiwanis Canyon (CCC). *Carter*: no data (AMNH, sent to Perth Museum). *Cherokee*: Scraper (UMMZ). *Cimarron*: 15 mi. N and 6 mi. W Boise City (ECSC). *Cotton*: 2 mi. E Randlett and 8 mi. W Randlett (CCC). *Creek*: Sapulpa (Schmidt, 1919:72). *Delaware*: Flint (UMMZ). *Harmon*: no data (FWCM). *Jefferson*: 16 mi. E Waurika (TU). *Kingfisher*: near Kingfisher (Hughes, 1954); Hennessey (Cope, 1894:386). *LeFlore*: 6 mi. W Page (Trowbridge,

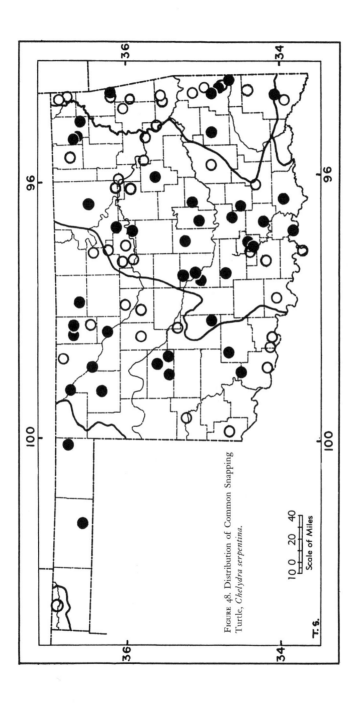

FIGURE 48. Distribution of Common Snapping Turtle, *Chelydra serpentina*.

Scale of Miles
10 0 20 40

T. S.

1937:300); 5 mi. N Heavener (KU); Slate Ford E Shadypoint (UMMZ). *Love*: 3 mi. S Thackerville (Carpenter, 1958a:71). *Mc-Curtain*: Little River bridge N Idabel (OU); 2 mi. SW Smithville (Trowbridge, 1937:300). *Murray*: Honey Creek above Turner Falls (McCoy, 1960a:41). *Muskogee*: 3 mi. NW Haskell (Burt, 1935:320); 0.5 mi. below Greenleaf Lake Dam (OSU); 7.3 mi. N Muskogee (UMMZ). *Noble*: 7 mi. SE Marland (Burt, 1935:320); Black Bear Creek (UMMZ). *Nowata*: 2 mi. N Delaware (Burt, 1935:320). *Osage*: vicinity Sand Springs, Tulsa County (UMMZ). *Ottawa*: Wyandotte, and just S Peoria (UMMZ). *Payne*: Stillwater, Lake Carl Blackwell, and near Coyle (OSU). *Pittsburg*: 2 mi. W McAlester (Burt, 1935:320). *Sequoyah*: Dwight Mission (Carpenter, 1958a:71); 11 mi. S Bunch, Adair County (UMMZ). *Tillman*: 13 mi. W Grandfield (CCC). *Tulsa*: [vicinity Tulsa] (Force, 1928:79; 1930:38). *Woods*: 13 mi. NW Alva (McCracken, 1966:3). *County unknown*: White Shield Creek (Anon., 1960b).

Chrysemys picta (Schneider)

Painted Turtles

Recognition.—Notch at tip of upper jaw flanked on either side by short projection (absent in young turtles); edges of scutes on carapace are even behind, so that posterior edge not sharply notched; pale middorsal stripe broad and conspicuous or narrow and obscure, depending upon subspecies (see *Remarks*).

Distribution.—Known only from southern McCurtain County in extreme southeastern Oklahoma, and reported once from the panhandle; two subspecies.

Remarks.—Two subspecies of *Chrysemys picta* in Oklahoma are recognized:

C. p. belli (Gray), Western Painted Turtle.—Plastron reddish around edges, having large central dark area with branches extending outward; middorsal stripe narrow and ill defined.

C. p. dorsalis Agassiz, Southern Painted Turtle.—Plastron

yellowish, lacking dark markings; middorsal stripe broad and distinct.

To my knowledge specimens of the western painted turtle have not been collected in Oklahoma. Marr (1944:489) wrote that *belli* ". . . was observed rather commonly in Beaver Co., Okla., but unfortunately none were secured." Smith (1956:149) reported *belli* in some of the southernmost counties in Kansas, and McCracken (1966:5) reported a specimen from 12 miles north of the Oklahoma border near Anthony, Harper County, Kansas. It would seem that *belli* occurs along the northern border of Oklahoma, and that it is possibly most abundant in the northwestern part of the state.

The distribution of southern painted turtles in Oklahoma is uncertain. All records for *dorsalis* are from the Coastal Plain in the Red River drainage, and are the westernmost records for the subspecies (see Bragg and Bragg, 1957).

Specimen examined.—McCurtain: 3 mi. NE Idabel (OU).

Additional records.—McCurtain: 2 mi. E and 0.5 mi. S Harris (Bragg and Bragg, 1957); Waterfall Creek at State Highway 87, S Idabel (OSU); Grassy Lake (CCC).

Deirochelys reticularia miaria Schwartz

Western Chicken Turtle

*Recognition.—*Neck long, about two-thirds length of carapace when extended; chin and throat pale yellow with indistinct striping; posterior surface of thighs marked with conspicuous, narrow, vertical, alternating black and yellow stripes; plastron mostly pale yellow, usually with black along sutures; prominent, elongate black mark on bridge.

*Distribution.—*Southeastern Oklahoma; known as far north and west as Seminole, Cleveland, and Marshall counties (map, Fig. 49).

Remarks.—Chicken turtles reach their northwesternmost extent of range in the Oak-Woodland of Oklahoma, and probably are more abundant than the relatively few records indicate. A skeleton was found near the edge of a small, shallow, wooded stream having a few deep holes (Marshall County). Two other turtles were collected from ponds—one that had aquatic vegetation (Choctaw County, Fig. 7) and one that lacked vegetation (Marshall County). Another individual was active at dusk on a paved highway (Cleveland County). Two hatchlings were seined from a small slough in April, 1953 (McCurtain County). A captive female deposited a total of 11 eggs; dates of deposition were July 15, 26, and 28, 1957 (Marshall County).

See Bonn and McCarley (1953:468), Carpenter (1956:41), Schwartz (1956:498), Webb (1950).

Specimens examined (OU except as indicated).—*Choctaw*: Red River Fisheries. *Cleveland*: 15 mi. E Norman. *Marshall*: vicinity Willis. *McCurtain*: 2 mi. SE Harris (TTC). *Seminole*: 5 mi. N Sasakwa (ECSC); Bowlegs.

Additional records.—*Bryan*: 15 mi. SE Colbert (CCC). *Marshall*: Shay (Carpenter, 1955a:40). *McCurtain*: 2 mi. S Pollard (OSU).

Graptemys geographica (Lesueur)

Map Turtle

Recognition.—Carapace lacking the conspicuous, middorsal blackened knobs or spots of the Mississippi and Ouachita map turtles; rear edge of carapace not strongly notched; striped pattern on head with small yellow spot behind eye, but spot separated from eye by short, vertical, pale line; crushing surface of upper jaw lacking median ridge; cutting edge of lower jaw smooth; plastron yellowish without dark markings (dark lines along sutures between scutes in young turtles); head much enlarged in large females (when carapace 7 to 10 inches long).

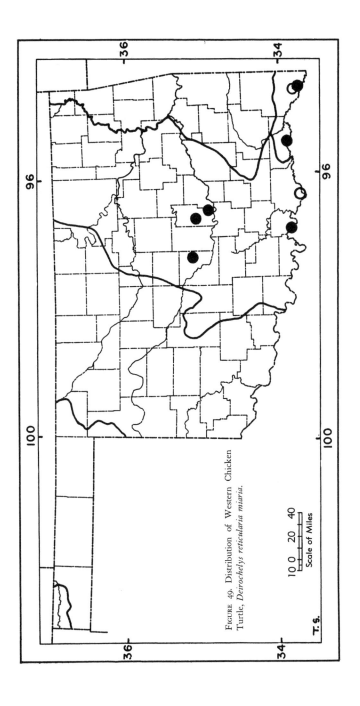

FIGURE 49. Distribution of Western Chicken Turtle, *Deirochelys reticularia miaria.*

Distribution.—Known only from Delaware County in northeastern Oklahoma.

Remarks.—The occurrence of this species in Oklahoma is based on three individuals (OU 7272–74; one exchanged to FMNH) obtained by a University of Oklahoma field party on June 12, 1927, from the Elk River, a tributary of the Grand River. Proper collecting techniques probably will reveal a more widespread distribution for the map turtle in eastern Oklahoma. Its known distribution elsewhere suggests restriction to the Arkansas River drainage.

Specimens examined.—*Delaware*: 6 mi. NE Grove (Ortenburger, 1929b:28, OU).

Graptemys kohni (Baur)

Mississippi Map Turtle

Recognition.—Carapace having blackened knobs or spots middorsally; posterior edge of carapace sharply notched; curved mark behind eye, usually continuous with pale stripe on neck and extending anteriorly under eye; head broadened in large adult females (when carapace 8 to 9 inches long); prominent pale stripes on anterior surface of forelimb not exceeding five or six; hatchlings usually having dark radiating plastral pattern confined mostly to sutures.

Distribution.—Eastern Oklahoma; known as far west as Okmulgee County (map, Fig. 50).

Remarks.—*Graptemys kohni* occurs in both the Red and Arkansas river drainages and seems to be confined mostly to the Interior Highlands. Although the patterns on the side of the head distinguishing *G. kohni* and *G. p. ouachitensis* (Cagle, 1954:184) are intermediate in some places where the two species occur together, the head patterns and other characteristics (com-

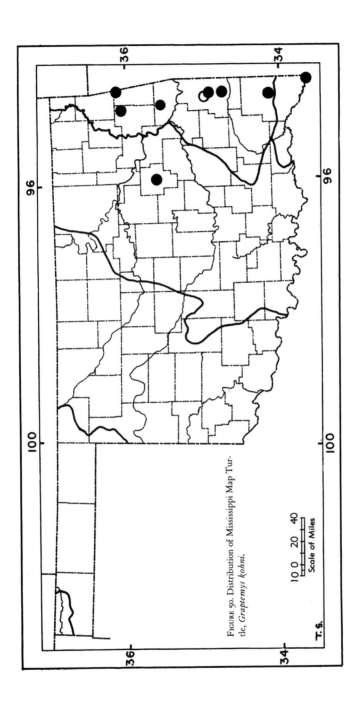

FIGURE 50. Distribution of Mississippi Map Turtle, *Graptemys kohni*.

pare comments under *Recognition*) serve to differentiate the relatively few available specimens of the two species from Oklahoma. Individuals of both species have been taken at the same place in McCurtain County. *Graptemys pseudogeographica pseudogeographica* does not occur in Oklahoma (Fred R. Cagle, personal conversation).

Specimens examined (OU except as indicated).—*Adair*: 4 mi. NW Watts. *Cherokee*: 1 mi. NE Scraper (TU); 2 mi. S Scraper. *LeFlore*: 6 mi. S Wister; 1.5 mi. E Zoe. *McCurtain*: Mountain Fork River, Beavers Bend State Park; Red River, 1 mi. W Arkansas-Oklahoma state line. *Okmulgee*: no data. *Sequoyah*: Sallisaw Creek near Dwight Mission (ECSC).

Additional record.—*LeFlore*: Wister (CM).

Graptemys pseudogeographica ouachitensis Cagle

Ouachita Map Turtle

Recognition.—Carapace having blackened knobs or spots middorsally; rear edge of carapace sharply notched; large, roundish, pale blotch behind eye, and small yellow blotch under eye; large postocular blotch connected to upper longitudinal stripe in some specimens; pale stripes on neck often orange in life; head not broadened even in largest females (when carapace about 9 inches long); many (more than five or six) pale stripes on anterior surface of forelimb; hatchlings usually having dark, broad and extensive plastral pattern not confined to sutures.

Distribution.—Eastern Oklahoma; known as far west as Kay, Noble, and Comanche counties (map, Fig. 51).

Remarks.—The Ouachita map turtle extends westward into the Oak-Woodland in tributaries of both the Red and Arkansas river drainages. The species is found in rivers, streams, and

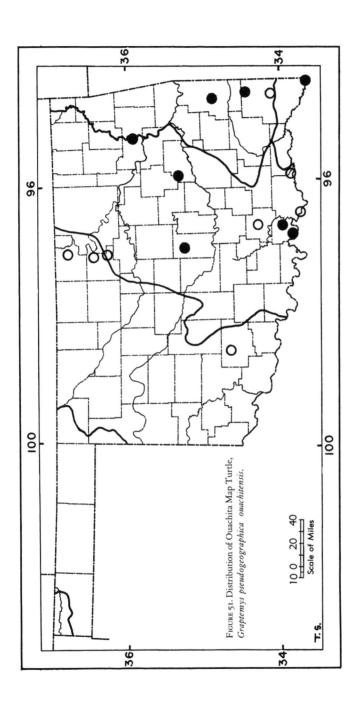

FIGURE 51. Distribution of Ouachita Map Turtle,
Graptemys pseudogeographica ouachitensis.

Scale of Miles

10 0 20 40

T. S.

impoundments, and frequently basks on emergent debris. The extent of range westward probably is determined by the permanency of water in the major rivers and streams, which may be intermittent or dry in western Oklahoma in the summer.

See Bonn and McCarley (1953:468), Cagle (1953:15), Carpenter (1956: 41; 1958c), Carr (1949:9; 1952:211), Webb (1961; 1962:436).

Specimens examined (OU except as indicated).—*LeFlore*: 6.5 mi. W Heavener. *Marshall*: UOBS; 4 mi. E and 2 mi. S Madill. *McIntosh*: 5 mi. SE Henryetta, Okmulgee County (ECSC). *McCurtain*: 2 mi. SW Smithville; Red River, 1 mi. W Arkansas-Oklahoma state line. *Pottawatomie*: 5 mi. SW Shawnee. *Wagoner*: Flat Creek Resort Area on Fort Gibson Reservoir (ECSC).

Additional records.—Bryan: Red River (OSU); Washita arm, Lake Texoma (UI); Lake West (CCC). *Comanche*: Medicine Creek, Fort Sill (Carr, 1949:9; 1952:211); Wichita Mts. (USNM). *Johnston*: no data (Carr, 1949:10; symbol on map represented by FMNH 15469). *Kay*: E Ponca City (UMMZ 89625 from this locality is recorded from Noble County by Cagle, 1953:14). *McCurtain*: Beavers Bend State Park (FWCM). *Noble*: Black Bear Creek and Red Rock Creek [both at intersection with U.S. Highway 177] (Moore and Rigney, 1942:80). *County unknown*: Dogtown Creek, Arkansas River (perhaps Dog Creek in Rogers County, USNM).

Kinosternon flavescens flavescens (Agassiz)

Yellow Mud Turtle

Recognition.—Head uniform olive, lacking distinct stripes on sides; chin and throat yellowish; carapace uniform olive or brownish; plastron yellow, often with black growth annuli and dark sutures, hinged in front and behind; pectoral scute triangular; ninth (and tenth) marginal larger than eighth (not enlarged in turtles less than two inches long); tail having horny clawlike tip; carapace not more than six inches in length.

Distribution.—Western Oklahoma; known as far east as Payne, Pontotoc, and Love counties (map, Fig. 52).

Remarks.—Yellow mud turtles do inhabit the Oak-Woodland, but they are most abundant in the Grassland in permanent or temporary waters. Individuals have been found in small roadside puddles of muddy water two to six inches deep (Harmon County), beneath wet vegetation in a recently dried-up part of Dog Creek (Woods County), in wet sand on the bank of the South Canadian River (Dewey County), and with *Pseudemys scripta* in a small pond under a bridge (Beckham County); one individual was taken on top of Black Mesa, north of Kenton (Cimarron County). Rain seems to be a stimulus for movement, as individuals are often seen on highways in rainy weather.

The easternmost published records of the species in Oklahoma are Okmulgee (Force, 1925b:82) and Tulsa (Force, 1930:37) counties. The Okmulgee record is based on OU 857, which is cataloged as *Terrapene carolina*. I am unable to account for the species in Tulsa County; Dr. Albert P. Blair told me that *flavescens* does not inhabit the vicinity of Tulsa.

See Cahn (1937:60), Carpenter (1955c; 1956:41; 1959c:34), Carter and Cox (1968), Dundee (1950c), Mahmoud (1967; 1969), Ortenburger and Freeman (1930:187), Smith and Leonard (1934:195).

Specimens examined (OU except as indicated).—*Alfalfa*: N Salt Fork on highway N Cherokee (KU); 3 and 10 mi. E Cherokee; 6 mi. S and 4 mi. E Cherokee. *Beaver*: 2.8 mi. E Gate. *Beckham*: 2 and 5 mi. S Carter; 8 mi. SW Carter. *Blaine*: 6 mi. S Watonga. *Cimarron*: 3 mi. N Kenton; 18 mi. E Kenton. *Cleveland*: several within 3 mi. radius Norman. *Comanche*: 6 mi. SE Lawton. *Cotton*: 2 mi. W Emerson; 4 mi. W Temple; 11.8 mi. E Randlett (TTC). *Dewey*: 4 mi. SW Taloga; 0.5 mi. NW Taloga. *Garvin*: Maysville. *Greer*: Granite; 2 mi. N Willow. *Harmon*: 7 mi. SW Hollis; 11 mi. N

Hollis; 2 and 5 mi. E. Vinson. *Harper*: 4 mi. N Fort Supply, Woodward County; near Gate, Beaver County. *Jackson*: 1 mi. NE El Dorado (TTC); near Elmer; 3 mi. E Duke; 2 mi. N Headrick. *Jefferson*: 9 mi. E Waurika. *Kingfisher*: 6 mi. E Kingfisher. *Kiowa*: Cooperton; Kiowa-Tillman county line. *Love*: 15 mi. W Marietta. *Major*: 3 mi. S Cleo Springs; 7 mi. E Orienta. *McClain*: no data. *Pontotoc*: 10 mi. W Ada (ECSC). *Roger Mills*: 7 mi. NW Durham; 3 mi. N Cheyenne. *Texas*: 4 mi. S Hooker (KU). *Tillman*: 3.8 mi. E Grandfield (TTC); 5 mi. E Davidson; 2 mi. E Frederick. *Woods*: 2–3 mi. W Edith; 2 mi. W and 1 mi. S Waynoka; 4 mi. S Waynoka. *Woodward*: 5 mi. E and 1 mi. N Woodward; 6 mi. S and 4 mi. W Freedom, Woods County.

Additional records.—Alfalfa: 6.5 mi. NE Ingersoll (Ortenburger and Freeman, 1930:187); 3 mi. NW Augusta (Smith and Leonard, 1934:195). *Beckham*: 4 mi. SW Sayre (Burt and Hoyle, 1935:195). *Blaine*: 2 mi. E Canton (KU). *Canadian*: "Elkino, Okla. Terr." (presumably El Reno, FMNH). *Cimarron*: 7 mi. S Boise City (Ortenburger, 1927c:48). *Comanche*: Lawton (Smith and Leonard, 1934:195). *Dewey*: 5 mi. SW Canton, Blaine County (Smith and Leonard, 1934:195). *Garfield*: 10 mi. E Enid (CCC). *Greer*: 1 mi. N Granite and 2 mi. S Mangum (OSU). *Harmon*: 6 mi. N Hollis (FWCM); 4 mi. E Hollis and 8 mi. SE Hollis (Ortenburger and Freeman, 1930:187). *Major*: vicinity Waynoka, Woods County (UMMZ). *Payne*: [Rifle Range Pond, 2 mi. N Stillwater, UMMZ] (Moore and Rigney, 1942:80); Cimarron River, 4 mi. W Perkins (OSU). *Pottawatomie*: 9 mi. W Shawnee (ECSC). *Stephens*: 1 mi. E Corum (CCC). *Texas*: 8 mi. SE Guymon (Ortenburger and Freeman, 1930:187). *Woods*: 7 mi. W Carmen, Alfalfa County (Burt, 1935:319); several vicinity of Alva (McCracken, 1966:4).

Kinosternon subrubrum hippocrepis Gray

Mississippi Mud Turtle

*Recognition.—*Head dark gray or slate; side of head with two prominent yellow stripes (behind eye and behind angle of jaws); head stripes often broken or partly interrupted; plastron

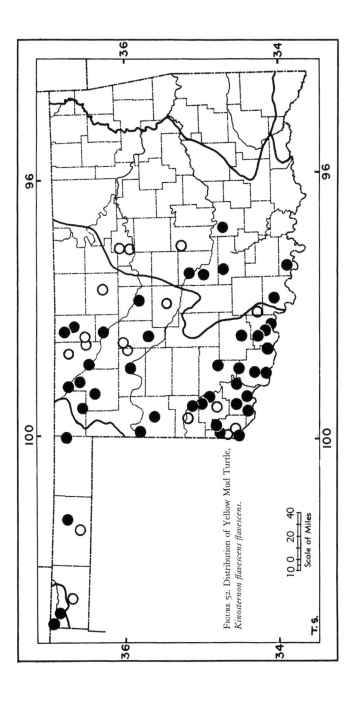

FIGURE 52. Distribution of Yellow Mud Turtle, *Kinosternon flavescens flavescens*.

hinged in front and behind; pectoral scute triangular; tail having horny clawlike tip; carapace not more than five inches in length. Young about one inch long having three blunt, longitudinal keels on carapace.

Distribution.—Eastern Oklahoma; known as far west as Tulsa, Pontotoc, and Carter counties (map, Fig. 53).

Remarks.—The Mississippi mud turtle, the eastern counterpart of the yellow mud turtle, is found in the Interior Highlands and the Oak-Woodland in the eastern half of Oklahoma. Specimens have been taken from large impoundments, small ponds, and small creeks and streams in Marshall County. Captives have eaten insects (house flies, carabid and tiger beetles, mayflies, cicadas, grasshoppers, crickets, dead bees, and June bugs (*Phyllophaga*) from the surface of the water, as well as chopped fish, vertebrate meat scraps, and some stonewort (*Chara*); live juveniles of *Trionyx* and *Pseudemys* were partly eaten by adult mud turtles.

The specimen from Tulsa County mentioned by Ortenburger (1927a:99) and Force (1928:79), and originally having a number corresponding to that of a snake (Dundee, 1950c:138), is now catalogued as OU 27471.

See Bonn and McCarley (1953:468), Carpenter (1956:41), Force (1930:38), Mahmoud (1967; 1969), Webb (1961:194).

Specimens examined (OU except as indicated).—*Atoka*: 17 mi. S Lehigh, Coal County. *Hughes*: 3.5 mi. S Wetumka (ECSC). *Johnston*: Tishomingo Fish Hatchery (ECSC). *Latimer*: Wilburton; 7 mi. W Wilburton. *LeFlore*: 1.5 mi. E Zoe. *Marshall*: UOBS; 2 mi. W Willis; 2 mi. NW Lebanon; near Shay. *Mayes*: 4 mi. S Salina. *McCurtain*: 3 mi. SE Tom; 4 mi. SE Harris. *Okmulgee*: no data. *Pittsburg*: 12 mi. W McAlester (ECSC). *Pontotoc*: Ada and 7 mi. NE Ada (ECSC). *Tulsa*: no data.

Additional records.—*Bryan*: 5 mi. SW Colbert (TNHC). *Carter*: Walnut Creek, 3 mi. E Wilson (CCC). *Choctaw*: Red River

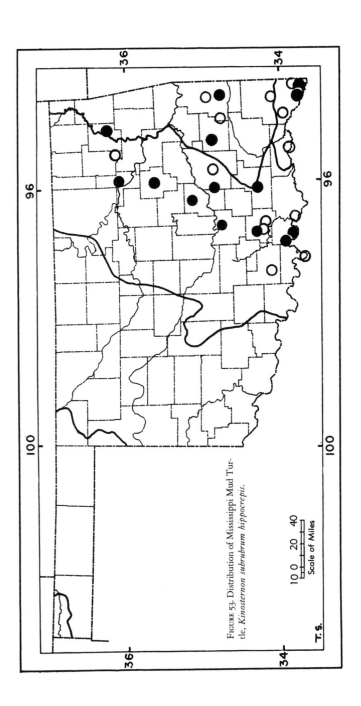

FIGURE 53. Distribution of Mississippi Mud Turtle, *Kinosternon subrubrum hippocrepis*.

Scale of Miles
10 0 20 40

T. S.

Fisheries (CCC). *Johnston*: Milburn (Dundee, 1950c); 4 mi. N Tishomingo (OSU). *LeFlore*: Wister (CM); Talihina City Lake and below Wister Dam (OSU). *Love*: 13 mi. S Thackerville (Carpenter, 1958a:71). *McCurtain*: 11 mi. W Americana and 4 mi. S Tom (Burger, Smith and Smith, 1949:132); 5 mi. N Broken Bow (OSU); 7 mi. W Garvin (FMNH). *Pittsburg*: 1 mi. W McAlester (McCoy, 1960a:41). *Rogers*: vicinity Inola and Chouteau Creek (UMMZ). *Tulsa*: Mohawk Park (UMMZ).

Macroclemys temmincki (Troost)

Alligator Snapping Turtle

Recognition.—Tail long, about as long as carapace; plastron small, having nine shields with abdominals forming part of bridge; carapace with three, jagged longitudinal keels, and having supramarginals; top of head with well defined scutes.

Distribution.—Eastern Oklahoma; known as far west as Kay and Pontotoc counties; an isolated record from Woods County (map, Fig. 54).

Remarks.—Alligator snapping turtles have been taken from deep permanent waters in the Arkansas and Red River drainages in eastern Oklahoma. Although Wickham (1922a) reported a specimen from near the mouth of the Washita River before the construction of Denison Dam and the impounding of Lake Texoma in 1944, alligator snappers have not been found in Lake Texoma, and the range of the species probably does not extend beyond Denison Dam in the Red River drainage. The geographic range of *Macroclemys* extended farther to the west in former times (Hibbard, 1963). The westernmost record in modern times, possibly based on a waif, is the isolated one from Woods County, which is represented by a carapace-plastron and skull said to have been obtained in 1935 near Hopeton, from North Eagle Chief Creek, a tributary of the Cimarron River. A

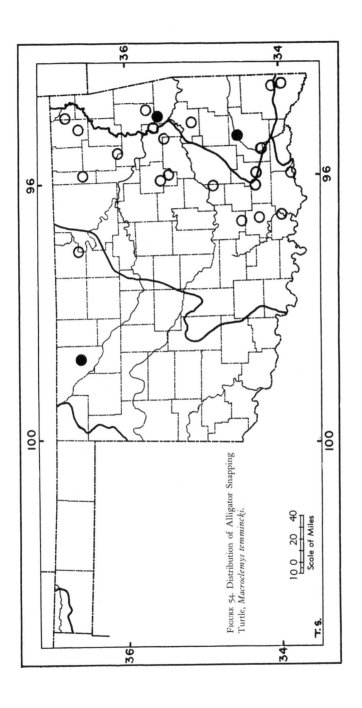

FIGURE 54. Distribution of Alligator Snapping Turtle, *Macroclemys temmincki.*

captive from Tenkiller Reservoir (at UOBS) ate dead fish and live turtles of the genera *Graptemys, Pseudemys,* and *Chelydra* (plastral length, 16 cm).

See Anon. (1950b; 1951; 1952a; 1955b; 1956c; 1959b; 1960d), Carpenter (1956:41), Glass (1949), Trowbridge (1937:300).

Specimens examined.—Pushmataha: Kiamichi River, 3 mi. SW Clayton (OU). *Sequoyah*: Tenkiller Reservoir (OU). *Woods*: North Eagle Chief Creek near Hopeton (NWSC). There is a mounted specimen (OU) that lacks data as to locality of collection.

Additional records (Glass, 1949, except as indicated).—*Atoka*: Potapo Creek, near Atoka (Anon., 1959b); Muddy Boggy River near Atoka (Anon., 1960d); Magee Creek, 15 mi. SE Atoka. *Bryan*: mouth of Blue River (McCoy, 1960a:41). *Cherokee*: Illinois River, 2 mi. S Cookson Ford. *Craig*: Big Cabin Creek near Vinita. *Haskell*: Sans Bois Creek S Stigler. *Hughes*: Coal Creek near Stuart. *Johnston*: Blue River, 6 mi. N and 14 mi. E Tishomingo. *Kay*: S Ponca City. *Marshall*: Washita River at Aylesworth Ferry [locality now inundated by Washita arm of Lake Texoma] (Wickham, 1922a). *McCurtain*: Mountain Fork River, 14 mi. SE Broken Bow (Trowbridge, 1937:300); Mountain Fork River at bridge on U.S. Highway 70. *McIntosh*: Rocky Ford on Dirty Creek, 6 mi. SW Keefeton, Muskogee County. *Muskogee*: "on the bayou between Muskogee and Braggs" (Anon., 1950b); Greenleaf Lake near Braggs (Anon., 1956c). *Okmulgee*: Deep Fork River near Henryetta; 3 mi. S and 1 mi. W Okmulgee. *Ottawa*: Little Cabin Creek (Anon., 1952a). *Pontotoc*: Blue River, southern part of county (Anon., 1951). *Pushmataha*: Kiamichi River near Antlers. *Rogers*: Verdigris River near Inola. *Washington*: Caney Creek near Ochelata. *Counties unknown*: Bird Creek; Grand River; Grand Lake area (OSU); Red River (USNM, skull).

Pseudemys floridana hoyi (Agassiz)

Missouri Slider

*Recognition.—*Cutting edge of lower jaw finely "toothed";

median ridge on crushing surface of upper jaw; head and neck blackish (not greenish) with pale, longitudinal striping; plastron yellowish without dark markings, or with scattered dark marks or smudges of interrupted pattern at least anteriorly and posteriorly.

Distribution.—Eastern Oklahoma; known as far west as Noble, Caddo, and Carter counties (map, Fig. 55).

Remarks.—The Slider, *Pseudemys concinna hieroglyphica* (Holbrook), probably ranges into eastern Oklahoma and occasionally hybridizes with the Missouri Slider. The two species closely resemble one another but can be distinguished as follows (Conant, 1958:56):

P. c. hieroglyphica—Second costal scute (as viewed from left side), having pale C-shaped figure in upper right corner; plastron, bridge, and lower surface of marginals usually well patterned.

P. f. hoyi—Second costal scute having pale vertical lines, lacking distinct C-shaped figure; plastron unmarked or slightly patterned; inconspicuous markings on bridge and lower surface of marginals.

Perhaps *Pseudemys concinna* and hybrids are confined to the Interior Highlands, but not having studied the relationships of the two species in Oklahoma, I have arbitrarily referred all sliders in the state to *Pseudemys floridana. Pseudemys concinna* is said to be partial to rivers, and *P. floridana* to lakes.

Slider turtles are abundant but seldom trapped in hoop nets. In Lake Texoma the few turtles obtained by me seemed to prefer shallow-water mud flats. Captives ignored insects, but occasionally ate chopped fresh fish and some *Chara*. Egg-laden females were found on highways on July 29, 1955 (Murray County), and July 21, 1959 (Carter County); the female obtained on the latter date had a plastral length of 26.5 cm and had enlarged ovarian follicles of a size indicating deposition of at least two clutches each breeding season.

See Anderson (1965:54), Carpenter (1956:41), Dundee (1950c:139, species of *Pseudemys* not indicated), Harwood (1931:98), Laughlin (1959:84), Trowbridge (1937:300), Webb (1961:194).

Specimens examined (OU except as indicated).—*Carter*: 7.3 mi. N Ardmore (TTC). *Johnston*: Tishomingo Fish Hatchery (ECSC). *Latimer*: 2 mi. N Wilburton. *LeFlore*: 0.5 mi. N Zoe; 6.5 mi. W Heavener. *Marshall*: UOBS. *Mayes*: 7.5 mi. S Pryor; 4 mi. S Salina. *McCurtain*: 14–15 mi. SE Broken Bow; 2 mi. SW Smithville; 6 mi. NE Idabel (RGW); 2.7 mi. W Battiest. *Murray*: 1 mi. N Sulphur (KU). *Pontotoc*: Wintersmith Lake in Ada (ECSC). *Pushmataha*: 1 mile S Kosoma; 4 mi. N Miller. *Sequoyah*: 2 mi. NE Gore. *Tulsa*: Sand Springs Lake.

Additional records.—*Caddo*: Fort Cobb (Yarrow, 1882:32). *Cherokee*: 1 mi. NE Scraper (TU); Scraper (UMMZ). *Creek*: Sapulpa (AMNH). *Delaware*: Grand Lake (Anderson, 1965:54, county not mentioned, presumably Delaware). *LeFlore*: 8.5 mi. E Fanshawe (TNIIC); Wister (CM). *Mayes*: E Chouteau (UMMZ). *McCurtain*: Beavers Bend State Park (FWCM); 5 mi. N Beavers Bend State Park (OU); 3 mi. S Broken Bow (OSU). *Noble*: [Otoe Reservation] (Moore and Rigney, 1942:80). *Okmulgee*: Okmulgee City Lake (McCoy, 1960a:41). *Osage*: Okesa, and Big Hominy Creek (UMMZ). *Pittsburg*: McAlester (Harwood, 1931:98); Lake McAlester (Laughlin, 1959:84). *Tulsa*: Mohawk River (UMMZ).

Pseudemys scripta elegans (Wied-Neuwied)

Red-eared Turtle

Recognition.—Enlarged red (in life) oblong blotch (expanded longitudinal stripe) behind eye; plastron partly or mostly blackish (large females) or marked with separate black blotches on each scute; head and neck greenish with pale longi-

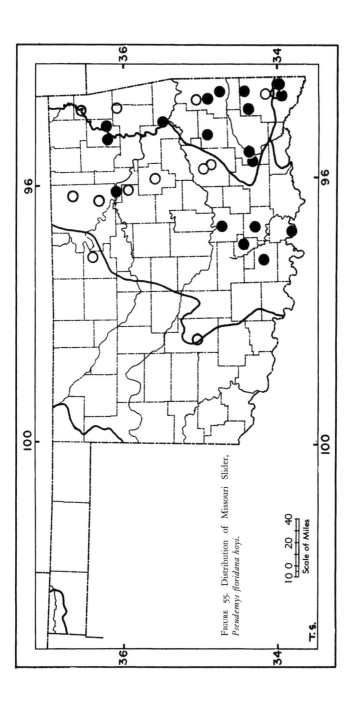

FIGURE 55. Distribution of Missouri Slider, *Pseudemys floridana hoyi*.

T. S.

10 0   20   40

Scale of Miles

tudinal striping; cutting edge of lower jaw smooth; median ridge on crushing surface of upper jaw. Some adult males (with long fingernails) have soft body parts dark with obscure pattern, and a buffy carapace and plastron with black concentrated along sutures.

Distribution.—Throughout the state (map, Fig. 56).

Remarks.—The widespread red-eared turtle is abundant in lakes, ponds, rivers, and streams. Individuals have been found in temporary waters, such as a small, shallow, prairie pond with a grass-herb bottom (Jefferson County) and a small pool under a bridge (Beckham County). There is a report of one individual taken from a water tank of an abandoned mine (Latimer County). Another individual was seined (with hundreds of crawfish) from the Washita River in February, 1951, when thin ice covered the water near the shore and snow covered the banks (Grady County). Captives ate insects and lettuce.

See Anon. (1950a; 1955c, species not mentioned, most turtles probably *Pseudemys scripta*); Bonn and McCarley (1953:468), Carpenter (1955c; 1956:41; 1959c:34), Dundee (1950c, species of *Pseudemys* not indicated), Force (1930:38), Harwood (1931: 98), Laughlin (1959: 84), McCoy (1968), Webb (1961:197; 1962:436), Webb and Ortenburger (1955:88).

Specimens examined (OU except as indicated).—*Alfalfa*: 3 mi. E Cherokee. *Beaver*: 2 mi. E Gate. *Beckham*: 2–3 mi. S Carter; 6 mi. SW Carter. *Bryan*: Durant. *Choctaw*: Red River Fisheries (RGW). *Cleveland*: 2–4 mi. S Norman. *Coal*: 2 mi. N Coalgate (ECSC). *Comanche*: near Lawton; Wichita Mts. Wildlife Refuge. *Cotton*: 2.5 mi. E Devol (KU). *Creek*: 3 mi. S Kiefer. *Garvin*: Maysville. *Grady*: Chickasha. *Grant*: 2.5 mi. W Medford (ECSC). *Greer*: N Reed; E Granite (RGW). *Hughes*: 3 mi. S Holdenville (ECSC). *Jefferson*: 2.2 mi. E Ringling (RGW). *Kiowa*: 1 mi. E Mountain Park. *Latimer*: Wilburton; 7 mi. W Wilburton. *LeFlore*: 6.5 mi. W Heavener. *Love*: 5 mi. S Thackerville; 20 mi. S Marietta.

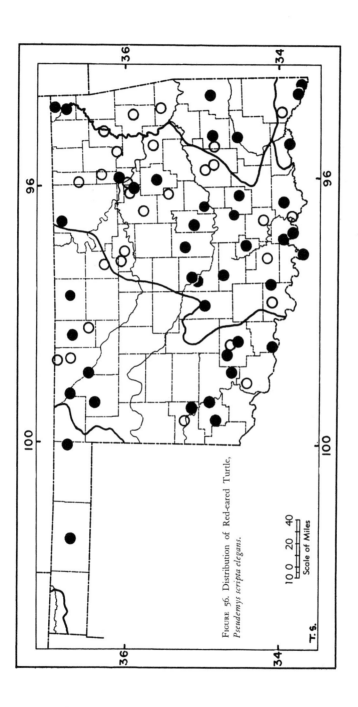

FIGURE 56. Distribution of Red-eared Turtle, *Pseudemys scripta elegans.*

10 0   20   40
Scale of Miles

T. S.

Marshall: UOBS; 1 mi. NW Lebanon. *McClain*: 4 mi. SW Norman, Cleveland County. *McCurtain*: 4 mi. S Tom; 2 mi. SE Harris (TTC). *Murray*: Sulphur; Platt National Park. *Okmulgee*: no data. *Osage*: 9 mi. N and 1 mi. E Shidler (ECSC). *Ottawa*: 4.3 mi. NE Fairland; 1 mi. S Quapaw (KU). *Pontotoc*: 2 mi. E Stonewall (ECSC). *Pottawatomie*: 5 mi. SW Shawnee. *Pushmataha*: Clayton. *Seminole*: Bowlegs. *Texas*: no data. *Tulsa*: no data. *Woods*: 2 mi. W Edith; 2 mi. W and 1 mi. S Waynoka. *Woodward*: 5 mi. E and 1 mi. N Woodward.

Additional records.—Alfalfa: 2 mi. W Goltry (Burt, 1935:321). *Beckham*: 0.5 mi. S Sayre (Ortenburger and Freeman, 1930:188); 1 mi. S Sayre (USNM); 4 mi. W Sayre (Burt, 1935:321). *Bryan*: Washita arm of Lake Texoma (TCWC); 5 mi. W Colbert (TNHC). *Carter*: 3 mi. N Ardmore (Burt and Hoyle, 1935:198). *Cherokee*: Illinois River, 30 mi. from Muskogee, Muskogee County (FMNH). *Comanche*: Medicine Creek, Fort Sill (FMNH). *Creek*: 2 mi. W Bristow (Burt, 1935:321); Sapulpa (FMNH). *Jefferson*: 18.3 mi. W Ringling (CCC). *Johnston*: 1 mi. N Milburn (Carpenter, 1958a:71). *Latimer*: 2 mi. N Gowen, and 1 mi. E Wilburton (Burt, 1935:321); 6 mi. SW Wilburton (USNM). *LeFlore*: 2 mi. SW Heavener (Burt, 1935:321); Wister (CM). *Love*: 1 mi. N Red River bridge on U.S. Highway 77 (Burt and Hoyle, 1935:198). *Marshall*: Newberry Creek, Lake Texoma (SESC). *Mayes*: Grand River (OSU). *McCurtain*: Little River, 5.5 mi. N Valliant (OSU). *Muskogee*: no data (Ortenburger, 1927a:100). *Noble*: Black Bear Creek (UMMZ). *Okfuskee*: 16 mi. NE Okemah (ECSC). *Payne*: [Stillwater, 2 mi. N Stillwater (OSU); Lake Carl Blackwell (OSU, UMMZ)] (Moore and Rigney, 1942:80). *Pittsburg*: Lake Taliwanda, McAlester (Harwood, 1931:98); Lake McAlester (Laughlin, 1959:84). *Rogers*: vicinity Inola (UMMZ). *Sequoyah*: 3.1 mi. S Marble City (UA); Dwight Mission (Carpenter, 1958a:71). *Tillman*: 2 mi. W Manitou (OU). *Tulsa*: Mohawk Park, and vicinity Collinsville (UMMZ); 2 mi. W Jenks (OSU). *Washington*: 3 mi. N Ochelata (Burt, 1935:321); 2 mi. N Ochelata (TNHC). *Woods*: Alva, and 14 mi. N and 4 mi. W Alva (McCracken, 1966:6).

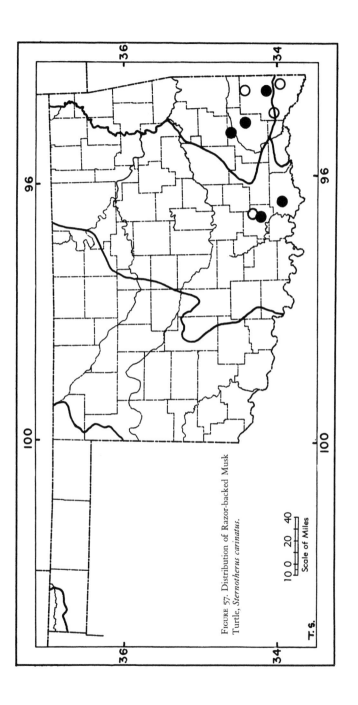

FIGURE 57. Distribution of Razor-backed Musk Turtle, *Sternotherus carinatus*.

Sternotherus carinatus (Gray)

Razor-backed Musk Turtle

Recognition.—Head and carapace having brownish streaks or spots; gular shield absent; pectoral scute quadrangular; carapace high and sharply arched in adults; tip of tail lacking distinct nail or claw; size not more than six inches in length. Young about one to two inches long with three longitudinal keels on carapace.

Distribution.—Southeastern Oklahoma; known only from McCurtain, Pushmataha, Johnston, and Bryan counties (map, Fig. 57).

Remarks.—Although extending into adjacent faunal regions, *Sternotherus carinatus* is most common in the Coastal Plain, where it is found in permanent ponds, lakes, streams, and rivers of the Red River drainage; the westernmost known tributary is the Blue River.

See Carpenter (1956:41), Mahmoud (1967; 1969), Trowbridge (1937:299).

Specimens examined (all OU).—*Bryan*: Durant. *Johnston*: Blue River, 2 mi. N Milburn. *McCurtain*: Mountain Fork River at mouth of Cedar Creek, and at Beavers Bend State Park. *Pushmataha*: Buffalo Creek, 5 mi. NW Tuskahoma; Little River.

Additional records.—*Johnston*: 7 mi. W Wapanucka (near bridge on State Highway 7, CCC). *McCurtain*: Little River, 5.5 mi. NE Valliant (OSU); Mountain Fork River, 14 mi. SE Broken Bow (Trowbridge, 1937:299); 3 mi. S Smithville (FMNH 21252, formerly OU 17360, bearing locality data of 2 mi. SW Smithville *fide* Trowbridge, 1937).

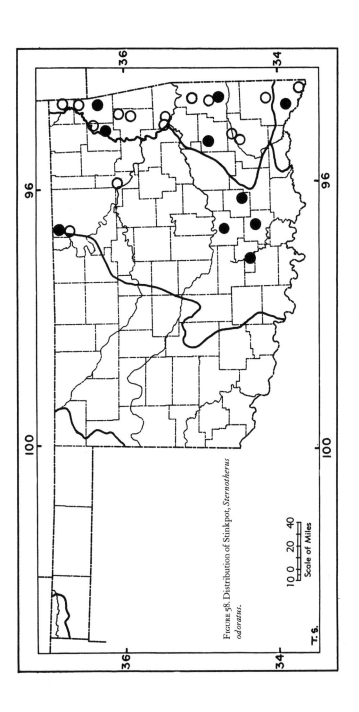

FIGURE 58. Distribution of Stinkpot, *Sternotherus odoratus*.

T. S.

Sternotherus odoratus (Latreille)

Stinkpot

Recognition.—Head dark olive with two prominent yellow stripes on side; limbs buff with fine pattern of black dots and streaks; gular shield present, and pectoral scute quadrangular; tip of tail lacking large cornified nail; carapace not more than six inches in length. Young about one to two inches long, blackish, with three blunt longitudinal keels on carapace, white-edged marginals, and a marbled black and yellow plastron.

Distribution.—Eastern half of Oklahoma; known as far west as Osage and Murray counties (map, Fig. 58).

Remarks.—Stinkpots occur in rivers, streams, and ponds in the Interior Highlands and Oak-Woodland. Honey Creek in the Arbuckle Mountains (Fig. 10), a clear, swift-flowing tributary of the turbid Washita River, is the westernmost known habitat of the stinkpot.

See Burt (1935:319), Force (1930:37), Mahmoud (1967; 1969).

Specimens examined (OU except as indicated).—*Coal*: 0.5 mi. E Coalgate (ECSC). *Delaware*: Spavinaw Creek (KU). *Johnston*: 12 mi. W Wapanucka. *Latimer*: 2 mi. N Wilburton; 6.5 mi. W Wilburton. *LeFlore*: 1.5 mi. E Zoe. *Mayes*: 2 mi. S Salina; 4 mi. S Salina. *McCurtain*: 1.5 mi. W Idabel (TCWC). *Murray*: Honey Creek below Turner Falls. *Osage*: Grainola (ECSC). *Pontotoc*: 2 mi. SE Ada (ECSC).

Additional records.—*Cherokee*: Scraper (UMMZ); Illinois River N Tahlequah (OSU). *Delaware*: Elk River at Camp Kemp (McCoy, 1960a:41). *Johnston*: 7 mi. W Wapanucka (CCC). *Latimer*: Lake Wilson, 4 mi. W and 4 mi. N Wilburton (FMNH 16081–83, cataloged as *odoratus,* were formerly OU 11321–22 and 11364 and were cataloged as *S. carinatus*). *LeFlore*: 2 mi. SW Heavener (Burt, 1935:319); 5.2 mi. E Zoe (FMNH); oxbow lake at Slate Ford E Shadypoint (OSU). *Mayes*: Spavinaw (UMMZ). *McCurtain*: 8.6

mi. N Beavers Bend State Park (OU); Waterfall Creek S Tom (OSU). *Murray*: Honey Creek above Turner Falls (OSU). *Osage*: [near Shidler, UMMZ] (Moore and Rigney, 1942:80). *Ottawa*: Lost Creek (McCoy, 1960a:41). *Pontotoc*: Wintersmith Lake in Ada (Carter and Cox, 1968). *Pushmataha*: Clayton Lake (OSU); 4 mi. E Tuskahoma (USNM). *Sequoyah*: near Gore (UMMZ); Swimmers Creek, 10 mi. E Gore (UMMZ). *Tulsa*: Tulsa (UMMZ).

Terrapene carolina triunguis (Agassiz)

Three-toed Box Turtle

Recognition.—Land turtles with hind feet stumpy and club-like, usually having three toes; carapace usually uniform tan or pale brownish, but occasionally having pattern of pale and dark spots or lines; carapace having slightly raised, longitudinal, middorsal ridge posteriorly; plastron with movable parts in front and behind that close tightly against upper shell; plastron butterscotch yellow, usually lacking dark marks, and widest across femoral scutes; interfemoral suture short, less than half length of interabdominal suture.

Distribution.—Eastern Oklahoma; known as far west as Alfalfa, Canadian, and Carter counties (map, Fig. 59).

Remarks.—Three-toed box turtles are found in the eastern half of Oklahoma in the Interior Highlands and Oak-Woodland; they seem partial to wooded hillsides, whereas ornate box turtles seem more abundant in open, grassy lowlands and valleys. In eastern Oklahoma, where man has removed much of of the forest cover (cultivation, lumbering, industrialization), the numbers of individuals of *Terrapene carolina* have probably decreased; the removal of forest cover would seem to favor the eastern dispersal of *Terrapene ornata*. In eastern Oklahoma *Terrapene carolina* is observed much less often on highways than is *Terrapene ornata*. The western extent of range of *caro-*

lina is limited by the Grassland, although one specimen (OU 28805) is reported from Alfalfa County.

In the field individuals have been observed eating mushrooms; captives have eaten grasshoppers, crickets, cockroaches, beetle larvae (grubs), small dead fish (*Lepomis* and *Pimephales*), a dead lizard (*Cnemidophorus*), and have defecated intact persimmon seeds. Two mounted individuals (reported to have been found in coitus) were discovered on April 18, 1959 (Pushmataha County).

See Adler (1958:13), Bonn and McCarley (1953:468), Carpenter (1955c; 1956:41; 1957a; 1957c; 1959c:34), Day (1962), Force (1925a:27; 1925b:83; 1930:38), Milstead (1969:54, Fig. 10A–D, 64), Trowbridge (1937:300), Wickham (1922b).

Specimens examined (OU except as indicated).—*Carter*: N Ardmore. *Cleveland*: 2–4 mi. S Norman. *Delaware*: 6 mi. NW Grove; 3.6 mi. S South West City, Missouri. *Garvin*: Maysville; 1 mi. N Paoli. *Hughes*: 2 mi. N Yeager. *Latimer*: 3 mi. N Red Oak; 2–3 mi. N Wilburton. *LeFlore*: 3 mi. N Howe; Zoe; 3.5 mi. SW Stapp; 6.5 mi. W Heavener; 5 mi. E Big Cedar. *Marshall*: 2 mi. W Willis. *McClain*: 4 mi. NW Purcell. *McCurtain*: 2 mi. SW Smithville; 9 mi. N Broken Bow. *Ottawa*: 11 mi. NW Grove, Delaware County. *Pittsburg*: 1 mi. N Crowder; 8 mi. E Stuart, Hughes County. *Pontotoc*: 8 mi. W Ada. *Pottawatomie*: Shawnee. *Pushmataha*: 0.5 mi. S Clayton (TTC). *Seminole*: Bowlegs. *Sequoyah*: 2 mi. NE Gore; 0.5 mi. E Gore. *Tulsa*: no data. *Wagoner*: 5 mi. N Muskogee, Muskogee County.

Additional records.—*Alfalfa*: Great Salt Plains Refuge [2 mi. E Cherokee, OU] (Carpenter, 1958a:71). *Atoka*: Limestone Gap (Stone, 1903:539). *Bryan*: Bokchito (UI); Colbert, and 2 mi. NW Colbert (TNHC). *Canadian*: near Cogar, Caddo County (Carpenter, 1958a:71). *Carter*: 12 mi. N Ardmore (TU). *Creek*: 16 mi. N Bristow (Smith and Leonard, 1934:196); Sapulpa (Schmidt, 1919); [10 mi E] Drumright (Adler, 1958:13). *Cherokee*: no data (Carpenter, 1958a:71). *Garvin*: Fort Arbuckle [9 mi. W Davis, Murray County] (Taylor, 1895:581). *Hughes*: 9 and 14 mi. N Holdenville

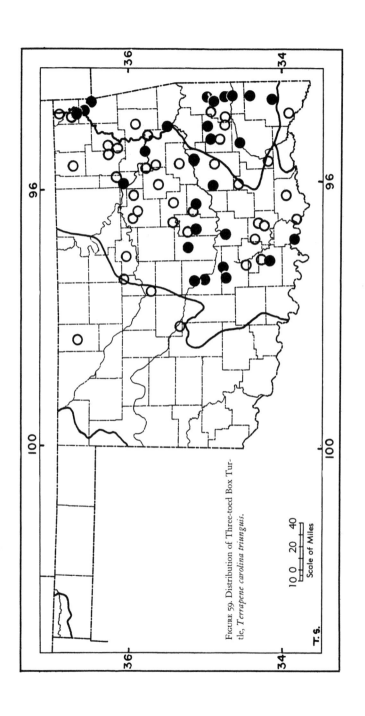

FIGURE 59. Distribution of Three-toed Box Turtle, *Terrapene carolina triunguis.*

Scale of Miles

10 0 0 20 40

T. S.

(OU). *Johnston*: Mill Creek (Taylor, 1895:581); 5 mi. N Milburn (Carpenter, 1955a:40); Blue River bridge on State Highway 7 W Wapanucka (OU). *Latimer*: Robbers Cave State Park (NWSC); 25 mi. N Clayton, Pushmataha County (TTC); 3 mi. W Talihina, LeFlore County (TNHC). *LeFlore*: 5 mi. E Talihina (TNHC); 27 mi. N Talihina (Carpenter, 1958a:71, locality reported in Haskell County). *Logan*: SW part of county (Smith and Acker, 1940); 2 mi. S Orlando (Burt, 1935:321, locality reported in Pittsburg County). *Mayes*: vicinity Chouteau, and Pryor Creek (UMMZ). *McCurtain*: 4 mi. N Broken Bow (OU); 1 mi. W Garvin and 2 mi. E Garvin (FMNH). *McIntosh*: no data (Carpenter, 1955a;40). *Muskogee*: Fort Gibson (Taylor, 1895:581); 1–2 mi. E Fort Gibson, and 7 mi. E Fort Gibson (FWCM); 5 mi. N Boynton, and 5 mi. NW Haskell (Burt, 1935:320). *Nowata*: Delaware (Burt and Burt, 1929b:13). *Okfuskee*: 7 mi. E Okemah, and 1 mi. SE Paden (Burt, 1935:320). *Okmulgee*: [near Okmulgee, UMMZ] (Force, 1925:27). *Ottawa*: 7 mi. E and 2 mi. N Miami (KU); 10–12 mi. S Miami (CM). *Payne*: Stillwater (Smith and Leonard, 1934:196). *Pittsburg*: 1 mi. SE Alderson, and 2 mi. SE McAlester (Burt, 1935:321); 14 mi. W McAlester (OU); 6.2 mi. SW Eufaula, McIntosh County (Richard L. Lardie, personal communication). *Pushmataha*: Antlers (TNHC); 4 mi. NNE Clayton (CCC). *Rogers*: 8 mi. E Claremore (Burt and Burt, 1929b:13). *Seminole*: 5 mi. NW Seminole (OU). *Tulsa*: Tulsa (Burt, 1935:321); Mohawk Park and Garnett (UMMZ).

Terrapene ornata ornata (Agassiz)

Ornate Box Turtle

Recognition.—Land turtles with hind feet stumpy and club-like, and having four toes; carapace having contrasting, mostly streaked pattern of yellow on black; plastron with movable parts in front and behind that close tightly against upper shell; plastron having contrasting black and yellow marks, and widest across abdominal scutes; interfemoral suture long, more than half length of interabdominal suture.

Distribution.—Throughout the state except for extreme eastern parts (map, Fig. 60).

Remarks.—Ornate box turtles are most abundant in the grasslands and open woodlands in the western part of the state, where many are killed on highways in the spring. Although almost statewide, ornate box turtles seem to avoid the Interior Highlands. I am unable to account for the record of *Terrapene ornata* from LeFlore County (Ortenburger, 1927a:99), which is presumably based on a specimen in the collections at The University of Oklahoma. *Terrapene ornata* is possibly becoming more abundant in eastern Oklahoma (see account of *Terrapene carolina triunguis*).

Some individuals have been found in water. A turtle that was startled in shallow water of a small pond in a rocky stream submerged to a depth of about six inches and wedged itself among rocks on the bottom (Marshall County), and Harold A. Dundee informed me that he observed several box turtles in a shallow prairie pond near Tulsa. Ornate box turtles have also been found burrowing in wet sand at the edge of the Red River in Harmon County. An individual captured and preserved in the field disgorged leaves and flowers of the spiderwort (*Tradescantia*).

See Anon. (1962), Bonn and McCarley (1953:468), Burt (1931a:15), Carpenter (1955c, 1956:41, 1959c:34), Carter and Cox (1968), Day (1962), Force (1930:38), Legler (1960:554), McMullen (1940), Milstead (1967:169, Fig. 1C; 1969:95, Fig. 16 B–C), Ortenburger and Bird (1933:60), Ortenburger and Freeman (1930:187), Trowbridge (1937:300).

Specimens examined (OU except as indicated).—*Alfalfa*: 9–10 mi. E Cherokee; 10 mi. NE Cherokee; 7 mi. SE Cherokee. *Beaver*: Gate. *Beckham*: 1.5 mi. NE Elk City (RGW). *Bryan*: Durant; 4.7 mi. E Bokchito. *Carter*: 2 mi. S Ardmore. *Choctaw*: 5 mi. E Soper. *Cimarron*: 7 mi. S Boise City; 5.5 mi. E Kenton. *Cleveland*: several

within 3 mi. radius Norman. *Comanche*: 5 mi. W Lawton; 4 mi.
W Indiahoma; Wichita Mts. Wildlife Refuge. *Cotton*: 0.5 mi. W
Taylor (RGW); 10 mi. W Walters; SW corner of county along
Red River. *Craig*: 3.8 mi. E Welch; 10 mi. W Vinita. *Custer*:
Weatherford. *Delaware*: 7 mi. NE Grove; near Turkey Ford.
Dewey: 1 mi. N Taloga. *Ellis*: 24 mi. S Arnett. *Garfield*: 8 mi. N
Enid. *Garvin*: Maysville. *Grady*: near Tuttle. *Grant*: Medford (Los
Angeles County Museum). *Harmon*: 7 mi. SW Hollis; 8 mi. N
Hollis; 0.5 mi. W McQueen. *Harper*: near Gate, Beaver County;
8 mi. W Buffalo. *Haskell*: 4.5 mi. N Kinta. *Hughes*: 2 mi. N
Yeager. *Jefferson*: 14 mi. W Ringling; 3 mi. N Petersburg. *Latimer*:
Wilburton. *Major*: 7 mi. E Orienta; 3 and 7 mi. S Cleo Springs.
Marshall: UOBS. *McClain*: no data. *McIntosh*: 9.5 mi. E Checotah.
Nowata: South Coffeyville (RGW). *Oklahoma*: 6 mi. S Oklahoma
City. *Osage*: 3 mi. N Wynona; 6.5 mi. E Pawhuska. *Ottawa*: 2.6 mi.
W Miami. *Pawnee*: near Quay. *Pottawatomie*: Shawnee. *Roger
Mills*: 7 mi. NW Durham; 1 mi. E and 1 mi. N Durham. *Seminole*:
Bowlegs. *Stephens*: Comanche. *Texas*: 8 mi. SE Guymon. *Tillman*:
3.2 mi. W Manitou. *Wagoner*: 14.5 mi. N Wagoner. *Woods*: 2 mi.
W and 1 mi. S Waynoka; 2.5 mi. W Edith. *Woodward*: 6 mi. S and
4 mi. W Freedom, Woods County; 5 mi. E Woodward; 3.5 mi.
WNW Woodward.

Additional records.—Alfalfa: 2 mi. S Aline (Smith and Leonard,
1934:196); 2 mi. W Goltry (Burt, 1935:320); 6.5 mi. NE Ingersoll
(Ortenburger and Freeman, 1930:187); 6 mi. E and 2 mi. S Ingersoll (USNM). *Atoka*: 18 mi. NE Atoka (FMNH). *Beckham*: 4 mi.
SW Sayre (Burt and Hoyle, 1935:197); 6.7 mi. E Sayre (UI).
Blaine: 3 mi. E Canton (Smith and Leonard, 1934:196). *Bryan*: 1.7
mi. SW Caddo (Richard L. Lardie, personal communication); Col-
bert (TNHC); 2 mi. SE Durant (FMNH). *Caddo*: Fort Cobb
(Taylor, 1895:582). *Carter*: 3 mi. S Ardmore (Burt and Hoyle,
1935:197). *Cherokee*: SE Peggs (UMMZ). *Cimarron*: 3 mi. N
Kenton (Ortenburger, 1927c:48); 13 and 17 mi. N Felt, 4 and 11
mi. SW Boise City, and 18.5 mi. N Boise City (UI). *Cleveland*: 4 mi.
S Norman (Burt and Burt, 1929b:13). *Craig*: Vinita (UMMZ).
Creek: vicinity Sapulpa (Schmidt, 1919:73). *Dewey*: 5 mi. SW

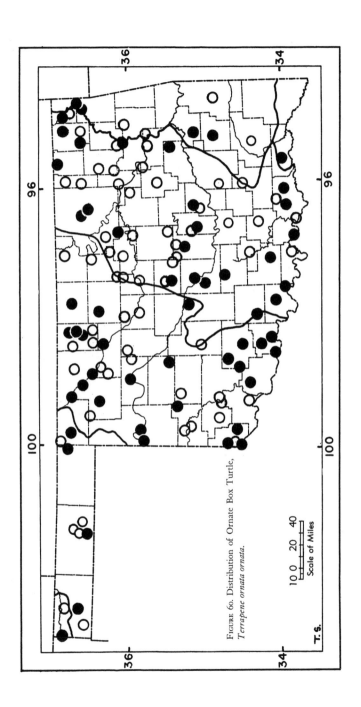

FIGURE 60. Distribution of Ornate Box Turtle,
Terrapene ornata ornata.

Scale of Miles

10 0 20 40

T. S.

Canton, Blaine County (Smith and Leonard, 1934:196). *Greer*: 3 mi.
N Blair and 9 mi. NW Blair, Jackson County (Burt and Hoyle,
1935:197); between Mangum and Reed (OU). *Harmon*: 1 mi. W
and 1 mi. N Hollis, 4 mi. S and 5 mi. W Hollis, and 5 mi. N Hollis
(FWCM). *Harper*: Cimarron River S Englewood, Kansas (Smith
and Leonard, 1934:196). *Hughes*: 2 mi. W Holdenville (Burt,
1935:320). *Jackson*: 11 mi. S and 2 mi. E Altus (ECSC). *Johnston*:
11 mi. W Wapanucka (Carpenter, 1955a:40). *Kay*: 6 mi. NE Newkirk (Burt and Hoyle, 1935:197). *Kingfisher*: 12 mi. NW Okarche
(Carpenter, 1955a:40); 4.3 mi. W Hennessey (OSU). *Kiowa*: 2 mi.
S Lugert (McCoy, 1960a:41). *LeFlore*: no data (Ortenburger,
1927a:99). *Lincoln*: 10 mi. E Meeker (USNM). *Logan*: 4 mi. N
Mulhall (Burt, 1931a:15); 3 mi. N Guthrie (USNM); Cimarron
River N Oklahoma City, Oklahoma County (McMullen, 1940:23).
Love: 4 mi. E Marietta (Carpenter, 1958a:71). *Major*: 5 mi. S
Sherman (Burt, 1935:320); Graver [= Griever] Creek (UMMZ,
some mammals from this locality in the UMMZ were listed as 9 mi.
SW Togo by Blair, 1939:99, 103, 119); vicinity Waynoka, Woods
County (UMMZ). *Mayes*: between Mazie and Chouteau (UMMZ).
Murray: no data (Smith and Leonard, 1934:196). *Muskogee*: 3 mi.
NW Haskell (Burt, 1935:320); 1–2 mi. E Fort Gibson (FWCM);
near Muskogee (UMMZ); no data [Muskogee] (Ortenburger,
1927a:99, FMNH). *Noble*: 5 mi. E Marland (Burt, 1935:320);
Morrison (UMMZ); 2 mi. N Orlando, Logan County (USNM).
Oklahoma: 2 mi. S Harrah (Burt, 1935:320); 6 mi. N Oklahoma
City (Burt and Burt, 1929b:13). *Okmulgee*: no data (UMMZ).
Ottawa: 5 mi. S Miami (CM); 6 mi. W Wyandotte (FMNH).
Pawnee: vicinity Pawnee (UMMZ). *Payne*: Cushing (OSU); 2 mi.
E Cushing (Burt, 1935:320); Stillwater (Smith and Leonard,
1934:196); 3 mi. S Stillwater (OSU). *Pittsburg*: 6 mi. SE Stuart
(Carter, 1966:33). *Pontotoc*: 7 mi. SE Ada (Carter, 1966:33).
Pottawatomie: 4 mi. W McLoud (Burt, 1935:320); 5 mi. S Aydelotte
(OSU). *Pushmataha*: no data (Carter, 1966:33). *Rogers*: 1 mi. W
Catoosa (UI); SW Oologah (UMMZ). *Seminole*: 6 mi. W Seminole
(Burt, 1935:320). *Texas*: Optima, 4 mi. E Guymon, and several
vicinity Hardesty (KU). *Tulsa*: no data (Burt, 1935:320); Garnett

(UMMZ). *Washington*: 4 mi. N Copan (Burt, 1935: 320); 7 mi. N Ochelata (Burt and Burt, 1929a:460). *Washita*: 2 mi. E Canute (UI). *Woods*: 2 mi. NE Waynoka (Burt, 1935:320); several vicinity of Alva (McCracken, 1966:4–5); 12 mi. W Alva (Smith and Leonard, 1934:196). *Woodward*: Fort Supply (Cope, 1894:386).

Trionyx muticus muticus Lesueur

Midland Smooth Softshell Turtle

Recognition.—Flattened turtles having skin covering carapace, an elongate nose, and fleshy, movable lobes covering horny parts of jaws; septal ridges absent; anterior edge of carapace smooth, lacking tubercles; back having dusky dots and streaks, or a blotched brownish pattern; dorsum of young often having pale orangish tinge in life.

Distribution.—Throughout the state (map, Fig. 61).

Remarks.—Found in rivers and streams and large, permanent impoundments, smooth softshells have been caught in gill nets, hoop nets, and on trotlines, but they seem less abundant than spiny softshells.

See Anon. (1960c, species of softshell not mentioned), Bonn and McCarley (1953:469), Carpenter (1956:41), Carter and Cox (1968), Force (1930:38, see account of *Trionyx spiniferus*), Moore and Rigney (1942:80), Webb (1961:194; 1962:434, 435, 436, 544, 558, 572, 573, Pl. 45, Pl. 49 [Fig. 1]).

Specimens examined (OU except as indicated).—*Alfalfa*: 2 mi. E Great Salt Plains Reservoir Dam (ECSC). *Cleveland*: 4 mi. SE Norman. *Hughes*: 4 mi. N Atwood (KU). *Johnston*: 5 mi. NNW Milburn (ECSC). *Kay*: 8 mi. E Ponca City. *LeFlore*: Poteau River below Wister Dam. *Love*: 9 mi. E Marietta. *Major*: 7 mi. E Orienta. *Marshall*: UOBS. *McIntosh*: 4 mi. W Onapa. *Oklahoma*: Lake Overholser. *Payne*: 3 mi. E Ripley (UMMZ); 19 mi. SE Stillwater

(UMMZ). *Pontotoc*: 10 mi. N Ada (ECSC). *Pottawatomie*: 5 mi. SW Shawnee. *Roger Mills*: no data. *Sequoyah*: 2 mi. NE Gore. *Tulsa*: Arkansas River at Tulsa (UMMZ). *Woodward*: 5 mi. E and 1 mi. N Woodward.

Additional records.—Alfalfa: 6.5 mi. NE Ingersoll (Ortenburger and Freeman, 1930:188). *Comanche*: Camp Boulder, Wichita Mts. Wildlife Refuge (Ortenburger and Freeman, 1930:188). *McCurtain*: no data (Ortenburger 1927a:100). *Payne*: Cimarron River at Perkins (OSU). *Pushmataha*: no data (Ortenburger, 1927a:100).

Trionyx spiniferus (Lesueur)
Spiny Softshell Turtles

Recognition.—Flattened turtles having skin covering carapace, an elongate nose, and fleshy movable lobes covering horny parts of jaws; septal ridges present; tubercles on anterior edge of carapace (small in hatchlings); carapace smooth in females but "sandpapery" to touch in males; carapace of large females having brownish mottled and blotched pattern.

Distribution.—Throughout the state; two subspecies (map, Fig. 62).

Remarks.—Two subspecies of *Trionyx spiniferus* are recognized:

T. s. hartwegi (Conant and Goin), Western Spiny Softshell Turtle.—Carapace marked with small black spots and circular marks or with brownish mottling and scattered black marks.

T. s. pallidus Webb, Pallid Softshell Turtle.—Carapace uniformly tan or brownish (small turtles not more than two inches) or marked either with small whitish dots posteriorly or with pale brown blotched pattern lacking scattered black marks.

Trionyx s. hartwegi is found in the Arkansas River drainage, and *T. s. pallidus* in the Red River drainage. So far as is known,

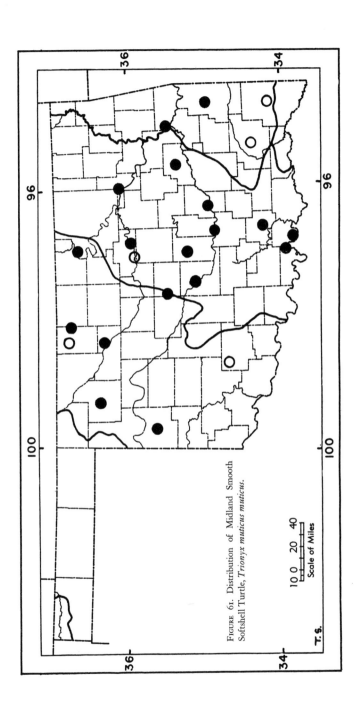

FIGURE 61. Distribution of Midland Smooth Softshell Turtle, *Trionyx muticus muticus.*

there is no intergradation between the two subspecies in Oklahoma. Both subspecies are known from LeFlore and Pontotoc counties. In LeFlore County, a specimen from Black Fork Creek, 1.5 miles east Zoe, is *hartwegi*, and one from the Kiamichi River, 5 miles east Big Cedar, about nine airline miles distant, is *pallidus*. In Pontotoc County, two specimens of *pallidus* are recorded from Ada, and 3.5 miles south Ada in the drainage of Clear Boggy Creek, and three specimens of *hartwegi* are from 7 miles northeast Ada in the South Canadian River drainage.

Spiny softshells are frequently caught in gill nets, hoop nets, and on trotlines and set lines, and can be expected to occur in permanent lakes and rivers having either clear or turbid waters. Soft substrates of sand or mud seem to be preferred, but individuals have been taken in places having gravel bottoms. Force (1930:38) reported several individuals from the Arkansas River near Tulsa as *spiniferus*—four of them (UMMZ 95032) are *Trionyx muticus*; Force's data, later utilized by me (1962:569, table 8), thus refer at least partly to *muticus*.

See Anon. (1960c, species of softshell not mentioned), Bonn and McCarley (1953:468), Carpenter (1956:41), Dundee (1950c:139), Trowbridge (1937:301), Webb (1956; 1961:194; 1962:434, 436, 544, 563, 564, Pls. 36, 48 [Fig. 1], 49 [Fig. 1]).

Specimens examined (OU except as indicated). *Alfalfa*: 2 mi. S Cherokee. *Atoka*: 10 mi. E Atoka; 7 mi. SW Daisy. *Caddo*: Fort Cobb (ANSP). *Choctaw*: 2 mi. NW Boswell. *Cleveland*: Norman. *Comanche*: Wichita Mts. Wildlife Refuge. *Garvin*: 8 mi. S Elmore City (ECSC). *Jackson*: 6 mi. E El Dorado. *Johnston*: Tishomingo Fish Hatchery, and 5 mi. NW Milburn (ECSC). *Kiowa*: no data (FMNH). *LeFlore*: 1.5 mi. E Zoe; 5 mi. E Big Cedar. *Marshall*: 4 mi. SW Kingston (KU); UOBS. *Mayes*: Spavinaw (UMMZ). *McCurtain*: 2 mi. SW Smithville; Red River (USNM). *Osage*: Big Hominy Creek (UMMZ). *Pontotoc*: 7 mi. NE Ada, and 3.5 mi. S Ada (ECSC). *Pottawatomie*: 5 mi. SW Shawnee. *Pushmataha*: 5 mi. NW Tuskahoma. *Rogers*: 5 mi. W Claremore (UMMZ); near

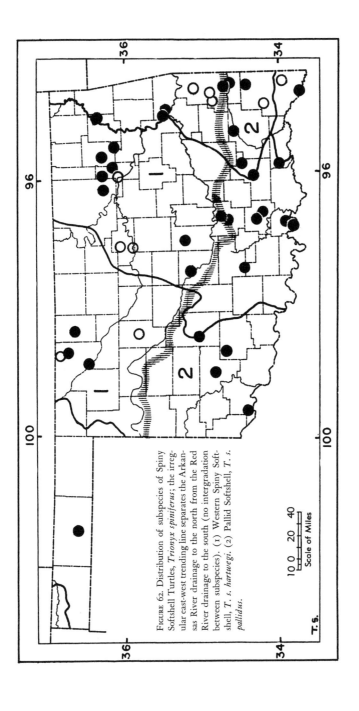

FIGURE 62. Distribution of subspecies of Spiny Softshell Turtles, *Trionyx spiniferus*; the irregular east-west trending line separates the Arkansas River drainage to the north from the Red River drainage to the south (no intergradation between subspecies). (1) Western Spiny Softshell, *T. s. hartwegi*. (2) Pallid Softshell, *T. s. pallidus*.

Garnett, Tulsa County, and 4 mi. NE Inola (UMMZ). *Sequoyah*:
2 mi. NE Gore; 1 mi. E Vian (TU). *Texas*: 5 mi. SE Guymon.
Tulsa: Bird Creek near Skiatook (TU). *Woods*: Waynoka
(FMNH); 2.5 mi. W Waynoka; 1 mi. S Waynoka; 8 mi. NW
Alva (ECSC).

Additional records.—Blaine: no data (CCC). *LeFlore*: Holston
Creek near Red Oak, Latimer County (MCZ); Shadypoint (KKA);
Wister (Conant and Goin, 1948:9); 6.5 mi. W Heavener, and 6 mi.
W Page (Trowbridge, 1937:301). *McCurtain*: 14 mi. SE Broken
Bow (Trowbridge, 1937:301); 18 mi. N Wright City (OSU).
Payne: Stillwater (McCoy, 1960a:41); Cimarron River at Wildhorse
Creek (OSU). *Pontotoc*: Wintersmith Lake in Ada (Carter and
Cox, 1968). *Tulsa*: Arkansas River at Tulsa (Force, 1930:38, see
Remarks, account of *Trionyx spiniferus*). *Woods*: 8 and 10 mi. NW
Alva, 12 mi. N and 6 mi. W Alva, and 10 mi. N and 4 mi. W Alva
(McCracken, 1966:6).

ORDER CROCODILIA—ALLIGATOR

Alligator mississippiensis (Daudin)

American Alligator

Recognition.—Large, blackish, lizardlike reptiles with pale
crossbands on back, and pale, mostly vertical marks on sides of
body and tail (markings obscure in adults); four toes; only
innermost three fingers and toes clawed; elongate snout with
nostrils elevated at tip; tail compressed.

Distribution.—Vagrant individuals occasional in extreme
southeastern Oklahoma.

Remarks.—In Pliocene times the alligator probably ranged
throughout the state (Woodburne, 1959). Today, however, it
seems to be only an occasional visitor in extreme southeastern
Oklahoma. Blair (1950b) reported an alligator that was shot in
Rock Creek, a tributary of Little River, about 7 miles east of

Eagletown, McCurtain County, only a few hundred feet west of the Oklahoma-Arkansas boundary.

Lane (1909) first reported the alligator in Oklahoma on the basis of a female, regarded as a migrant, obtained from a bayou of the South Canadian River within five miles of the University of Oklahoma, Norman. Later, Cross (in Snider, 1917:199) mentioned another alligator from a small lake near Durant, Bryan County. Recently, Hibbard (1960:9) stated that the alligator previously ranged as far westward as the site of Denison Dam (which impounds Lake Texoma on the Red River); records indicate that it inhabited this area "... for a period of 12 years prior to 1953."

Baby "alligators" bought in pet stores that escape or are liberated may be subsequently recovered in Oklahoma. The pet-store "alligators" are often the spectacled caiman (*Caiman sclerops*), a neotropical crocodilian that is not native to the United States. The spectacled caiman is easily distinguished from the American alligator by a curved, transverse ridge just in front of the eyes (absent in American alligator).

ORDER SQUAMATA, SUBORDER SAURIA—LIZARDS

Anolis carolinensis carolinensis Voigt

Carolina Anole

Recognition.—Green, often brown (individuals capable of changing color), with a partly strawberry-colored throat (folds of skin in males extensible into prominent "throat fan"); widened "pads" with transverse grooves underneath fingers and toes; femoral pores lacking; dorsal scales small and granular.

Distribution.—Southeastern Oklahoma in McCurtain, Choctaw, Bryan, LeFlore, and Pushmataha counties (map, Fig. 63).

Remarks.—Characteristic of the Coastal Plain, the range of

139

the Carolina anole extends westward in floodplain habitats of the Red River and its tributaries (as far as White Grass Creek, Bryan County), and northward into the Ouachita Mountains along rivers and streams, where it is found in wooded valleys and ravines (Eagle Fork Creek in LeFlore County, and Little River in Pushmataha County). Individuals are most frequently seen on shrubby vegetation or on tree trunks. Ortenburger (field notes of June 11, 1925) found anoles in small trees 15 to 20 feet above ground, and recorded one male as being pale pea green with a reddish brown middorsal region.

See Taylor and Laughlin (1964:42–43), Trowbridge (1937:293).

Specimens examined (all OU).—*Choctaw*: Red River Fisheries. *LeFlore*: several within 6 mi. radius Page; several within 7.5 mi. radius Zoe; several within 3.5 mi. radius Stapp. *McCurtain*: 1–2 and 15 mi. N Broken Bow; 14 mi. E Broken Bow; 13–14 mi. SE Broken Bow; 2 mi. SW Smithville; Beavers Bend State Park; 1 mi. W Arkansas state line on Red River. *Pushmataha*: 2 mi. E Nashoba; 7.4 mi. NE Cloudy.

Additional records.—*Bryan*: 4.5 and 8.5 mi. SE Bennington (Taylor and Laughlin, 1964:42). *McCurtain*: Little River bridge NE Idabel (Blair and Lindsay, 1961); 7 mi. N Broken Bow, and State Game Preserve (OSU).

Cnemidophorus gularis gularis Baird and Girard[1]

Spotted Whiptail

Recognition.—Striped lizards having tiny, granular scales on back and sides of body; venter uniformly whitish, or with chin

---

[1] The use of the trinomial *C. g. gularis* is in accordance with the publication of the *nomen nudum, C. g. rauni* (H. M. Smith and E. H. Taylor, *Herpetology of Mexico*, Eric Lundberg reprint, 1966:28), and the presumed forthcoming publication of the study of geographic variation of *Cnemidophorus gularis*.

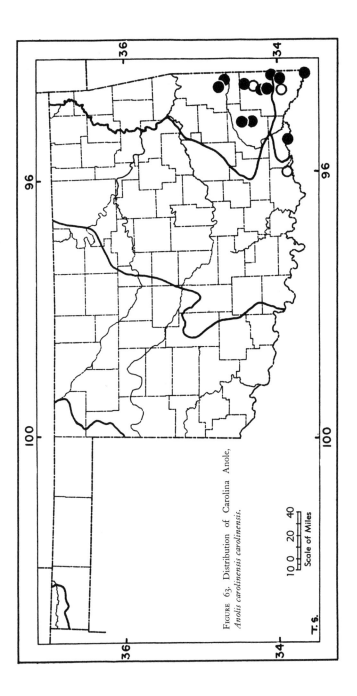

FIGURE 63. Distribution of Carolina Anole,
Anolis carolinensis carolinensis.

pinkish and chest blue black; belly with eight longitudinal rows of large squarish scales; small patch of scales on underside of forearm (postantebrachial scales) abruptly larger than surrounding scales; pale spots posteriorly on back in black areas (at least lateralmost) between pale stripes; body lacking green suffusion. Young striped with grayish tail, and lacking pale spots in black areas between pale stripes.

Distribution.—Southern Oklahoma; known as far north as Beckham and Murray counties, and as far east as Pushmataha County (map, Fig. 64).

Remarks.—The distribution of spotted whiptails to the north and east terminates in Oklahoma. The distribution northward is perhaps affected by the southwestern filter barrier (see page 49). The eastern extent of range probably is limited by the Interior Highlands, although one specimen (OU 1833) is reported from the Ouachita Mountains in Pushmataha County.

Individuals are found in flat or hilly areas of the Grassland and Oak-Woodland, usually on hard-packed soils having small rocks and a low sparse cover of grasses and herbs. Captives burrow in soft soils. In Harmon County individuals have been found in cultivated fields. The species is abundant in the mesquite plains in southwestern Oklahoma (Fig. 11) and in the Arbuckle Mountains. In most places *Cnemidophorus sexlineatus* (page 144) seems to differ from *gularis* in that it is found in loose-soiled, especially sandy, places. I have never found individuals of the two species together; Ortenburger and Freeman (1930:181), however, detected no difference in habitat, and found individuals of both species ". . . within the same few square yards" (floodplain of Red River, 7 miles southwest Hollis, Harmon County). There are also records of both species from the same locality in Comanche, Jackson, Love, and Murray counties.

Reports of *gularis* from Tulsa County (Ortenburger, 1927a:94;

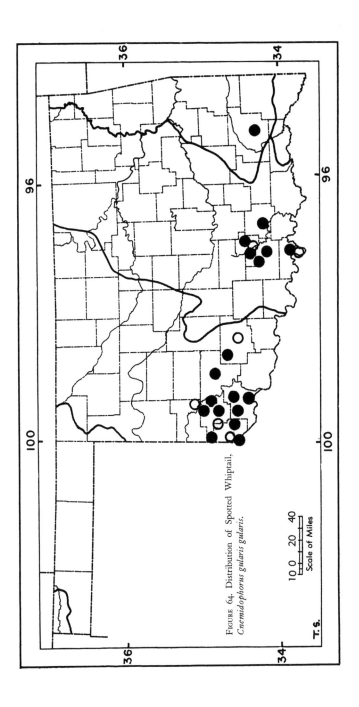

FIGURE 64. Distribution of Spotted Whiptail, *Cnemidophorus gularis gularis*.

Scale of Miles

10 0 20 40

T. S.

Force, 1928:78) presumably are based on specimens of *C. sexlineatus*. Force (1930), in her later survey of the herpetofauna of the county, did not report *gularis*.

See Burt (1931b:120, 144), Carpenter (1956:42), McCoy (1958), Taylor (1938:521).

Specimens examined (OU except as indicated).—*Carter*: Lake Woodford; 5 mi. N Ardmore. *Comanche*: Wichita Mts. Wildlife Refuge. *Greer*: Granite; 2 mi. N Willow; 4 mi. W Mangum; Salt Fork Red River S Mangum. *Harmon*: 7 mi. SW Hollis; 3 mi. S Gould; near Carl; 4 mi. N Carl. *Jackson*: near Elmer; 4 mi. W Altus; 6 mi. SE Duke (RGW). *Johnston*: 4 mi. N Tishomingo; 1 mi. SW Ravia. *Kiowa*: 10 mi. NW Roosevelt. *Love*: 4 mi. S Marietta. *Murray*: Sulphur, Platt National Park; Price's Falls; Turner Falls. *Pushmataha*: 2 mi. E Cloudy.

Additional records.—*Beckham*: [SE part of county along North Fork of Red River] (Baird and Girard, 1854:211, Pl. X, Figs. 1–4). *Comanche*: Fort Sill (AMNH). *Greer*: 1 mi. N Granite, 3 mi. S Mangum, 5 mi. SE Mangum, and 3 mi. SW Reed (OSU); 2 mi. W Reed (McCoy, 1958). *Harmon*: 5.5 mi. S Hollis and 5 mi. N Hollis (FWCM); 4 mi. W Reed, Greer County (OSU). *Jackson*: SW Olustee (UMMZ). *Love*: 5 mi. N Thackerville (reported by Burt and Burt, 1929b:9, as *gularis-sexlineatus* intergrades; AMNH 36992–93 determined as *gularis* by R. G. Zweifel). *Murray*: Dougherty (Burt, 1931b:114); Honey Creek above Turner Falls, and Camp Classen (OSU).

Cnemidophorus sexlineatus viridis Lowe

Prairie Lined Racerunner

Recognition.—Striped lizards with tiny, granular scales on back and sides of body; belly whitish or pale bluish having eight longitudinal rows of large squarish scales; postantebrachial scales not enlarged; pale spots lacking in black areas between pale stripes on back; middorsal stripe(s) brownish; green suffusion often on anterior part of body in life. Young black with yellow stripes and blue tail, and lacking green.

Distribution.—Throughout the state (map, Fig. 65).

Remarks.—Lowe (1966) recently recognized a western subspecies of *Cnemidophorus sexlineatus, C. s. viridis.* Judging from the distribution map prepared by Stebbins (1966, Map 108; account of species read by Lowe, p. ix), *viridis* occurs throughout Oklahoma, except for a small, perhaps intergrading, area in extreme southeastern Oklahoma, occupied by the subspecies *sexlineatus.* The principal characteristics differentiating the two subspecies are the number of pale longitudinal stripes (six in *sexlineatus*; seven or eight [brownish middorsal stripe may or may not be divided] in *viridis*), and the presence (*viridis*) or absence (*sexlineatus*) of a greenish suffusion (in life) on the body. The two subspecies are also distinguished by differences in average number of scales around midbody and between the paravertebral stripes (counts low in *viridis*, high in *sexlineatus*). Until the status of the two subspecies in southeastern Oklahoma is clarified, all racerunners in Oklahoma are conveniently referred to *viridis*.

The species is abundant in many different kinds of habitats—from shrubby wooded hillsides in the Ouachita Mountains to short-grass plains having yucca and sage in the panhandle. There are several records of individuals on the banks and floodplains of rivers and creeks among sedges, willows, assorted weeds, grass clumps, and brush. In Osage County, individuals were found under large rocks deeply set in the ground in a well-grazed pasture. In general, *sexlineatus* seems to prefer loose, sandy soils in which they dig burrows and take refuge when pursued. Lined racerunners have been eaten by *Lampropeltis calligaster* and *Masticophis flagellum testaceus.* See account of *Cnemidophorus g. gularis.*

See Bonn and McCarley (1953:469), Burt (1931b:83, 120, 140,

145

144), Burt and Hoyle (1935:202), Carpenter (1956:42; 1958b:114, 115; 1959a; 1959c:34; 1960a; 1960c; 1961; 1962), Carpenter et al. (1961:193), Carter and Cox (1968), Force (1925a:26; 1925b:82; 1930:28, 32), Glass and Dundee (1950), Harney (1955:85), Jenni (1954), Ortenburger and Bird (1933:60), Ortenburger and Freeman (1930:181), Taylor (1938:521), Trowbridge (1937:294).

Specimens examined (OU except as indicated).—*Adair*: 4 mi. NW Watts. *Alfalfa*: 6 mi. N and 8 mi. E Cherokee; 3 and 9 mi. E Cherokee; 5 mi. N Cherokee. *Beaver*: near Gate; 4 mi. E Forgan; Cimarron River, 1 mi. S Kansas state line (KU). *Beckham*: 5 mi. S Carter. *Blaine*: Salt Creek Canyon (KU); 4 mi. SW Geary. *Bryan*: 3 mi. SE Yuba (UMMZ); near Durant. *Caddo*: 4 mi. S Hinton. *Carter*: 11 mi. W Ardmore. *Cherokee*: 4 mi. NE Welling. *Choctaw*: 1 mi. W Sawyer; 10 mi. S Hugo; 2 mi. S Grant; 4.2 mi. W Fort Towson. *Cimarron*: 7 mi. S Boise City; 3 mi. N Kenton; 2 mi. W Kenton and 6.9 mi. E Kenton (TTC). *Creek*: Drumright (KU). *Cleveland*: several within 3 mi. radius Norman. *Coal*: 5 mi. W Coalgate. *Comanche*: Wichita Mts. Wildlife Refuge. *Delaware*: near Turkey Ford. *Dewey*: 1 mi. N Taloga; 5 mi. SW Canton, Blaine County (KU). *Garvin*: Maysville. *Grady*: 7 mi. S Chickasha. *Harmon*: 7 mi. SW Hollis; 11 mi. N Hollis; 7 mi. SW Vinson. *Harper*: near Gate, Beaver County; Cimarron River S Englewood, Kansas (KU). *Haskell*: no data. *Jackson*: near Elmer. *Jefferson*: 2.2 mi. E Ringling; 18.3 mi. W Ringling. *Johnston*: 2.5 mi. N Milburn. *Kay*: Ponca City; 8 mi. E Ponca City. *Latimer*: several within 6 mi. radius Wilburton. *LeFlore*: 6 and 18 mi. SW Wister; 5 and 13 mi. E Big Cedar; 1 mi. SW Talihina; 6.5 mi. W Heavener; 1.5 and 5.2 mi. E Zoe; 4 mi. E Page; 6 mi. SW Page; 2.5 mi. N Stapp. *Logan*: Guthrie; 5 mi. S Guthrie; 6 mi. W Guthrie. *Love*: 17.5 mi. W Marietta; 20 mi. S Marietta; 1.5 mi. W Rubottom; Red River bridge S Marietta (KU). *Major*: 3 mi. S Cleo Springs. *Marshall*: UOBS; 0.5 mi. E Lebanon; 8 mi. W Kingston; 0.5 mi. E Powell; 0.2 mi. S Marshall-Johnston county line on U.S. Highway 70; 0.5 mi. E Cumberland. *Mayes*: 5 mi. NW Locust Grove. *McClain*: 5 and 10 mi. S Norman, Cleveland County; 6 mi. E Blanchard. *McCurtain*:

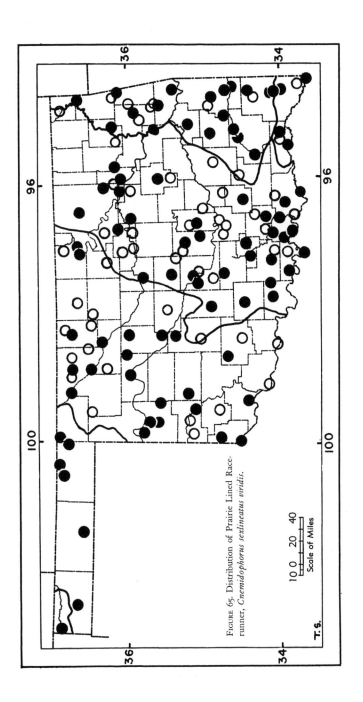

FIGURE 65. Distribution of Prairie Lined Race-runner, *Cnemidophorus sexlineatus viridis.*

Scale of Miles

10 0 20 40

Beavers Bend State Park; Smithville; 7 mi. S Broken Bow; 10 mi. SE Broken Bow; 2 mi. N Broken Bow; 1 mi. W Oklahoma-Arkansas state line on Red River. *Murray*: Price's Falls; Sulphur, Platt National Park (KU). *Muskogee*: Camp Gruber, near Braggs. *Oklahoma*: 2 mi. SE Oklahoma City. *Okmulgee*: Okmulgee. *Osage*: 7 mi. W Skiatook, Tulsa County; 5 and 14 mi. E Pawhuska. *Pawnee*: near Quay. *Pottawatomie*: Shawnee; 3.5 mi. NE Shawnee; St. Louis. *Pushmataha*: 4 mi. E Tuskahoma; 1.5 mi. SW Kosoma; 0.5 mi. S Clayton (TTC). *Roger Mills*: 2 mi. N Cheyenne; 6 mi. NE Durham; 2 mi. S Roll; Hammon. *Rogers*: 1 mi. W Catoosa. *Seminole*: Bowlegs. *Sequoyah*: 1 mi. W Muldrow; 1–2 mi. N Marble City; Dwight Mission. *Stephens*: 8 mi. E and 2 mi. N Duncan. *Texas*: 8 mi. SE Guymon. *Tulsa*: 5 mi. SW Tulsa; 2 mi. S Sand Springs. *Washita*: western part of county between Cordell and Carter, Beckham County. *Woods*: 1–3 mi. W Edith; 2.5 mi. W and 1 mi. S Waynoka; 12 mi. W Alva (KU).

Additional records.—Adair: 3 mi. S Bunch (KU); 2 mi. W Proctor (UI). *Alfalfa*: 3 mi. E Byron (OSU); 6.5 mi. NE Ingersoll (Ortenburger and Freeman, 1930:181); 2 mi. W Goltry (Burt, 1935:325). *Atoka*: 14 mi. NE Stringtown (UI). *Beckham*: 2 mi. SE Erick and 4 mi. SW Sayre (Burt and Hoyle, 1935:202). *Bryan*: 5 mi. E Caddo (SESC); Colbert and 5 mi. SW Colbert (TNHC). *Caddo*: Kiwanis Canyon (OSU); Fort Cobb (USNM). *Canadian*: "Elkino, Okla. Terr." (presumably El Reno, FMNH). *Carter*: 5 mi. S and 2 mi. W Ardmore (Carpenter, 1958a:72). *Cherokee*: 4 mi. SE Cookson (KU); 11 mi. SW Tahlequah (UI). *Cleveland*: Noble (Burt, 1931b:89). *Comanche*: near Lawton (Smith and Leonard, 1934:193). *Cotton*: 1 mi. N Red River (Smith and Leonard, 1934:193). *Creek*: 1 mi. SW Oakhurst, Tulsa County (Burt, 1935:325); Sapulpa (Burt, 1931b:89). *Delaware*: Dripping Springs (KU). *Garfield*: 1 mi. SE Hillsdale (Burt, 1935:325). *Grant*: 2 mi. N Pond Creek (Smith and Leonard, 1934:193). *Greer*: near Mangum (USNM). *Harmon*: 7 mi. SW and 1.5 mi. E Hollis (Carpenter et al., 1961:193). *Hughes*: 4 mi. SE Non (Burt, 1931b:89); 5 mi. W Holdenville (Burt, 1935:325). *Johnston*: 6 mi. N Milburn (Carpenter, 1958a:72); 5 mi. N Milburn and 1 mi. S Ravia (Carpenter,

1956:42); 7 mi. W Wapunucka (CCC). *Kay*: Salt Fork of Arkansas, near Ponca City (OSU); 6 mi. NE Newkirk (Burt and Hoyle, 1935:202). *LeFlore*: Page (USNM); 1 mi. E Fanshawe (Burt, 1935:325); Wister (Burt, 1931b:89). *Love*: 4 mi. N Marietta (Burt, 1935:325); Thackerville and 5 mi. N Thackerville (reported as *gularis-sexlineatus* intergrades by Burt and Burt, 1929b:9; AMNH 36985 and 36994 determined as *sexlineatus* by R. G. Zweifel). *Major*: 5 mi. S Sherman (Burt, 1935:325). *Mayes*: 1.5 mi. S Chouteau (KU). *McClain*: near Payne Center (UMMZ). *McCurtain*: 6 mi. SW Eagletown (UMMZ); 5 mi. S Broken Bow (OSU); within 2 mi. radius Tom (UI); between Bethel and Broken Bow [5 mi. E Bethel] (Burt, 1931b:89, FMNH). *Murray*: Turner Falls (OU); Camp Classen (SESC). *Noble*: 5 mi. E Perry (OSU); 8 mi. N Perry (Burt, 1935:325). *Oklahoma*: 2 mi. S Harrah (Burt, 1935:325); Oklahoma City (FMNH). *Okmulgee*: 1 mi. NE Dewar (Burt, 1935:325). *Osage*: 4 mi. W Pawhuska (Burt and Hoyle, 1935:202); vicinity Turley, Tulsa County (UMMZ); 7 mi. NNW Tulsa, Tulsa County (TNHC). *Ottawa*: Miami (Cope, 1894:387). *Pawnee*: Black Bear Creek near Pawnee (OSU); 2 mi. SE Pawnee (Burt, 1935:325). *Payne*: several within 4.5 mi. radius Stillwater, 9 mi. SW Stillwater, Ripley Bluffs, and Cushing (OSU). *Pittsburg*: McAlester (UA). *Pontotoc*: 2 mi. S Ada (Carter, 1966:34); 7 mi. NE Ada and 10 mi. W Ada (ECSC). *Pottawatomie*: 4 mi. E Shawnee (Burt, 1935:325); Shawnee Lake (OSU). *Pushmataha*: 7 mi. SE Clayton (TNHC). *Seminole*: 4 mi. E Seminole (Burt, 1935:325). *Tillman*: 1–2 mi. S Davidson (CCC). *Tulsa*: Tulsa (Blair, 1961); Garnett (UMMZ); Red Fork (Burt, 1931b:89); near Cincinnati (USNM, locality unknown). *Woods*: 7 mi. W Carmen, Alfalfa County (Burt, 1935:325); several vicinity Alva (McCracken, 1966:10) Waynoka (UMMZ, USNM); Whitehorse Springs (Burt, 1931b:89). *Woodward*: Fort Supply (Cope, 1894:387).

Cnemidophorus tesselatus (Say)

Checkered Whiptail

Recognition.—Large lizards with tiny, granular scales on back and sides of body; belly whitish (some specimens have a few black specks on chest) with eight longitudinal rows of large squarish scales; back and sides of body have pale longitudinal stripes and barlike spots (orange posteriorly in life) in black fields, forming a checkered pattern. Young black and white striped with pale specks and wavy middorsal stripe.

Distribution.—Known only from the northwestern corner of Cimarron County in the panhandle.

Remarks.—*Cnemidophorus tesselatus* is a uniparental or unisexual (all female) species that most likely reproduces parthenogenetically; males are rarely found. This whiptail is confined to the Mesa de Maya, and seems to be abundant on the rocky slopes of the buttes and mesas. Individuals are unwary and easily captured (see Glass and Dundee, 1950).

Specimens examined.—*Cimarron*: 2 mi. W Kenton (TTC); 5 mi. E Kenton (OU).

Additional records.—*Cimarron*: 5 mi. N Kenton (Glass and Dundee, 1950); 2 mi. E Kenton (OSU); 8 mi. S Kenton (ECSC).

Crotaphytus collaris collaris (Say)

Eastern Collared Lizard

Recognition.—Large, spotted, mostly greenish (males) or orange and buff (females), with relatively large distinct heads and long tails; two interrupted, black collars on neck and shoulder; tiny granular scales on back and sides (see colored frontispiece).

Distribution.—Throughout the state (map, Fig. 66).

Remarks.—Although considered to be distributed statewide, the known records indicate that collared lizards avoid the Coastal Plain. Commonly referred to as "mountain boomers," collared lizards live in rocky habitats, and seem to be more abundant in western than eastern Oklahoma. Individuals are abundant in the Arbuckle and Wichita mountains. In the western part of the state, collared lizards are often found along the eroded banks of creeks and streams. In Stephens County three lizards were found associated with an isolated group of four small boulders in a large, open, grassy field. In northeastern Oklahoma lizards were observed sunning on rocks of road cuts. In the southeast, lizards were taken in wooded areas on bouldered slopes or rock outcrops near creeks and streams. Captives have eaten crickets, cockroaches, moths, blister beetles, and phalangids; one ate a *Lygosoma*. Collared lizards have been eaten by individuals of *Agkistrodon contortrix* (Comanche County) and *Sistrurus catenatus* (Kiowa County). Nine eggs, averaging 13 by 21 mm, were deposited by a captive on June 19, 1951 (Stephens County).

See Blair and Blair (1941), Bonn and McCarley (1953:469), Burt (1928b:11; 1931a:14), Burt and Hoyle (1935:198, 205), Carpenter (1956:41), Carter and Cox (1968), Force (1925a:26; 1925b:83; 1930:27, 32), Hallowell (1854:145 [footnote]; 1857: 238–239), McCoy (1958), Ortenburger and Freeman (1930:178), Stejneger (1890:103, Pl. 12, Fig. 2), Trowbridge (1937:294), Webb and Ortenburger (1955:88).

Specimens examined (OU except as indicated).—*Adair*: 5–6 mi. N Marble City, Sequoyah County. *Atoka*: 3.5 mi. E Stringtown. *Beaver*: Cimarron River, 1 mi. S Kansas state line (KU). *Beckham*: Elk City; 2 mi. E and 10 mi. S Erick. *Blaine*: Roman Nose State Park; Salt Creek Canyon (KU). *Caddo*: 5 mi. E Weatherford, Custer County. *Canadian*: Devils Canyon. *Carter*: Ardmore. *Cimarron*: 3 mi. N Kenton; 5 mi. E Kenton. *Cleveland*: several within 6 mi. radius Norman; 2 mi. E Noble. *Comanche*: Wichita Mts. Wildlife Refuge; Craterville Park, 3.5 mi. N Cache; 2 mi. N Cache; 9 mi. NW Cache. *Cotton*: 1 mi. S Temple City Lake; 2 mi. NW Temple City. *Creek*: Drumright (KU). *Custer*: 2 mi. S Weatherford (SWSC). *Garvin*: Maysville. *Grady*: 6 mi. NE Chickasha. *Greer*: 4.5 mi. N Mangum; 1 mi. NW Reed. *Harmon*: 7 mi. SW Hollis;

3.4 mi. N Carl; 1 mi. W junction Elm Fork Red River and State Highway 30. *Harper*: near Gate, Beaver County. *Jackson*: near Elmer, 0.8 mi. W Salt Fork Red River; 6 mi. W Altus; near Headrick. *Jefferson*: 3 mi. S Addington; 3 mi. SW Waurika; Ryan (KU). *Johnston*: Blue River bridge on State Highway 7; 1 mi. S Connerville; Ravia Quarry. *Kay*: Ponca City; 8 mi. E Ponca City. *Kiowa*: Cooperton; 10 mi. NW Meers, Comanche County; 1.2 mi. S Snyder (TTC). *Latimer*: Wilburton; 2 and 7 mi. N Wilburton; 9–10 mi. SW Wilburton; 2 mi. N Red Oak. *LeFlore*: 6 and 18 mi. SW Wister; 10 mi. S Wister; 6 and 10 mi. W Heavener; 1.5 mi. N Zoe; Spring Mt., 6 mi. SW Page. *Logan*: Guthrie; 3 mi. S Guthrie. *Love*: 6 mi. W Lebanon, Marshall County (TTC); 0.5 mi. W Courtney. *Major*: 8 mi. S Cleo Springs; 4.5 mi. W junction U.S. Highways 281 and 15 (TTC). *McClain*: near Goldsby; 6 mi. W Norman and 5 mi. SW Norman, Cleveland County. *McCurtain*: 13 mi. N Bethel. *Murray*: Turner Falls; Sulphur (KU). *Noble*: 10 mi. N Stillwater, Payne County. *Oklahoma*: 5 mi. NE Oklahoma City. *Okmulgee*: Okmulgee. *Osage*: Reservoir Hill. *Pawnee*: Quay. *Pontotoc*: 1.3 mi. W Fittstown; near Ada. *Pottawatomie*: Shawnee; 5 mi. NE Shawnee; St. Louis. *Pushmataha*: 7 mi. NE Daisy, Atoka County; 4 mi. W Sardis. *Roger Mills*: Strong City. *Rogers*: 2 mi. NE Catoosa. *Seminole*: Bowlegs. *Sequoyah*: 1 mi. N Marble City; 8 mi. N Sallisaw. *Stephens*: 10 mi. E Duncan. *Texas*: 8 mi. SE Guymon. *Tillman*: 1 mi. N Frederick. *Tulsa*: Tulsa. *Wagoner*: no data. *Washita*: 5 mi. S and 5 mi. W Weatherford, Custer County (SWSC). *Woods*: Waynoka and Alva (NWSC); 2 mi. W Edith.

Additional records.—Adair: 18.4–20.6 mi. S Stilwell (UA); 4 mi. S Stilwell (UI). *Beckham*: Gypsum Bluffs on [North Fork of] Red River [SE part of county] (Baird and Girard, 1854:206). *Caddo*: Fort Cobb (Yarrow, 1882:53 and Cope, 1900:258; reported by both as *C. wislinzeni*, but determined as *collaris* by James R. Dixon); 2 mi. E Fort Cobb (KU). *Cimarron*: 2 mi. E Kenton (OSU). *Coal*: 2 and 6 mi. N Coalgate (ECSC); Lehigh (AMNH); 6 mi. S Non, Hughes County (Burt, 1931a:14). *Comanche*: 17 mi. NW Lawton (Burt, 1931a:14); Fort Sill, and Cache (USNM). *Creek*: near Sapulpa (Schmidt, 1919:71); 2 mi. W Bristow, 1 mi. NW Milfay, and 4 mi.

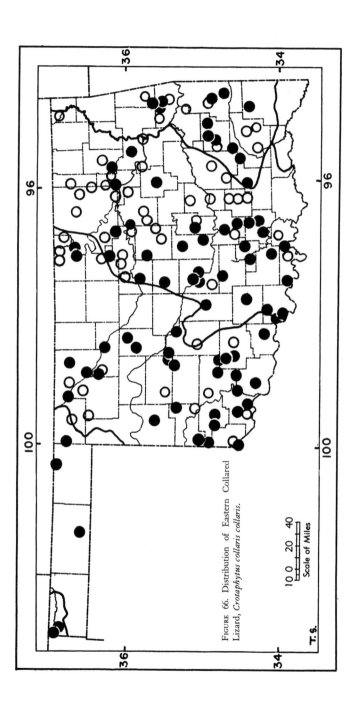

FIGURE 66. Distribution of Eastern Collared Lizard, *Crotaphytus collaris collaris*.

SW Sapulpa (Burt, 1935: 322). *Custer*: below Foss Reservoir Dam (Carter, 1966:33). *Greer*: 4 mi. W Mangum (UMMZ); 3 mi. SW Reed and 5 mi. SE Reed (OSU); 2 mi. W Reed (McCoy, 1958). *Harmon*: 3 and 5 mi. S Hollis (FWCM). *Harper*: 7 mi. S Buffalo (UA). *Haskell*: near Cartersville (Carter, 1966:33). *Hughes*: 2 mi. N Calvin (Burt, 1931a:14); near Wetumka (UMMZ). *Jackson*: 9 mi. SW Olustee (UMMZ). *Kay*: 4 mi. W Lyman, Osage County (Burt, 1935:322); 6 mi. SE Chilocco and 6 mi. NE Newkirk (Burt and Hoyle, 1935:199); 13 mi. E Newkirk (KU). *Kiowa*: 3 mi. E Lone Wolf (KU). *Latimer*: 2 mi. N Gowan (Burt, 1935:322); Coon Creek near Robbers Cave State Park (CCC). *LeFlore*: Wister (AMNH, CM). *Lincoln*: near Sparks (ECSC); 3 mi. S Sac and Fox Agency (Burt, 1935:322). *Logan*: 3 mi. S Guthrie (Burt, 1935:322); 2 mi. N Mulhall (Burt and Burt, 1929b:8). *Love*: 16 mi. S Ardmore, Carter County (Burt and Burt, 1929b:8). *Major*: 6 mi. NE Sherman (Burt, 1935:322). *Marshall*: Glasses Creek N Madill (CCC). *McClain*: Payne (UMMZ). *Muskogee*: 3 mi. NW Haskell (Burt, 1935:322). *Noble*: 5 mi. N Sumner (Burt, 1935:322). *Oklahoma*: 7 mi. N Oklahoma City (Burt and Hoyle, 1935:199). *Osage*: 12 mi. from Barnsdall (FMNH); 2 mi. SE Avant, 10 mi. SW Bartlesville, Washington County, and 4 mi. W Pawhuska (Burt and Hoyle, 1935:199); 5 mi. N Sand Springs, Tulsa County (UMMZ); 2 mi. N Sand Springs, Tulsa County (TNHC). *Ottawa*: Miami (Cope, 1894:386). *Pawnee*: 2 mi. N Pawnee and 2 mi. SE Pawnee (Burt, 1935:322). *Payne*: [Stillwater (OSU, UMMZ) and Lake Carl Blackwell (OSU)] (Moore and Rigney, 1942:78); 2 mi. E Cushing and 4 mi. W Quay (Burt, 1935:322). *Pittsburg*: Kiowa (SESC); South McAlester (Stone, 1903:540). *Pontotoc*: 17 mi. S Ada (FWCM). *Pushmataha*: 1 mi. S Nashoba, and Finley (TNHC); 5 mi. N Finley (FMNH); between Cloudy and Pickens (CCC). *Rogers*: 1 mi. W Catoosa (UI); near Claremore (MCZ); 6 mi. W Claremore (Burt and Hoyle, 1935:199). *Seminole*: 5 mi. NW Wewoka (Burt, 1935:322). *Sequoyah*: 5 mi. E Tenkiller Dam (KU); 4 mi. NE Sallisaw (UMMZ). *Tulsa*: 7 mi. NNW Tulsa (TNHC); Garnett (UMMZ); Turley and Sperry (KU). *Wagoner*: about 4 mi. ENE Fort Gibson, Muskogee County (restricted type locality, see p. 331). *Washington*: Bartlesville (CM, USNM).

Woods: 1.5 mi. E Tegarden (OSU); Whitehorse Springs (FMNH). *Woodward*: Fort Supply (Cope, 1894:386); 16 mi. SW Freedom, Woods County (Ortenburger and Freeman, 1930:178). *County unknown*: 1 mi. W Springhill (Burt, 1935:322; Springhill not found in Okfuskee County as reported, but a "Spring Hill" near Oklahoma City, Oklahoma County).

Eumeces anthracinus pluvialis Cope

Southern Coal Skink

Recognition.—Brownish lizards having smooth, flat, over-lapping scales; wide, brownish black band on sides of body flanked by thin pale lines; faint middorsal stripe usually lacking; no stripes on head; one postmental; no postnasal. Young blackish with whitish labial spots and blue tails.

Distribution.—Eastern Oklahoma; known as far west as Creek, Johnston, and Marshall counties (map, Fig. 67).

Remarks.—Coal skinks are found in the Interior Highlands and sparingly in the Oak-Woodland. Individuals have been found under rocks, logs, and other debris on wooded hillsides and in valleys, most often in lowlands along rivers and streams. Two lizards from Latimer County were found "on trees" (field notes, A. I. Ortenburger). A record of this species from Comanche County (Ortenburger, 1926a:138; 1927a:95) is considered erroneous.

See Carpenter (1956:42), Force (1930:29), Smith and Smith (1952:691), Trowbridge (1937:294).

Specimens examined (OU except as indicated).—*Adair*: 9.4 mi. SSW Stilwell (KU). *Bryan*: near Durant. *Cherokee*: McSpadden Falls. *Latimer*: several within 2.5 mi. radius Wilburton. *LeFlore*: 3.5 mi. NE Page; 5 mi. E Page. *McCurtain*: 14 mi. E Broken Bow; 14 mi. SE Broken Bow; 1 mi. W Tom; near Idabel; Beavers Bend State Park; Little River bridge, NE Idabel. *Ottawa*: 2 mi. S Peoria, and 5.5 mi. SE Quapaw (KU). *Pushmataha*: 7.4 mi. NE Cloudy; Little River between Pickens and Cloudy. *Tulsa*: Parthenia Park.

Additional records.—Adair: 5 mi. S Kansas, Delaware County (Smith and Smith, 1952:689). *Cherokee*: Camp Egan (McCoy, 1960a:42). *Choctaw*: Fort Towson (Cope, 1900:663; Hurter and Strecker, 1909:23). *Creek*: Heyburn Lake Recreational Area (INHS). *Johnston*: 3 mi. NW Reagan (CCC). *Marshall*: 1 mi. W Shay (Carpenter, 1958a:72). *Pushmataha*: [4 mi. E Tuskahoma] (Ortenburger, 1927a:95).

Eumeces fasciatus (Linnaeus)

Five-lined Skink

Recognition.—Scales smooth, flat, and overlapping; blackish or brownish with pale stripes on body; median stripe bifurcating at base of head; in some specimens dorsum uniform olive brown with slightly darker sides; sides of head reddish in large males; length of body not more than 3.5 inches; postnasal present; supralabials usually seven (four small ones in front of eye); two large postlabials; young have blue tails.

Distribution.—Eastern half of Oklahoma; known as far west as Caddo and Comanche counties (map, Fig. 68).

Remarks.—This species and the little ground skink (*Lygosoma*) are the most frequently collected skinks in Oklahoma. The five-lined skink is generally a woodland species, being found on hillsides and in lowlands, usually among leaf litter and under rocks and fallen logs, but occasionally climbing trees (observed once on pine tree); skinks of this species also frequent rocky, grassy areas, and trash piles in urban areas. In central Oklahoma these skinks are abundant in spring and early summer but scarce in the hot months of July and August. Recorded numbers of eggs per clutch are 7 (Cherokee County), 9 (Washington County, June 14), and 6 and 9 (Delaware County).

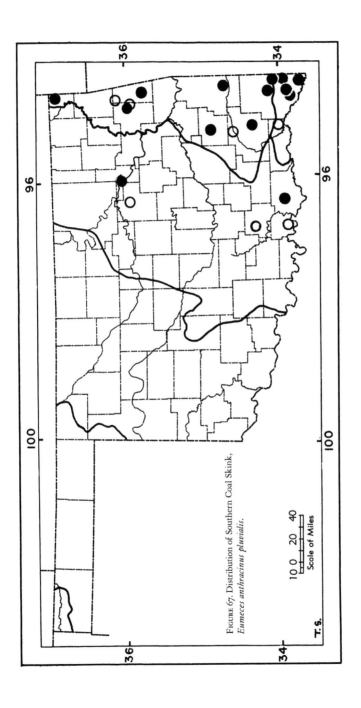

FIGURE 67. Distribution of Southern Coal Skink, *Eumeces anthracinus pluvialis.*

Of 209 Oklahoma specimens, 17 (8%) had eight supralabials (resembling *laticeps*) but all had two large postlabials. Only seven lizards (3%) had seven supralabials on one side and eight on the other side of the head. Taylor (1936:199, 202) noted that many specimens from Oklahoma had one postmental (usually two in *fasciatus*). Of 182 specimens, 63 (35%) had one postmental (partly separated, in some, by short, incomplete lateral sutures from one or both sides).

The record of *fasciatus* from 6 miles northeast of Grove, Delaware County (Ortenburger, 1929b:27), is based on an individual of *Eumeces laticeps*.

See Bonn and McCarley (1953:469), Carpenter (1956:42; 1959c:34), Carter and Cox (1968), Fitch (1954:137), Force (1930:29), Moore and Rigney (1942:79), Smith (1950:186, Fig. 130A; 1956:192, Fig. 138A), Taylor (1932:264, 265; 1936:59), Trowbridge (1937:294).

Specimens examined (OU except as indicated).—*Adair*: 3 mi. NNW Chewey; 4 mi. NW Watts; 4 mi. N Stilwell; 9.4 mi. SSW Stilwell (KU). *Cherokee*: Scraper; 3.6 mi. N Scraper; 4 mi. NE Welling; 2 and 5 mi. S Welling; Camp Egan; 4 mi. N and 5 mi. E Tahlequah (KU). *Choctaw*: 2 mi. SW Grant. *Cleveland*: 2–3 mi. S Norman; 6 mi. NE Norman. *Coal*: 4 mi. W Tupelo. *Comanche*: 9 mi. SE Cache. *Delaware*: near Flint; near Cayuga; 1 mi. E Kansas (KU). *Garvin*: Maysville. *Hughes*: 6 mi. S Weleetka, Okfuskee County. *Latimer*: several within 9 mi. radius Wilburton. *LeFlore*: 1 mi. E Zoe; 3 mi. W Zoe; 3.5 mi. SW Stapp; 5 and 13 mi. E Big Cedar. *Logan*: Guthrie. *McClain*: 5 mi. SW Norman, Cleveland County; 6 mi. E Blanchard. *McCurtain*: State Game Preserve; Beavers Bend State Park; several within 5 mi. radius Broken Bow; 10 mi. SE Broken Bow; 14 mi. E Broken Bow; 6 mi. E Sherwood; 9 mi. S Haworth; several within 4 mi. radius Harris; 7 mi. SE Eagletown; 2 mi. N Tom; 2 mi. E Bokhoma; 2 mi. SW Smithville; 4 mi. S Bethel; near Idabel; 6 mi. N Idabel. *Murray*: no data. *Okmulgee*: Okmulgee. *Oklahoma*: no data. *Ottawa*: near Wyandotte; 2.5 mi. SW Peoria (KU). *Payne*: near Quay; near Lake Carl Black-

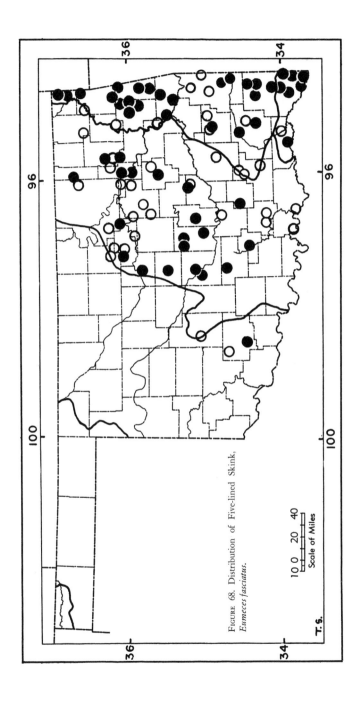

FIGURE 68. Distribution of Five-lined Skink,
Eumeces fasciatus.

well. *Pottawatomie*: Shawnee; 12 mi. W Shawnee; St. Louis. *Push-mataha*: 3 mi. NE Cloudy; 0.5 mi. S Clayton (TTC). *Rogers*: 5 mi. W Claremore. *Seminole*: Bowlegs. *Sequoyah*: 3 mi. NE Gore; 4.5 mi. SW Sallisaw; 13 mi. N Sallisaw; Dwight Mission. *Tulsa*: 9 mi. SE Tulsa; near Bixby. *Wagoner*: 2 mi. S Catoosa, 6 mi. SE Catoosa and 8 mi. SE Catoosa, Rogers County. *Washington*: near Bartlesville (KU).

Additional records.—Adair: 6 mi. S Kansas, Delaware County (TNHC, TTC); 4 mi. W Stilwell (UI); 1 mi. NW Chewey (TTC). *Atoka*: 14 mi. NE Stringtown (UI); 1.1 mi. NW Farris (AMNH); Limestone Gap (Stone, 1903:541). *Bryan*: 3.5 mi. N Colbert and 5 mi. SW Colbert (TNHC). *Caddo*: Fort Cobb (Cope, 1900:640; Taylor, 1936:210, 223). *Cherokee*: Hanging Rock (UI); Camp Muskogee and Tahlequah (OSU). *Choctaw*: 7 mi. W Fort Towson (FMNH). *Comanche*: Wichita Mts. Wildlife Refuge (Ortenburger, 1926a:138). *Craig*: 4 mi. SW Whiteoak (Burt and Hoyle, 1935:203). *Creek*: Drumright (USNM); Sapulpa (Taylor, 1936:210); 2 mi. W Bristow, 1 mi. NW Milfay, and 1 mi. SW Oakhurst, Tulsa County (Burt, 1935:326). *Delaware*: 3 mi. S Cleora (OU). *Hughes*: 10 mi. E Wetumka (UMMZ). *Johnston*: 9 mi. NW Milburn (Carpenter, 1958a:72); near Tishomingo (OU). *Latimer*: 3 mi. N Red Oak (Ortenburger, 1929a:11). *LeFlore*: Sugarloaf Mt. and Wister (Stone, 1903:541); Panama (KU); Coal Creek (Cope, 1900:650; probably *fasciatus,* certainly not the young of *E. obsoletus,* as described by Cope on p. 647; based on USNM 3113, which is no longer extant). *Marshall*: near Shay (Howard McCarley, personal communication). *Mayes*: 3 mi. S Locust Grove (OU); 2 mi. N Locust Grove (TU); 5 mi. S Locust Grove (OSU, TNHC); Cedar Crest Lake (OSU). *McCurtain*: 10 mi. E Broken Bow (OSU); 2 mi. SW Tom (UI); 2.5 mi. NE Idabel (TCWC). *Muskogee*: Greenleaf Lake State Park (ECSC). *Noble*: 5 mi. E Perry (McCoy, 1960a:41). *Okmulgee*: Bald Hill (Burt and Hoyle, 1935:203). *Osage*: Reservoir Hill (OU); Okesa (UMMZ). *Pawnee*: 2 mi. SE Pawnee (Burt, 1935:326). *Payne*: several within 4 mi. radius Stillwater, and Ripley Bluffs (OSU); Lake Carl Blackwell, 9 mi. W Stillwater (FWCM); 14 mi. N Stillwater (UMMZ).

Pittsburg: South McAlester (Stone, 1903:541). *Pontotoc*: 7 mi. NE Ada (Carter, 1966:34). *Pushmataha*: 1 mi. S Nashoba (TNHC). *Rogers*: 6 mi. E Catoosa (Dundee and Burger, 1948); 3 mi. SW Verdigris (TU); 7 mi. W Claremore (KU); 19 mi. E Tulsa, Tulsa County (OSU); 6 mi. W Claremore (Burt and Hoyle, 1935:203). *Sequoyah*: 10 mi. NE Gore (OSU). *Tulsa*: Tulsa (FWCM, USNM); 2 mi. S Sand Springs (OU); 1 mi. N Red Fork (OU); Garnett (UMMZ).

Eumeces laticeps (Schneider)

Broad-headed Skink

Recognition.—Scales smooth, flat, and overlapping; body brownish with blackish lateral band, with stripes on back, and with median stripe bifurcating at base of head; body occasionally uniform olive brown with slightly darker sides; heads broadened and sides reddish in large males; maximum length of body exceeding 3.5 inches; postnasal present; supralabials eight (five small ones in front of eye); postlabials small; young have blue tails.

Distribution.—Eastern Oklahoma; known as far west as Tulsa, Pottawatomie, and Love counties (map, Fig. 69).

Remarks.—Broad-headed skinks are arboreal in forested or savanna regions (deciduous trees so far as known), and the quality and quantity of wooded areas probably affects the westward dispersal of the species. The specimen from Love County was found foraging on a sand bank of the Red River, and one from McCurtain County was taken in wet bottomlands in a pile of driftwood with one individual of *Eumeces fasciatus*. The remarks of Trowbridge (1937:295), in his account of *Eumeces obsoletus*—"25 feet from the ground in trees . . . (and) . . . from hollow trees"—probably refer to *E. laticeps* (certainly not *obsoletus*).

Of 43 Oklahoma specimens, all have 8 supralabials except five, in which counts were 7 on one side and 8 on the other in three, 8-9 in one, and 7-7 in another (thus resembling *fasciatus*) which had no postlabials and had a snout–vent length of 90 mm.

See Bonn and McCarley (1953:469), Carpenter (1956:42), Carter and Cox (1968), Taylor (1932:264, 265, Pl. XX, Fig. 4; 1936:569, Pl. XIII, Fig. 4).

Specimens examined (all OU).—*Choctaw*: Sawyer. *Delaware*: 6 mi. NW Grove. *Johnston*: 2.5 mi. N Milburn. *Latimer*: 1 mi. N Wilburton. *LeFlore*: 1.5 and 5.2 mi. E Zoe; 6.5 mi. W Heavener; 6 mi. SW Page. *Love*: 20 mi. S Marietta. *Mayes*: no data. *McCurtain*: 10 mi. S Idabel; Little River N Idabel; 2 mi. SW Smithville; Beavers Bend State Park; 1 mi. W Arkansas state line on Red River; 6 mi. E Broken Bow; 3.5 mi. S and 1 mi. E Tom. *Pottawatomie*: Shawnee. *Pushmataha*: near Nashoba; 10 mi. SW Pickens, McCurtain County. *Sequoyah*: Dwight Mission.

Additional records.—*Bryan*: 5 mi. SW Colbert (Bonn and McCarley, 1953:469). *Johnston*: 4 mi. N Milburn (Carpenter, 1958a: 72). *LeFlore*: Wister (CM). *Marshall*: near Shay (Howard McCarley, personal communication). *McCurtain*: 14 mi. SE Broken Bow (Trowbridge, 1937); Tom (UI); 5 mi. S Broken Bow and 6 mi. SE Eagletown (OSU). *Pontotoc*: 2 mi. S Ada (ECSC). *Rogers*: 2 mi. NE Garnett, Tulsa County (UMMZ). *Tulsa*: Red Fork and Garnett (UMMZ).

Eumeces obsoletus (Baird and Girard)

Great Plains Skink

Recognition.—Scales smooth, flat, and overlapping; scales of body tannish, most edged with black; black most concentrated on sides of body; scale rows oblique on sides. Young (body less than two inches long) black with bluish tails and whitish spots on chin and sides of head.

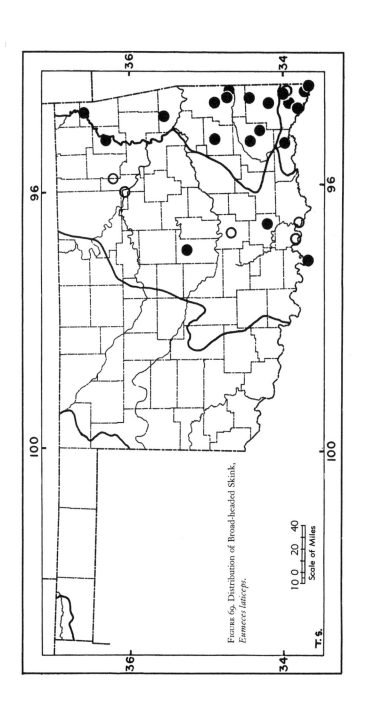

FIGURE 69. Distribution of Broad-headed Skink, *Eumeces laticeps*.

Scale of Miles

10 0 20 40

Distribution.—Western Oklahoma; known as far east as Craig, Mayes, Okmulgee, Pontotoc, and Johnston counties (map, Fig. 70).

Remarks.—These skinks are limited eastward by the Interior Highlands. Individuals are found on wooded or grassy hillsides, often under flat rocks among limestone outcroppings; these skinks also are found in flat, sparsely vegetated, sandy or rocky areas (among clumps of sage, and one in a pile of dead yuccas in Cimarron County) and in backyards and gardens of urban areas. Trowbridge's observations (1937:295) of *obsoletus* in McCurtain County probably refer to *Eumeces laticeps* (see account of that species).

See Carter and Cox (1968), Dundee (1950a:29), Fitch (1955: 62), Force (1930:29), McCoy (1958), Marr (1944:483), Moore and Rigney (1942:79), Ortenburger and Bird (1933:61), Taylor (1936:62, 65, 312, 313, 314).

Specimens examined (OU except as indicated).—*Alfalfa*: Cherokee; 4 mi. E Cherokee. *Beaver*: near Gate. *Beckham*: 2 mi. W and 6.5 mi. S Erick. *Blaine*: Roman Nose State Park; 2.6 mi. N Watonga. *Caddo*: 8 mi. W Hinton (RGW). *Cimarron*: 8 mi. SW Boise City; 2 mi. W Kenton (TTC). *Comanche*: Cache; 4 mi. N Cache; Wichita Mts. Wildlife Refuge. *Craig*: near Vinita. *Custer*: Weatherford. *Ellis*: 5 mi. NNE Shattuck. *Grady*: near Chickasha. *Harmon*: 1 mi. E Red River bridge. *Harper*: near Gate, Beaver County. *Kay*: Ponca City; 8 mi. E Ponca City. *Kiowa*: Cooperton. *Mayes*: 1.5 mi. S Chouteau (KU). *McClain*: 4 mi. N Wayne. *Murray*: Sulphur (KU); 1–2 mi. W Turner Falls. *Nowata*: 14 mi. NW Lenapah (ESCS). *Okmulgee*: no data. *Osage*: 13 mi. W Pawhuska. *Pawnee*: near Quay. *Pontotoc*: 5 mi. S Ada, and 5 mi. S Fittstown (ECSC). *Rogers*: 3 mi. W Catoosa. *Tulsa*: Tulsa; 15 mi. NE Tulsa. *Woods*: Alva (KU, NWSC); 1.6 mi. E Tegarden. *Woodward*: 16 mi. SW Freedom, Woods County; Alabaster Caverns.

Additional records.—*Alfalfa*: islands on Salt Plains (OSU). *Blaine*: gypsum hills W Hitchcock (FWCM). *Carter*: 10 mi. SE

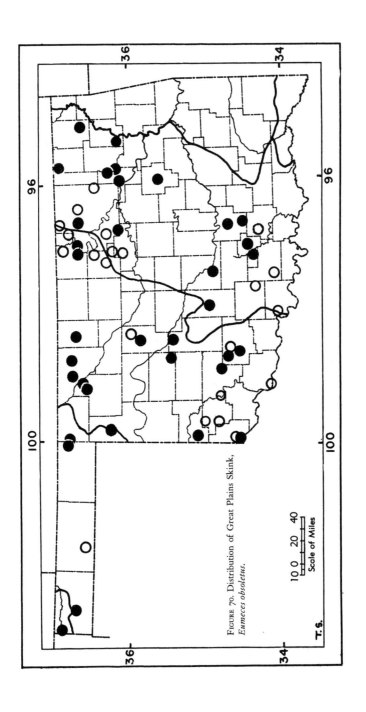

FIGURE 70. Distribution of Great Plains Skink, *Eumeces obsoletus.*

Scale of Miles

T. S.

Healdton (ECSC). *Cimarron*: N Kenton (Blair, 1950c). *Comanche*: Medicine Park (TNHC). *Greer*: 12 mi. N Reed (FWCM); 2 mi. W Reed (McCoy, 1958). *Harmon*: several within 7 mi. radius Hollis (FWCM); 2 mi. SW Reed, Greer County (Carpenter, 1958a:72). *Jefferson*: 5 mi. W Waurika (CCC). *Johnston*: 3 mi. NW Reagan (CCC). *Kay*: 4 mi. W Lyman, Osage County (Burt, 1935:327); 6 mi. NE Newkirk (Burt and Hoyle, 1935:203). *Kiowa*: 2 mi. S Lugert (OSU). *Noble*: Otoe Indian Reservation (OSU); 5 mi. E Perry (McCoy, 1960a:41). *Osage*: 2 mi. SE Avant and 4 mi. W Pawhuska (Burt and Hoyle, 1935:203); 1 mi. S Grainola (ECSC). *Pawnee*: 2 mi. N Pawnee and 2 mi. SE Pawnee (Burt, 1935:327). *Payne*: Stillwater (OSU, UMMZ); 14 mi. W Stillwater (UMMZ). *Rogers*: 1 mi. W Catoosa (UI). *Stephens*: Alma (Taylor, 1936:320). *Texas*: Goodwell (OU). *Tillman*: 2 mi. S Davidson (CCC). *Tulsa*: near Garnett (UMMZ).

Eumeces septentrionalis obtusirostris Bocourt

Southern Prairie Skink

Recognition.—Scales smooth, flat, and overlapping; dark dorsolateral stripe (reduced in some specimens to narrow "lines" of spots) separated from black lateral band by thin, pale, longitudinal line; pale, dark-edged middorsal stripe usually present in specimens from eastern counties, but poorly defined or absent in specimens from western counties; no postnasal; two postmentals; young have blue tails.

Distribution.—Central Oklahoma; known as far east as Cherokee and LeFlore counties and as far west as Woods and Kiowa counties (map, Fig. 71).

Remarks.—Records of most southern prairie skinks are from the Oak-Woodland, where they have been collected under logs in open, sandy places or foraging among dry oak leaves in wooded areas.

The relative size of the frontonasal (large and in broad con-

166

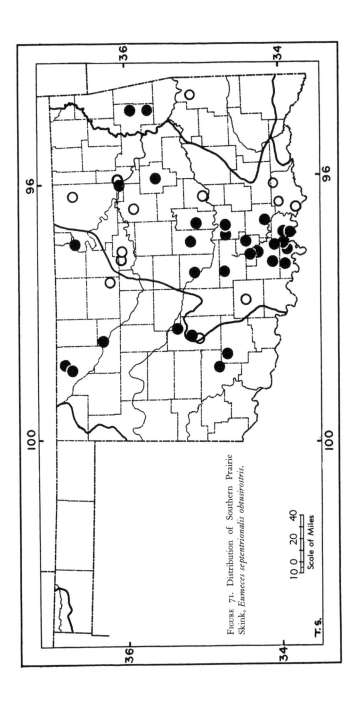

FIGURE 71. Distribution of Southern Prairie Skink, *Eumeces septentrionalis obtusirostris*.

Scale of Miles
10 0 20 40

T. S.

tact with anterior loreal in *obtusirostris*; small and not in contact with anterior loreal in *septentrionalis*) has been utilized as the principal criterion for differentiating *obtusirostris* and the northern subspecies, *Eumeces septentrionalis septentrionalis*. One specimen from Woods County (KU 8954, which has one large postmental), one from Major County, two of four specimens from one locality in Kay County that have small frontonasals resembling *E. s. septentrionalis*, and one from Osage County having a frontonasal split longitudinally—all of these suggest intergradation with the subspecies *septentrionalis* along the northern border of Oklahoma. Other Oklahoma specimens examined have large frontonasals, but in some they do not quite contact the anterior loreals. For convenience all Oklahoma specimens are referred to the subspecies *obtusirostris*.

Ortenburger's report of *Eumeces brevilineatus* and *Eumeces pachyurus* from Oklahoma (1927a:95) are based on specimens of *Eumeces septentrionalis* (Smith and Slater, 1949:443).

See Carpenter (1956:42; 1959c:34), Cope (1900:658), Force (1930:29).

Specimens examined (OU except as indicated).—*Caddo*: no data. *Canadian*: Devils Canyon. *Carter*: 5 mi. SE Ardmore; 10 mi. W Ardmore; just S Murray County line on U.S. Highway 77. *Cherokee*: 2 mi. W Cookson (KU); 8 mi. NE Tahlequah. *Cleveland*: near Norman; 2 mi. S Norman. *Comanche*: Wichita Mts. Wildlife Refuge. *Garvin*: Maysville. *Johnston*: near Tishomingo. *Kay*: 8 mi. E Ponca City. *Kiowa*: Cooperton. *Love*: 6 mi. W Lebanon, Marshall County (TTC); 7.5 mi. N Marietta; 4 mi. E Oswalt; 4 mi. E and 3 mi. S Oswalt. *Major*: "on dunes" (presumably along Cimarron River). *Marshall*: UOBS; 4 and 8 mi. N UOBS. *Murray*: 4 mi. W Turner Falls; Platt National Park. *Okmulgee*: no data. *Pontotoc*: 0.5–2 mi. SE Ada and 10 mi. W Ada (ECSC). *Pottawatomie*: Tecumseh. *Seminole*: Bowlegs. *Tulsa*: 6 mi. W Tulsa. *Woods*: 12 mi. W Alva (KU); 10 mi. NW Alva (NWSC).

Additional records.—Bryan: 7 mi. N Durant and 10 mi. N Bennington (Laughlin, 1964:61); 4 mi. E Colbert (Howard McCarley, personal communication). *Caddo*: Fort Cobb (Smith and Slater, 1949:443); Devils and Kiwanis canyons (OSU). *Carter*: 5 mi. W Ardmore and 6 mi. S Ardmore (Smith and Slater, 1949:443). *Creek*: Heyburn Lake Recreational Area (INHS). *Garfield*: near Hayward (ECSC). *Hughes*: 7 mi. N Calvin (ECSC). *LeFlore*: Panama (KU). *Murray*: Camp Classen (OSU). *Osage*: Osage Hills State Park (Smith and Slater, 1949:444). *Payne*: Stillwater (OSU); 2 mi. S Stillwater (Moore and Rigney, 1942:79); Lake Carl Blackwell (FWCM). *Stephens*: Lake Duncan (Smith and Slater, 1949:444). *Tulsa*: Tulsa (FWCM, MCZ).

Holbrookia maculata Girard

Earless Lizards

Recognition.—Scales on back small, flat, and granular; scales on upper lip strongly overlapping, in shinglelike fashion; ear opening lacking; two blackish bars or spots on each side of body; complete tail slightly shorter than length of body.

Distribution.—Western Oklahoma; known as far east as Alfalfa, Logan, Cleveland, and Jefferson counties; an isolated record from Mayes County; two subspecies (map, Fig. 72).

Remarks.—Axtell (1956) recognized two subspecies of *Holbrookia maculata* in Oklahoma:

H. m. maculata Girard, Northern Earless Lizard.—Back having separate brown blotches (not joined across back to neighboring lateral blotches by thin dark lines as in *perspicua*); body marked with a sprinkling of whitish dots (especially males) and ill-defined, pale dorsolateral stripes.

H. m. perspicua Axtell, Oklahoma Earless Lizard.—Back having distinct, dark brown blotches, often joined across back and to dark blotches on sides by thin dark lines; whitish dots and dorsolateral stripes lacking.

169

The subspecies intergrade in western Oklahoma, *maculata* being found mostly in the High Plains, and *perspicua* in the Grassland. Earless lizards are generally characteristic of flat, sparsely vegetated places, such as plowed, fallow, overgrazed, or cultivated fields, and "prairie dog towns," but individuals have been captured in sandy areas along rivers and streams, and once, by the side of a road in patches of weeds on damp, sandy soil (Roger Mills County). Individuals startled by me have taken refuge in small mammal burrows, or in the bases of yuccas.

Data obtained from 112 specimens of *H. m. maculata* (52 males, 60 females) are: femoral pores averaging 11.7, extremes 7–15; transverse rows of ventral scales from gular fold to anus, 68.3, 58–77; internasals, 3.5, 2–5; hind leg/snout–vent length, 0.76, 0.64–0.87 in 49 males, and 0.69, 0.57–0.78 in 58 females. Males tend to have slightly longer legs and tails than females; males utilized in calculating the ratios ranged from 38 to 56 mm in snout–vent length, whereas females ranged from 41 to 56 mm.

An individual having characteristics of *perspicua* (OU 29025), obtained by Dr. Arthur N. Bragg on July 28, 1948, is recorded from northeastern Oklahoma in Mayes County, and is isolated from the nearest records to the west. Perhaps there has been inadequate collecting in the intervening area, or the clearing of land in parts of eastern Oklahoma has recently favored the eastward spread of *Holbrookia*, or the data on collection may be untrustworthy. Possible corroboration of the record from Mayes County is provided by Hallowell (1854:146), who recorded three specimens from "Creek boundary; very abundant in that region," and later (1857:239) mentioned "many specimens we have from the Creek and Cherokee countries. . . . " Malnate (personal communication) wrote that Hallowell's specimens probably referred to seven specimens (ANSP 8242–48), collected by Dr. Woodhouse in the "Cherokee country." Although the ANSP specimens may have come from

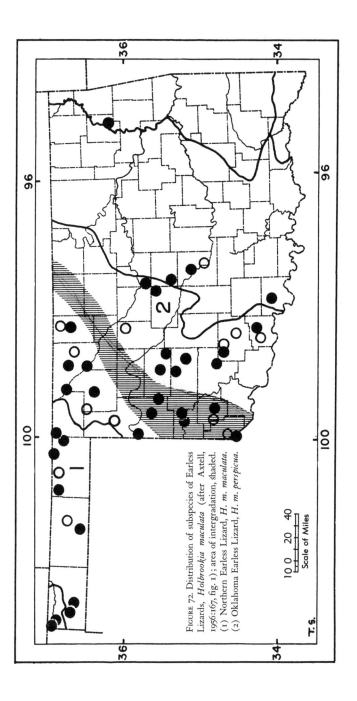

FIGURE 72. Distribution of subspecies of Earless
Lizards, *Holbrookia maculata* (after Axtell,
1956:167, fig. 1); area of intergradation, shaded.
(1) Northern Earless Lizard, *H. m. maculata*.
(2) Oklahoma Earless Lizard, *H. m. perspicua*.

T. S.

eastern Oklahoma, the Creek and Cherokee countries extended into western Oklahoma (Fig. 1) at that time, and it is likely that the seven ANSP specimens came from somewhere in the western half of the state along the east-west trending Creek-Cherokee boundary.

See McCoy (1958), Marr (1944:481), Ortenburger and Bird (1933:60), Ortenburger and Freeman (1930:178–179), Smith and Acker (1940:65), Webb and Ortenburger (1955:88).

Specimens examined (OU except as indicated).—*Alfalfa*: Great Salt Plains, 2–4 and 9 mi. E Cherokee; east bank Salt Fork Arkansas River. *Beaver*: 2 mi. N Turpin (KU); Cimarron River, 1 mi. S Kansas state line (KU); vicinity Gate. *Beckham*: 3 mi. N Sayre; 8 mi. E and 2.2 mi. S Sayre. *Canadian*: 2 mi. S Piedmont. *Cimarron*: 7 mi. S Boise City; 8 mi. W Boise City; 5.5 mi. E Kenton; 3 and 5 mi. N Kenton. *Cleveland*: 2.5 mi. NE Norman; 1 and 6 mi. N Norman. *Comanche*: Wichita Mts. Wildlife Refuge. *Cotton*: near Walters. *Custer*: W Arapaho (SWSC); Weatherford. *Greer*: 4 mi. N Mangum. *Harmon*: 6–7 mi. S Hollis. *Harper*: near Cimarron River, S Englewood, Kansas (KU); vicinity Gate. *Jefferson*: 17.5 mi. W Ringling. *Kiowa*: Cooperton. *Logan*: SW part of county. *Mayes*: State Highway 82, 2.7 mi. N Locust Grove. *Oklahoma*: SW Oklahoma City. *Roger Mills*: 6 mi. NE Durham; Strong City; Hammon. *Texas*: 8 mi. SE Guymon. *Washita*: Cloud Chief; Bessie. *Woods*: Cimarron River, 2.5 mi. W and 1 mi. S Waynoka; 2.5 mi. W Edith; 12 mi. W Alva (KU). *Woodward*: 5 mi. E and 1 mi. N Woodward.

Additional records.—*Alfalfa*: 3 mi. E Byron (OSU). *Beaver*: Maple Ranch, near Forgan (OSU). *Beckham*: 7 mi. W Sayre (Burt, 1935:322). *Blaine*: Salt Creek Canyon (FWCM). *Cimarron*: 8 mi. N junction U.S. Highway 64 and New Mexico state line (OSU). *Cleveland*: Lexington (UI). *Comanche*: Meers (Axtell, 1956:171); near Lawton (Smith and Leonard, 1934:192); Lawton (FMNH). *Cotton*: 33 mi. S Lawton, Comanche County (FMNH). *Ellis*: no data (UMMZ). *Greer*: 2 mi. W Reed (McCoy, 1958); 3 mi. SW Reed (OSU); 2 mi. W and 1 mi. S Reed (FWCM). *Harmon*: 5 mi. W Reed, Greer County (OSU); 5 mi. N Hollis, 4–5 mi. S Hollis, and 1 mi. N and 1 mi. W Hollis (FWCM). *Texas*: 9 mi. SE Hooker (Ortenburger, 1927c:47; Ortenburger and Freeman, 1930:178). *Woodward*: Fort Supply (Cope, 1894:386). *Woods*: 7 mi. S Alva (McCracken, 1966:7).

Lygosoma laterale (Say)

Ground Skink

Recognition.—Scales smooth, flat, and overlapping; size small, length of body not more than two inches; back brownish or bronze, often with small black specks; sides of body blackish; belly whitish or pale yellow; part of lower eyelid transparent, forming a "window" through which lizard can see when eye shut; no supranasals, frontonasal in contact with rostral.

Distribution.—Eastern Oklahoma; known as far west as Woods, Beckham, and Harmon counties (map, Fig. 73).

Remarks.—Although the small ground skink is found in the Grassland, individuals are most abundant in the Interior Highlands and Oak-Woodland. Lizards are found most often under leaf cover, logs, rocks, or trash in wooded or grass herb areas, usually where the vegetation is dense close to the ground. Five eggs (two partly buried) were found on the surface of slightly moist, hard-packed sand under a log (Marshall County) on July 23, when all eggs measured approximately 7 x 12 mm and weighed 0.5 gram; all hatched on July 31. Captives have been eaten by individuals of *Crotaphytus* and *Sceloporus undulatus hyacinthinus*. On two occasions, one lizard was discovered in a small, vertical earthen burrow (diameter slightly larger than girth of lizard) under a flat board. One of the westernmost specimens (OU 27796) was obtained near a cattle tank in Beckham County. Another of the westernmost localities is in Woods County, where six specimens were collected "from a seep area

173

covered with *Populus* and *Rhus* in the sand dunes of Little Sahara State Park" (McCracken, 1966:11).

See Bonn and McCarley (1953:469), Carpenter (1956:42; 1958b:114; 1959c:34), Cope (1900:623; USNM 3152, presumably from Oklahoma), Fitch and Greene (1965), Force (1930:28), Harney (1955:85), Ortenburger and Freeman (1930:181); Trowbridge (1937:294).

Specimens examined (OU except as indicated).—*Adair*: Tyner Creek; 4 mi. N Stilwell; 9.4 mi. SSW Stilwell (KU). *Atoka*: 13 mi. SE Atoka. *Beckham*: 7 mi. N and 0.1 mi. E Sayre. *Bryan*: Durant. *Canadian*: Devils Canyon. *Carter*: Ardmore; 5 mi. SE Ardmore. *Choctaw*: no data. *Cleveland*: 3–4 mi. S Norman; 6 mi. NE Norman. *Comanche*: Wichita Mts. Wildlife Refuge. *Creek*: Sapulpa. *Delaware*: 6 mi. NE Grove; 3 mi. S Cleora. *Dewey*: 5 mi. W Canton, and 5 mi. SW Canton, Blaine County (KU). *Garvin*: Maysville. *Harmon*: 1.5 mi. SW Reed, Greer County. *Latimer*: 3 mi. N Red Oak; 8 mi. NW Wilburton; 2 mi. N Wilburton; 6 mi. SW Wilburton; Robbers Cave State Park (NWSC). *LeFlore*: 15 mi. S Heavener; 6.5 mi. W Heavener; 5 mi. E Big Cedar; Wister; 1.5 mi. E Zoe. *Logan*: no data. *Love*: 20 mi. S Marietta; 3.5 mi. SE Thackerville. *Marshall*: UOBS; 5.5 mi. W. and 2 mi. S Kingston; 4 mi. NE Kingston; 0.2 mi. S. Johnston County line on U.S. Highway 70. *Mayes*: no data. *McCurtain*: 1 mi. W Tom; near Bokhoma; Beavers Bend State Park; 2 mi. SW Smithville; Broken Bow; 13 mi. SE Broken Bow; 14 mi. E Broken Bow. *Murray*: Price's Falls. *Okmulgee*: no data. *Osage*: near Okesa. *Ottawa*: 2.5 mi. S Peoria (KU). *Payne*: 1 mi. N and 1 mi. E Ripley. *Pottawatomie*: Shawnee; 3 mi. W Shawnee. *Pushmataha*: 4 mi. E Tuskahoma; 1.5 mi. W Kosoma; 0.5 mi. S Clayton (TTC). *Seminole*: Seminole; Bowlegs. *Stephens*: 10 mi. E Duncan; 2 mi. S and 1 mi. W Duncan. *Tulsa*: 1 mi. N Red Fork; Oakhurst; 9 mi. SE Tulsa. *Wagoner*: 2 mi. S Catoosa, Rogers County.

Additional records.—*Adair*: 4 mi. W Stilwell, and 5 mi. SE Stilwell (UI); 5 mi. S Kansas, Delaware County (UMMZ). *Atoka*: Limestone Gap (Stone, 1903:541). *Blaine*: Roman Nose State Park

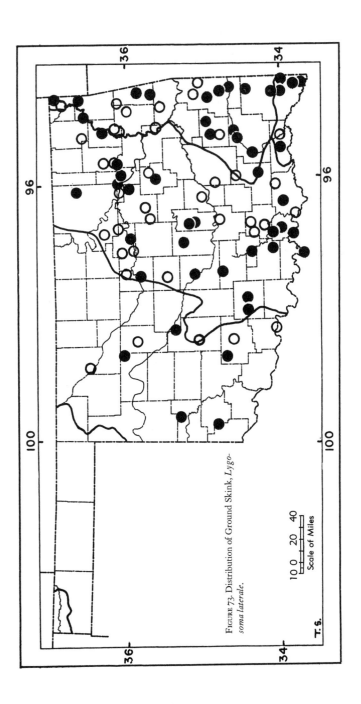

FIGURE 73. Distribution of Ground Skink, *Lygosoma laterale.*

(CCC). *Bryan*: Colbert (TNHC); 5 mi. SW Colbert, and 9 mi. E Caddo (SESC). *Caddo*: Devils Canyon (OSU); Fort Cobb (USNM). *Carter*: 2 mi. W Ardmore (Carpenter, 1958a:72). *Cherokee*: Hanging Rock (UI); Fred Darby Boy Scout Camp, near mouth Barren Fork Creek (OSU). *Choctaw*: [7 mi. W Fort Towson] (Ortenburger, 1927a:95, FMNH). *Comanche*: Fort Sill (AMNH). *Cotton*: "near the mouth of Cache creek" (Baird and Girard, 1854:212). *Craig*: 4 mi. SW Whiteoak (Burt and Hoyle, 1935:202). *Creek*: 2 mi. W Bristow, 1 mi. NW Milfay, 2 mi. E Sapulpa, and 4 mi. SW Sapulpa (Burt, 1935:326). *Hughes*: no data (Carter, 1966:34). *Johnston*: 2 mi. W Connerville, and 4 mi. S Mill Creek (ECSC); 5 mi. NW Tishomingo (SESC). *Latimer*: 1 mi. S Red Oak (SESC); 25.3 mi. N Clayton, Pushmataha County (TTC). *LeFlore*: just N Page (Burt, 1935:326); near Page (UMMZ); Slate Ford E Shadypoint (OSU); Panama (KU); Gilmore (SESC); Sugarloaf Mt. (Stone, 1903:541). *Logan*: 1 mi. N Mulhall (Burt, 1935:326). *Mayes*: 5 mi. SW Locust Grove (TNHC); Cedar Crest Lake (OSU); 1.4 mi. S and 1.4 mi. E Naples (UMMZ, locality not found; a Naples in Grady County). *McCurtain*: 2 mi. N Broken Bow (FMNH); 3 and 4.5 mi. E Eagletown (UI). *Murray*: Dougherty (FMNH); Honcy Creek, Camp Classen (OSU); Turner Falls (FWCM). *Muskogee*: Greenleaf Lake State Park (ECSC). *Oklahoma*: 7 mi. N Oklahoma City (Burt, 1935:326). *Okmulgee*: Bald Hill (Burt and Hoyle, 1935:202); 3 mi. W Okmulgee (TU). *Ottawa*: Wyandotte (Stone, 1903:541). *Pawnee*: 2 mi. SW Pawnee (Burt, 1935:326); presumably near Quay (Ortenburger, 1930a:94). *Payne*: several within 5 mi. radius Stillwater (OSU); 15 mi. SE Stillwater (Burt, 1931a:14); near Perkins (OSU); 4 mi. W Quay (Burt, 1935:326). *Pittsburg*: 6 mi. SE Stuart, Hughes County (Carter, 1966:34). *Pontotoc*: 7 mi. NE Ada (Carter, 1966:34). *Rogers*: 6 mi. W Claremore (Burt and Hoyle, 1935:202); 6 mi. E Catoosa (Dundee and Burger, 1948:1); 19 mi. E Tulsa, Tulsa County (OSU). *Sequoyah*: 3.1 mi. S Marble City (UA); Dwight Mission (Carter, 1966:34). *Tulsa*: 2 mi. S Sand Springs (OU); Red Fork (UMMZ). *Woods*: Little Sahara State Park, 3 mi. S Waynoka (McCracken, 1966:11; Carter 1966: 34).

Ophisaurus attenuatus attenuatus Baird

Western Slender Glass Lizard

Recognition.—Lizards resembling snakes in lacking legs, but having ear openings and movable eyelid; deep groove or tuck of skin along each side of body; distinct dark middorsal stripe, and longitudinal dark stripes below lateral tuck of skin; tail long, slightly more than twice length of body (unregenerated), and easily broken, often into more than one piece.

Distribution.—Eastern Oklahoma; known as far west as Woods, Roger Mills, and Kiowa counties (map, Fig. 74).

Remarks.—Glass lizards are secretive, burrowing in loose soil in grassy, brushy areas, but they are sometimes found under logs or assorted bits of trash. One recently killed individual was found on a highway at 10:30 p.m. (Marshall County), suggesting nocturnal habits. Most records suggest a preference for the grassy parts of the Oak-Woodland and an avoidance of the forested parts of the Ozark and Ouachita mountains. Blair (1961) suggested that relatively tall grass influences the distribution of glass lizards. The known previous distribution of tall grass prairie in western Oklahoma, a fossil vertebra (Pleistocene) from Harper County (Etheridge, 1960), and the report of USNM 5129 from between the Arkansas and Cimarron rivers in New Mexico (Van Denburgh, 1924:211) indicate a receding range. See account of *Ophisaurus ventralis* (page 58).

See Blair (1950a), Bonn and McCarley (1953:469), Carpenter (1956:42; 1959c:34), Carter and Cox (1968), Force (1925a:26; 1925b:83; 1930:28), Hallowell (1854:145), Webb and Ortenburger (1955:89).

Specimens examined (OU except as indicated).—*Alfalfa*: no data. *Bryan*: near Durant. *Caddo*: Caddo Canyon. *Carter*: 5 mi. NW Ardmore. *Cleveland*: 1–3 mi. S Norman. *Coal*: near Coalgate.

Comanche: Wichita Mts. Wildlife Refuge. *Cotton*: Walters. *Grady*: 3.8 mi. W Blanchard, McClain County. *Johnston*: 3–4 mi. N Milburn. *Marshall*: 7 mi. W Kingston. *McClain*: 4 mi. N Wayne. *McCurtain*: near Idabel. *Muskogee*: no data. *Nowata*: Wann. *Okmulgee*: no data. *Pawnee*: near Quay. *Payne*: Lake Carl Blackwell. *Pottawatomie*: Shawnee. *Seminole*: Seminole. *Tulsa*: no data. *Woods*: 2.5 mi. W and 0.5 mi. S Waynoka; 12 mi. W Alva (KU).

Additional records.—*Bryan*: vicinity Burns Run Resort [near Cartwright] (Bonn and McCarley, 1953:469). *Caddo*: Fort Cobb (Yarrow, 1882:46); Kiwanis Canyon (Carpenter, 1958a:72). *Canadian*: Methodist [Devils] Canyon (Carter, 1966:34). *Comanche*: Fort Sill, Medicine Bluff Creek (UMMZ). *Garvin*: 6.5 mi. W and 0.5 mi. N Stratford (ECSC). *Hughes*: 5 mi. E Gerty (ECSC). *Johnston*: Mannsville (OSU); Tishomingo Refuge (ECSC). *Kingfisher*: Hennessey (Cope, 1894:387). *Kiowa*: Quartz Mountain State Park, near Lugert (CCC). *Major*: 6 mi. NE Sherman (Burt, 1935:324). *Muskogee*: Muskogee (UI). *Okmulgee*: Schulter (ECSC). *Payne*: several within 6 mi. radius Stillwater (OSU). *Pontotoc*: 7 mi. SW Ada (Carter, 1966:34). *Roger Mills*: Berlin (OSU). *Rogers*: 1 mi. N Claremore (FWCM); 10 mi. E Tulsa, Tulsa County (OSU). *Sequoyah*: 4 mi. N Gore (KU). *Tulsa*: Tulsa, and Red Fork (UMMZ); near Cincinnati (USNM, locality unknown).

Phrynosoma cornutum (Harlan)

Texas Horned Lizard

Recognition.—"Horned toads" having a flattened body with two rows of soft, movable, spinelike scales on sides, and pale middorsal stripe on back; large, immovable spines projecting from back of head.

Distribution—Western Oklahoma; known as far east as Ottawa, LeFlore, and Choctaw counties (map, Fig. 75).

Remarks.—"Horned toads" are less abundant in eastern

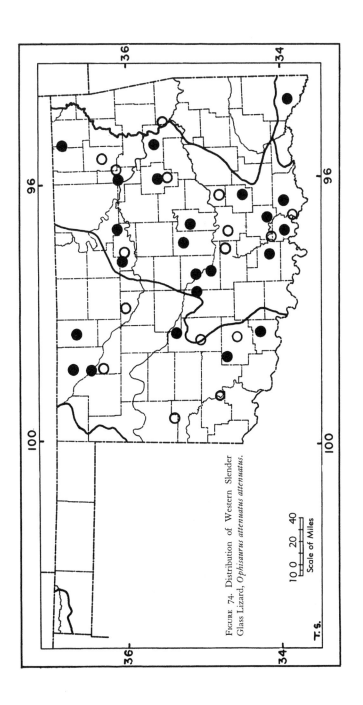

FIGURE 74. Distribution of Western Slender Glass Lizard, *Ophisaurus attenuatus attenuatus.*

T. S.

10 0   20   40

Scale of Miles

Oklahoma than in the western part of the state. Records suggest that the Texas horned lizard may be found statewide, but that it is rare in the wooded and mountainous Interior Highlands. These lizards are commonly found in rather open, sandy, or loose-soiled areas where they can burrow; one lizard, however, was found under a rock on a hard-packed substratum (Harmon County). Individuals are often observed along dirt roads, and in urban areas in gardens, vacant lots, and cultivated fields.

Pleistocene jaws of *Phrynosoma* sp. have been reported from northwestern Arkansas (Gilmore in Dowling, 1958:3, 7), and suggest that the range of the species is receding to the west. But where human activity has increased the amount of sparsely vegetated, open area in previously wooded parts of eastern Oklahoma, the eastward dispersal of the Texas horned lizard may be favored.

See Bonn and McCarley (1953:469), Burt and Hoyle (1935: 201), Carpenter (1956:42), Carter and Cox (1968), Force (1930:28), Hallowell (1854:145), McCoy (1958), Ortenburger and Freeman (1930:179–180), Marr (1944:482), Vanderpol (1955).

Specimens examined (OU except as indicated).—*Alfalfa*: several within 10 mi. radius Cherokee. *Beaver*: near Gate. *Beckham*: 2 mi. W and 6.5 mi. S Erick; 6 mi. SE Erick; 5 mi. S Carter. *Blaine*: 5 mi. S Canton (KU). *Bryan*: N Burris Run Resort on private beach, WNW Cartwright. *Caddo*: 10 mi. N Carnegie. *Choctaw*: Hugo (KU). *Cimarron*: 3 mi. N Kenton; 7 mi. S Boise City; 15 mi. W and 4 mi. N Boise City. *Cleveland*: several within 4 mi. radius Norman; 7–8 mi. E Norman. *Comanche*: Cache; 5 mi. N Cache; Wichita Mts. Wildlife Refuge. *Creek*: Drumright. *Custer*: Weatherford. *Dewey*: 5 mi. E Seiling; 5.5 mi. SW Canton, and 5 mi. W Canton, Blaine County (KU). *Ellis*: 5 mi. NNE Shattuck. *Garvin*: Maysville. *Greer*: 2 mi. N Willow; 1 mi. S and 1 mi. W Reed. *Harmon*: 7 mi. SW Hollis; 3 mi. W Vinson; 3 mi. W Reed, Greer County. *Harper*: near Gate, Beaver County. *Jackson*: 3 mi. S El Dorado; 2 mi. S

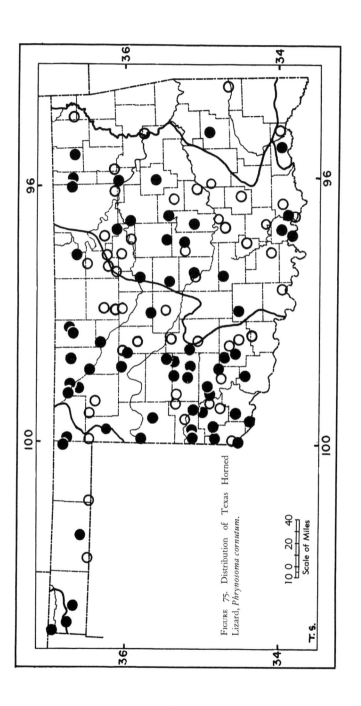

FIGURE 75. Distribution of Texas Horned Lizard, *Phrynosoma cornutum*.

Duke. *Kay*: Ponca City. *Kingfisher*: 2 mi. N Okarche. *Kiowa*: Cooperton; 2 mi. W Hobart; 7 mi. W Lone Wolf. *Latimer*: Wilburton. *Lincoln*: 3.5 mi. E Meeker. *Logan*: Guthrie. *Major*: Cleo Springs; 3 mi. S Cleo Springs. *Marshall*: Willis; 5 mi. S Madill. *Nowata*: Coody's Bluff. *Okfuskee*: 11 mi. E Prague, Lincoln County. *Oklahoma*: Oklahoma City; 4 mi. N Oklahoma City. *Okmulgee*: Okmulgee. *Osage*: 2 mi. W Bartlesville, Washington County. *Pawnee*: near Quay. *Pottawatomie*: Shawnee. *Roger Mills*: Strong City; 5 mi. NE Durham. *Seminole*: Bowlegs. *Stephens*: 40 mi. E Cache, Comanche County. *Texas*: 8 mi. SE Guymon. *Tillman*: 1 mi. W Manitou. *Tulsa*: Tulsa. *Washington*: 2 mi. E Bartlesville. *Washita*: 3 mi. S Cordell; 15 mi. N Cordell; Cloudchief (SWSC); 10 mi. SW Weatherford, Custer County (SWSC). *Woods*: 10 mi. E Edith; 2.5 mi. W Edith; 2.5 mi. W and 1 mi. S Waynoka; Alva (KU, NWSC). *Woodward*: 6 mi. S and 4 mi. W Freedom, Woods County.

Additional records.—*Beaver*: SW corner township (UA). *Beckham*: Elk City, Sayre, and 4 mi. SW Sayre (Burt and Hoyle, 1935:201). *Blaine*: Canton Reservoir (INHS); Roman Nose State Park (CCC). *Bryan*: Durant, and Colbert (TNHC); 5 mi. SW Colbert (SESC). *Caddo*: Fort Cobb (Reeve, 1952:902); Rock Mary [3 mi. W Hinton] (Cope, 1900:435). *Canadian*: "Elkino, Okla. Terr." (presumably El Reno, FMNH). *Carter*: Ardmore (Reeve, 1952:902). *Choctaw*: Fort Towson (Yarrow, 1882:67). *Coal*: 2 mi. N Coalgate (ECSC). *Comanche*: Medicine Park (TNHC); near Lawton (Smith and Leonard, 1934:193). *Cotton*: 1 mi. SE Junction City (Burt, 1935:324; located 2 mi. S Geronimo, Comanche County, but no longer in existence, Shirk, 1965:113). *Custer*: below Foss Reservoir Dam (ECSC). *Ellis*: extreme NW corner of county (Carpenter, 1958a:72). *Garfield*: 5 mi. S Enid (Burt and Hoyle, 1935:201); 1 mi. N Bison (Reeve, 1952:902). *Greer*: 3 mi. W and 1 mi. S Reed (UI); 2 mi. W Reed (McCoy, 1958); 4 mi. E Reed and 5 mi. SE Mangum (OSU); Granite (KU). *Harmon*: 1 mi. W and 2 mi. N Hollis, and 6 mi. S Hollis (FWCM). *Hughes*: 0.5 mi. E Lamar (ECSC). *Jefferson*: near Grady (Carpenter, 1955a:40). *Johnston*: 0.5 mi. S Tishomingo (Carter, 1966:33). *Kay*: 1 mi. S Ponca City (Burt, 1935:324). *Kingfisher*: Hennessey (Cope,

1894:387). *Kiowa*: near Roosevelt (Vanderpol, 1955). *LeFlore*: near Rich Mt., Arkansas (FMNH). *Major*: 8 mi. NW Togo (Burt, 1935:324). *McClain*: near Canadian River bridge (OU). *Murray*: Platt National Park (Carpenter, 1955a:40). *Muskogee*: Fort Gibson (Cope, 1900:435). *Noble*: 1 mi. S Perry, and 4 mi. N Perry (Burt and Burt, 1929b:9); 2 mi. SE Sumner, 2 mi. N Orlando, Logan County, and 2 mi. S Three Sands, Kay County (Burt, 1935:324). *Okfuskee*: 3 mi. E Okemah (Burt, 1935:324). *Oklahoma*: Crutcho [eastern part of Oklahoma City] (Burt, 1935:324). *Osage*: near Sand Springs, Tulsa County (UMMZ); Reservoir Hill (USNM). *Ottawa*: Afton (USNM). *Pawnee*: Pawnee (Burt and Hoyle, 1935:201). *Payne*: Stillwater and Ripley Bluffs (OSU); 3 mi. SE Ripley, and 5 mi. S Stillwater (Burt, 1935:324). *Pittsburg*: 15 mi. W McAlester (Carter, 1966:33). *Pontotoc*: Ada (UMMZ); 7 mi. NE Ada (Carter, 1966:33). *Pottawatomie*: Shawnee Lake (OSU). *Rogers*: 2 mi. NE Garnett, Tulsa County (UMMZ). *Texas*: near Texhoma (AMNH). *Tulsa*: Garnett (UMMZ). *Washington*: Bartlesville (CM); near Bartlesville (Carter, 1966:33); Foster's Ranch near Bartlesville (UMMZ). *Washita*: 1.7 mi. E Canute (UI). *Woods*: Whitehorse Springs (FMNH). *Woodward*: Woodward (USNM); Fort Supply (Cope, 1894:387).

Phrynosoma modestum Girard

Round-tailed Horned Lizard

Recognition.—"Horned toads" having flattened body; sides of body lacking soft, movable, spinelike scales; large, immovable spines projecting from back of head; back gray without distinct markings except for pair of large dark smudges on neck.

Distribution.—Known only from the panhandle in northwestern Cimarron County.

Remarks.—The only specimen known from Oklahoma (OU 30825) was found on a bluff above Lake Carl Etling, Black Mesa State Park, about 13 miles northeast of Boise City, Cimarron County, by Gene Grubitz III on July 25, 1962.

That *modestum* should be found in western Oklahoma is not totally unexpected, since the species has been reported in Texas from Donley and Hemphill counties (Cope, 1900:439) and from Motley County (Reeve, 1952:870); and in northern New Mexico from San Miguel County (Van Denburgh, 1924:210). Maslin (1959:73) discussed a doubtful record from Custer County, Colorado.

Scelporus undulatus Sonnini and Latreille

Prairie, Plateau, and Fence Lizards

Recognition.—Spiny, rough lizards having scales on back keeled and pointed; back with dark spots and pale dorsolateral stripes, or with dark, wavy crossbands; throat and sides of belly blue in some specimens.

Distribution.—Throughout the state; four subspecies (map, Fig. 76).

Remarks.—McCoy (1960b, 1961a) studied the relationships of the subspecies of *Sceloporus undulatus* in Oklahoma. The four subspecies can be distinguished as follows:

S. u. consobrinus Baird and Girard, Southern Prairie Lizard.— Back having obscure dorsolateral whitish stripes with brownish spots medially, and lacking narrow, undulate, dark brown crossbars; males having brilliant blue, black-bordered belly and throat patches that nearly touch or are confluent medially.

S. u. erythrocheilus Maslin, Eastern Plateau Lizard.—Narrow, brown, wavy crossbands on back, obscure middorsally in some specimens; whitish dorsolateral stripes (in young) lacking or indistinct in adults; lips and chin yellow or red orange in some specimens; dorsal scales usually 44 or more, averaging 48, ranging from 41 to 55.

S. u. garmani Boulenger, Northern Prairie Lizard.—Distinct

184

dorsolateral whitish stripes bordered medially by brownish spots; back lacking dark brown, wavy crossbands; blue belly patches of males widely separated, not edged medially with black; throat lacking bluish patches or marked with few black or blue spots.

S. u. hyacinthinus (Green), Northern Fence Lizard.—Back with narrow, undulate, dark brown crossbands and lacking distinct dorsolateral stripes; dorsal scales usually less than 44, averaging 42, ranging from 35 to 49.

Sceloporus u. erythrocheilus is confined to the Mesa de Maya, and there is no evidence of intergradation with *garmani* to the east in the panhandle. Individuals of *erythrocheilus* are found on boulders and outcroppings on the slopes of buttes and mesas, or on fallen trees and debris in sandy areas near creeks, or in trees (mostly hackberry) to a height of 10 to 12 feet. Some adult males have red orange lips in the breeding season. One of four collected on May 31 had bright orange (mostly on the lower lip and chin), two had pale yellow, and one had no contrast in color; only one of three males collected on June 17 had red. The crossbanded dorsal pattern seems to be more obscured in adult males than females.

Sceloporus u. hyacinthinus is confined mostly to the Interior Highlands, intergrading with *garmani* in the Oak-Woodland. Individuals of *hyacinthinus* are mostly arboreal, but are occasionally found on fallen trees, logs, and among trash piles. Two sluggish lizards were found under rocks on a cold, windy day. A gravid female, obtained on May 20, contained eight oviducal eggs (Coal County). A large captive female ate a *Lygosoma*.

Sceloporus u. garmani is found in western Oklahoma in the Grassland and High Plains, and to the east in parts of the Oak-Woodland; in southwestern Oklahoma it intergrades with *consobrinus*. Individuals of *garmani* are mostly terrestrial in northern Oklahoma, where they are seen on grassy, rocky knolls, or in open, sandy, sparsely vegetated places, or among piles of debris. In south central Oklahoma (Murray and Stephens counties) lizards resembling *garmani* are arboreal in habit, like *consobrinus* and *hyacinthinus*, and are probably intergrades. A gravid female contained nine oviducal eggs on June 8 (Stephens County).

Sceloporus u. consobrinus is restricted to southwestern Oklahoma (see page 49 concerning southwestern filter barrier). Oklahoma specimens of *consobrinus* are distinguished from *garmani* on the basis of the less distinct dorsolateral stripes and the ventral coloration in males (counts of femoral pores about the same in the two subspecies). In the Wichita Mountains individuals of *consobrinus* have been observed on trunks of oak trees, on large boulders partly shrouded by vegetation, or in brush piles. In Beckham County along Timber Creek, almost topotypic individuals (KU 84673–76), which more closely resemble *garmani* than *consobrinus*, were found on fallen trees and logs and cement supports of a bridge.

See Bonn and McCarley (1953:469), Burt (1928a:2; 1935:323), Carpenter (1956:41; 1958b:114, 115; 1959b; 1959c:34; 1960c; 1961; 1962), Carpenter et al. (1961:193), Carter and Cox (1968), Force (1925a:26; 1925b:83; 1930:27, 32), Harney (1955:85), Maslin (1956:291), McCoy (1958), Ortenburger and Bird (1933:60, 61), Ortenburger and Freeman (1930:179), Trowbridge (1937:294), Webb and Ortenburger (1955:88).

Specimens examined (OU except as indicated).—*Adair*: 4 mi. N Stilwell; 5 mi. S Bunch; 1 mi. E and 5 mi. S Kansas, Delaware County (KU). *Alfalfa*: 3 to 9 mi. E Cherokee; 7 mi. NE Cherokee. *Atoka*: 13 mi. SE Atoka. *Beaver*: near Gate; 1 mi. S Kansas state line on Cimarron River (KU). *Beckham*: 3.8 mi. E Sayre (KU). *Bryan*: Durant. *Caddo*: Kiwanis Canyon; 8 mi. W Hinton (TTC). *Canadian*: near Wheatland, Oklahoma County. *Carter*: Ardmore; 5 mi. S and 2 mi. W Ardmore. *Cherokee*: 4 mi. NE Welling; 5 mi. S Welling; McSpadden Falls; near Barber (KU); 2 mi. N Fort

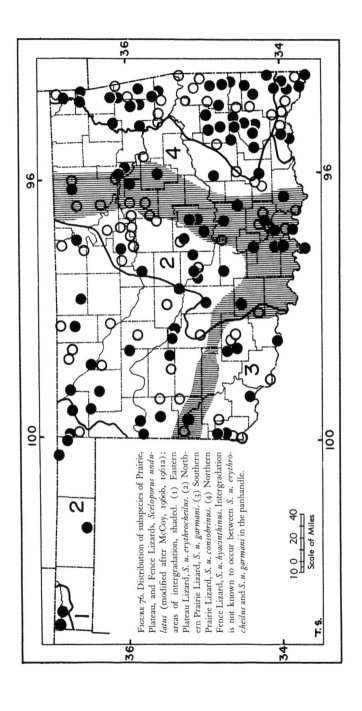

FIGURE 76. Distribution of subspecies of Prairie, Plateau, and Fence Lizards, *Sceloporus undulatus* (modified after McCoy, 1960b, 1961a); areas of intergradation, shaded. (1) Eastern Plateau Lizard, *S. u. erythrocheilus*. (2) Northern Prairie Lizard, *S. u. garmani*. (3) Southern Prairie Lizard, *S. u. consobrinus*. (4) Northern Fence Lizard, *S. u. hyacinthinus*. Intergradation is not known to occur between *S. u. erythrocheilus* and *S. u. garmani* in the panhandle.

10 0 20 40

Scale of Miles

T. S.

Gibson, Muskogee County. *Choctaw*: 1 mi. W Sawyer; 2 mi. SW Grant. *Cimarron*: several within 3 mi. radius Kenton; 6.9 mi. E Kenton (TTC). *Cleveland*: several within 7 mi. radius Norman; 15 mi. E Norman. *Coal*: 4 mi. W Tupelo. *Comanche*: Wichita Mts. Wildlife Refuge; 17 mi. NW Lawton; 5 mi. N Cache. *Cotton*: 1 mi. N Red River (KU). *Creek*: near Sapulpa (KU). *Custer*: Weatherford; 1 mi. E Weatherford and 2 mi. W Weatherford (SWSC). *Delaware*: 6 mi. NE Grove; 6 mi. NW Grove; near Flint; 1 mi. E Kansas (KU). *Dewey*: 5 mi. W Canton and 5.5 mi. SW Canton, Blaine County (KU). *Ellis*: 23 mi. S Arnett. *Garvin*: Maysville. *Grady*: 3 mi. N Chickasha. *Grant*: 4 mi. S Jefferson (TTC). *Harmon*: 11 mi. N Hollis; 3 mi. W Vinson. *Harper*: near Gate, Beaver County; 3 mi. S Buffalo. *Jackson*: near Elmer. *Johnston*: near Tishomingo. *Kay*: 8 mi. E Ponca City. *Latimer*: several within 4 mi. radius Wilburton; 8 mi. NW Wilburton; 3 mi. N Red Oak; 25.3 mi. N Clayton, Pushmataha County (TTC). *Logan*: Guthrie. *Love*: 7.5 mi. N Marietta; 20 mi. S Marietta; near Red River bridge (KU). *LeFlore*: several within 7 mi. radius Zoe; 5 mi. E Big Cedar; 3.5 mi. SW Stapp; 6.5 mi. W Heavener; several within 6 mi. radius Page; 8 mi. N Talihina; 18 mi. SW Wister. *Marshall*: 2 mi. E Willis; 1 mi. E Powell; 2 mi. S Shay; 0.2 mi. S Johnston-Marshall county line on U.S. Highway 70. *Mayes*: 4 mi. S Locust Grove. *McClain*: 6 mi. E Blanchard; 6 mi. W Norman, Cleveland County. *McCurtain*: 10 mi. SE Broken Bow; 2 and 11 mi. N Broken Bow; 8 mi. N and 6 mi. E Eagletown; 1 mi. W Oklahoma-Arkansas state line on Red River; 2 mi. SW Smithville; Little River S Broken Bow; 1.5 mi. E Harris; 0.5 mi. E Bethel. *Murray*: Dougherty; Turner Falls. *Okmulgee*: Okmulgee. *Osage*: Osage Hills State Park, near Okesa. *Ottawa*: 4 mi. S Wyandotte. *Payne*: 4 mi. W Stillwater. *Pittsburg*: 15 mi. W McAlester. *Pontotoc*: Ada; 5 mi. E Ada (KU). *Pottawatomie*: Shawnee; St. Louis. *Pushmataha*: 1 mi. S Kosoma; 4 and 14 mi. E Tuskahoma; 3 mi. NE Cloudy; near Nashoba; 4 mi. W Sardis; just N Finley; 0.5 mi. S Clayton (TTC). *Roger Mills*: 3 mi. N Cheyenne; 6 mi. NE Durham. *Seminole*: Seminole; Bowlegs. *Sequoyah*: 15 mi. N Sallisaw. *Stephens*: 7 mi. N Duncan (TTC). *Texas*: 8 mi. SE Guymon. *Tulsa*: Tulsa; 9 mi. SE Tulsa. *Woods*: several within 3 mi. radius Edith; 2.5 mi. W and 1 mi. S Waynoka. *Woodward*: 5 mi. E Woodward; Fort Supply.

Additional records.—Adair: 4 mi. NW Watts (Ortenburger, 1929b:27); 4 mi. W Stilwell, 4 mi. S Stilwell, and 5 mi. SE Stilwell (UI); 5 mi. S Stilwell (TNHC); Tyner Creek, S Proctor (OSU). *Alfalfa*: 1 mi. E Byron (OSU). *Atoka*: near Atoka (UMMZ); 4 mi. E Atoka (SESC); 14 mi. SE Stringtown (UI); Limestone Gap (Stone, 1903:540). *Beckham*: Elk City, and 0.5 mi. W Mayfield (McCoy, 1961a:83); 3.5 mi. W Sayre (KU); 1 mi. S Sayre (Burt, 1935:323); junction North Fork Red River and Timber Creek, 4 mi. ESE Sayre (restricted type locality, see page 332). *Blaine*: Canton (OSU); Roman Nose State Park (OU). *Bryan*: 5 mi. SW Colbert (TNHC, SESC). *Caddo*: Fort Cobb (USNM). *Canadian*: "Elkino, Okla. Terr." (presumably El Reno, FMNH). *Cherokee*: Camp Egan, and 3 mi. S Welling (OSU); Hanging Rock (UI, OSU); 4 mi. W and 5.4 mi. SW Scraper (UMMZ); 6 mi. S Kansas, Delaware County (TNHC). *Choctaw*: Fort Towson (Cope, 1900:373, 375). *Cimarron*: 2–3 mi. E Kenton, and 1 mi. W Dinosaur Monument (OSU). *Cleveland*: Noble (FMNH). *Comanche*: Fort Sill (UMMZ); Medicine Park (TNHC). *Creek*: Drumright (KU); 15 mi. E Drumright (McCoy, 1960b:44); 2 mi. W Bristow, 1 mi. NW Milfay, and 4 mi. SW Sapulpa (Burt, 1935:324); Oilton (OSU). *Custer*: 2 mi. E Clinton (RWA). *Delaware*: Dripping Springs (UMMZ). *Garvin*: 4 mi. N Stratford (ECSC). *Greer*: 2 mi. W Reed (McCoy, 1958; 1961a:83). *Harmon*: 7 mi. SW Hollis (Ortenburger and Freeman, 1930:179); 7 mi. S Hollis, and 3 mi. N Hollis (FWCM). *Harper*: 4.5 mi. N Laverne (UMMZ). *Haskell*: near Cartersville (Carter, 1966:33). *Johnston*: 4 mi. N Milburn (Carpenter, 1958a:72); Blue River near Reagan, and 3 mi. E Russett (OU). *Kay*: Salt Fork Arkansas River S Ponca City (OSU); Newkirk (USNM). *Latimer*: near Damon (OU); 5 mi. N Wilburton (UMMZ). *LeFlore*: Shadypoint (OSU); Wister (OSU, CM, AMNH); Gilmore (SESC); 15 mi. S Heavener (OU); 1 mi. E Fanshawe (Burt, 1935:324); Sugarloaf Mt. (Stone, 1903:540); near mouth Poteau River (Cope, 1900:373). *Lincoln*: 3 mi. S Sac and Fox Agency (Burt, 1935:324). *Major*: 18 mi. E Fairview (UMMZ);

7 mi. S and 3 mi. E Bouse Junction [12 mi. S Waynoka, junction State Highway 15 and U.S. Highway 281] (OSU). *Marshall*: 8 mi. W Kingston, and 1 mi. SE Shay (OU). *McCurtain*: several within 5 mi. radius Beavers Bend State Park, near Bokhoma, 25 mi. W Broken Bow, 14 mi. E Broken Bow, Glover River W Battiest, 3 mi. NW Battiest, 1 mi. W Pickens, and 1.5 mi. S Bethel (OU); 10 mi. E Broken Bow, Eagletown, 9 mi. S Valliant, and Idabel (OSU); 6 and 8 mi. SW Eagletown, and 2 mi. E Garvin (UMMZ). *Murray*: Camp Classen (OSU). *Muskogee*: Greenleaf Lake (OSU); 3 mi. NW Haskell (Burt, 1935:324). *Okmulgee*: 3 mi. W Okmulgee (TU). *Osage*: Reservoir Hill (USNM); near Hominy (OSU); 3 mi. W Pawhuska, and 7 mi. W Bartlesville, Washington County (Burt and Hoyle, 1935:201); Delaware Creek (FMNH); 15 mi. NW Bartlesville, Washington County (AMNH). *Ottawa*: 2 mi. S Peoria (KU). *Pawnee*: 2 mi. SE Pawnee (Burt, 1935:324). *Payne*: several within 5 mi. radius Stillwater, 8 mi. E Stillwater, 9 mi. S and 1 mi. W Stillwater, Lake Carl Blackwell, Ripley Bluffs, near Perkins, and Cushing (OSU); 4 mi. W Quay (Burt, 1935:323); 1 mi. S and 1 mi. E Mehan (FWCM). *Pittsburg*: 3 mi. SW Gowen, Latimer County (Burt, 1935:324). *Pottawatomie*: 5 mi. NE Shawnee (OSU). *Pushmataha*: 5 mi. N Snow (SESC); 5 mi. N Honobia (OU); 7 mi. SE Clayton, and 8 mi. S Finley (TNHC). *Roger Mills*: Hammon (OU). *Seminole*: 4 mi. E Seminole (OSU). *Sequoyah*: Swimmer's Creek below Tenkiller Dam (KU); 10 mi. NE Gore (OSU); 3.1 mi. S Marble City (UA). *Stephens*: 6 mi. E Comanche (Carpenter, 1958a:72). *Tillman*: 1–2 mi. S Davidson (CCC). *Tulsa*: 3 mi. N Tulsa (OSU). *Woodward*: Southern Plains Experimental Range, 1 mi. S Woodward (OSU); near Mooreland (McCoy, 1961a:84). *Woods*: Alva, and 18 mi. W and 3 mi. N Alva (McCracken, 1966:8); 11 mi. NW Alva (ECSC).

Uta stansburiana stejnegeri Schmidt

Desert Side-blotched Lizard

Recognition.—Scales small (dorsal scales more than 80), overlapping and keeled on back becoming granular and nonkeeled on sides of body, larger on belly; blackish spot on sides behind forelimbs; small, pale spots on back and sides of body (whitish, blue or orange in life); blue tails in males; dorsolateral pale stripes usually in females.

Distribution.—Known only from Harmon County in extreme southwestern Oklahoma.

Remarks.—The desert side-blotched lizard presumably has recently moved eastward along the sandy floodplain of the Red River, having been reported from Childress and Hardeman counties, Texas, and Harmon County, Oklahoma (Carpenter et al., 1961; Preston and Pratt, 1962). The species seems to be most abundant on the Texas side of the Red River; the only known locality in which they are found on the Oklahoma side, based on 13 specimens (OU 30848-60), is approximately 7 miles southwest and 1.5 miles east of Hollis, Harmon County. Ortenburger collected several reptiles from the floodplain of the Red River in the 1920's but found no *Uta* (the locality, given in other species accounts herein, is recorded as 7 miles southwest Hollis).

ORDER SQUAMATA, SUBORDER SERPENTES—SNAKES

Agkistrodon contortrix (Linnaeus)

Copperheads

Recognition.—Poisonous snakes having deep facial pit between eye and nostril, and no labial entering eye; head wider than neck; most subcaudals undivided; broad chestnut or brownish bands across body; dorsal scales keeled in 23 rows at midbody; anal plate single.

Distribution.—Eastern and central Oklahoma; known as far west as Ellis and Kiowa counties; two subspecies (map, Fig. 77).

Remarks.—Gloyd and Conant (1934, 1938, 1943) have studied

191

the relationships of copperheads. The two subspecies of *Agkistrodon contortrix* in Oklahoma are distinguished by differences in pattern:

A. c. laticinctus Gloyd and Conant, Broad-banded Copperhead.—Crossbands on body as broad on back as on sides, extending to edges of belly and blending with ventral coloration.

A. c. mokasen (Daudin), Northern Copperhead.—Crossbands on body hourglass shaped, constricted in middle of back and wider on sides, not extending to belly.

Broad-banded copperheads occur principally in the Oak-Woodland, but are also found in wooded, shrubby areas in the Grassland. Gloyd (1969:224) notes that his new subspecies, *A. c. phaeogaster*, intergrades with *A. c. laticinctus* in northern Oklahoma. Northern copperheads seem to be characteristic of the Interior Highlands. Gloyd and Conant (1943) referred a specimen found in the valley of the Arkansas River (northern LeFlore County, judging from symbol on map) to the southern copperhead, *A. c. contortrix*, which has narrower crossbands (three scales or less and bands sometimes broken on back) middorsally, and a paler (pale brown to tan) ground color than *A. c. mokasen*. Perhaps *A. c. contortrix* occurs in the Coastal Plain in southeastern Oklahoma, but its distribution in the state is uncertain. For convenience all specimens from eastern Oklahoma are referred to *A. c. mokasen*.

Copperheads seem most common in rocky, wooded country, but individuals also have been taken in sparsely wooded, mostly grass-herb areas having a scattered cover of logs. Although principally nocturnal, copperheads have been found in daytime in thick grassy cover, or in early morning along creek banks. An individual from Carter County ate two shrews and a small mouse. Another was found in a barn coiled in a chicken's nest, where adjacent brooding chickens were not disturbed. The

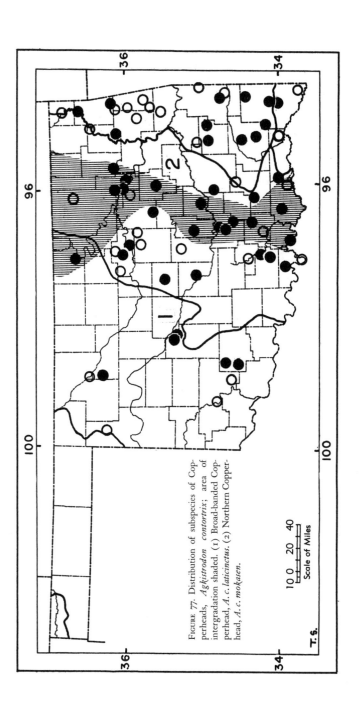

FIGURE 77. Distribution of subspecies of Copperheads, *Agkistrodon contortrix*; area of intergradation shaded. (1) Broad-banded Copperhead, *A. c. laticinctus*. (2) Northern Copperhead, *A. c. mokasen*.

T. S.

10 0 20 40
Scale of Miles

westernmost record in Ellis County suggests that copperheads occur in the shinnery (see page 36).

Of 99 copperheads from Oklahoma (including both subspecies), all have 23 scale rows at midbody (except one having 25), 25 or 27 rows anteriorly, and 19 or 21 posteriorly. Ventrals in 48 males average 151.3 (146–155), and in 39 females 149.5 (144–155); caudals in 51 males average 47.1 (43–51), and in 45 females 45.6 (41–54). Supralabials usually average 8 (7–10), and infralabials usually 10 (9–12).

See Bonn and McCarley (1953:470), Dundee and Burger (1948), Carpenter (1956:43; 1958b:115), Carter and Cox (1968), Chenoweth (1948), Diener (1961), Fitch (1960:129, 205, 210), Force (1930:37), Jenni (1955), McCoy (1961b), Mahaffey (1954:10), Ortenburger and Freeman (1930:186), Sturgis (1939:19), Trowbridge (1937:298).

Specimens examined (OU except as indicated).—*Atoka*: 4.5 mi. E Atoka. *Bryan*: Durant (SESC). *Caddo*: Kiwanis Canyon; Devils Canyon (SWSC). *Canadian*: Devils Canyon (SWSC). *Carter*: Ardmore; 1 mi. E Gene Autry. *Choctaw*: 2 mi. NW Boswell. *Cleveland*: 6 mi. E Noble. *Comanche*: West Cache [creek] (SWSC); Wichita Mts. Wildlife Refuge. *Creek*: 12 mi. S Bristow. *Delaware*: 6 mi. NE Grove; Dripping Springs; 1 mi. N and 1 mi. E Moseley [Moseley is 4.5 mi. E Flint]. *Hughes*: no data. *Johnston*: 3 mi. W Bromide. *Kay*: Ponca City. *Latimer*: 1 mi. N Wilburton; 3 mi. N Wilburton; 9 mi. N Wilburton; 2 mi. S Red Oak (SESC). *LeFlore*: 1.5 mi. E Zoe. *Love*: no data. *Major*: 20 mi. S Waynoka, Woods County (NWSC). *Marshall*: UOBS; 6 mi. N Willis; 2 mi. S Shay. *Mayes*: Locust Grove (NWSC). *McCurtain*: Beavers Bend State Park; 1 mi. N Broken Bow; 1–2 mi. SW Smithville; 2.5 mi. N Smithville; N side Little River at State Highway 3. *Okmulgee*: no data. *Oklahoma*: no data. *Osage*: NW edge Tulsa, Tulsa County. *Payne*: near Ripley; SE Stillwater (UA). *Pittsburg*: 5 mi. SE Stuart, Hughes County (ECSC). *Pontotoc*: 2 and 16 mi. SE Ada, and 7 mi. NE Ada (ECSC). *Pushmataha*: 2 mi. E Cloudy; 18 mi. S Tuskahoma. *Rogers*: 5 and 6 mi. E Catoosa. *Seminole*: 1 mi. E and 0.5 mi. S

Bowlegs. *Tulsa*: Tulsa; 5 mi. SW Tulsa; 9 mi. SE Tulsa. *Wagoner*: 2 mi. S Catoosa, and 6 mi. SE Catoosa, Rogers County.

Additional records.—Adair: Cookson Hills, 4 mi. S Stilwell (UI); 0.5 mi. E and 0.5 mi. N Proctor, and near Bunch (KU); 5 mi. S Kansas, Delaware County (McCoy, 1960a:43). *Atoka*: Limestone Gap (Stone, 1903:542). *Bryan*: 10 mi. SE Bennington (TNHC). *Cherokee*: Camp Muskogee (OSU); Fred Darby Boy Scout Camp, near mouth Barren Fork Creek (FWCM). *Choctaw*: Fort Towson (Ortenburger, 1925:87). *Creek*: Sapulpa (Schmidt, 1919:72). *Ellis*: "killed in west Gage" (Mahaffey, 1954:11). *Haskell*: 4 mi. S and 3 mi. E Quinton, Pittsburg County (HAD). *Johnston*: 3 mi. N Troy (OU); Tishomingo (OSU). *Kiowa*: Quartz Mountain State Park, near Lugert (CCC); vicinity Mountain Park (source of supply for Regal Reptile Ranch in Quartz Mountain State Park). *LeFlore*: Rich Mt., 1 mi. E Page (OSU); Sugarloaf Mt. (Stone 1903:542). *Lincoln*: 3 mi. S Agra (McCoy, 1960a:43); NE part of county (Anon., 1961:19). *Love*: just N Red River on U.S. Highway 77 (FMNH). *Mayes*: 5 mi. SW Locust Grove, and Pensacola Dam (TNHC). *McCurtain*: 3 mi. N Tom (ECSC). *Murray*: Camp Classen (McCoy, 1960a:43). *Osage*: Okesa (UMMZ); Osage Hills State Park (OSU, USNM). *Ottawa*: W Wyandotte near Grand Lake (Chenoweth, 1948). *Payne*: several within 6 mi. radius Stillwater, Lake Carl Blackwell, and Ripley Bluffs (OSU); 10 mi. SW Stillwater (KKA). *Pottawatomie*: 12 mi. radius Shawnee (Webster, 1936:21). *Rogers*: 18 mi. E Tulsa, Tulsa County (OSU); Catoosa (UMMZ). *Sequoyah*: Dwight Mission (CCC). *Tulsa*: 1.5 mi. N Tulsa (TNHC); 3 mi. N Tulsa (OSU); Oakhurst (USNM). *Woods*: 2 mi. S Waynoka (McCracken, 1966:28).

Agkistrodon piscivorous leucostoma (Troost)

Western Cottonmouth

Recognition.—Poisonous snakes having deep facial pit between eye and nostril and one labial touching eye; head wider than neck; most subcaudals undivided; brownish, broad-banded pattern on body, most distinct in young, but indistinct (back mostly blackish) in adults; belly usually with scattered dark smudges; dorsal scales keeled in 25 rows at midbody; anal plate single.

Distribution.—Eastern Oklahoma; known as far west as Tulsa, Comanche, and Cotton counties (map, Fig. 78).

Remarks.—Cottonmouths occur principally in the Interior Highlands, but their range extends westward into the Oak-Woodland, generally in the lowlands of river floodplains having rocky bluffs suitable for hibernation. A dead cottonmouth, which was found on February 5, 1951, near the watercourses of the golf course on the campus of the University of Oklahoma, Norman, Cleveland County, is presumed to be a waif. The westernmost records are from two localities along Cache Creek, where several cottonmouths were collected near Geronimo, Comanche County, and near Temple, Cotton County. Captive cottonmouths have been found at the annual rattlesnake hunts held at Waurika in Jefferson County (William A. Carter, personal communication). Six young were born on September 7 (Cotton County). Captives readily ate frogs (*Rana pipiens*), and one ate a large coachwhip, *Masticophis f. flagellum.*

See Anon. (1959e), Bonn and McCarley (1953:471), Carpenter (1956:43; 1958b:115), Curd (1950), Dundee and Burger (1948), Force (1930:37), Kinsey (1956), Laughlin (1959), Trowbridge (1937:299).

Specimens examined (OU except as indicated).—*Adair*: 4 mi. NW Watts; 5 mi. S Bunch. *Choctaw*: 8 mi. S Hugo. *Cotton*: 3 mi. W Temple. *Craig*: 3 mi. E Vinita. *Johnston*: 7 mi. W Wapanucka; Tishomingo Fish Hatchery. *Latimer*: 1–2 mi. N Wilburton; 8 mi. NW Wilburton. *LeFlore*: 6.5 mi. W Heavener; 5 mi. E Big Cedar; near Zoe; 6 mi. SW Page; 3.5 mi. SW Stapp; 4 mi. W Wister. *Marshall*: UOBS. *McCurtain*: 11 mi. W Idabel; 7 mi. N Idabel; 9 mi. E Broken Bow; 1–2 mi. SW Smithville. *Murray*: Price's Falls. *Pushmataha*: 4 mi. E Tuskahoma. *Rogers*: 20 mi. E Tulsa, Tulsa

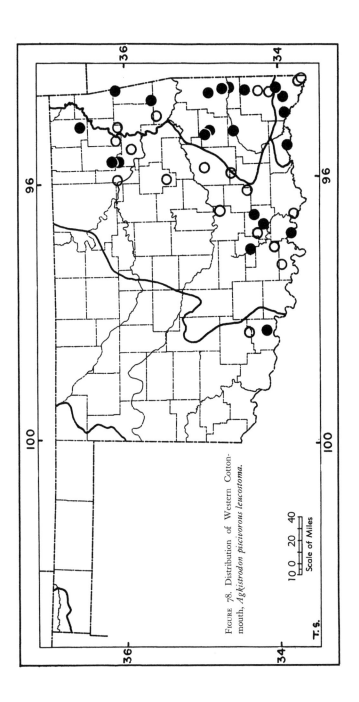

FIGURE 78. Distribution of Western Cotton-mouth, *Agkistrodon piscivorous leucostoma*.

10 0   20   40
Scale of Miles

T. S.

County; 6 mi. E Catoosa; 2.5 mi. N State Highway 33 bridge over Verdigris River (KU). *Wagoner*: 6 and 8 mi. SE Catoosa and 4 mi. S Catoosa, Rogers County (KU).

Additional records.—Atoka: Kiowa City Lake, 5 mi. S and 1 mi. E Kiowa, Pittsburg County (ECSC). *Bryan*: vicinity Colbert (Bonn and McCarley, 1953:471). *Carter*: Lake Murray State Park (Carter, 1966:35). *Coal*: 1.5 mi. E Lehigh (ECSC). *Comanche*: Cache Creek just east of Geronimo (Carter, 1966:35). *Johnston*: 7.5 mi. S Mill Creek (Howard McCarley, personal communication). *LeFlore*: Wister (CM). *Love*: near Oswalt (OU). *Marshall*: Northcutt Ranch [near Willis] (Carpenter, 1955a:41). *Mayes*: 2 mi. S Chouteau (UMMZ); Camp Garland, 5 mi. S Locust Grove (OSU, USNM); Spring Creek, 7 mi. S and 3 mi. E Locust Grove (McCoy, 1960a:43). *McCurtain*: McCurtain County Game Refuge (Anon., 1959e); Grassy Lake (Kinsey, 1956; Curd, 1950); Idabel (UMMZ); Beavers Bend State Park (OU); SE Broken Bow (AMNH); 8 mi. S Millerton, and mouth Mountain Fork River (OSU); 2 mi. SW Tom (UI). *Okmulgee*: 5 mi. N Henryetta (ECSC). *Pittsburg*: Lake McAlester (Laughlin, 1959:83). *Pontotoc*: near Steedman (ECSC). *Rogers*: Tulsa Fin and Feather Club (OSU). *Sequoyah*: 10 mi. NE Gore (McCoy, 1960a:43). *Tulsa*: Mohawk Park (Dundee and Burger, 1948). *Wagoner*: Verdigris River near Wagoner (KKA).

Arizona elegans blanchardi Klauber
Kansas Glossy Snake

Recognition.—Straw or buff snakes having pattern of dark-edged brownish blotches on back and smaller ones on sides; belly whitish, unmarked; usually short, dark, postocular stripe; snout slightly pointed with rostral enlarged and extending backward between internasals; dorsal scales smooth in 29 or 31 rows at midbody; anal plate single.

Distribution.—Western Oklahoma; known as far east as Cleveland County (Map, Fig. 79).

Remarks.—Glossy snakes are nocturnal, occurring in the

198

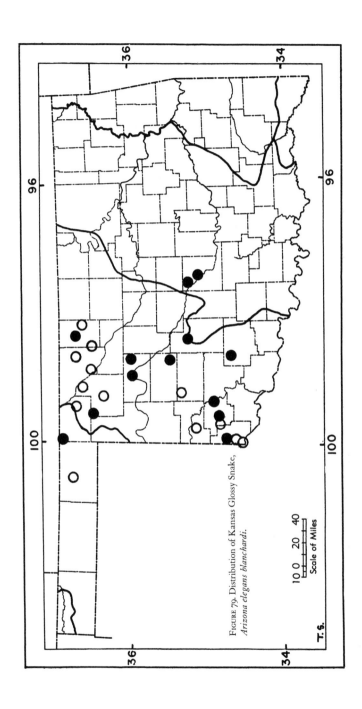

FIGURE 79. Distribution of Kansas Glossy Snake, *Arizona elegans blanchardi.*

Scale of Miles

10 0 20 40

T. S.

Grassland in loose-soiled areas that permit burrowing, or among cover associated with human habitation (one found in a barn; another foraging at night at a gas station).

See Blanchard (1924a:Table), Burt and Hoyle (1935:208), Burt (1935:331), Klauber (1946:321, 332), Ortenburger and Bird (1933:61), Smith and Leonard (1934:194).

Specimens examined (OU except as indicated).—*Alfalfa*: 3 mi. E Cherokee. *Caddo*: 7 mi. W Binger (FMNH). *Cleveland*: Norman; 0.5 and 2–4 mi. W Norman; 18 mi. NW Norman. *Comanche*: Wichita Mts. Wildlife Refuge. *Custer*: 2 mi. N Weatherford (SWSC). *Dewey*: 6 mi. W Canton, Blaine County; 0.5 mi. NW Taloga. *Greer*: 5.7 mi. E Mangum; 1 mi. NW Granite. *Harmon*: 3 mi. N McKnight. *Harper*: 2 mi. S Kansas state line on Cimarron River S Englewood, Kansas. *Woodward*: 1 mi. W Fort Supply.

Additional records.—*Alfalfa*: Salt Plains, and 5 mi. W Carmen (OSU); 4 mi. N Jet (ECSC). *Beaver*: 2 mi. S Beaver (Klauber, 1946:333). *Beckham*: 6 mi. E Erick (Burt and Hoyle, 1935:208). *Greer*: 1 mi. W and 1 mi. S Reed (OSU). *Harmon*: several within 7 mi. radius Hollis (FWCM). *Harper*: 3 mi. S Selmans (OSU). *Washita*: 5 mi. NE Canute (Burt and Hoyle, 1935:208). *Woods*: Alva (Ortenburger, 1925:85); Waynoka (Klauber, 1946:333); 6 mi. NE Waynoka (Burt, 1935:331). *Woodward*: 5 mi. E Woodward, and 3 and 7 mi. SW Freedom, Woods County (OSU).

Carphophis amoenus vermis (Kennicott)[2]

Western Worm Snake

Recognition.—Small snakes, usually not more than one foot in length; head and body uniform dark gray; unmarked, salmon pink belly, pink of belly extending upward on sides to third row of dorsal scales; dorsal scales smooth in 13 rows throughout length of body; anal plate divided.

[2] Donald R. Clark, Jr., (*Herpetologica*, 24: 104–12, 1968) proposes recognition of this snake as a distinct species, *Carphophis vermis*.

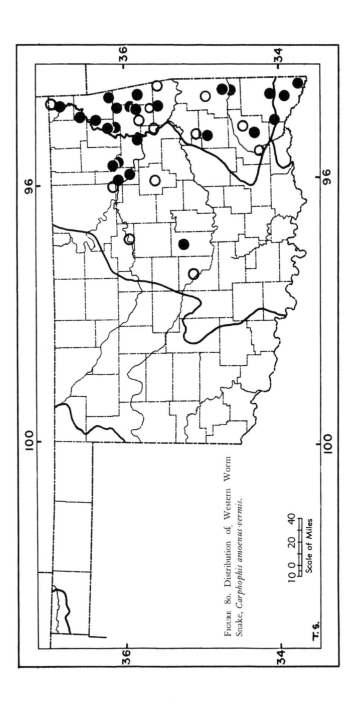

FIGURE 80. Distribution of Western Worm Snake, *Carphophis amoenus-vermis.*

Scale of Miles

10 0 20 40

T. S.

Distribution.—Eastern Oklahoma; known as far west as Payne and Cleveland counties (map, Fig. 80).

Remarks.—Worm snakes occur in the Oak-Woodland, but are most common in the Interior Highlands. Individuals burrow and are found under rocks or logs in wooded areas in uplands or lowlands; one was uncovered in a back yard of a residential section in northwestern Tulsa. A young thrush that was shot along the Kiamichi River in LeFlore County had partly swallowed a *Carphophis*.

See Force (1930:29).

Specimens examined (OU except as indicated).—*Adair*: 3 mi. NNW Chewey; 4 mi. N Stilwell. *Cherokee*: 2–3 mi. N Scraper; 2 mi. E Welling; Camp Egan. *Delaware*: Dripping Springs; 3 mi. S Cleora. *Latimer*: Robbers Cave State Park (NWSC). *LeFlore*: 2–6 mi. SW Page; 5 mi. E Big Cedar. *Mayes*: 4 mi. N Locust Grove; Camp Garland, 5 mi. S Locust Grove; near lower Spavinaw Lake. *McCurtain*: near Tom; 6 mi. N Idabel; 25 mi. W Broken Bow; Beavers Bend State Park. *Ottawa*: near Wyandotte; 4 mi. E junction Neosho River bridge and U.S. Highway 60. *Pottawatomie*: Shawnee. *Pushmataha*: 3 mi. NE Cloudy. *Rogers*: 1 mi. W Catoosa; 6–8 mi. E Catoosa. *Sequoyah*: 2 mi. N Marble City. *Tulsa*: Tulsa; E Bixby; near Red Fork; 9 mi. SE Tulsa. *Wagoner*: 6 mi. SE Catoosa, and 2 mi. S Catoosa, Rogers County; 2 mi. S Okay (KU).

Additional records.—*Adair*: 4 mi. W Stilwell, and 4 mi. S Stilwell (UI). *Cherokee*: 6 mi. S Kansas, Delaware County (TTC); 13 mi. E Fort Gibson, Muskogee County, and 8 mi. E Tahlequah (OSU); Camp Muskogee, and 14 mi. NW Hanging Rock (OSU); 4 mi. SE Cookson (KU). *Cleveland*: near Norman (Van Vleet, 1902:168). *Haskell*: 4 mi. S and 3 mi. E Quinton, Pittsburg County (HAD). *LeFlore*: Wister (Stone, 1903:542); Rich Mt., 2 mi. E Page (UMMZ). *Mayes*: Cedar Crest Lake (OSU). *Muskogee*: Greenleaf Lake (McCoy, 1960a:43). *Okmulgee*: 3 mi. W Okmulgee (TU). *Osage*: 2 mi. NE Tulsa, Tulsa County (TNHC). *Ottawa*: 3.5 mi. N and 4.5 mi. E Quapaw (UI). *Payne*: 1 mi. N and 3 mi. W Ripley

(McCoy, 1960a:43). *Pushmataha*: 1 mi. S Nashoba (TNHC); 4.5 mi. N Kiamichi River bridge, N Antlers (OU). *Rogers*: Verdigris, and 2 mi. NE Garnett, Tulsa County (UMMZ); Tulsa Fin and Feather Club (OSU). *Sequoyah*: near Dwight Mission (Carpenter, 1958a:73); Short (OSU). *Tulsa*: 1 mi. N Sand Springs, and 4 mi. N Tulsa (TNHC); 3 mi. N Tulsa (OSU).

Cemophora coccinea copei Jan

Scarlet Snake

Recognition.—Snout red and pointed; body having red, black-bordered blotches (black borders thin or interrupted on sides) separated by yellowish interspaces; belly whitish or pale yellow, unmarked; dorsal scales smooth in 19 rows throughout length of body; anal plate single.

Distribution.—Eastern Oklahoma; known as far west as Logan and Seminole counties (map, Fig. 81).

Remarks.—Scarlet snakes are secretive and fossorial, and little is known about them in Oklahoma. The species is found in the Interior Highlands and in parts of the Oak-Woodland, and is probably more abundant than the few records indicate. A juvenile was uncovered by a tractor next to a log in a cultivated field (Pittsburg County).

See Carter (1966:35), Force (1930:34), Williams, Brown, and Wilson (1966:85, Table 1), Williams and Wilson (1967:109, 115, 116).

Specimens examined.—*Okmulgee*: no data (OU). *Pittsburg*: just off Route 6 near McAlester (OU). *Seminole*: 2 mi. S and 5 mi. E Wewoka (ECSC).

Additional records.—*Creek*: Drumright (USNM). *Delaware*: 3.6 mi. N Flint (Long Beach State College). *Logan*: near Meridian (specimen in custody of Dr. Neil Douglas, Monroe, Louisiana, *fide* Bryan P. Glass in personal communication from George A. Moore).

Pittsburg: 3 mi. E Haywood (ECSC). *Tulsa*: Parthenia Park (Force, 1930:34, UMMZ).

Coluber constrictor flaviventris Say

Eastern Yellow-bellied Racer

Recognition.—Adults patternless, uniform dark blue to blackish in eastern Oklahoma, or pale bluish to greenish in western Oklahoma; belly unmarked, pale yellow or whitish, or having blue black smudging and small black dots in southeastern Oklahoma; lowermost preocular very small; dorsal scales smooth in 17 rows at midbody and 15 just in front of anal plate; anal plate divided. Young (not more than about 20 inches) bluish gray with yellow anteriorly, having scattered blue, yellow, and reddish brown dots, and middorsal row of large red brown blotches with smaller spots on sides; belly yellow with small yellowish brown spots, mostly anteriorly.

Distribution.—Throughout the state (map, Fig. 82).

Remarks.—Active in daytime, racers are frequently observed in many different habitats, often found in trees and near water. One was swimming in Lake Texoma about 75 yards from shore; another was found at the base of a man-made purple martin roost with a young bird of that species half-ingested; one was captured as it was attempting to eat a "horned toad"; a juvenile, the anterior part of its body missing (presumably prey), was found in the nest of a red-tailed hawk. See account of *Elaphe guttata*.

Auffenberg (1955:100–101) indicated the occurrence of the southern black racer, *Coluber constrictor priapus*, and intergradation of that subspecies with the eastern yellow-bellied racer in eastern Oklahoma. The two specimens seen by Auffenberg (from Adair and Pushmataha counties) were considered as intergrades between *flaviventris* and *priapus*. The subspecies

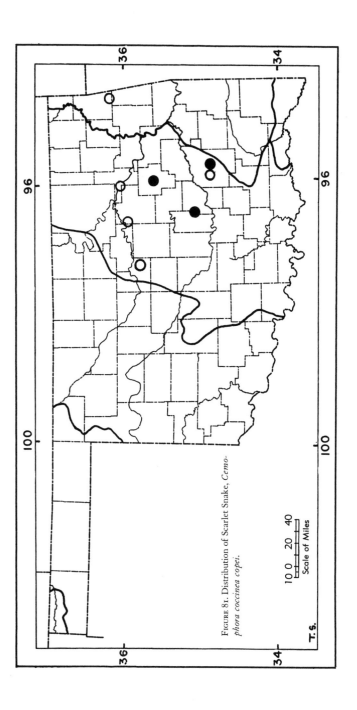

FIGURE 81. Distribution of Scarlet Snake, *Cemophora coccinea copei.*

priapus, found principally in the southeastern United States, is distinguished from *flaviventris* by its uniformly slate black ventral surface, its mostly whitish chin (often with black marks), and its blackish dorsal surface. None of the specimens seen by me are referable to *priapus*, but many from southeastern Oklahoma (LeFlore, Latimer, Pushmataha, and McCurtain counties) have small black spots on the belly, and some have a dark smudging; the features of *priapus* are most pronounced in one snake from McCurtain County (OU 1712, 2 mi. N Broken Bow). Intergradation between *priapus* and *flaviventris* seems evident in southeastern Oklahoma, but further relationships remain to be worked out by future investigators. For convenience I have referred all Oklahoma racers to *flaviventris*.

See Bonn and McCarley (1953:470), Burt and Burt (1929b: 10), Burt and Hoyle (1935:205), Carpenter (1956:43; 1958b:114; 1959c:34), Force (1925a:27; 1925b:83; 1930:31), Mahaffey (1954:10), Ortenburger (1928c:186–87), Trowbridge (1937:296).

Specimens examined (OU except as indicated).—*Adair*: 6 mi. N Marble City, Sequoyah County; 4 mi. NW Watts. *Alfalfa*: 9 mi. N Driftwood (KU). *Beaver*: near Gate. *Blaine*: Roman Nose State Park; 3 mi. W Hitchcock; 9 mi. SW Okeene. *Bryan*: Durant (SESC). *Caddo*: 2 mi. S Hinton. *Canadian*: 3 mi. SE Mustang. *Carter*: 5 mi. NW Ardmore; 5 mi. S and 2 mi. W Ardmore. *Cherokee*: Camp Egan; 1 mi. S Welling; 3 mi. E Tahlequah. *Cimarron*: 3 mi. N Kenton. *Cleveland*: several within 4 mi. radius Norman; 7 mi. E Norman; 8 mi. NNE Norman. *Comanche*: Wichita Mts. Wildlife Refuge; 15 mi. W Lawton; 6 mi. S and 10 mi. E Lawton. *Creek*: Drumright. *Custer*: Weatherford (SWSC). *Delaware*: 3 mi. NW Moseley [Moseley is 4.5 mi. E Flint]. *Garvin*: Maysville. *Greer*: 3 mi. SW Mangum. *Harper*: near Gate, Beaver County. *Hughes*: near Wetumka. *Jackson*: 9 mi. W Altus. *Johnston*: 2.5 mi. NW Ravia. *Kay*: 8 mi. E Ponca City. *Kiowa*: Cooperton. *Latimer*: vicinity of Wilburton; 9 mi. N Wilburton; Robbers Cave State Park (NWSC). *LeFlore*: 6 mi. S Talihina; 6–7 mi. W Heavener; 18.7 mi. SE Heavener; near Zoe; 4 mi. E Page; Spring Mt., 6

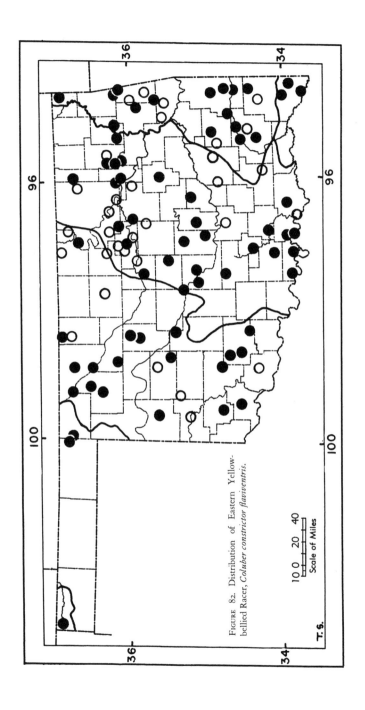

FIGURE 82. Distribution of Eastern Yellow-bellied Racer, *Coluber constrictor flaviventris*.

mi. SW Page; 5 mi. E Big Cedar. *Logan*: Guthrie. *Love*: 2 mi. W Marietta; 1.5 mi. W Rubottom. *Major*: 10.5 mi. E Chester (RGW). *Marshall*: UOBS; 2 mi. W Willis; 8 mi. W Kingston. *Mayes*: Locust Grove; 2 mi. S Chouteau. *McClain*: 6 mi. NW Blanchard. *McCurtain*: 2 mi. SW Smithville; 1–2 mi. N Broken Bow; 7 mi. E Broken Bow; 14–15 mi. SE Broken Bow; 2 mi. E Harris; 1.5 mi. W Harris. *Murray*: Dougherty; Price's Falls. *Oklahoma*: eastern part of county. *Okmulgee*: Okmulgee. *Osage*: NW edge Tulsa, Tulsa County. *Ottawa*: 2 mi. S Peoria (KU). *Pawnee*: near Quay. *Payne*: no data. *Pottawatomie*: Shawnee; 3.5 mi. NE Shawnee; St. Louis. *Pushmataha*: 4 mi. E Tuskahoma; Clayton; 7.8 mi. N Finley. *Roger Mills*: Strong City. *Rogers*: 6 mi. E Catoosa; 7 mi. W Claremore; 2 mi. NE Verdigris. *Seminole*: Bowlegs. *Tulsa*: Tulsa; 9 mi. SE Tulsa; 6 mi. W Tulsa; 5 mi. E Tulsa. *Wagoner*: 6 mi. SE Catoosa, Rogers County. *Washington*: Bartlesville (KU). *Woods*: 2.5 mi. W Waynoka; 4 mi. S Waynoka; 2 mi. W Edith; 12 mi. W Alva (KU). *Woodward*: 5 mi. E and 1 mi. N Woodward; 6 mi. E Woodward; 16 mi. SW Freedom, Woods County.

Additional records.—Adair: 3 mi. NE Proctor (Auffenberg, 1955:100); 4 mi. S Stilwell (OU); 3 mi. S Bunch (KU). *Alfalfa*: 6 mi. N and 2 mi. E Cherokee (McCoy, 1960a:43). *Atoka*: NE Farris (Carpenter, 1958a:73). *Beckham*: 1 mi. S Sayre and 4 mi. W Sayre (Burt, 1935:329). *Bryan*: Colbert and 5 mi. SW Colbert (TNHC). *Creek*: Sapulpa (AMNH). *Custer*: 6 mi. NW Custer (Burt, 1935:329). *Garfield*: 10 mi. E Enid (CCC). *Johnston*: 5 mi. S Tishomingo (ECSC). *Kay*: 4 mi. W Lyman, Osage County (Burt, 1935:329); 6 mi. SE Chilocco (Burt and Hoyle, 1935:206). *Latimer*: 2 mi. N Gowen (Burt, 1935:329). *LeFlore*: just N Page (Burt, 1935:329); Wister (Burt and Burt, 1929b:10). *Lincoln*: 9 mi. N Stroud (Burt, 1935:329). *Mayes*: Camp Garland, 5 mi. S Locust Grove (OSU). *McCurtain*: 1 mi. N Bethel (CCC); 7.5 mi. S Sherwood (OU). *Noble*: 5 mi. N Sumner (Burt, 1935:329). *Osage*: Okesa (UMMZ). *Pawnee*: N Keystone (AMNH); 2 mi. SE Pawnee (Burt, 1935:329); Cleveland (Mahaffey, 1954:10). *Payne*: near Coyle, Logan County (OSU); Boomer Lake, Yost Lake, 5 mi. N and 5 mi. E Stillwater, and several within 2 mi. radius Stillwater (OSU); 5 mi. S Stillwater (Burt, 1935:329); 2

mi. NE Ripley (UA). *Pittsburg*: 4 mi. E Stuart, Hughes County (ECSC); 2 mi. SE Alderson (ECSC). *Pontotoc*: 2 mi. E Ada (McCoy, 1960a:43); 7 mi. NE Ada (ECSC). *Pushmataha*: 1 mi. S Nashoba (Auffenberg, 1955:100). *Rogers*: 6 mi. W Claremore (Burt and Hoyle, 1935:206); near Claremore (MCZ); 12 mi. NE Tulsa, Tulsa County (TNHC). *Sequoyah*: Swimmer's Creek below Tenkiller Dam (KU); Dwight Mission and 10 mi. NE Gore (Carpenter, 1958a:73). *Tillman*: 12 mi. E Frederick (CCC). *Tulsa*: 1 mi. S Red Fork (TNHC); Garnett (UMMZ). *Washington*: 4 mi. N Ochelata (Burt and Burt, 1929a:456). *Washita*: 4.9 mi. E Elk City, Beckham County (RWA). *Woods*: several vicinity Alva (McCracken, 1966:16).

Crotalus atrox Baird and Girard

Western Diamondback Rattlesnake

Recognition.—Poisonous snakes with rattle (horny segments) or horny "button" on tip of tail; top of head with many small scales between large supraoculars; facial pit between eye and nostril; head wider than neck; tail pale gray to whitish, having contrasting black rings; only two internasals touching rostral; dorsal pattern of brownish, white-edged, diamond-shaped blotches (less distinct posteriorly) that join one another; most subcaudals single; dorsal scales keeled usually in 25 (or 27) rows at midbody; anal plate single.

Distribution.—Irregular; generally throughout the state except in the panhandle and north central part of Oklahoma (map, Fig. 83).

Remarks.—In Oklahoma, western diamondbacks seem to prefer terrain having a dissected topography, such as rocky or mountainous habitats, eroded canyons and ravines, or bluffs along rivers. Individuals are abundant in the Wichita Mountains and Gypsum Hills in western Oklahoma. Most rattlers obtained in the annual "rattlesnake roundups" near Okeene (every April since 1939), and in other "hunts" near Waynoka and Waurika, are western diamondbacks. *Crotalus atrox* probably occurs throughout the Interior Highlands, but seems less abundant in eastern than western Oklahoma. To the west, *atrox* is limited by the High Plains; the absence of *atrox* in north central Oklahoma is perhaps due to the lack of rocky places suitable for hibernation sites. See account of *Crotalus viridis*.

See Anon. (1946, 1954a, 1954b, 1954c, 1956b, 1957, 1958, 1959d), Boyer (1957), Carpenter (1958b:115), Carter and Cox (1968), Hughes (1947, 1950), Jenni (1955, 1958, 1966), Kinsey (1952), Klauber (1930:8, 9, 24, 25, 26, 27, 29, 30, 31, 32, 43; 1956:547, 561, 589, 968, 997, 1045, 1054, 1082), Kolb (1946), Ortenburger and Freeman (1930:186), Trowbridge (1937:229), Van Vleet (1902:173).

Specimens examined (OU except as indicated).—*Blaine*: Watonga; near Hitchcock; Okeene (SWSC); 8–9 mi. SW Okeene; Salt Creek Canyon (KU). *Comanche*: 5 mi. N Cache; Wichita Mts. Wildlife Refuge. *Cotton*: 2 mi. S Devol. *Greer*: 2.7 mi. W Reed. *Harmon*: 5 mi. N Carl; NW Reed, Greer County. *Kiowa*: Cooperton; 7 mi. E Mountain Park. *Latimer*: 2, 5 and 9 mi. N Wilburton. *LeFlore*: 2.5 mi. NW Stapp; Zoe; Talihina; near Wister; Spring Mt., 6 mi. SW Page; 5 mi. E Big Cedar. *Major*: 7 mi. E Orienta; Glass Mts., and Orienta (NWSC). *Murray*: few within 3 mi. radius Turner Falls. *Okmulgee*: no data. *Pushmataha*: 4 mi. E Tuskahoma. *Woods*: near Waynoka. *Woodward*: 4 mi. E Quinlan, and 15 mi. SW Freedom, Woods County (NWSC).

Additional records.—*Adair*: no data (Anderson, 1965:297). *Alfalfa*: presumably near Byron (Klauber, 1956, I:547). *Blaine*: 15 mi. SW Okeene (OSU); Roman Nose State Park (Allen et al., 1960). *Cherokee*: Cherokee Game Management, near Tahlequah (Anon., 1958). *Comanche*: Craterville Park (TTC); Cache (Smith, 1950:301; 1956:315). *Garvin*: Sparks Ranch near Hennepin (Anon., 1959d). *Greer*: 1 mi. W Granite (OSU); 3.5 mi. E and 1.5 mi. N Reed (OU). *Harmon*: several within 7 mi. radius Hollis (FWCM). *Haskell*: 4 mi. SE McCurtain (Mahaffey, 1954);

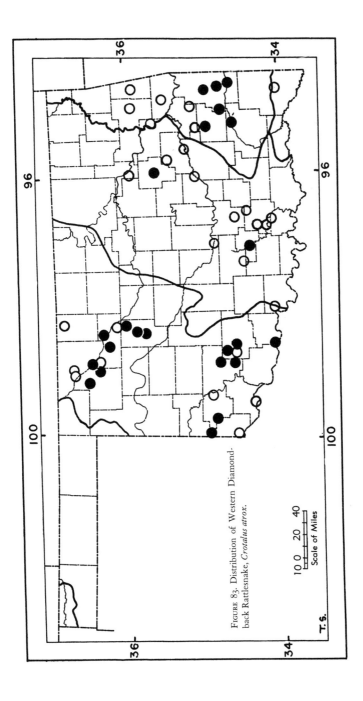

FIGURE 83: Distribution of Western Diamond-
back Rattlesnake, *Crotalus atrox*.

4 mi. S and 3 mi. E Quinton, Pittsburg County (HAD). *Hughes*: 5 mi. NE Lamar (ECSC). *Jackson*: Red River, SW Olustee (Anon., 1957); 14 mi. S Olustee (UMMZ). *Jefferson*: near Waurika (Carter, 1966:36). *Johnston*: 5 mi. E Pontotoc (Carter, 1966:36); 6 mi. SE Mill Creek, and S Ravia along Washita River (ECSC). *Major*: 8 mi. N and 1 mi. W Okeene, Blaine County (OSU); 12 mi. S Waynoka, Woods County (UMMZ). *Marshall*: 8 mi. SW Tishomingo, Johnston County (Carter, 1966:36). *McClain*: 2 mi. N Byars (ECSC). *McCurtain*: presumably near Broken Bow (Kolb, 1946). *McIntosh*: Deep Fork River, near Hitchita (Anon., 1946); 3 mi. S Eufaula (ECSC). *Muskogee*: Camp Gruber, near Braggs (Anon., 1954b). *Pontotoc*: Frank Vincent Ranch, 9 mi. SE Fittstown (ECSC). *Sequoyah*: Dwight Mission (CCC). *Tulsa*: Limbo Mts. near Glenpool (Story, 1958). *Woods*: 5 mi. SW Waynoka (UMMZ); Freedom (OSU); 25 mi. W Alva (McCracken, 1966:29); near Whitehorse (Ortenburger and Freeman, 1930:186).

Crotalus horridus horridus Linnaeus

Timber Rattlesnake

Recognition.—Poisonous snakes with rattle (horny segments) or horny "button" on tip of tail; top of head with many small scales between large supraoculars; facial pit between eye and nostril; head wider than neck; tail black (obscure banded pattern in young); dorsal pattern of blackish chevrons or bar-like blotches across back; most subcaudals single; dorsal scales keeled, usually in 23 (or 25) rows at midbody; anal plate single.

Distribution.—Eastern Oklahoma; known as far west as Payne, McClain, and Love counties (map, Fig. 84).

Remarks.—Timber rattlers are found principally in wooded, rocky habitats in the Interior Highlands and Oak-Woodland. Individuals have been collected in lowlands along rivers and streams, in dry stream beds, along dirt roads at night, and under trash in rockless, grassy places; the westernmost record

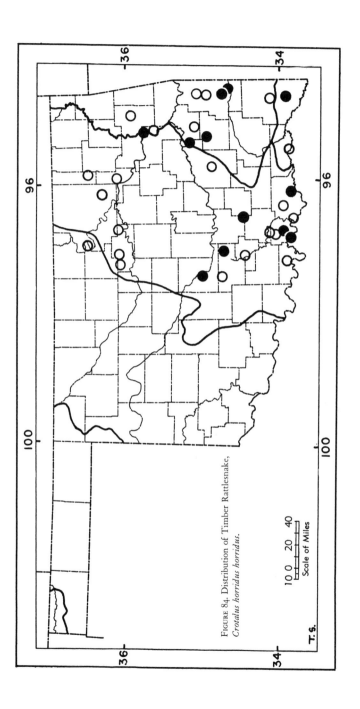

FIGURE 84. Distribution of Timber Rattlesnake, *Crotalus horridus horridus*.

Scale of Miles

10 0 20 40

T. S.

(McClain County) is that of a specimen found along the wooded floodplain of the South Canadian River.

Specimens from southeastern Oklahoma are more like the Canebrake Rattlesnake, *Crotalus horridus atricaudatus*, than *C. h. horridus* in having contrasting patterns, blackish postocular and reddish middorsal stripes, most ventrolateral blackish spots anteriorly with pale centers, and 25 rows of dorsal scales at midbody. Intergradation, at least, seems to occur in southeastern Oklahoma between *horridus* and *atricaudatus*. Snakes resembling *atricaudatus* are found in the Coastal Plain. In 16 Oklahoma specimens (most from the southeastern part of the state), ventrals in 9 males average 169.3 (166–172), and in 6 females, 174.3 (172–177); subcaudals in 10 males average 26.7 (25–28) and in 6 females, 22.3 (20–27); body blotches average 24.4 (20–27) in 16 specimens, and the dorsal scale rows at midbody usually number 25 (69%).

See Anon. (1956a, 1959a), Bonn and McCarley (1953:471), Bragg (1948), Carpenter (1956:43), Force (1930:37), Klauber (1956, II:1233, probably *horridus*), Trowbridge (1937:299).

Specimens examined (OU except as indicated).—*Bryan*: near Albany. *Garvin*: 6 mi. W Stratford (ECSC). *Haskell*: 3.5 mi. N Quinton, Pittsburg County. *Latimer*: 7 mi. N Wilburton. *LeFlore*: 4 mi. W Page; 6 mi. SW Page; 3.5 mi. SW Stapp; 1.5 mi. E Zoe. *Marshall*: UOBS; 5.2 mi. N Willis; 3 mi. W Kingston. *McClain*: no data; 7 mi. NW Purcell. *McCurtain*: 7 mi. N Idabel. *Muskogee*: Fort Gibson. *Pontotoc*: Rhynes Ranch, SE corner of county (ECSC).

Additional records.—*Bryan*: 4 mi. SE Colbert (TNHC); near Durant (Anon., 1959a). *Cherokee*: 4 mi. N and 4 mi. E Tahlequah (UMMZ). *Choctaw*: near Red River bottoms (Mahaffey, 1954, probably *horridus*). *Cleveland*: near Norman (Van Vleet, 1902:173; possibly based on OU 3770, listed under "Specimens examined" as having no data from McClain County). *Garvin*: near Maysville (ECSC). *Haskell*: Sans Bois (Gloyd, 1940:178). *Johnston*: Randolph Bottoms, 4 mi. E Russett (Carpenter, 1958a:74); 5 mi. SE Tishomingo (ECSC). *LeFlore*: Poteau (Klauber, 1956, II:1233, probably based on *horridus*); Wister (Gloyd, 1940:178). *Love*: 7.5 mi. W Marietta (SESC). *Marshall*: Catfish Bay, Lake Texoma (Anon., 1956a); 4 mi. S Kingston and 2 mi. NW Madill (OU). *McCurtain*: 10 mi. N Broken Bow (TU). *Murray*: near Davis (ECSC). *Muskogee*: Camp Gruber Scout Reservation, near Braggs (FWCM). *Noble*: 12 mi. S and 8 mi. E Ponca City, Kay County (ECSC). *Osage*: 16 mi. W Skiatook, Tulsa County (TNHC). *Payne*: Stillwater, and 10 mi. NW Stillwater (Gloyd, 1940:178); Dripping Springs near Quay, Lake Carl Blackwell, and Game Farm (OSU). *Pittsburg*: McAlester (MU). *Tulsa*: E Tulsa (Force, 1930:37). *Washington*: Caney River E Ramona (UMMZ).

Crotalus viridis viridis (Rafinesque)

Prairie Rattlesnake

Recognition.—Poisonous snakes with rattle (horny segments) or horny "button" on tip of tail; top of head with many small scales between large supraoculars; facial pit between eye and nostril; head wider than neck; usually several internasals touching rostral; bands on tail brownish, not black; dorsal pattern of nonconnecting, brownish blotches with narrow white edges (less distinct and not white-edged posteriorly); most caudals single; dorsal scales keeled, usually in 27 (or 25) rows at midbody; anal plate single.

Distribution.—Western Oklahoma; known as far east as Blaine County (map, Fig. 85).

Remarks.—Prairie rattlesnakes are abundant on the High Plains, including the Mesa de Maya, where individuals have been taken on the rocky slopes of mesas, in flat, short-grass areas along creeks, and in Beaver County "from a prairie dog mound" (William A. Carter, personal communication). A collared lizard and kangaroo rat are recorded as items of food. Nineteen young were born on August 26 (Cimarron County).

Elsewhere in western Oklahoma, in territory occupied by the western diamondback, there are few records of occurrence for *viridis*; *Crotalus atrox*, so far as known, does not occur on the High Plains. In most places the two species seem to prefer different habitats—*viridis* in mostly nonrocky, flat, sparsely vegetated places, and *atrox* in rocky, mountainous, or dissected terrain; McCracken (1966:29), however, reported *atrox* from "brushy areas or even on open plains" and *viridis* as "often found on rocky hillsides." Both species seem to be abundant in the vicinity of Hollis, Harmon County, where Mr. John R. Preston of the Fort Worth Children's Museum wrote me that "there is much overlap in the habitat requirements, both species being collected in buffalo grass, mesquite, and prickly pear associations; however, *atrox* is commonly found in woodrat dens in the summer, but *viridis* has never been seen in this situation. Both species are rather common along section line roads, but *viridis* is noticeably so along the terracelike escarpments south of Hollis. Here the habitat is short grass, scattered mesquite, and gypsum outcroppings." There are few recent reports of *viridis* beyond the extreme western border of Oklahoma. Possibly there has been decimation of the species and a receding range to the west because of the alteration of previously suitable open plains by man.

Crotalus viridis was erroneously reported from Comanche County by Webb and Ortenburger (1955:91); the two specimens that formed the basis of that report were collected by Frank B. McMurray in Beaver County. Baird and Girard (1854:190, Pl. I) recorded a specimen (USNM 4227) that "was collected the 5th of June in the Witchita [*sic*] mountains," but the itinerary of Marcy and McClellan (1854:24) indicates that on that date their expedition was in the southeastern part of Beckham County.

See Amaral (1929:89, Table I), Ortenburger and Freeman (1930:186), Hallowell (1854:18), Van Vleet (1902:173).

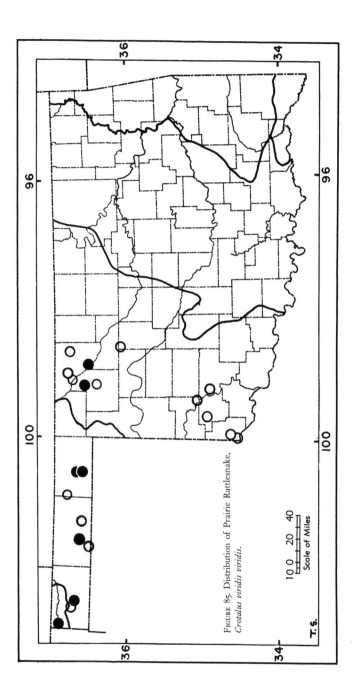

FIGURE 85. Distribution of Prairie Rattlesnake, *Crotalus viridis viridis.*

Specimens examined (OU except as indicated).—*Beaver*: 18 mi. S and 6 mi. W Beaver; 13 mi. S and 6 mi. W Beaver. *Cimarron*: 7 mi. S Boise City; 3 mi. SE Kenton; 3 mi. N Kenton; 2 mi. W Kenton (TTC). *Texas*: 5.5 mi. SW Guymon (RGW). *Woods*: Waynoka (NWSC). *Woodward*: 16 mi. SW Freedom, Woods County.

Additional records.—*Beaver*: 2 mi. S and 4 mi. E Turpin (ECSC). *Beckham*: SE part of county (Baird and Girard, 1854:190; see section "Remarks"). *Blaine*: "Cross Timbers," along North Fork of Canadian River near 36° N Lat. and 98° 30′ W Long. (Stejneger in Amaral, 1929:87; see account of *Caudisona lecontei* on p. 328). *Cimarron*: 8 mi. W Boise City (ECSC). *Greer*: 10 mi. N Reed (FWCM). *Harmon*: 3 mi. W Hollis (UA); several within 6 mi. radius Hollis (FWCM). *Kiowa*: Lone Wolf (Van Vleet, 1902:173). *Texas*: near Texhoma (AMNH); 8 mi. SE Guymon (Ortenburger, 1927c:48). *Woods*: [Whitehorse Springs] (Ortenburger, 1927a:99, FMNH); Alva, and near Freedom (McCracken, 1966:30). *Woodward*: north of Mooreland (Carter, 1966:36).

Diadophis punctatus arnyi Kennicott

Prairie Ringneck Snake

Recognition.—Small dark gray snakes, having narrow, pale orange band or "ring" on neck, broken in some specimens; belly orange with black dots usually arranged irregularly; underside of tail red; dorsal scales smooth in 15 or 17 rows at midbody; anal plate divided.

Distribution.—Throughout the state (map, Fig. 86).

Remarks.—Gregarious, secretive, and burrowing, ringneck snakes are abundant in early spring under cover of one sort or another, often small limestone rocks on grassy or wooded hillsides. Records of occurrence indicate that individuals are less abundant in western than in eastern Oklahoma. In the western part of the state, ringnecks are associated with river floodplains, and small creeks and streams in ravines and canyons.

Snakes in eastern Oklahoma have 17 scale rows at midbody, whereas those in the Grassland of western Oklahoma have 15. Some snakes from southeastern Oklahoma are referable to the Mississippi ringneck snake, *Diadophis punctatus stictogenys*, in having 15 scale rows and black spots arranged in two parallel rows on the belly. Of 11 specimens from McCurtain County, nine have 15 scale rows. In eastern Oklahoma belly patterns are variable; spots are arranged irregularly, or in a single row, or in a double row. Further study is needed to determine the status of *stictogenys* in southeastern Oklahoma.

See Blanchard (1942:71–73, 75, 77, 79), Bonn and McCarley (1953:469), Burt (1935:328), Carpenter (1956:43; 1959c:34), Carter and Cox (1968), Force (1925a:27; 1925b:83; 1930:30), Kassing (1961:193), Ortenburger and Freeman (1930:182), Trowbridge (1937:295), Webb and Ortenburger (1955:89).

Specimens examined (OU except as indicated).—*Adair*: 9.4 mi. SSW Stilwell (KU); 3 mi. S Kansas. *Atoka*: Kiowa City Lake, 5 mi. S and 1 mi. E Kiowa, Pittsburg County (ECSC). *Blaine*: Roman Nose State Park; Longdale (NWSC). *Canadian*: 3 mi. SE Mustang. *Carter*: Ardmore; 5 mi. SE Ardmore. *Cherokee*: 2 mi. W Cookson, and 4 mi. N and 5 mi. E Tahlequah (KU); 0.5 mi. N Hanging Rock; 3 mi. N Scraper; 2 mi. S Scraper. *Cleveland*: 5 mi. S Norman; 17 mi. E Norman. *Comanche*: 5 mi. N Cache; Wichita Mts. Wildlife Refuge. *Creek*: Drumright. *Custer*: Weatherford (SWSC). *Delaware*: 6 mi. NE Grove; 3 mi. S Cleora. *Garvin*: Maysville. *Grady*: between Blanchard, McClain County, and Chickasha. *Kay*: 1 mi. E Ponca City. *Latimer*: 1.5 mi. N Wilburton; 8 mi. NW Wilburton. *LeFlore*: 15 mi. S Heavener; 5 mi. E Page; 6 mi. SW Page. *Logan*: Guthrie. *Marshall*: UOBS. *Mayes*: 4–5 mi. S Locust Grove. *McClain*: 5 mi. SW Norman, Cleveland County. *McCurtain*: 2 mi. E Idabel; Beavers Bend State Park; 4 mi. SE Smithville, and 10 mi. E Broken Bow (OSU); 3.3 mi. N Broken Bow. *Murray*: Sulphur (KU); Dougherty; Arbuckle Mts. *Oklahoma*: Oklahoma

City. *Okmulgee*: Okmulgee. *Osage*: near Okesa; 2 mi. NE Sand Springs, Tulsa County. *Ottawa*: 4 mi. S and 3.5 mi. E Quapaw, and 1 mi. S and 2 mi. E Quapaw (KU); Wyandotte. *Payne*: near Ripley. *Pottawatomie*: Shawnee; 5 mi. E Shawnee. *Roger Mills*: Antelope Hills, 6 mi. NE Durham. *Rogers*: 8 mi. E Catoosa; 1 mi. W Catoosa. *Seminole*: Bowlegs. *Stephens*: Lake Duncan. *Tulsa*: Tulsa; 2 mi. S Sand Springs; 5–7 mi. W Tulsa; 9 mi. SE Tulsa; Red Fork. *Wagoner*: 2 mi. S Catoosa, Rogers County; 2 mi. S Okay (KU). *Woodward*: W Quinlan.

Additional records.—Alfalfa: Salt Fork River, N Cherokee (McCoy, 1960a:42). *Atoka*: 14 mi. SE Stringtown (INHS). *Beaver*: Berend's Draw [near Gate] (UMMZ). *Bryan*: 11 mi. NW Durant (Laughlin, 1964:62). *Canadian*: Methodist Camp, Devils Canyon (ECSC). *Cherokee*: 4 mi. SE Cookson (KU). *Choctaw*: 7 mi. W Fort Towson (FMNH). *Cimarron*: 6 mi. N Kenton (Carter, 1966:34); Lake Carl Etling, Black Mesa State Park (ECSC). *Cleveland*: 2 mi. S Norman (Carpenter, 1959c:34); 8 mi. NNE Norman (OU). *Comanche*: Fort Sill (Blanchard, 1942:80). *Cotton*: near mouth Cache Creek (McCoy in Smith, Maslin, and Brown, 1965:30–31; if "mouth" of Cache Creek is correct, the county is more likely Cotton than Comanche; I can find no evidence that the reported collector, Amiel W. Whipple, was near Cache Creek, see p. 11). *Creek*: 2 mi. W Bristow (Burt, 1935:238). *Custer*: 2 mi. E Clinton (RWA). *Garvin*: 4 mi. N Stratford (ECSC). *Hughes*: 10 mi. E Wetumka (UMMZ). *Jefferson*: 6 mi. S Waurika (ECSC). *Johnston*: 2 mi. W Connerville, and 4 mi. S Mill Creek (ECSC). *Kay*: 3 mi. NE Ponca City (OSU). *Kingfisher*: Hennessey (Cope, 1894:387). *Kiowa*: 2 mi. S Lugert (McCoy, 1960a:42). *Latimer*: 1 mi. S Robber's Cave, and Wilburton (TCWC). *LeFlore*: Wister (Blanchard, 1942:80); Sugarloaf Mt. (Stone, 1903:541). *Major*: 3 mi. W Bouse Junction [12 mi. S Waynoka, Woods County, junction State Highway 15 and U.S. Highway 281] (McCoy, 1960a:42). *Mayes*: Camp Scott, about 6 mi. S Locust Grove on Spring Creek (OSU). *Murray*: Camp Classen (OSU). *Muskogee*: 3 mi. S and 3 mi. W Porum (HAD); Greenleaf Lake (UMMZ). *Noble*: 5 mi. E Perry (OSU). *Osage*: 4 mi. W Pawhuska, and 2 mi. SE Avant

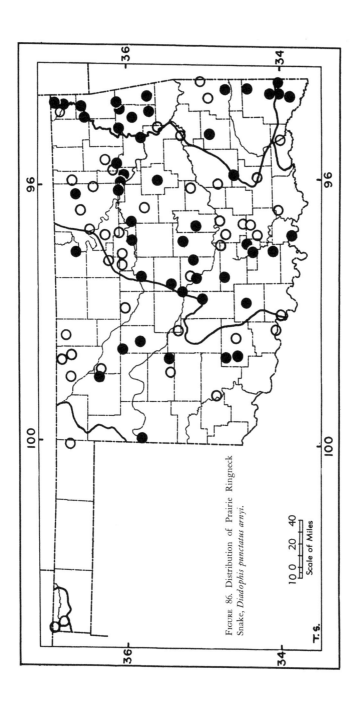

FIGURE 86. Distribution of Prairie Ringneck Snake, *Diadophis punctatus arnyi*.

Scale of Miles

10 0 20 40

T. S.

(Burt and Hoyle, 1935:205); S Fairfax (OSU). *Ottawa*: Miami (FWCM). *Pawnee*: 2 mi. SE Pawnee, and 2 mi. N Pawnee (Burt, 1935:328). *Payne*: Lake Carl Blackwell, and several within 5 mi. radius Stillwater (OSU); 4 mi. W Quay (Burt, 1935:328). *Pittsburg*: 5 mi. SE Stuart, Hughes County (Carter, 1966:34). *Pontotoc*: 7 mi. NE Ada (Carter, 1966:34); 10 mi. W Ada, and 5 mi. S Fittstown (ECSC). *Rogers*: 2 mi. NE Garnett, Tulsa County (UMMZ); 6 mi. E Catoosa (Dundee and Burger, 1948); near Claremore (MCZ); 7 mi. W Claremore (KU); 6 mi. W Claremore (Burt and Hoyle, 1935:205); Tulsa Fin and Feather Club (OSU). *Washington*: Bartlesville (AMNH). *Woods*: 1.5 mi. E Tegarden (McCoy, 1960a:42); Alva, and 12.5 mi. N and 6 mi. W Alva (McCracken, 1966:14).

Elaphe guttata emoryi (Baird and Girard)

Great Plains Rat Snake

Recognition.—Pale gray or buff snakes, having brownish or red brown blotches with narrow dark outlines; large middorsal blotches more than 35 on body, slightly narrowed and bandlike across back; dark stripes on neck usually uniting to form point between eyes; belly checkered or smudged with dark marks; dorsal scales smooth or weakly keeled, usually in 27 (or 29) rows at midbody; anal plate divided.

Distribution.—Throughout the state (map, Fig. 87).

Remarks.—Although records of occurrence are relatively scattered, and lacking in northeastern Oklahoma, the known distribution of the species indicates that it occurs throughout the state. Great Plains rat snakes are less frequently observed than black rat snakes (*Elaphe obsoleta*), and there is little known about them in Oklahoma. Individuals may prefer the vicinity of water; in the Wichita Mountains, one was captured in dense grass and brush along West Cache Creek, and two were collected along the shore of Lake Lawtonka. In Kiowa County one

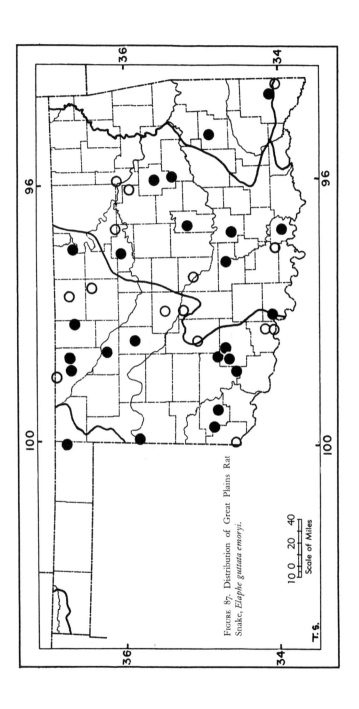

FIGURE 87. Distribution of Great Plains Rat Snake, *Elaphe guttata emoryi*.

Scale of Miles

10 0 20 40

T. S.

was found in "a cave 60 feet deep" (field notes of A. I. Ortenburger). A hibernating aggregation of 6 *Elaphe guttata* and 27 *Coluber constrictor* was discovered during removal of the cement foundation of a house on December 17, 1963 (west of Alva, Woods County).

Records of *guttata* from Drumright, Creek County, and from Cleveland County (Ortenburger, 1925:85) are based on young specimens of *Elaphe obsoleta*.

See Carpenter (1958b:115), Dowling (1951), Twente (1955: 388).

Specimens examined (OU except as indicated).—*Alfalfa*: 7 mi. NE Jet. *Beaver*: near Gate. *Blaine*: 2–6 mi. N Watonga. *Comanche*: Wichita Mts. Wildlife Refuge; Lake Lawtonka. *Garvin*: Pauls Valley. *Greer*: 3 mi. S Mangum. *Harmon*: NW Reed, Greer County. *Jefferson*: near Waurika (ECSC). *Kay*: 3 mi. N and 5 mi. E Ponca City. *Kiowa*: 3 mi. E Snyder; 10 mi. NW Meers, Comanche County. *Latimer*: 0.5 mi. W Wilburton. *Major*: E Glass Mts. *Marshall*: 5 mi. S Madill. *McCurtain*: Beavers Bend State Park. *Okmulgee*: Okmulgee; 4 mi. SE Henryetta. *Payne*: 3 mi. S Stillwater (OSU). *Pontotoc*: 10 mi. SW Ada (ECSC). *Roger Mills*: 6 mi. NE Durham. *Seminole*: Seminole. *Woods*: 1.5 mi. E Tegarden (OSU); 12 mi. W Alva (KU); 7 mi. W Alva, and 8 mi. NW Alva (ECSC).

Additional records.—*Caddo*: Fort Cobb (Ortenburger, 1925:85). *Canadian*: no data (Carpenter, 1958a:74). *Carter*: 8 mi. SE Ardmore (ECSC). *Cleveland*: 2 mi. S Norman (Carpenter, 1958a:74). *Cotton*: 12 mi. S Temple (UMMZ); 1.5 mi. S Temple City Lake (Carpenter, 1958a:74). *Creek*: Sapulpa (Blanchard, 1921:122). *Garfield*: 5 mi. SE Hunter (Burt, 1935:330). *Grady*: near Minco (Carpenter, 1958a:74). *Grant*: 1 mi. E Medford (Burt and Hoyle, 1935:207). *Harmon*: 3 mi. W and 2.5 mi. S Hollis (FWCM). *McCurtain*: 3 mi. W Eagletown (UMMZ). *Pawnee*: near Quay (Ortenburger, 1930a:94). *Tulsa*: Tulsa (USNM). *Woods*: Merrihew Cave (Twente, 1955:388).

Elaphe obsoleta obsoleta (Say)

Black Rat Snake

Recognition.—Adults large (up to at least 5.5 feet), blackish above with scattered whitish flecks and red between scales, and often with obscure blotched pattern; belly mostly whitish, especially chin and throat, but often smudged or clouded with pale gray; dorsal scales smooth or weakly keeled in 25, 27 or 29 rows at midbody; anal plate divided. Young having conspicuous blotched pattern; large, dark purplish middorsal blotches, often with pale centers, fewer than 35 on body, mostly squarish or rectangular, and slightly biconcave anteroposteriorly; belly having contrasting checked pattern with pigment especially concentrated posteriorly and on underside of tail.

Distribution.—Eastern Oklahoma; known as far west as Woodward, Roger Mills, and Kiowa counties (map, Fig. 88).

Remarks.—Black rat snakes are frequently observed in daytime in wooded or shrubby areas of the Interior Highlands, Oak-Woodland, and parts of the Grassland. Both young and adults climb trees and shrubs, and are often associated with human habitation. One individual was found at night coiled in the pulpy interior of a large log near a copperhead and a speckled kingsnake, each species about one foot apart (Marshall County); another was found coiled in a mockingbird nest built about two feet above the ground in a wild rose bush, and had eaten two mourning dove eggs (ornithological identifications by Dr. George M. Sutton). The only other data for the black rat snake are these: two eggs of a brood that was found in a tree stump in August hatched in September (Marshall County), and a young rat snake about 110 mm long was eaten by a speckled kingsnake 104 mm long.

See Bonn and McCarley (1953:470), Burt (1935:330), Carpenter (1956:43; 1958b:115; 1959c:34), Carter and Cox (1968),

Dowling (1951), Dundee (1950b), Force (1925a:27; 1925b:83; 1930:31), Gehlbach (1956), Ortenburger and Freeman (1930: 184), Trowbridge (1937:296), Van Vleet (1902:170).

Specimens examined (OU except as indicated).—*Adair*: Proctor. *Alfalfa*: 7 mi. NE Jet. *Atoka*: 7 mi. SW Daisy; 5 mi. N Atoka. *Blaine*: Roman Nose State Park. *Bryan*: Durant. *Canadian*: 24 mi. W Oklahoma City, Oklahoma County. *Carter*: Ardmore. *Cherokee*: 6 mi. NE Tahlequah. *Cleveland*: several within 4 mi. radius Norman; Noble; Moore; 6 mi. E Norman. *Comanche*: 12 mi. E Lawton; 5 mi. N Cache; Wichita Mts. Wildlife Refuge; Lake Lawtonka. *Creek*: Drumright. *Delaware*: 7 mi. NE Grove. *Garvin*: Maysville. *Grant*: 2 mi. W Lamont (ECSC, albino). *Haskell*: 3.5 mi. E Stigler. *Hughes*: 2 mi. N Yeager. *Johnston*: 2.5 mi. NW Ravia. *Kay*: Ponca City; 8 mi. E Ponca City. *Kiowa*: Cooperton. *Latimer*: Wilburton; 7 mi. W Wilburton; 7 and 9 mi. N Wilburton. *LeFlore*: 5 mi. E Big Cedar; 6.5 mi. W Heavener; 1.5 mi. E Zoe; near Wister. *Logan*: 2 mi. S and 2 mi. E Guthrie. *Major*: 7 mi. SE Cleo Springs; 7.7 mi. E Chester (RGW). *Marshall*: several within 2 mi. radius Willis; 7 mi. N and 2 mi. E Willis. *Mayes*: Locust Grove. *McCurtain*: 10 and 14 mi. SE Broken Bow; 4 mi. S Smithville; 6 mi. N Idabel; 1 mi. W Oklahoma-Arkansas state line on Red River. *Murray*: Dougherty; Price's Falls; Platt National Park (KU). *Muskogee*: 6 mi. E Fort Gibson. *Okmulgee*: Okmulgee. *Osage*: 7 mi. NE Sand Springs, Tulsa County. *Ottawa*: 3 mi. SW Peoria (KU). *Pawnee*: near Quay. *Payne*: Stillwater; 2 mi. W Stillwater; Lake Carl Blackwell. *Pittsburg*: 11 mi. E McAlester. *Pottawatomie*: Shawnee; 7 mi. E Shawnee. *Pushmataha*: 4 mi. E Tuskahoma. *Roger Mills*: 7 mi. N Cheyenne. *Seminole*: Bowlegs; Seminole. *Stephens*: Duncan. *Tulsa*: Tulsa; 4 mi. S Tulsa; 7 mi. NE Tulsa. *Wagoner*: 2 mi. S Catoosa, and 6 mi. SE Catoosa, Rogers County. *Washita*: Corn. *Woods*: Alva (NWSC).

Additional records.—*Adair*: 5 mi. S Kansas, Delaware County (UMMZ). *Bryan*: 1 mi. N Denison Dam (TCWC); 10 mi. N Bennington (TNHC). *Blaine*: SW Okeene (TNHC). *Canadian*: Methodist Camp, Devils Canyon (ECSC). *Cherokee*: 3 mi. E Tahlequah (FWCM); Scraper (UMMZ); Camp Muskogee (OSU);

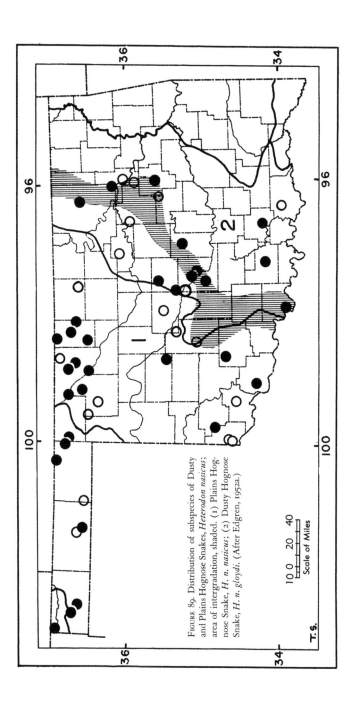

FIGURE 89. Distribution of subspecies of Dusty and Plains Hognose Snakes, *Heterodon nasicus*; area of intergradation, shaded. (1) Plains Hognose Snake, *H. n. nasicus*; (2) Dusty Hognose Snake, *H. n. gloydi*. (After Edgren, 1952a.)

Scale of Miles

5 mi. E Muskogee, and 11 mi. E Tahlequah (OU). *Coal*: 4 mi. NE
Coalgate (Carpenter, 1958a:74). *Creek*: Sapulpa (Schmidt, 1919:
71). *Garfield*: 5 mi. W Garber (CCC). *Haskell*: 4 mi. S and 3 mi.
E Quinton, Pittsburg County (HAD). *Johnston*: 1 mi. E and 4 mi.
S Tishomingo (ECSC). *LeFlore*: Poteau (UA); 0.5 mi. NE Braden
(OSU). *Marshall*: 9 mi. E Madill (SESC). *Mayes*: Chouteau
(UMMZ). *McCurtain*: 7.6 mi. S Broken Bow (TTC); Smithville
(TU). *Noble*: 5 mi. N Orlando, Logan County (Burt, 1935:330).
Okfuskee: 3 mi. W Okfuskee (ECSC); 3 mi. E Okemah (ECSC).
Oklahoma: 2 mi. E Oklahoma City (Carpenter, 1958a:74). *Payne*:
6 mi. E Cushing (Burt, 1935:330). *Pontotoc*: 7 mi. NE Ada (Carter,
1966:34). *Rogers*: 6 mi. E Catoosa (Dundee and Burger, 1948);
Tulsa Fin and Feather Club (OSU). *Sequoyah*: 10 mi. NE Gore
(OSU); 1 mi. S Marble City (UA); Dwight Mission (Carpenter,
1958a:74). *Tulsa*: 3 mi. E Bixby (Burt, 1935:330); Broken Arrow
(FWCM); Mohawk Park, and Garnett (UMMZ); Red Fork (UI).
Woodward: Fort Supply (Cope, 1894:387).

Farancia abacura reinwardti Schlegel

Western Mud Snake

Recognition.—Shiny, black or blue black snakes, having alternating black and red orange bars on belly; internasals fused into
single scale; no preocular; dorsal scales smooth (keeled above
anus in some specimens), in 19 rows throughout length of body;
anal plate divided.

Distribution.—Known only from McCurtain County in extreme southeastern Oklahoma.

Remarks.—The western mud snake is confined to the Coastal
Plain. Two specimens were found active on a highway on a
rainy night; data concerning another are: "born Sept. 20, 1947
from egg laid Aug. 14." See Burger (1948) and Curd (1950).

Specimens examined (all OU).—*McCurtain*: 10 mi. S Eagletown;
20 mi. SE Idabel, S Tom; Little River bridge on U.S. Highway 70.

Additional records.—McCurtain: Grassy Lake (Curd, 1950, OSU); 1 mi. W Oklahoma-Arkansas state line on State Highway 87, E edge Idabel, and 11 mi. S Idabel (ECSC).

Heterodon nasicus Baird and Girard

Dusty and Plains Hognose Snakes

Recognition.—Heavy-bodied snakes with upturned snout; rostral enlarged, broadened, and keeled above; several small scales behind rostral separating internasals and prefrontals; dorsal pattern of brownish blotches; belly mostly blackish with pale areas orange in life; dorsal scales keeled in 23 (or 21) rows at midbody; anal plate divided.

Distribution.—Western Oklahoma; known as far east as Tulsa, Okmulgee, and Bryan counties; two subspecies (map, Fig. 89).

Remarks.—Edgren (1952b) recognized two subspecies of *Heterodon nasicus* in Oklahoma:

H. n. nasicus Baird and Girard, Plains Hognose Snake.— Large, dark brown middorsal blotches, usually more than 35 in males and more than 40 in females; blotches well defined.
H. n. gloydi Edgren, Dusty Hognose Snake.—Blotches fewer than 35 in males and fewer than 40 in females; blotches ill defined.

The range map presented by Smith and Smith (1962:7, Fig. 3) suggests that *H. n. nasicus* is found mostly in the High Plains, and *H. n. gloydi* mostly in the Oak-Woodland. Edgren (1952a: 211–213) designated specimens from Caddo, Cleveland, Osage, and Okmulgee counties as intergrades between the two subspecies; the easternmost specimen of *nasicus* was from Creek County, and the westernmost specimen of *gloydi* from the Neutral Strip (see Fig. 3). Intergradation seems to occur throughout most of the Oak-Woodland. The subspecies *gloydi* seems to be weakly defined in Oklahoma, and the status of both subspecies remains to be worked out by future investigators.

Hognose snakes are harmless and rarely bite, but when intimidated they may flatten the head and neck, hiss, open the mouth, and roll over with belly up and "play possum." They have thus earned the name of "puff (or spreading) adders." The species is often found in loose-soiled areas; many specimens in western Oklahoma have been collected in sandy areas along the Canadian River. One snake was found in an open field under a pile of corn stalks; others have been found under rocks in Osage County (Harold A. Dundee, personal communication). A gravid female from Beaver County measured 360 mm in length.

See Force (1930:30), Moore and Rigney (1942:79), Ortenburger and Bird (1933:61), Ortenburger and Freeman (1930: 183).

Specimens examined (OU except as indicated).—*Alfalfa*: 4 mi. E Cherokee; 4 mi. S Salt Plains Dam; 2 mi. S Carmen; 9 mi. N Driftwood (KU). *Beaver*: near Gate; Cimarron River, 1 mi. S Kansas-Oklahoma state line (KU). *Carter*: no data. *Cimarron*: 7 mi. S Boise City; 11 mi. W Boise City; 8 mi. SW Boise City; 3 mi. N Kenton; 1 mi. SE of NW corner of state. *Cleveland*: 3 mi. W Norman; 3 mi. E Noble. *Comanche*: Wichita Mts. Wildlife Refuge. *Custer*: Weatherford. *Harmon*: 3 mi. W Reed, Greer County (RGW). *Harper*: near Gate, Beaver County. *Jefferson*: 4 mi. ESE Ryan. *Johnston*: 3 mi. E and 4 mi. N Tishomingo (ECSC). *McClain*: no data. *Oklahoma*: near Wheatland; Edmond. *Okmulgee*: Okmulgee. *Osage*: NW edge Tulsa, Tulsa County; 6.5 mi. E Pawhuska. *Pottawatomie*: Shawnee. *Texas*: 8 mi. SE Guymon. *Tillman*: 4.2 mi. W Frederick. *Woods*: 3 mi. S Waynoka; 1.5 mi. W Edith; 10 mi. SW Alva; 12 mi. W Alva (KU). *Woodward*: 11 mi. SW Freedom, Woods County.

Additional records.—*Beaver*: 5 mi. E Texas-Beaver county line on State Highway 3 (OSU). *Bryan*: Durant (Laughlin, 1964:62).

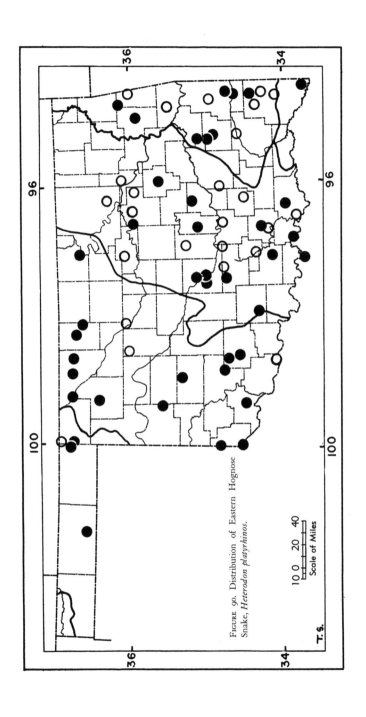

FIGURE 90. Distribution of Eastern Hognose Snake, *Heterodon platyrhinos*.

Scale of Miles

10 0 20 40

T. ᴤ.

Caddo: Fort Cobb (Cope, 1900:777). *Canadian*: Methodist Camp, Devils Canyon (ECSC); El Reno, North Fork Canadian River (FMNH). *Cimarron*: 5 mi. W Boise City, and S Graham [Graham is about 5 mi. E Kenton on Cimarron River] (OSU). *Cleveland*: 2 mi. S Norman (AMNH). *Creek*: Drumright (FMNH). *Grant*: Lamont (ECSC). *Harmon*: 3 mi. W Hollis (UA); several within 6 mi. radius Hollis (FWCM). *Jackson*: Altus (TTC). *McClain*: 4 mi. NW Newcastle (ECSC). *Okfuskee*: just E Okfuskee (ECSC). *Payne*: Stillwater (Moore and Rigney, 1942:79). *Texas*: 1 mi. N Guymon (OSU). *Tulsa*: 6 mi. S Tulsa (McCoy, 1960a:42); S Glenpool (KKA). *Woodward*: Fort Supply (Cope, 1894:387); Southern Great Plains Experimental Range, 1 mi. S Woodward (KKA). *Woods*: 8 mi. NW Alva, 12 mi. N and 6 mi. W Alva, 9 mi. N and 3 mi. W Alva (McCracken, 1966:15).

Heterodon platyrhinos Latreille

Eastern Hognose Snake

Recognition.—Heavy-bodied snakes with spadelike snout; rostral scale slightly enlarged and keeled; one small azygous scale separating internasals; body usually with pattern of dark brown blotches on pale brownish or yellowish, but some specimens are uniformly dark brown; belly usually light with pale gray smudging, but may be black posteriorly; underside of tail paler than belly; dorsal scales keeled in 25 rows at midbody; anal plate divided.

Distribution.—Throughout the state (map, Fig. 90).

Remarks.—*Heterodon platyrhinos* also displays the bluffing, defensive behavior of *H. nasicus*. Judging from field data, the principal habitat of this species in western Oklahoma seems to be vegetated places along floodplains of rivers and streams. Individuals have been found under logs and trash; one was captured while motionless and outstretched in the branches of a small shrub about two feet above the ground. One snake ate

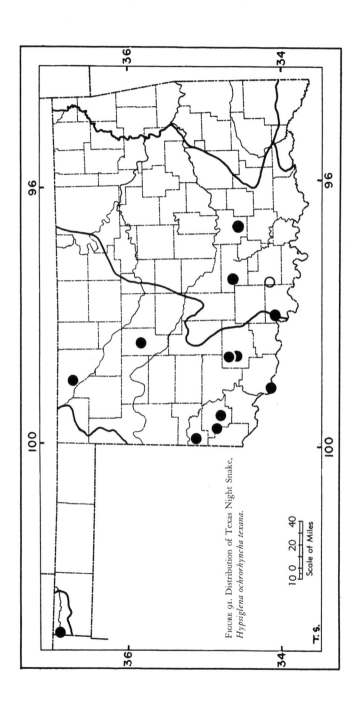

FIGURE 91. Distribution of Texas Night Snake, *Hypsiglena ochrorhyncha texana*.

two ranid frogs. A captive laid two eggs on July 19, two on the 20th, two the 22nd, two the 23rd, and 17 eggs on July 24 (Marshall County); average measurements and weight of these eggs were 18.6 x 28.6 (18–20 x 24–30) mm, and 4.8 (3.9–6.0) grams.

See Bonn and McCarley (1953:469), Carpenter (1956:43; 1958b: 114), Carter and Cox (1968), Edgren (1957:134; 1961); Force (1925a:27; 1925b:83; 1930:30), Klau and David (1952, based in part on Oklahoma specimens), Mahaffey (1954, possibly *nasicus*), Ortenburger and Bird (1933:61), Ortenburger and Freeman (1930:182), Smith and Leonard (1934:193–194), Trowbridge (1937:295), Van Vleet (1902:169).

Specimens examined (OU except as indicated).—*Adair*: 5.5 mi. S Kansas, Delaware County (TTC). *Alfalfa*: 4 mi. E Cherokee; 3 and 7 mi. NE Jet. *Beaver*: near Gate. *Bryan*: near Durant. *Carter*: Ardmore. *Cherokee*: 2 mi. NE Eldon. *Cleveland*: vicinity Norman. *Comanche*: 5 mi. N Cache; Wichita Mts. Wildlife Refuge. *Creek*: Drumright. *Garvin*: Maysville. *Harmon*: 7 mi. SW Hollis; 0.5 mi. W Madge (KU). *Harper*: near Gate, Beaver County. *Haskell*: 2.5 mi. SE Quinton, Pittsburg County. *Hughes*: near Wetumka. *Jackson*: 6 mi. S Altus. *Johnston*: no data. *Kay*: Ponca City. *Kiowa*: Cooperton; 7 mi. SE Cooperton. *Latimer*: Wilburton; 2 mi. N Wilburton; 8 mi. NW Wilburton. *LeFlore*: 5.2 mi. E Zoe; 5 mi. E Big Cedar. *Love*: 4 mi. SE Thackerville. *Marshall*: UOBS. *McClain*: 4 mi. N Purcell; near Washington. *McCurtain*: 2 mi. SW Smithville; Tom. *Okmulgee*: Okmulgee. *Roger Mills*: Hammon. *Seminole*: Bowlegs. *Stephens*: near Comanche. *Texas*: 8 mi. SE Guymon. *Washita*: Bessie. *Woods*: 1.5 mi. W Edith; Alva; 12 mi. W Alva (KU). *Woodward*: 4.5 mi. E and 1 mi. N Woodward.

Additional records.—*Adair*: near Westville (Carpenter, 1958a: 73). *Blaine*: Canton Dam (McCoy, 1960a:42). *Bryan*: Colbert (TNHC). *Coal*: 2 mi. N Coalgate (ECSC). *Creek*: Sapulpa (Schmidt, 1919:71); 3 mi. W Brown's Creek on State Highway 33 (OSU). *Garvin*: 1 mi. N Paoli (FMNH); 4.5 mi. N Stratford (ECSC). *Harper*: Cimarron River, S Englewood, Kansas (Smith and Leonard, 1934:193). *Johnston*: 0.5 mi. W Tishomingo

(TCWC). *Kingfisher*: 3 mi. W Cimarron River on State Highway 51 (McCoy, 1960a:42). *LeFlore*: 6 mi. N Stapp (Trowbridge, 1937); Wister (CM). *McCurtain*: 1 mi. S Bethel, State Game Refuge, and Beavers Bend State Park (CCC). *Murray*: Dougherty (Ortenburger, 1925). *Osage*: 16 mi. W Skiatook, Tulsa County (TNHC). *Payne*: Stillwater, and 3 mi. E Stillwater (OSU). *Pittsburg*: 5 mi. SE Stuart, Hughes County (Carter, 1966:34). *Pontotoc*: 7 mi. NE Ada (Carter, 1966:34). *Pottawatomie*: within 12 mi. radius Shawnee (Webster, 1936:21). *Pushmataha*: 3 mi. E Tuskahoma (FMNH). *Sequoyah*: Dwight Mission (CCC). *Tillman*: 5.5 mi. S Grandfield (CCC). *Tulsa*: no data (Ortenburger, 1927a:96). *Woodward*: 0.5 mi. N and 2.5 E Woodward (OSU).

Hypsiglena ochrorhyncha texana Stejneger

Texas Night Snake

Recognition.—Relatively small snakes (rarely exceeding one and a half feet); pupils vertically elliptical; head gray with light-edged, dark postocular stripe; dorsal pattern of gray or brownish spots; three large elongate brown black blotches, often fused, on neck; belly whitish, unmarked; dorsal scales smooth in 21 (or 23) rows at midbody; anal plate divided.

Distribution.—Western Oklahoma; known as far east as Blaine and Pontotoc counties (map, Fig. 91).

Remarks.—Night snakes penetrate the Oak-Woodland but seem most abundant in the Grassland, and are doubtless more abundant than the few records of occurrence indicate. Individuals are nocturnal and frequent rocky areas having a dissected topography, where they may be found by day under rocks, especially after rains. A characteristic defensive posture that can be induced by intimidation is a flattening of the head and body, with occasional hissing and orientation of the body in a slightly raised spiral with the head at the apex. See account of *Leptotyphlops dulcis*.

235

Dixon (1965) has shown that *ochrorhyncha* and *torquata* are distinct species. Based on a study of specimens of *ochrorhyncha*, principally from the Mexican plateau, Dixon was unable to distinguish the two subspecies *H. o. jani* and *H. o. texana*, and suggested that *texana* be a synonym of *jani*. Nevertheless, until spotted night snakes are studied from elsewhere in the range of the genus, the name *texana* is retained for Oklahoma specimens. See Dundee (1950a), Kuntz (1940).

Specimens examined (OU except as indicated).—*Beckham*: 6 mi. SW Erick. *Blaine*: Roman Nose State Park. *Cimarron*: 3 mi. N Kenton; 5 mi. E Kenton. *Comanche*: 3.5 mi. N Cache; 5 mi. NW Cache; Wichita Mts. Wildlife Refuge. *Garvin*: 7.5 mi. NW Elmore City (ECSC). *Greer*: 2–3 mi. SW Mangum. *Harmon*: NW Reed, Greer County. *Jefferson*: near Waurika (ECSC). *Pontotoc*: Byrd's Mill Spring near Fittstown (ECSC). *Tillman*: 2 mi. S Davidson. *Woods*: 1.6 mi. E Tegarden.

Additional records.—*Carter*: 2 mi. W Healdton (ECSC). *Greer*: 2.5 mi. S Mangum (FMNH); 3 mi. W and 1 mi. S Reed (OSU).

Lampropeltis calligaster calligaster (Harlan)

Prairie Kingsnake

Recognition.—Blotched snakes, some having short, dark, dorsolateral streaks on neck; middorsal blotches brownish or red brown, narrowly outlined in black, oriented transversely and broken into spots in some specimens, and alternating with small dark blotches on sides; belly with irregular, cloudy markings, or with well-defined markings, or nearly immaculate; dorsal pattern often obscure in adults, but prominent in young; dorsal scale rows smooth in 25 rows at midbody; anal plate single.

Distribution.—Throughout the state (map, Fig. 92).

Remarks.—An eastern species for which records of occurrence

236

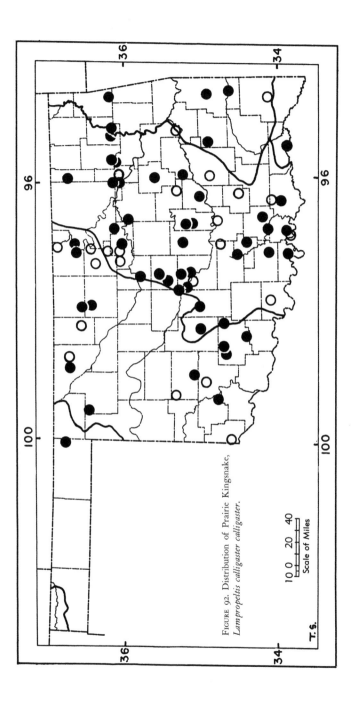

FIGURE 92. Distribution of Prairie Kingsnake,
Lampropeltis calligaster calligaster.

10 0 20 40

Scale of Miles

T. s.

are lacking for most of the panhandle, the prairie kingsnake is considered to occur throughout the state because of its distribution in neighboring states. Most records are in the Grassland and Oak-Woodland. Individuals are not uncommon around human habitation and are often found dead on highways. The snake representing the westernmost known record (Beaver County) was active late at night on a dirt road after a rain. Each stomach of two snakes contained one *Cnemidophorus sexlineatus*.

The individual of this species reported from Sapulpa by Schmidt (1919:71) was redetermined as *Elaphe guttata* by Blanchard (1921:122).

See Bonn and McCarley (1953:470), Carpenter (1956:43; 1958b:115; 1959c:34), Carter and Cox (1968), Fitch (1954:137), Force (1930:32), Kern (1956), Trowbridge (1937:297).

Specimens examined (OU except as indicated).—*Beaver*: near Gate. *Bryan*: near Durant. *Caddo*: 5 mi. S Anadarko. *Canadian*: 3 mi. SE Mustang. *Carter*: 2 mi. E Ardmore. *Choctaw*: Red River Fisheries. *Cleveland*: several within 6 mi. radius Norman; 5 mi. E Hollywood; 1 mi. S Moore. *Comanche*: 7 mi. S Lawton; 3 mi. E Meers; 2.5 mi. SE Sterling; Wichita Mts. Wildlife Refuge. *Creek*: Drumright (KU). *Delaware*: near Flint. *Garfield*: 10 mi. N Enid. *Grady*: Chickasha. *Grant*: 4 mi. W Pond Creek. *Greer*: 1 mi. S Quartz Mountain State Park. *Hughes*: no data. *Johnston*: 3.2 mi. N Milburn; 10 mi. N Madill, Marshall County. *Kay*: Ponca City; 8 mi. E Ponca City. *Latimer*: 10 mi. W Wilburton. *LeFlore*: 6.5 mi. W Heavener; 5 mi. E Big Cedar. *Logan*: Guthrie. *Love*: 1.3 mi. W Marietta. *Marshall*: Shay. *Mayes*: 0.5 mi. E Grand River on State Highway 33; Locust Grove. *McClain*: 2 mi. W Newcastle. *McIntosh*: 4.8 mi. E Hughes County line on State Highway 9. *Murray*: 4 mi. S Wynnewood, Garvin County; Platt National Park. *Oklahoma*: 12 mi. NW Oklahoma City; 3 mi. S Oklahoma City; near Oklahoma City. *Okmulgee*: near Okmulgee. *Osage*: NW edge Tulsa, Tulsa County. *Pawnee*: near Quay. *Payne*: no data. *Pottawatomie*: Shawnee. *Rogers*: 5.6 mi. E Catoosa. *Seminole*: Seminole;

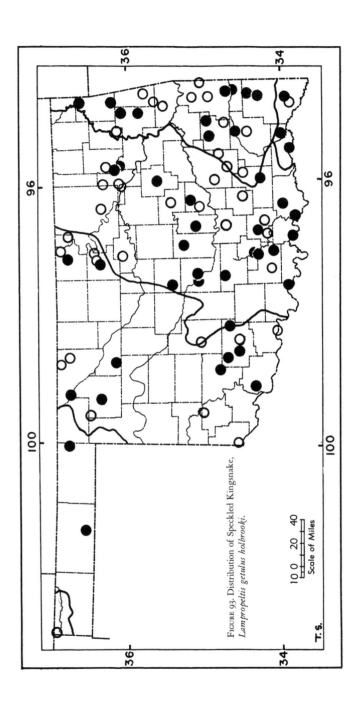

FIGURE 93. Distribution of Speckled Kingsnake, *Lampropeltis getulus holbrooki.*

T. S.

Scale of Miles

Bowlegs. *Tulsa*: 5 and 6 mi. SW Tulsa. *Wagoner*: 2 mi. S Catoosa, Rogers County. *Washington*: near Bartlesville (KU). *Washita*: 3 mi. E Rocky. *Woods*: 12 mi. W Alva (KU). *Woodward*: north side Fort Supply Dam.

Additional records.—Alfalfa: 4 mi. W and 3 mi. S Jet (Carter, 1966:35). *Bryan*: 5 mi. E Caddo (SESC). *Coal*: 6 mi. N Coalgate (ECSC). *Garvin*: near Stratford (Carter, 1966:35). *Harmon*: 2.7 mi. W Hollis (FWCM). *Jefferson*: 18.3 mi. W Ringling (Carpenter, 1958a:74). *Johnston*: 3 mi. S Tishomingo (ECSC). *Kay*: 6 mi. NE Newkirk (Burt and Hoyle, 1935:210). *Kiowa*: Hobart (OSU). *Latimer*: 3 mi. W Wilburton (Carter, 1966:35). *Marshall*: UOBS (Carpenter, 1955a:40). *McClain*: Johnson's Pasture, 1 mi. S and 3 mi. W Norman, Cleveland County (OU). *McCurtain*: 5 mi. N entrance Beavers Bend State Park (Carpenter, 1955a:40). *Muskogee*: 2.5 mi. S Porum (HAD). *Noble*: 9 mi. N Perry (Burt and Burt, 1929b:11); 12 mi. N Stillwater, Payne County (UMMZ). *Okfuskee*: 4 mi. N Weleetka (ECSC). *Payne*: [within 3 mi. radius] Stillwater (Moore and Rigney, 1942); Sanborn Lake, Lake Carl Blackwell, and 1 mi. S Yost Lake (OSU). *Pawnee*: near Otoe Reservation, Noble County (OSU). *Pittsburg*: 11 mi. W McAlester (ECSC). *Pontotoc*: 7 mi. NE Ada (Carter, 1966:35). *Tulsa*: Tulsa (Blair, 1961); 3 mi. S Tulsa, and 7 mi. NE Tulsa (TNHC). *Washita*: 4.9 mi. E Elk City, Beckham County (RWA). *Woods*: Alva (Blanchard, 1921: 121).

Lampropeltis getulus holbrooki Stejneger

Speckled Kingsnake

*Recognition.—*Black snakes having small, pale yellow or white spot on almost every dorsal scale; back having narrow, short, pale crossbars separating black blotches in some specimens; belly evenly checked with black and pale yellow; dorsal scale rows smooth in 21 (or 23) rows at midbody; anal plate single.

*Distribution.—*Throughout the state (map, Fig. 93).

Remarks.—Speckled kingsnakes occur in many kinds of habitats, and, judging from casual observations, seem to be slightly more abundant than prairie kingsnakes. Individuals of *getulus* have been found on steep, rocky hillsides under rocks (McCurtain County), foraging in flat, mostly grassy places (Choctaw County), in decayed interiors of large logs (Marshall County), sunning outstretched across rock about 11:00 a.m. (Woodward County), by flood pools of the Kiamichi River (LeFlore County), in a small mammal burrow with head protruding (McClain County), in inhabited and urban areas (Cleveland County), and often in wooded areas along river floodplains. A female from near Noble, Cleveland County, laid 12 eggs on June 15, of which 11 hatched on August 17. See account of *Elaphe obsoleta* and *Natrix sipedon.*

The Sonora Kingsnake, *Lampropeltis getulus splendida,* characterized by a blotched pattern (narrow pale bands separating black blotches) on back, 23 scale rows at midbody, and a mostly black belly and head, has been reported from southwestern Oklahoma. Blanchard (1921:31) referred USNM 1697 to *splendida*; it is illustrated on Plate VII in Baird and Girard (1854) and seems to have a mostly black venter. Webb and Ortenburger (1955:90) discussed OU 26893 from the Wichita Mountains and referred it to *splendida*, and FMNH 69430 from the same place is cataloged as *splendida*; both snakes resemble *splendida* except for the speckled heads and evenly checkered black and yellow bellies.

Characteristics applicable to *splendida* have been noted in some individuals of *holbrooki.* Five of 71 Oklahoma specimens have 23 scale rows at midbody (*splendida*), but some *holbrooki* have 23 instead of 21 scale rows (Blanchard, 1921:25, 34, 105). Both young and adults of *holbrooki* may have pale yellow, black-speckled crossbars separated by black areas, as in *splendida*; this pattern is most often seen in young snakes. Adults having this pattern are mostly from western Oklahoma. In some specimens the narrow crossbars are solid pale yellow (not black-speckled). No Oklahoma specimen examined by me has shown all the characteristics of *splendida*, nor is there any indication that a population of *splendida* exists in Oklahoma. The two subspecies *holbrooki* and *splendida* may intergrade in south-western Oklahoma, with the Red River acting as a filter barrier (see page 49).

See Blanchard (1932), Carpenter (1956:43; 1957b; 1958b:115; 1959c:34), Carter and Cox (1968), Force (1925a:27; 1925b:83; 1930:32–33), Kassing (1961:187, probably *getulus*), Ortenburger and Freeman (1930:184), Trowbridge (1937:297).

Specimens examined (OU except as indicated).—*Atoka*: 15 mi. SE Atoka. *Beaver*: Gate. *Bryan*: near Durant; near Colbert. *Carter*: 5 mi. SE Ardmore; just S Murray County line on U.S. Highway 77. *Cherokee*: near Scraper; 4 mi. NE Welling. *Choctaw*: 8 mi. S Hugo; 4 mi. W Fort Towson. *Cleveland*: 4 mi. S Norman; 2 mi. E Noble. *Comanche*: 11 mi. W Lawton; 6 mi. SW Sterling; Wichita Mts. Wildlife Refuge. *Delaware*: 7 mi. NE Grove; Dripping Springs; 1 mi. E Kansas (KU). *Garvin*: Maysville. *Hughes*: near Wetumka. *Jefferson*: near Petersburg. *Johnston*: Ballard Park near Reagan. *Kay*: no data. *Kiowa*: Cooperton. *Latimer*: Wilburton; 3 mi. N Red Oak; Robbers Cave State Park (NWSC). *LeFlore*: 6 mi. SW Page; 5 mi. E Big Cedar. *Major*: 11.5 mi. E Chester (TTC). *Marshall*: UOBS. *McClain*: 5 mi. W Norman, Cleveland County. *McCurtain*: 6 mi. N Idabel; 1 mi. SW Smithville; 6 mi. E Sherwood. *Murray*: Dougherty; Arbuckle Mts. *Noble*: no data. *Oklahoma*: 1 mi. SE Oklahoma City. *Okmulgee*: Okmulgee. *Pottawatomie*: Shawnee. *Pushmataha*: 4 mi. E Tuskahoma. *Rogers*: 1 mi. W Catoosa. *Seminole*: Bowlegs. *Texas*: 8 mi. SE Guymon. *Tillman*: E part of county. *Wagoner*: 2 mi. S Catoosa, Rogers County. *Woods*: 2 mi. W Edith. *Woodward*: 6 mi. E Woodward.

Additional records.—*Adair*: 5 mi. SE Stilwell, and 4 mi. S Stilwell (UI); 3 mi. S Bunch (KU). *Atoka*: 14 mi. NE Stringtown (UI). *Caddo*: Fort Cobb (Blanchard, 1921:40). *Carter*: Ardmore (AMNH); 11 mi. W Ardmore (KU). *Choctaw*: Fort Towson

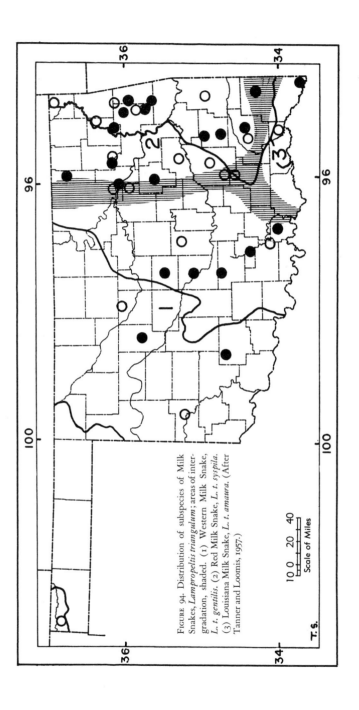

FIGURE 94. Distribution of subspecies of Milk Snakes, *Lampropeltis triangulum*; areas of intergradation, shaded. (1) Western Milk Snake, *L. t. gentilis*. (2) Red Milk Snake, *L. t. syspila*. (3) Louisiana Milk Snake, *L. t. amaura*. (After Tanner and Loomis, 1957.)

Scale of Miles

10 0   20   40

T. S.

(Blanchard, 1921:40). *Cimarron*: 4.6 mi. N and 2 mi. W Kenton (OU). *Coal*: 6 mi. N Coalgate (Carter, 1966:35). *Comanche*: Lawton (TTC). *Cotton*: "16th of May, between Cache creek and Red river" (Baird and Girard, 1854:200; locality near confluence of Cache Creek and Red River according to itinerary of Marcy and McClellan, 1854:9). *Greer*: 15 mi. NW Mangum (MU). *Harmon*: 4 mi. W and 5 mi. S Hollis (FWCM). *Hughes*: 2 mi. W Holdenville (Burt, 1935:332). *Johnston*: 1 mi. SW Ravia (Carpenter, 1955a:41); near Milburn (FWCM). *Kay*: 4 mi. W Lyman, Osage County (Burt, 1935:332); 6 mi. NE Newkirk (Burt and Hoyle, 1935:210). *Latimer*: 5 mi. W Talihina, LeFlore County (OSU). *LeFlore*: Rich Mt., 5 mi. SW Page, and 6 mi. W Heavener (Trowbridge, 1937); Wister, and Sugarloaf Mt. (Blanchard, 1921:36); Panama (KU). *Mayes*: Camp Garland [5 mi. S Locust Grove] (McCoy, 1960a: 43). *McCurtain*: 5 mi. S Broken Bow (KKA); 3 mi. S Smithville (Trowbridge, 1937); 1 mi. N Idabel (TCWC). *Noble*: near Red Rock (OSU). *Okfuskee*: no data (Carter, 1966:35). *Osage*: 2 mi. E Hominy (FWCM). *Pawnee*: [near] Otoe Reservation [Noble County] (McCoy, 1960a:43). *Payne*: [several within 4 mi. radius Stillwater] (Moore and Rigney, 1942: 79). *Pittsburg*: Haileyville (McCoy, 1960a:43); 3 mi. N Pittsburg (SESC); 10 mi. W McAlester (ECSC). *Pontotoc*: 2 mi. SE Ada (Carter, 1966:35). *Pushmataha*: 1 mi. S Nashoba (TNHC). *Rogers*: Tulsa Fin and Feather Club (OSU); 6 mi. W Claremore (Burt and Hoyle, 1935: 210). *Sequoyah*: Dwight Mission (CCC). *Tulsa*: Red Fork (Blanchard, 1921:41); Tulsa (Blair, 1961); 8 mi. W Collinsville (OSU); Oakhurst (USNM). *Woods*: Alva (FMNH); 12 mi. N and 4 mi. W Alva (McCracken, 1966:21). *Woodward*: Fort Supply (Blanchard, 1921:36).

Lampropeltis triangulum (Linnaeus)

Milk Snakes

Recognition.—Snakes having blotches or nearly ringed pattern of red or orange, white or yellow, and black; belly marked with red and/or black; dorsal scales smooth in 21 rows at midbody; anal plate single.

Distribution.—Throughout the state; three subspecies (map, Fig. 94).

Remarks.—Tanner and Loomis (1957) have most recently studied the relationships of the milk snakes. The three subspecies of *Lampropeltis triangulum* in Oklahoma are distinguished as follows:

L. t. amaura Cope, Louisiana Milk Snake.—Red of dorsal pattern extending onto belly; white rings on body and tail 23 or fewer, rarely 24; red rings much wider than whitish rings.

L. t. gentilis (Baird and Girard), Western Milk Snake.—Red of dorsal pattern extending onto belly; whitish rings on body and tail 24 (usually 26) or more; most red rings about same width as white rings because of black encroaching middorsally onto red rings.

L. t. syspila (Cope), Red Milk Snake.—Red of dorsal pattern not extending onto belly; large red blotches or saddles, surrounded by black, extending well down onto sides.

Lampropeltis t. amaura is associated with the lowland fauna of the Coastal Plain, *L. t. gentilis* with the Grassland and Oak-Woodland, and *L. t. syspila* with the Interior Highlands. Field data are scanty for milk snakes obtained in Oklahoma. No data are available for specimens of *amaura*, but, judging from their collection outside of Oklahoma, they can be expected to be found under the loose bark of partly rotted upright stumps and fallen logs or in their decayed interiors. An individual of *syspila* from Mayes County was found in the moist, decayed interior of a half-buried log, another from Pushmataha County was under a rock on a wooded hillside on a rainy morning, and one from Washington County was dug up in a ditching operation. Three individuals of *gentilis* from the Wichita Mountains were taken in a wooded, rocky area near Lost Lake.

Dr. Frederick Gehlbach (personal communication) supplied

data of collection for seven milk snakes captured in an oak woodland two miles north of Willis, Marshall County, on April 27, 1968. The day was cool and cloudy with intermittent showers, and the time of collection was 9:00 to 10:00 a.m. The milk snakes, as well as 57 snakes of the genera *Diadophis*, *Tantilla*, *Sonora*, and *Leptotyphlops* (only two of the latter) were found under flat-surfaced limestone rocks on sandy soil. When uncovered, one milk snake was in contact with a large *Sonora*, and two milk snakes backed down burrows. One small milk snake ate a *Tantilla* in a cloth sack. Body temperatures ranged from 18.0 to 21.0° C, air temperatures from 19.0 to 19.6° C, and ground temperatures under rocks from 18.5 to 19.2° C. Two small milk snakes, measuring about six inches in length, probably hatched the previous year; they differ from the larger milk snakes (about 14 to 20 inches long) in having brighter red (instead of orangish) body blotches and grayish (instead of yellowish) annuli. These milk snakes, having mottled black-white snouts, red on belly, and 24 or fewer white annuli on the body, seem most like *amaura*, but are probably *amaura-gentilis* intergrades.

A snake from Washita County, incorrectly identified as *gentilis* by Ortenburger (1927a:97), has since been identified as *Lampropeltis calligaster*.

See Carpenter (1958a:74), Force (1925a:27; 1925b:83; 1930: 34).

Specimens examined (OU except as indicated).—*Adair*: E Proctor (UA); 3 mi. S Bunch (KU). *Blaine*: Watonga (OSU). *Cherokee*: Blair Mts. near Barber, and 10 mi. ENE Tahlequah (KU). *Cleveland*: 3 mi. S Norman. *Comanche*: Wichita Mts. Wildlife Refuge. *Garvin*: Maysville. *Latimer*: Robbers Cave State Park (NWSC); 25.3 mi. N Clayton, Pushamataha County (TTC) *Marshall*: Madill. *Mayes*: 4 mi. S Locust Grove. *McCurtain*: State Game Preserve (ECSC); Tom. *Murray*: Turner Falls. *Oklahoma*: no data. *Okmulgee*: no data. *Pushmataha*: near Nashoba. *Rogers*:

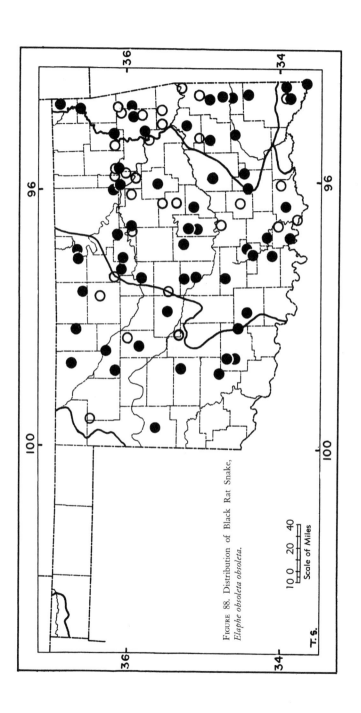

Figure 88. Distribution of Black Rat Snake, *Elaphe obsoleta obsoleta.*

1 mi. NE Catoosa. *Tulsa*: 1 mi. S Red Fork. *Washington*: 4 mi. E Dewey.

Additional records (Tanner and Loomis, 1957, except as indicated).—*Adair*: [5 mi. S] near Kansas, Delaware County. *Atoka*: Limestone Gap (Stone, 1903:542; Blanchard, 1921:177). *Beckham*: 2 mi. E Sayre (Burt and Hoyle, 1935:210). *Blaine*: gyp hills near Watonga. *Carter*: near Dickson (ECSC). *Cherokee*: Camp Muskogee (McCoy, 1960a:43); Welling. *Choctaw*: Fort Towson (Cope, 1889: 385). *Cimarron*: Black Mesa State Park, near Lake Carl Etling (private collection of William A. McCracken, personal communication from William A. Carter). *Creek*: Sapulpa. *Kingfisher*: Hennessey (Cope, 1894: 387). *LeFlore*: Wister (CM). *Marshall*: 2 mi. N Willis (Frederick Gehlbach, personal communication). *Mayes*: near Lower Lake Spavinaw (OU). *McIntosh*: 5 mi. NW Eufaula (McCoy, 1960a:43). *Osage*: 5 mi. N Sand Springs, Tulsa County. *Ottawa*: 3 mi. S and 4 mi. E Quapaw. *Pittsburg*: "South McAlester" (Stone, 1903:542; Blanchard, 1921:182); Kiowa (ECSC). *Pottawatomie*: 12 mi. from Shawnee (Webster, 1936:21). *Pushmataha*: Sulphur Canyon, 23 mi. NE Antlers (CCC). *Rogers*: 7 mi. W Inola.

Leptotyphlops dulcis (Baird and Girard)

Blind Snakes

Recognition.—Small (rarely more than one foot long), earthwormlike, pale brownish snakes; tail extremely short, blunt but pointed; eye visible as dark dot through overlying scale; all scales on body of same size (ventral scales not transversely widened).

Distribution.—Western Oklahoma; known as far east as Tulsa, Pottawatomie, Pontotoc, and Marshall counties; two subspecies (map, Fig. 96).

Remarks.—Klauber (1940), who provided the most comprehensive study of the blind snakes, considered the two forms in

Oklahoma as subspecies of *Leptotyphlops dulcis*, differentiating them as follows:

L. d. dulcis (Baird and Girard), Plains Blind Snake.—One supralabial (Fig. 95A); dorsal scales 223 or fewer; fifth dorsal not widened; occipitals not divided.

L. d. dissectus (Cope), New Mexico Blind Snake.—Two supralabials (Fig. 95B); dorsal scales 224 or more; fifth dorsal widened; one or both occipitals divided.

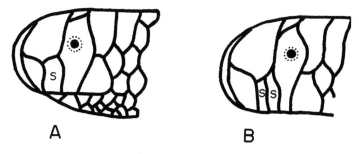

A   **B**

FIGURE 95. Sides of heads of *Leptotyphlops dulcis*; S, supralabial. (A) *L. d. dulcis*. (B) *L. d. dissectus*. (Redrawn from Klauber, 1940.)

The characters distinguishing the two forms overlap in specimens from southwestern Oklahoma, and individuals are not easily referred to either *dulcis* or *dissectus*. Klauber (1940:116) mentioned the possibility of hybridization, a view followed by Smith (1944:136) and Smith and Sanders (1952:216), who considered the forms as distinct species (*L. dulcis* and *L. myopicus dissectus*). Pending a thorough study of the *dulcis-myopicus-dissectus* complex, I have, for convenience, considered the area of overlap as a region of intergradation and *dulcis* and *dissectus* as subspecies. Among the characters that seem to be useful in distinguishing these subspecies are the variation in number of middorsal scales and pigmented dorsal scale rows, the number of supralabials (one or two), the number of divided occipitals, and the relative width of the fifth dorsal scale. Since I have not studied all of these characters in Oklahoma blind snakes, I have placed principal emphasis on whether the specimen has one or two supralabials.

Specimens having one supralabial on one side and two on the other side of the head are discussed as intergrades, and are recorded from Comanche, Harmon, Kiowa, Love, Marshall, Murray, and Pontotoc counties. The intergrades from Harmon and Kiowa counties were obtained by themselves; the specimens from the other counties were found along with specimens of *dulcis* (2 intergrades of 13, Comanche; 2 of 7, Love; 1 of 2, Marshall, and 1 of 5, Murray County); intergrades are known to have been found at the same time and place with specimens of *dissectus* only once (2 of 3, Pontotoc), although both are recorded from Cooperton, Kiowa County. Individuals of *dulcis* and *dissectus* are recorded from Comanche, Cleveland, Kiowa, and Pontotoc counties, and in two instances from the same locality (Norman, Cleveland County, and Cooperton, Kiowa County). A series of intergrades from Seminole County is as yet unstudied. On the basis of supralabials, *dissectus* seems to occur throughout most of northern Oklahoma in the western part of the state, whereas *dulcis* occurs in the mesquite plains of the southwest, a distribution corresponding in some degree to the distribution of the forms in the Texas panhandle, with *dulcis* below the caprock and *dissectus* above the caprock on the High Plains (Tinkle and Knopf, 1964:43–44). But in Oklahoma *dissectus* occurs east of the High Plains, and the distribution of the two forms may be affected by the southwestern filter barrier (see page 49). The distribution of blind snakes to the east is limited by the Interior Highlands.

In my experience, most blind snakes are found under small, flat rocks on open or partly wooded hillsides in early spring when frequent rains moisten the soil, and before the hot, dry, summer months. Thirteen individuals were found in a buffalo pasture under large rocks, some penetrating three feet beneath the surface (Comanche County); another was found in the moist, pulpy interior of a small log (Marshall County), and seven tightly clumped blind snakes (at least two escaped in soft earth) were taken under a small, flat rock (Love County). The specimen from Tillman County had been eaten by a Texas night snake (*Hypsiglena*). Surface activity has been reported in urban areas on sidewalks at 9:30 p.m., when the temperature was 72° F (erroneously stated as 92° F by Klauber, 1940:148), in Norman, Cleveland County, and on a cloudy morning in Weatherford, Custer County. Supplementary data about an "intergrade" from near the Red River southwest of Hollis, Harmon County (this is the same blind snake mentioned by Ortenburger and Freeman, 1930:182) consist of the time of observation (8:50 a.m.) and the rapidity of movement—about four or five feet a minute (field notes, A. I. Ortenburger).

The locality given for OU 12658 is Denton, Choctaw County (Force, 1936a:25; Klauber, 1940:112). So far as I am able to determine, there is no "Denton" in Choctaw County, and the specimen is presumed to have been taken at Denton, Texas. The geographically enigmatic record of *dulcis* from the panhandle in Cimarron County (Klauber, 1940:112; UMMZ 77541), which suggests a considerable overlap with the range of *dissectus*, has supported the contention that the two forms are specifically distinct. But the sleuthing of Harold A. Dundee (personal conversation) has shown the correct locality of UMMZ 77541 to be the Wichita Mts. Wildlife Refuge, Comanche County; the only other specimen from Cimarron County (OU 28170) is *dissectus*.

See Carpenter (1956:42), Carter (1966:34), Carter and Cox (1968), Dowling (1959:42, Fig. 1B), Dundee (1950a:29), Force (1930:29), McCoy (1960c), Moore and Rigney (1942:79), Stebbins (1954:350), Sturgis (1939:18), Webb and Ortenburger (1955:89).

Specimens examined (OU except as indicated).—*Beckham*: 7 mi. SW Erick; 10.5 mi. S and 2 mi. W Erick (KU). *Caddo*: 2 mi. E Fort Cobb (KU). *Canadian*: 7 mi. N Yukon. *Carter*: 5 mi. SE Ardmore; 5 mi. W and 2 mi. S Ardmore. *Cimarron*: 4 mi. N Kenton. *Cleveland*: Norman. *Comanche*: Wichita Mts. Wildlife Refuge. *Custer*: Weatherford (SWSC). *Harmon*: 6 mi. S Hollis; 7 mi. SW Hollis; NW Reed, Greer County; 6 mi. SW Vinson; 1 mi. W junction State Highway 30 and Elm Fork of Red River. *Kiowa*: Cooperton; Gotebo. *Love*: 6 mi. W Lebanon, Marshall County (TTC, TU). *Marshall*: 1 mi. E Powell; 5 mi. N Willis; UOBS. *Murray*: several within 2 mi. radius Turner Falls. *Pontotoc*: 1.5 mi. W Fittstown; 5 mi. S Fittstown, and 5 mi. S Ada (ECSC). *Tillman*: 2 mi. S Davidson. *Woods*: 1.6 mi. E Tegarden.

Additional records.—*Carter*: 12 mi. W Ardmore (UI). *Comanche*: 5 mi. N Cache (Klauber, 1940:112). *Garvin*: Table Top Mts., 7.5 mi. NW Elmore City (ECSC). *Greer*: 1 mi. N Granite (McCoy, 1960a:42). *Harmon*: 1 mi. W and 5 mi. S Hollis. (FWCM). *Jackson*: 8.5 mi. W and 2.5 mi. N Altus (ECSC). *Jefferson*: Waurika area (MU). *Kiowa*: 2 mi. S Lugert (OSU). *Love*: 3 mi. N Marietta (FMNH). *McClain*: 3 mi. E and 1 mi. S Blanchard (ECSC). *Murray*: Camp Classen (SESC). *Payne*: [several within 8 mi. radius] Stillwater (McCoy, 1960c). *Pottawatomie*: 12 mi. radius Shawnee (Webster, 1936:21). *Seminole*: 18 mi. S Seminole (ECSC). *Tulsa*: Tulsa (Force, 1928:79); Limestone (FMNH, MCZ). *Woods*: 2 mi. E and 12 mi. S Alva (McCracken, 1966:13); Alva (McCracken, 1966:13; Carter, 1966:34).

Masticophis flagellum (Shaw)

Coachwhips

Recognition.—Large adults black anteriorly and pale brown posteriorly, or entire body either mostly black or pale brown; pale scales posteriorly dark-edged imparting braided effect; belly anteriorly dark brown black, or pale with brown spots;

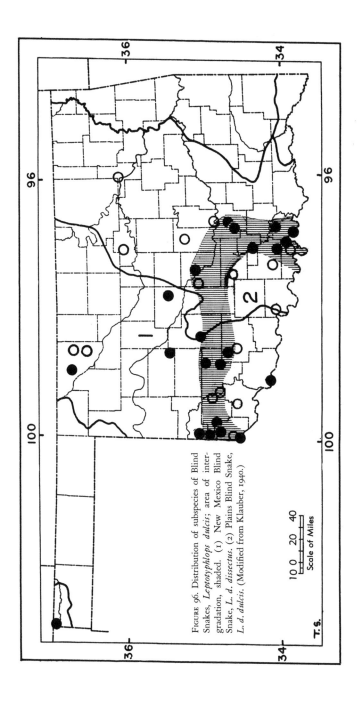

FIGURE 96. Distribution of subspecies of Blind Snakes, *Leptotyphlops dulcis*; area of intergradation, shaded. (1) New Mexico Blind Snake, *L. d. dissectus*. (2) Plains Blind Snake, *L. d. dulcis*. (Modified from Klauber, 1940.)

young (which sometimes resemble adults) pale brown with dark brown crossbars on neck; lowermost preocular very small; dorsal scales smooth in 17 rows at midbody and 13 just anterior to anal plate; anal plate divided.

Distribution.—Throughout the state; two subspecies (map, Fig. 97).

Remarks.—The two subspecies of *Masticophis flagellum* in Oklahoma are recognized as follows:

M. f. flagellum (Shaw), Eastern Coachwhip.—Adults uniform blackish or dark brown with posterior part of body pale brown or tannish, or black all over with posterior parts of body and tail tinted with tan or red; belly mostly black anteriorly, pale posteriorly corresponding to coloration on back. Young having crossbands separated by one or two scales, with belly having two rows of brown spots anteriorly.

M. f. testaceus (Hallowell), Western Coachwhip.—Adults pale brown or buff, often having brown bands across back and dark marks on many anterior dorsal scales; belly with edges of ventrals brown in some specimens and often having brown, mostly paired, spots anteriorly. Young resembling adults with crossbands anteriorly often separated by three scales, but not readily distinguished from young of *M. f. flagellum*.

Eastern coachwhips occur in the eastern half of Oklahoma, whereas western coachwhips occur in the western half of the state, with intergradation seemingly in the western part of the Oak-Woodland. Specimens of both subspecies have been taken from Kay, Pawnee, Payne, Oklahoma, Cleveland, McClain, Garvin, Comanche, and Marshall counties; some snakes from Logan and Murray counties are dark brown (not black) on the anterior part of the body, and are most like *flagellum*. Some specimens of *flagellum* from scattered localities have more or

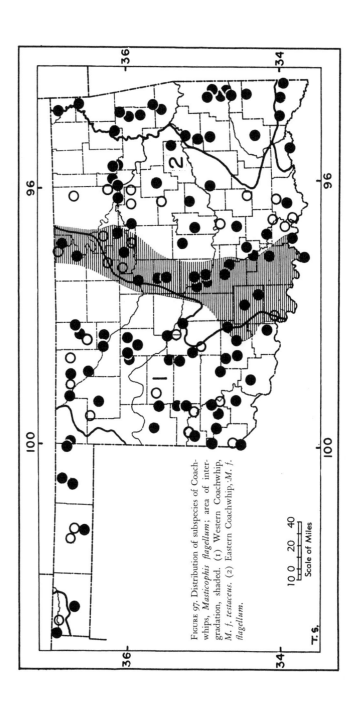

FIGURE 97. Distribution of subspecies of Coach-whips, *Masticophis flagellum*; area of inter-gradation, shaded. (1) Western Coachwhip, *M. f. testaceus*. (2) Eastern Coachwhip, *M. f. flagellum*.

Scale of Miles

10 0   20   40

T. 5.

less regularly spaced pale bands on the body. The westernmost specimen of *flagellum* is from Comanche County.

Snakes of this species are diurnal and frequently observed; a few have been noticed with their heads protruding from mammal burrows, and many are found dead on highways. Startled snakes often climb trees and shrubs, then remain motionless. Individuals of *testaceus* are frequent along wooded, sandy floodplains of rivers and streams, and often are reported in rattlesnake dens. Eight eggs were deposited on July 9 (Johnston County). Food items include the lizards *Holbrookia maculata* (*testaceus*), *Cnemidophorus sexlineatus* (both subspecies), and the racer *Coluber constrictor* (*testaceus*). A dead individual containing a *Sceloporus* in its stomach was found in the nest of a red-tailed hawk (Woods County).

Inquisitive behavior that may reflect courtship activities was observed in mid-July, 1954, Marshall County. In a thick grassy area with some scattered trees, a coachwhip moved directly toward me from a distance of some 30 feet away with approximately the anterior third of its body off the ground. As I stood still the snake stopped about one foot away and remained motionless in "cobra fashion" for about 10 seconds before moving away in the same manner. A few days later, about two miles distant, I observed what Bogert and Roth (1966) have interpreted as ritualistic combat of males. In a shrubby, sandy, terraced area, a pair of entwined coachwhips, with their heads at about the same level and not lifted off the ground, moved rapidly over the terrain and disappeared in a hollow log; the pair seemed undisturbed as I scurried to keep pace with them a few feet away.

Since Maslin's (1953) resurrection of *testaceus* for the reddish (nonfading in preservative) population in Colorado, and recognition of *flavigularis*, investigators have considered *flavigularis* as indistinguishable from the earlier-named *testaceus* (most recently by Smith, Maslin, and Brown, 1965:25), principally because of the occurrence of reddish (fading in preservative) individuals in Texas (most, if not all, of them seem to be from trans-Pecos Texas). Only an occasional coachwhip from western Oklahoma has a faint pink-red tinge in places, and are unlike the mostly uniform brick red snakes from parts of west Texas.

See Anderson (1965:211), Carpenter (1956:43; 1958b:114; 1959c:34), Carter and Cox (1968), Burt and Hoyle (1935:206), Dundee and Burger (1948), Force (1925a:27; 1925b:83; 1930: 30), Gehlbach (1956:369–370), Hallowell (1854:133, 146), Jenni (1955), Marr (1944:484), McCracken (1966:17), Ortenburger (1928c:97, 100, 101, Pl. XIX), Ortenburger and Freeman (1930:183–184), Smith (1961:199, Fig. 190), Smith and Leonard (1934:194), Trowbridge (1937:296), Webb and Ortenburger (1955:89), Yarrow (1883).

Specimens examined (OU except as indicated).—*Adair*: 5 mi. S Bunch. *Alfalfa*: 7 mi. NE Jet; 6 mi. S and 4 mi. E Cherokee. *Beaver*: near Gate; 8 mi. E and 4 mi. S Beaver (KU); 2 mi. W Forgan and 7 mi. E Forgan. *Beckham*: Elk City; 9 mi. S Elk City; 4 mi. SE Erick. *Blaine*: 9 mi. SW Okeene; 4 mi. SW Geary; Roman Nose State Park; Canton Dam (OSU); 1 mi. S Canton (KU). *Bryan*: no data. *Caddo*: 10 mi. N Carnegie; near Cogar; S Geary, Blaine County, at South Canadian River bridge. *Carter*: several within 5 mi. radius Ardmore. *Cherokee*: 5 mi. S Welling; 3 mi. N Scraper; McSpadden Falls; near Barber (KU). *Choctaw*: 10 mi. S Hugo. *Cimarron*: 3 mi. N Kenton; 7 mi. S Boise City. *Cleveland*: several within 7 mi. radius Norman. *Comanche*: 2 mi. E Sterling; Cache; 4–5 mi. N Cache; Lawton; 4 mi. W Lawton; 12–14 mi. W Lawton; Wichita Mts. Wildlife Refuge. *Cotton*: near Temple. *Creek*: Drumright. *Custer*: Weatherford (SWSC). *Delaware*: 6 mi. NE Grove. *Dewey*: 5.5 mi. SW Canton, 5 mi. W Canton, and 8 mi. SW Canton, Blaine County (KU). *Garvin*: Pauls Valley; Maysville. *Greer*: Granite; 0.5 mi. N Mangum. *Harmon*: 6 mi. S Hollis; near Carl; 1 mi. W Vinson; NW Reed, Greer County. *Harper*: near Gate, Beaver County. *Haskell*: 5 mi. W Stigler; 3 mi.

E and 4 mi. S Quinton, Pittsburg County (KU). *Hughes*: near
Wetumka. *Jackson*: 5 mi. N Altus. *Johnston*: Ravia Quarry. *Kay*:
Ponca City; 12 mi. E Newkirk (KU). *Kiowa*: Cooperton. *Latimer*:
2 mi. N Wilburton. *LeFlore*: 6 mi. S Stapp; 3.5 mi. SW Stapp;
Page; 5 mi. E Big Cedar; 2 and 18 mi. SW Wister; 6.5 mi. W
Heavener; 1.5 mi. E Zoe; 3 mi. N Zoe. *Logan*: 6 mi. NW Guthrie.
Love: 6 mi. S Thackerville. *Major*: 4 mi. S Cleo Springs; 4 mi. W
Meno. *Marshall*: several within 5 mi. radius Willis. *Mayes*: Locust
Grove; 4 mi. S Locust Grove. *McClain*: near Washington; just N
Purcell; 12 mi. W Norman, Cleveland County. *McCurtain*: 2 mi.
SW Smithville; 2.5 mi. NE Smithville; 7 mi. SE Eagletown; 1 and
25 mi. W Broken Bow. *McIntosh*: 7.5 and 11 mi. E Checotah.
Murray: Sulphur; Dougherty; Turner Falls. *Oklahoma*: no data;
Edmond. *Okmulgee*: Okmulgee. *Ottawa*: 7 mi. E and 2 mi. N
Miami (KU). *Pawnee*: near Quay. *Payne*: no data. *Pittsburg*: 4
mi. E Stuart, Hughes County. *Pontotoc*: 1.5 mi. W Fittstown.
Pottawatomie: Shawnee; 4 mi. NE Shawnee. *Pushmataha*: 2 mi. E
Cloudy. *Roger Mills*: Hammon; 7 mi. N Cheyenne. *Rogers*: 2 mi.
NE Catoosa. *Seminole*: Bowlegs. *Sequoyah*: 0.5 mi. S Marble City.
Stephens: Lake Duncan; Loco. *Texas*: 8 mi SE Guymon. *Tillman*:
1.3 mi. W Manitou. *Tulsa*: Tulsa; 6 mi. W Tulsa; 13 mi. NE Tulsa;
2 mi. W Sand Springs. *Wagoner*: 6 mi. SE Catoosa, and 2 mi. S
Catoosa, Rogers County (KU). *Washita*: 10 mi. S Weatherford,
Custer County (SWSC). *Woods*: 12 mi. W Alva (KU); 2.5 mi. N
Waynoka; 1.5 mi. W Edith. *Woodward*: 4 mi. E and 1 mi. N
Woodward; 3.5 mi. WNW Woodward; Boiling Springs State
Park.

Additional records.—Alfalfa: 3 mi. E Carmen (Burt, 1935:330).
Beckham: 4 mi. SW Sayre (Burt and Hoyle, 1935:206); 2 mi. S
and 3 mi. W Carter (TTC). *Bryan*: Durant, and 3.4 mi. E Caddo
(SESC); 7 mi. NW Colbert (Bonn and McCarley, 1953:470).
Caddo: Fort Cobb (Yarrow, 1883:153); Kiwanis and Devils canyons
(OSU). *Canadian*: Devils Canyon (Carpenter, 1958a:73). *Cimar-
ron*: 8 and 10 mi. E Kenton (OSU). *Coal*: [Lehigh] (Ortenburger,
1927a:96). *Creek*: 13 mi. W Sapulpa (OSU); Sapulpa (Ortenbur-
ger, 1928c:109); 4 mi. SW Sapulpa (Burt, 1935:330). *Custer*: 3 mi.
NE Butler (Burt, 1935:330). *Greer*: 2 mi. SW Reed (OU); 3 mi.

S Quartz Mt. State Park, Kiowa County (OSU). *Harmon*: several within 6 mi. radius Hollis (FWCM). *Jefferson*: near Waurika (MU; Carter, 1966:34). *Johnston*: 8 mi. SE Tishomingo (Carter, 1966:34). *Kay*: 6 mi. NE Newkirk (Burt and Hoyle, 1935:206). *LeFlore*: Wister (AMNH, CM). *Marshall*: 2 mi. E Kingston (OU). *Murray*: Camp Classen (OSU). *Noble*: 6 mi. E Perry (McCoy, 1960a:43). *Okfuskee*: 2 mi. W Okfuskee (ECSC). *Osage*: Osage Hills State Park (OSU); 14 mi. NW Turley, Tulsa County (UMMZ). *Pawnee*: 2 mi. N Pawnee (Burt, 1935:330). *Payne*: 15 mi. W Stillwater (MCZ); 2 mi. NE Ripley (UA); several within 4 mi radius Stillwater, Boomer Lake, Ripley Bluffs, and Lake Carl Blackwell (OSU). *Pontotoc*: 7 mi. NE Ada (ECSC). *Rogers*: Tulsa Fin and Feather Club (OSU); 6 mi. E Catoosa (UI). *Texas*: 9 mi. E Guymon (Ortenburger, 1927c:47); 1.8 mi. NE Optima (KU). *Tulsa*: Garnett, and Limestone (UMMZ); Red Fork (UI). *Woods*: Alva, and Whitehorse Springs (FMNH); Waynoka (UMMZ). *Woodward*: Fort Supply (Cope, 1894:387).

Natrix erythrogaster transversa (Hallowell)

Blotched Water Snake

Recognition.—Adults with brown-blotched pattern, or uniformly brownish, gray, or olive green, but usually having obscure blotches on back separated by narrow, dark-bordered, pale crossbars; belly pale yellow and underside of tail pale orange; ventral surface having small dark smudges along each side on each ventral (middle of belly unmarked); usually three postoculars; dorsal scales keeled usually in 23 (or 25, rarely 27) rows at midbody; anal plate divided. Young having conspicuous blotches on back alternating with row of spots on sides, the first one or two sets of blotches and spots on neck continuous as crossbands in some specimens.

Distribution.—Throughout the state (map, Fig. 98).

Remarks.—Blotched water snakes are frequently observed near sloughs and impoundments, and along rivers and streams.

Individuals sun on grassy shores, rocks, or on emergent debris, and are active both night and day. Recorded food items include a catfish and a ranid frog. A female from Cleveland County gave birth to one snake on August 15, another on the 23rd, was then killed and found to contain 15 unborn young.

Individuals having a uniform dorsum (no blotching) are referable to the yellow-bellied water snake, *Natrix erythrogaster flavigaster*. According to Conant (1949:5, 12) *transversa* and *flavigaster* intergrade in eastern Oklahoma, but I have not been able to study their relationships. For convenience I have referred all specimens to *transversa*.

Stone (1903:541) commented on a young snake from Vinita that differed from *Natrix erythrogaster*, referring it to "*Natrix* sp." That snake (ANSP 15516) is *Storeria dekayi* (Edmond V. Malnate, personal communication; Trapido, 1944:69).

See Bonn and McCarley (1953:470), Burt and Burt (1929a: 457), Burt and Hoyle (1935:212), Carpenter (1956:42; 1958b: 113), Carter and Cox (1968), Diener (1957:210), Force (1925a:27; 1925b:83; 1930:35), Laughlin (1959:83), Ortenburger and Freeman (1930:185), Smith and Leonard (1934: 195), Trowbridge (1937:297).

Specimens examined (OU except as indicated).—*Adair*: 2.2 mi. E Proctor. *Alfalfa*: 4 mi. W and 3 mi. S Jet (ECSC); Cherokee (AMNH, skin only). *Atoka*: 4.5 mi. E Atoka; 0.5 mi. S Lane. *Beckham*: 6 mi. SW Carter. *Carter*: Ardmore. *Cherokee*: 2 mi. E Welling; 6 mi. NE Tahlequah; 4 mi. W Tahlequah. *Choctaw*: Red River Fisheries (TTC). *Cimarron*: 3 mi. N Kenton. *Cleveland*: 1 mi. W Noble; 6 mi. E Norman; 3 mi. S Norman. *Coal*: 2 mi. S Lehigh; 2 mi. E Centrahoma. *Comanche*: Cache; Sterling; Wichita Mts. Wildlife Refuge. *Craig*: 3 mi. N Vinita. *Creek*: Drumright (KU). *Custer*: Weatherford (SWSC). *Delaware*: 6 mi. NW Grove; 1 mi. S Jay. *Dewey*: 10 mi. NW Canton, Blaine County (KU). *Garvin*: near Stratford (ECSC). *Harmon*: 6 mi. S Hollis; 11 mi. N Hollis. *Hughes*: 12 mi. S Holdenville (ECSC); near Wetumka.

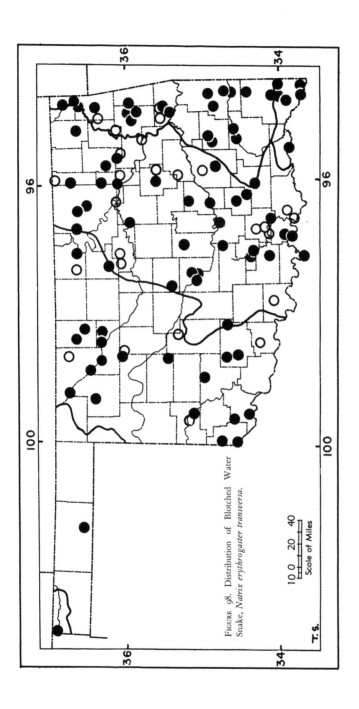

FIGURE 98. Distribution of Blotched Water Snake, *Natrix erythrogaster transversa*.

Scale of Miles
10 0 20 40

T. S.

Jackson: 10 mi. E El Dorado; 3 mi. E Duke. *Johnston*: Tishomingo Wildlife Refuge (ECSC). *Kay*: Ponca City. *Kiowa*: 6 mi. W Gotebo (SWSC). *Latimer*: 2, 7, and 9 mi. N Wilburton; 8 mi. W Wilburton; Robbers Cave State Park (NWSC). *LeFlore*: 5 mi. E Big Cedar; 4 mi. E Summerfield; 6 mi. SW Page; 3.5 mi. SW Stapp; 5 mi. E Zoe; 6–8 mi. W Heavener. *Love*: 6 mi. S Thackerville. *Major*: Cleo Springs; 5 mi. W Meno; 2 mi. E Togo. *Marshall*: UOBS; 2 mi. W Willis; 2 mi. S Shay; 7 mi. N and 2 mi. E Willis. *McClain*: 4 mi. SW Norman, Cleveland County. *McCurtain*: near Broken Bow; 9 and 15 mi. E Broken Bow; 2 mi. SW Smithville; Tom; 1.5 mi. S Harris; Idabel; 6 mi. N Idabel; Beavers Bend State Park. *Murray*: Dougherty; Price's Falls and Turner Falls. *Noble*: 5 mi. S and 3 mi. W Perry. *Oklahoma*: SW part Oklahoma City. *Okmulgee*: Okmulgee. *Osage*: 10 mi. N Fairfax; NW edge Tulsa, Tulsa County; 3 mi. N Wynona; 10 mi. E Pawhuska. *Ottawa*: 3 mi. E Wyandotte; 1.5 mi. E Turkey Ford. *Pittsburg*: no data (ECSC). *Pontotoc*: 7 mi. NE Ada (ECSC). *Pottawatomie*: Shawnee. *Pushmataha*: 4 mi. E Tuskahoma; 0.5 mi. S Clayton (TTC). *Rogers*: 5 mi. W Claremore. *Sequoyah*: 1 mi. N and 1 mi. E McKey; Dwight Mission. *Texas*: 8 mi. SE Guymon. *Tulsa*: Tulsa; Skiatook; Red Fork. *Wagoner*: 7 mi. W Inola, Rogers County. *Washington*: near Bartlesville (KU). *Woods*: 2 mi. W and 1 mi. S Waynoka; 0.5 mi. W Edith. *Woodward*: 5 mi. E and 1 mi. N Woodward.

Additional records.—Adair: 7 mi. NE Proctor (TNHC). *Beckham*: 4 mi. SW Sayre (Burt and Hoyle, 1935:212). *Blaine*: Canton Dam (McCoy, 1960a:42). *Bryan*: 5 mi. SW Colbert (SESC, TNHC); 6.5 mi. NW Colbert (TNHC). *Caddo*: Devils Canyon (McCoy, 1960a:42). *Cherokee*: Illinois River, 2 mi. E Park Hill (TU). *Cotton*: 11 mi. N and 2 mi. E Randlett (ECSC). *Delaware*: Spavinaw Lake (UMMZ). *Johnston*: Tishomingo Fish Hatchery (OSU); 0.5 mi. W Tishomingo (TCWC); Randolph Bottoms, 4 mi. E Russet (CCC). *Kay*: 3 mi. N Tonkawa (Burt and Burt, 1929b:12). *Jefferson*: 15 mi. E Waurika (CCC). *Latimer*: State Game Preserve (TU). *LeFlore*: Wister (CM). *Mayes*: Camp Garland, 5 mi. S Locust Grove (OSU). *McCurtain*: 2.5 mi. N Idabel, and 3 mi. N and 1 mi. E Harris (OU); 2 mi. SW Tom (UI). *Mc-*

Intosh: 5 mi. SE Henryetta, Okmulgee County (ECSC). *Murray*: Camp Classen. *Muskogee*: 7.3 mi. N Muskogee (UMMZ). *Okmulgee*: 6 mi. E Morris (UMMZ). *Payne*: [2 mi. radius Stillwater] (Moore and Rigney, 1942:79); Lake Carl Blackwell (OSU). *Pittsburg*: Lake McAlester (Laughlin, 1959:83). *Rogers*: Pea Creek, 5 mi. S Inola (UMMZ). *Sequoyah*: 10 mi. NE Gore (OSU); Sallisaw Creek, 3 mi. S Marble City (Diener, 1957:203). *Tulsa*: 2 mi. SE Alsuma (Burt, 1935:333); near Keystone, Payne County (restricted type locality, Cochran, 1961:223); Parthenia Park, and Mohawk Park (UMMZ); 5 mi. E Tulsa (OSU). *Washington*: 4 mi. SE Bartlesville (TNHC); 2 mi. S Kansas state line between Caney, Kansas, and Owen (Burt and Burt, 1929a:457). *Woods*: Alva (FMNH).

Natrix fasciata confluens Blanchard

Broad-banded Water Snake

Recognition.—Blotched snakes having fewer than 20 large, broad black blotches on back; blotches separated by narrow pale interspaces, wider on sides and often orange, especially on sides; large middorsal blotches fused with smaller blotches on sides forming bands in some specimens; belly with large, more or less squarish black marks; scales keeled in 21 or 23 rows at midbody; anal plate divided.

Distribution.—Southeastern Oklahoma; known only from Atoka, Bryan, Choctaw, McCurtain, and Pushmataha counties (map, Fig. 99).

Remarks.—*Natrix fasciata* is associated with the biota of the Coastal Plain. Field observations suggest a preference in habitat for quiet water; broad-banded water snakes have been collected or observed among brush and drift piles of backwater sloughs and cut-off pools near rivers, in a small pond of a road culvert, a large muddy pond by a railroad fill, abandoned stock ponds of the Red River Fisheries, and in Roebuck Lake (Bryan County), and Kiowa City Lake (Atoka County). Oklahoma specimens differ from some of those of *confluens* from other parts of the range of the subspecies in having an interrupted postocular dark stripe, usually indicated by small dark marks and smudges (instead of distinct stripe from eye to angle of jaw), and orange in pale areas on sides (instead of buff or mostly black).

Field data indicate that Ortenburger's record of this species from Comanche County (1926a:138; 1927a:97) is based on a specimen obtained in Pushmataha County.

See Bonn and McCarley (1953:470), Carpenter (1956:42; 1958b:113), Conant (1963:6), Curd (1950), Trowbridge (1937: 297).

Specimens examined (OU except as indicated).—*Atoka*: 5 mi. S and 1 mi. E Kiowa, Pittsburg County (ECSC). *Bryan*: near Durant. *Choctaw*: Red River Fisheries; 2 mi. SW Grant. *McCurtain*: 10 and 14–16 mi. SE Broken Bow; 14 mi. E Broken Bow; 6 mi. N Idabel; 3 mi. N and 1 mi. E Harris; 3.8 mi. SE Harris. *Pushmataha*: 4 mi. E Tuskahoma; Little River, near Cloudy.

Additional records.—*Bryan*: Red River, 1 mi. E Denison Dam (UI); 5 mi. SW Colbert (TNHC). *McCurtain*: 5.5 mi. N Idabel (OU); 10 mi. E Broken Bow, and mouth Mountain Fork River (OSU); Grassy Lake (Curd, 1950).

Natrix rhombifera rhombifera (Hallowell)

Diamond-backed Water Snake

Recognition.—Yellow-brown, gray, or olive snakes having dark brown chainlike pattern; belly mostly pale yellow having small irregular gray marks arranged mostly in two lateral rows; dorsal scales keeled in 25 or 27 rows at midbody; anal plate divided.

Distribution.—Throughout the state, except the panhandle (map, Fig. 100).

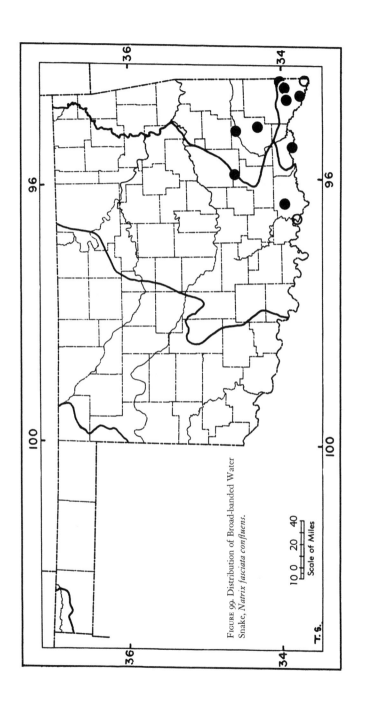

FIGURE 99. Distribution of Broad-banded Water Snake, *Natrix fasciata confluens*.

Remarks.—The diamond-backed water snake is frequently observed and can be expected to occur in the vicinity of most relatively permanent bodies of water. The distribution of the species in western Oklahoma seems to be limited by the High Plains, but individuals are expected to occur there along creeks and streams. The snakes bask on grassy banks and on debris in streams or rivers. They are also active at night; one was found at night in a shallow part of Lake Texoma (in a period of high water) with a live four-inch black bass in its mouth. These snakes also have been found some distance from water in grassy, weedy areas. One was captured in a decaying log near a water-filled ditch. Data on numbers of embryos within females, and corresponding dates of collection, are: 17, August 23 (Cleveland County); 46, May 31 (Stephens County); 17, September 8 (Choctaw County); and 34, July 21 (Marshall County). Data on numbers of young per brood are: 32 born on September 8 (Marshall County) and 16 born on September 16 (Choctaw County).

A specimen from 4 miles northwest Watts, Adair County, reported by Ortenburger (1929b:28) as *rhombifera*, is representative of *Natrix sipedon.*

See Anon. (1960a), Bonn and McCarley (1953:470), Carpenter (1955b; 1956:42; 1958b:113), Carter and Cox (1968), Force (1930:35), Hallowell (1854:137), Laughlin (1959), Ortenburger and Freeman (1930:185), Sisk and McCoy (1964), Smith and Leonard (1934:195), Trowbridge (1937:297), Van Vleet (1902: 171).

Specimens examined (OU except as indicated).—*Alfalfa*: 3 mi. E Cherokee. *Beckham*: 9 mi. S Sayre. *Blaine*: S Watonga along Canadian River. *Canadian*: 5 mi. S Yukon; 3 mi. SE Mustang. *Choctaw*: 2 mi. SW Grant; Red River Fisheries (TTC). *Cleveland*: several within 4 mi. radius Norman. *Comanche*: 5 mi. N Cache; Lake Lawtonka; Wichita Mts. Wildlife Refuge. *Cotton*: near Walters. *Custer*: Weatherford, and 5 mi. NE Weatherford (SWSC).

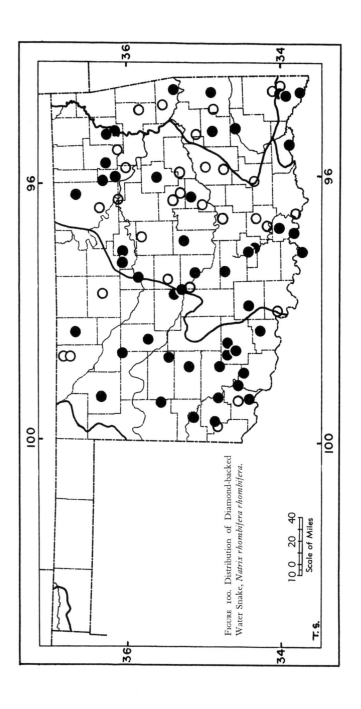

FIGURE 100. Distribution of Diamond-backed Water Snake, *Natrix rhombifera rhombifera.*

Dewey: 10 mi. NW Canton, Blaine County (KU). *Garvin*: Maysville. *Greer*: N Reed; Quartz Mt. State Park. *Hughes*: near Wetumka. *Jackson*: near Elmer; 12 mi. E Altus. *Kiowa*: Cooperton. *Latimer*: Wilburton; 3 and 6.5 mi. W Wilburton. *LeFlore*: 6.5 mi. W Heavener. *Logan*: 10 mi. NW Guthrie. *Love*: 3.5 mi. SE Thackerville. *Marshall*: UOBS; 3 mi. N Madill. *Mayes*: 5 mi. W Locust Grove; 6 mi. SE Pryor. *McCurtain*: near Broken Bow; 4 mi. W Harris; 6–7 mi. N Idabel; 7 mi. S Idabel; 13 mi. SE Idabel. *Murray*: Dougherty; 4 mi. SW Davis; Price's Falls. *Okmulgee*: Okmulgee. *Osage*: near Okesa. *Payne*: 2 mi. W Stillwater; Lake Carl Blackwell. *Pottawatomie*: Shawnee. *Pushmataha*: 4 mi. E Tuskahoma. *Roger Mills*: Hammon. *Rogers*: 5 mi. W Claremore. *Sequoyah*: 1 mi. W Muldrow. *Stephens*: Duncan. *Tillman*: 7 mi. S Snyder, Kiowa County. *Tulsa*: 7 mi. NE Tulsa; Skiatook. *Washita*: Cloud Chief (SWSC). *Woodward*: 6 mi. E Woodward.

Additional records.—Atoka: 4 mi. E Atoka (SESC). *Bryan*: 0.5 and 3.5 mi. N Colbert (SESC); 5 mi. SW Colbert (TNHC). *Cherokee*: Camp Muskogee (McCoy, 1960a:42). *Garfield*: 10 mi. E Enid (CCC). *Harmon*: 2 mi. SW Reed [Greer County] (Carpenter, 1958a:73). *Haskell*: 2.5 mi. SE Quinton, Pittsburg County (FMNH). *Hughes*: near Holdenville (Anon., 1960a). *Jackson*: Altus (TTC). *Jefferson*: 3 mi. S Waurika (Carpenter, 1958a:73). *Johnston*: 0.5 mi. W Tishomingo (TCWC); Blue River bridge at State Highway 7 (CCC). *LeFlore*: Wister (CM); 3 mi. E Summerfield (Trowbridge, 1937:297). *Lincoln*: 1 mi. S Agra (Burt, 1935: 334). *McClain*: 3 mi. NW Newcastle (ECSC). *McCurtain*: Beavers Bend State Park (OU); 10 mi. E Broken Bow (OSU). *McIntosh*: 5 mi. SE Henryetta, Okmulgee County (ECSC). *Murray*: Turner Falls (FWCM). *Okfuskee*: 3 mi. N Okemah (ECSC); 2 mi. W Weleetka (ECSC). *Oklahoma*: NE Oklahoma City (Carpenter, 1958a:73). *Osage*: Hominy (OSU). *Payne*: Stillwater, and 6 mi. N and 2 mi. E Stillwater (OSU); 8 mi. W Stillwater (FWCM); Boomer Lake (Sisk and McCoy, 1964). *Pittsburg*: Lake McAlester (Laughlin, 1959:83); 6 mi. NE Kiowa (SESC). *Pontotoc*: 7 mi. NE Ada (Carter, 1966:35). *Rogers*: Inola (UMMZ). *Sequoyah*: Dwight Mission (OU). *Tulsa*: Tulsa (UI, UMMZ); near Keystone, Payne

County (restricted type locality, Cochran, 1961:223); 1 mi. W Broken Arrow (Burt, 1935:334). *Woods*: 2 mi. N and 1.5 mi. E Alva, and 11 mi. N Alva (McCracken, 1966:23).

Natrix sipedon pleuralis Cope

Midland Water Snake

Recognition.—Dark brown, gray, or olive snakes, often with orangish tinge, having dark crossbands on anterior part of body and alternating dorsal and lateral blotches on posterior part of body; pattern distinct in young, but often obscure in adults; belly pattern mottled, usually with some fine gray stippling and small half-moon–shaped marks arranged mostly in two longitudinal rows, and having an over-all red orange or pale orange tint; underside of tail dark, well patterned; dorsal scales keeled in 21, 23 or 25 rows at midbody; anal plate divided.

Distribution.—Eastern Oklahoma; known as far west as Payne, Johnston, and Bryan counties (map, Fig. 101).

Remarks.—*Natrix s. pleuralis* is found in the vicinity of rivers, creeks, ponds, and sloughs. Individuals are most frequent in the Interior Highlands, and less abundant in the Oak-Woodland. One snake ate a tadpole of *Rana catesbeiana*, and another attempted to eat a mudpuppy (*Necturus*), which took its own tail in its mouth, thus preventing the snake from swallowing it (field note, author unknown, 4 mi. NW Watts, Adair County). One snake of this species was removed from the stomach of a speckled kingsnake (*Lampropeltis getulus*). Other data for the species are no more precise than: female obtained July 25 containing 28 eggs (McCurtain County) and another on June 25 containing 15 eggs (Delaware County).

The few specimens from north central Oklahoma may represent the northern water snake, *Natrix sipedon sipedon*, which is distinguished from *N. s. pleuralis* of the Interior Highlands in

269

having the dark markings on the sides wider than the pale spaces between them (narrower in *pleuralis*), and the markings on the belly scattered, diffuse, and irregularly arranged (usually in two rows in *pleuralis*). A juvenile specimen (OU 11120, Latimer County) has a pattern of crossbands, some of which touch each other middorsally, throughout the length of the body and tail. Pending a study of *Natrix sipedon* in Oklahoma, I have, for convenience, referred all specimens to *N. s. pleuralis*.

Records of *Natrix sipedon* from Rogers County (5 mi. W Claremore) and Sequoyah County (1 mi. W Muldrow) by Ortenburger (1929b:28) are based on specimens of *Natrix erythrogaster* and *Natrix rhombifera*, respectively. Records of the species from Kay and Cleveland counties (Ortenburger, 1927a:98), presumably based on OU specimens, have not been verified.

See Carpenter (1956:42), Diener (1957:210), Force (1930:35), Laughlin (1959), Trowbridge (1937:297).

Specimens examined (OU except as indicated).—*Adair*: 5 mi. S Bunch; 4 mi. NW Watts; 4 and 10 mi. N Stilwell; 2 mi. N Adair-Sequoyah county line. *Bryan*: vicinity Durant. *Cherokee*: 1 mi. E Welling; 2 mi. S Eldon; 2 mi. S Scraper. *Delaware*: 6 mi. NW Grove; 6 mi. NE Grove; near Flint; 6 mi. E Flint; near Kansas; Dripping Springs. *Johnston*: 0.5 mi. N Milburn. *Latimer*: vicinity Wilburton; 6 mi. S Wilburton; 8 mi. NW Wilburton. *LeFlore*: 5 mi. E Big Cedar; 6.5 mi. W Heavener; near Zoe; 6 mi. SW Page; 3.5 mi. SW Stapp. *Mayes*: 5 mi. S Locust Grove. *McCurtain*: 6.5 mi. S Broken Bow (TTC); Little River bridge, 25 mi. W Broken Bow; 15 mi. SE Broken Bow; 6 mi. E Broken Bow; 2 mi. N Broken Bow; 6 mi. E Sherwood; 2 mi. SW Smithville; 4 mi. NE Hochatown (TTC); Beavers Bend State Park. *Ottawa*: 3 mi. N Wyandotte. *Pushmataha*: near Cloudy; 1 mi. S Kosoma; 4 mi. E Tuskahoma. *Sequoyah*: 2 mi. NE Gore; Dwight Mission.

Additional records.—*Adair*: Tyner Creek near Proctor (OSU). *Cherokee*: 8 mi. S Moodys, and 3 mi. E and 4.8 mi. N Tahlequah

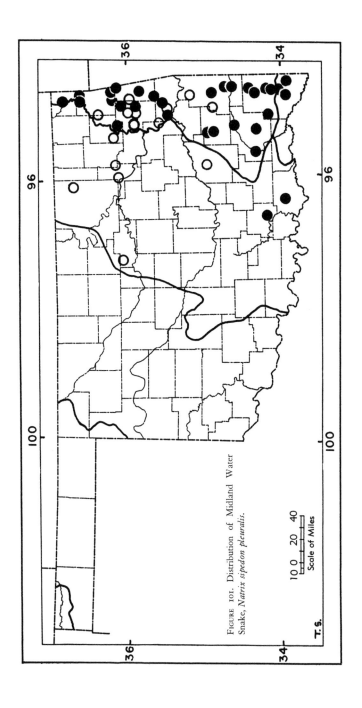

FIGURE 101. Distribution of Midland Water Snake, *Natrix sipedon pleuralis.*

(UMMZ); 15 mi. N Tahlequah (USNM); 10 mi. N Tahlequah (FWCM); McSpadden Falls, Camp Muskogee, 2 mi. W Tahlequah, Hulbert, and Illinois River at Tahlequah (OSU). *Delaware*: Turkey Ford (OSU); Lake Spavinaw (UMMZ). *Latimer*: Robbers Cave State Park (OSU). *LeFlore*: Wister (CM); NE Summerfield, James Fork, and Nigger Creek (Cross and Moore, 1952:398). *Mayes*: 2 mi. S Chouteau (UMMZ); Lake Spavinaw (UI); Cedar Crest Lake (OSU). *McCurtain*: Little River N Idabel (CCC). *Muskogee*: Greenleaf Creek above Greenleaf Lake (McCoy, 1960a:42). *Osage*: Osage Hills State Park (McCoy, 1960a:42). *Payne*: Lake Carl Blackwell (OSU). *Pittsburg*: Lake McAlester (Laughlin, 1959:83). *Rogers*: Tulsa Fin and Feather Club (McCoy, 1960a:42). *Sequoyah*: Sallisaw Creek near Marble City, and Swimmers Creek, 10 mi. E Gore (OSU). *Tulsa*: Tulsa (UMMZ, UI).

Opheodrys aestivus majalis (Baird and Girard)
Western Rough Green Snake

Recognition.—Long, slender, green (blue to blackish in preservative) snakes, having yellow, unmarked belly; scales keeled in 17 rows throughout length of body; anal plate divided.

Distribution.—Eastern Oklahoma; known as far west as Blaine, Comanche, and Tillman counties (map, Fig. 102).

Remarks.—Rough green snakes extend westward into the Grassland. Individuals have been found in open, grassy areas, climbing in shrubs, or with their heads protruding from burrows, and often along streams or rivers. One snake, presumably in hibernation, was discovered packed in hard clay a few inches below the surface on November 15 (Indian Springs, near Noble, Cleveland County) by Harold A. Dundee. Reproductive data are no more precise than: clutch of eight eggs (Oklahoma County); clutch of five eggs obtained on August 4 that hatched on August 7 (Cleveland County); and clutch of five eggs laid on July 13 that hatched August 29, with young measuring about 130 mm in body length (McCurtain County).

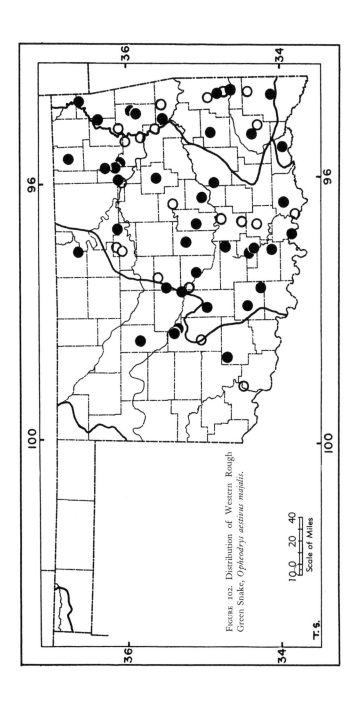

FIGURE 102. Distribution of Western Rough Green Snake, *Opheodrys aestivus majalis*.

Baird and Girard (1854:203, Pl. IX) recorded a green snake on the "13th of July at the head of Cache creek, near old Witchita [*sic*] village," apparently a locality in Comanche County, but according to the itinerary of Marcy and McClellan (1854:65), their camp on that date was between the confluence of the North Fork of the Red River and Otter Creek, which is in northwestern Tillman County. Morris and McReynolds (1965: 21 [map]) place "Wichita village" along the North Fork of the Red River in Kiowa County, and Shirk (1965:222) locates "Wichita" a few miles north of Fort Sill. For the time being, I have mapped the specimen in Tillman County as the western-most locality for the rough green snake in Oklahoma.

The name *majalis* was applied to rough green snakes occurring in Oklahoma by W. Leslie Burger in a dissertation for the degree of Master of Science at the University of Oklahoma, a study that is unpublished except for a brief abstract (1947).

See Bonn and McCarley (1953:469), Carpenter (1956:43; 1958b: 114; 1959c:34), Carter and Cox (1968), Force (1925a:27; 1925b:83; 1930:30), Kassing (1961:193), Trowbridge (1937:296), Ortenburger and Freeman (1930:183).

Specimens examined (OU except as indicated).—*Blaine*: Roman Nose State Park. *Bryan*: near Durant. *Caddo*: 2 mi. S Hinton. *Canadian*: 3 mi. SE Mustang; Devils Canyon (SWSC). *Carter*: Ardmore; 6 mi. SE Ardmore. *Cherokee*: near Welling; near Tahlequah; McSpadden Falls. *Choctaw*: near Hugo. *Cleveland*: Noble; several within 4 mi. radius Norman. *Comanche*: Wichita Mts. Wildlife Refuge. *Delaware*: 6 mi. NE Grove; 6 mi. NW Grove. *Garvin*: 6 mi. W Stratford, and 1.5 mi. NW Stratford (ECSC). *Grady*: Chickasha. *Hughes*: no data. *Kay*: Ponca City. *Latimer*: Wilburton; 2 and 7 mi. W Wilburton. *LeFlore*: 5 mi. E Big Cedar; 6.7 mi. S Heavener. *Marshall*: UOBS; 2 mi. S Shay. *Mayes*: near Lower Spavinaw Lake. *McCurtain*: 4.8 mi. N Beavers Bend State Park. *Murray*: Dougherty; 10 mi. S Davis; 4 mi. SW Davis; Price's Falls and Turner Falls. *Nowata*: no data. *Oklahoma*: Lake Overholser.

Okmulgee: Okmulgee. *Pawnee*: near Quay. *Pittsburg*: 5 mi. E Stuart, Hughes County. *Pottawatomie*: Shawnee. *Pushmataha*: no data. *Rogers*: 20 mi. NE Tulsa, Tulsa County; Twin Lakes (see map in Blair, 1938:474); 1 mi. NE Catoosa. *Seminole*: Bowlegs. *Sequoyah*: Illinois River, 0.5 mi. below Tenkiller Dam. *Stephens*: Duncan; Loco. *Tulsa*: Tulsa. *Wagoner*: 2 mi. S Catoosa, and 8 mi. SE Catoosa, Rogers County.

Additional records.—Bryan: 3 mi. E Colbert (TNHC). *Caddo*: Devils Canyon (OSU); Fort Cobb (Cope, 1900:786). *Cherokee*: Camp Muskogee (OSU). *Delaware*: Spavinaw Lake (UMMZ). *Johnston*: 13 mi. N Tishomingo (Carpenter, 1955a:40); 9 mi. N and 4 mi. E Tishomingo (ECSC). *LeFlore*: N Page (Burt, 1935:329); Wister (AMNH, CM); 5.2 mi. N Stapp, 1.5 mi. NE Zoe, and 6 mi. SE Page (Trowbridge, 1937). *Mayes*: 5 mi. S Locust Grove, and Cedar Crest Lake (OSU). *McClain*: 1.5 mi. N and 2.5 mi. W Newcastle (ECSC). *McCurtain*: 2 mi. SW Smithville (Trowbridge, 1937). *Murray*: Camp Classen (OSU). *Muskogee*: Braggs (McCoy, 1960a:43). *Okfuskee*: 1 mi. SE Castle (Burt, 1935:329). *Oklahoma*: 4 mi. NE Edmond (Burt, 1935:329). *Payne*: several within 2 mi. radius Stillwater, and S Boomer Lake Dam (OSU). *Pontotoc*: 7 mi. NE Ada (Carter, 1966:34); 5 mi. S Fittstown (ECSC). *Pushmataha*: Little River between Cloudy and Pickens, McCurtain County (OU). *Sequoyah*: Dwight Mission (ECSC). *Tillman*: confluence North Fork of Red River and Otter Creek (see *Remarks*). *Tulsa*: Mohawk Pond (UMMZ); Dawson, 5 mi. NE Tulsa (UI); Red Fork (UI, UMMZ). *Wagoner*: 5 mi. SE Mazie, Rogers County (TNHC); 2 mi. S Okay (UI).

Pituophis melanoleucus sayi (Schlegel)

Bullsnake

Recognition.—Large, yellow, buff, or straw-colored snakes having brown, red brown, or brown black middorsal blotches and smaller blotches on sides; usually short, dark band behind eye to angle of jaw and less distinct band between eyes; sutures of supralabials usually dark; tail having dark-ringed appearance; belly pale yellow with dusky marks; rostral enlarged; four prefrontals; dorsal scales keeled (first four or five rows smooth) in 31 to 35, usually 33, rows at midbody; anal plate single.

Distribution.—Western Oklahoma; known as far east as Delaware and McIntosh counties (map, Fig. 103).

Remarks.—The occurrence of the bullsnake in Delaware County and a report of the species from Mena, Polk County, Arkansas (Dowling, 1957:23), suggest that bullsnakes may occur throughout the state; the Interior Highlands, however, apparently serve as a barrier to the eastward spread of the species. Bullsnakes are abundant in western Oklahoma; they have been discovered basking in the sun on several occasions (field notes, A. I. Ortenburger), and they are often found dead on highways. Adults are diurnal, whereas juveniles are often nocturnal. Individuals are often captured in urban and residential areas. One snake, obtained about 6:00 a.m. south of Snyder in Kiowa County, had just eaten a ground squirrel (*Citellus tridecemlineatus*).

See Anon. (1952b), Bonn and McCarley (1953:470), Carpenter (1956:43; 1958b:115), Force (1925a:27; 1925b:83; 1930:32), Ortenburger and Bird (1933:61), Ortenburger and Freeman (1930:184), Stull (1940:98).

Specimens examined (OU except as indicated).—*Alfalfa*: several within 4 mi. radius Cherokee; 1 mi. N and 2 mi. E Jet; 6 mi. W Jet; 5.3 mi. S and 4.4 mi. E Driftwood (KU). *Beaver*: near Gate; 1 mi. S Turpin (KU). *Beckham*: 4 mi. SE Erick. *Blaine*: Greenfield; 4 mi. S and 2 mi. W Okeene. *Caddo*: 1 mi. E Hinton. *Canadian*: El Reno; 1 mi. W Calumet. *Cimarron*: Kenton; 5 mi. E Kenton; 3 mi. N Kenton; 7 mi. S Boise City. *Cleveland*: Norman; 6 mi. SE Norman; 7 mi. E Norman; 2 mi. N Hollywood. *Comanche*: Wichita Mts. Wildlife Refuge; 4.5 mi. E and 2 mi. S Sterling. *Cotton*: 2.3 mi. W Taylor. *Custer*: Weatherford. *Delaware*: near Upper Spavinaw

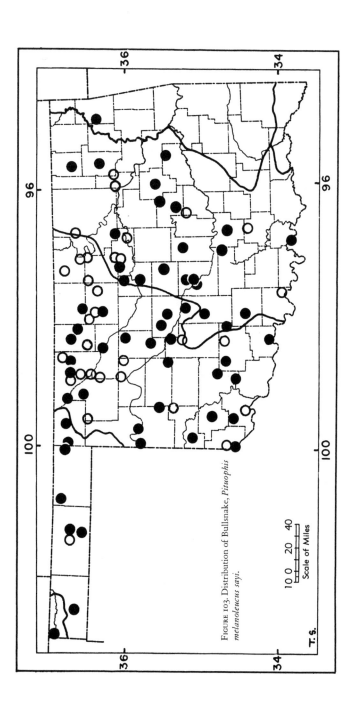

FIGURE 103. Distribution of Bullsnake, *Pituophis melanoleucus sayi*.

10 0   20   40

Scale of Miles

T. S.

Lake. *Ellis*: just N South Canadian River bridge on U.S. Highway 283. *Garfield*: 6 mi. S Enid; 1.3 mi. N Waukomis (TTC). *Garvin*: 1 mi. N and 3.5 mi. W Stratford (ECSC). *Grady*: Tuttle; Chickasha; 7 mi. W eastern county line. *Grant*: 15 mi. E and 1 mi. S Nash. *Greer*: 4 mi. N Mangum. *Harmon*: 3 and 7 mi. SW Hollis. *Harper*: near Gate, Beaver County; 3 mi. N Buffalo. *Jackson*: 1.6 mi. N Duke. *Kiowa*: Cooperton; 2 mi. S Snyder. *Logan*: 2 mi. E Guthrie; 1.7 mi. N Mulhall. *Marshall*: 1 mi. E Powell (RGW). *Major*: 6 mi. S Cleo Springs. *McClain*: 8 mi. S Norman, Cleveland County. *McIntosh*: 5 mi. N Checotah. *Nowata*: 1 mi. E Nowata. *Okfuskee*: 3 mi. S Okemah, and 16 mi. NE Okemah (ECSC). *Oklahoma*: eastern part of county. *Okmulgee*: Okmulgee. *Pawnee*: near Quay. *Payne*: Lake Carl Blackwell. *Pontotoc*: no data (ECSC). *Pottawatomie*: Shawnee. *Roger Mills*: Hammon; 6 mi. NE Durham; 4.5 mi. N Roll. *Rogers*: no data. *Stephens*: Duncan. *Texas*: 8 mi. SE Guymon; 1 mi. SW Optima (KU). *Woods*: 1.5 mi. W and 2 mi. N Edith; 12 mi. W Alva (KU); Alva (NWSC). *Woodward*: 10.5 mi. SW Freedom, Woods County.

Additional records.—Alfalfa: 3 mi. E Carmen (Burt, 1935:331). *Beckham*: 4 mi. NE Elk City (Burt, 1935:331). *Caddo*: 3 mi. W Binger (FMNH). *Comanche*: 4 mi. W Elgin (OU). *Dewey*: 5 mi. NW Canton, Blaine County (Smith and Leonard, 1934:194); 3.1 mi. SE Seiling (OSU). *Garfield*: 5 mi. N Enid (Burt and Hoyle, 1935:209); 1 mi. SE Hillsdale (Burt, 1935:331); 4 mi. S Garber (KKA). *Harmon*: several within 6 mi. radius Hollis (FWCM). *Hughes*: 13 mi. N Holdenville (ECSC). *Jackson*: 5 mi. S Olustee (UMMZ). *Jefferson*: 2 mi. E Grady (CCC). *Johnston*: 2 mi. W Connerville (CCC). *Kay*: 5 mi. S Ponca City, Grainville, and 101 Ranch [locality not found] (Burt, 1935:331). *Logan*: 2 mi. N Guthrie (Burt, 1935:331). *Major*: 3 mi. W Orienta (SWSC); 12 mi. S and 4.5 mi. W Waynoka, Woods County (TTC). *Noble*: 4 mi. E Marland (Burt, 1931a:15); 4 mi. N Billings (Burt, 1935:331). *Osage*: 3 mi. E Burbank (Burt, 1935:331). *Payne*: 9 mi. N Stillwater (FWCM); Stillwater (UMMZ); 1 mi. W Stillwater, 5 mi. S Stillwater, and Yost Lake road, 1 mi. E State Highway 177 (OSU); 5 mi. N Cushing (KKA). *Pontotoc*: 8 mi. ENE Fittstown (Carter and Cox, 1968). *Texas*: 5 mi. N Guymon (OSU). *Tulsa*: Tulsa (UI); 3 mi. N Tulsa (TU); Garnett (UMMZ). *Woods*: 2 mi. E Tegarden (OSU); 10 mi. N Waynoka (SESC); 4 mi. W Capron, and Cimarron River S Waynoka (Burt, 1935:331); Whitehorse Springs (Ortenburger, 1925). *Woodward*: Fort Supply (Cope, 1894:387).

Regina grahami Baird and Girard

Graham's Water Snake

Recognition.—Back dark brown, gray, or olive, with pale mid-dorsal stripe and wide, pale ventrolateral stripe (on first three dorsal scale rows) bordered below by narrow, blackish line (occasionally irregular or zigzag on adjacent parts of first row of dorsal scales and ventrals); belly whitish without markings, or having blackish line or row of dots posteriorly; dorsal scales keeled in 19 rows at midbody; anal plate divided.

Distribution.—Eastern Oklahoma; known as far west as Kingfisher and Beckham counties (map, Fig. 104).

Remarks.—Although there are relatively few records of occurrence for Graham's water snake in Oklahoma, the western limit of its geographic range probably is the High Plains; the species seems to avoid the Interior Highlands. Known field data suggest a preference for the vicinity of ponds, sloughs, small creeks, and headwater streams. One individual was found about one foot above ground in a clump of small willows near the edge of West Cache Creek, Comanche County. A captive female, approximately 720 mm in body length, gave birth to 19 young on September 1 (Boomer Lake, Payne County).

See Burt (1935:333), Burt and Burt (1929b:11), Carpenter (1959c:34), Conant (1960:26), Force (1925a:27; 1925b:83; 1930:35), Laughlin (1959), Smith and Leonard (1934:195).

Specimens examined (OU except as indicated).—*Atoka*: Kiowa

City Lake, 5 mi. S and 1 mi. E Kiowa, Pittsburg County (ECSC). *Beckham*: 4 and 5 mi. S Carter. *Canadian*: 10 mi. W Oklahoma City, Oklahoma County. *Cleveland*: 2–3 mi. S Norman. *Comanche*: Wichita Mts. Wildlife Refuge; Fish Hatchery, Medicine Park. *Craig*: 9.5 mi. W Vinita. *Hughes*: 7 mi. NE Holdenville (ECSC). *Kay*: 2 mi. NE Blackwell. *Marshall*: Cowan Creek, W Willis. *McClain*: 8 mi. SW Norman, Cleveland County. *Muskogee*: 3 mi. SW Warner. *Oklahoma*: NW edge Oklahoma City. *Okmulgee*: Okmulgee. *Osage*: NW edge Tulsa, Tulsa County. *Ottawa*: 2 mi. SW Miami. *Payne*: Boomer Lake (ECSC). *Pittsburg*: 6 mi. SE Stuart, Hughes County (ECSC). *Pottawatomie*: 3 mi. N and 9 mi. E Shawnee. *Tulsa*: 8 mi. NE Tulsa.

Additional records.—Choctaw: 10 mi. S Hugo (Carpenter, 1955a:41). *Creek*: near Kiefer (ECSC). *Garfield*: 5 mi. E Garber (CCC). *Johnston*: Blue River bridge area N Tishomingo (CCC). *Kingfisher*: 3 mi. E Hennessey (McCoy, 1960a:42). *McCurtain*: 3 mi. N and 1 mi. E Harris (Carpenter, 1958a:73). *Noble*: 12 mi. N Perry (Burt and Burt, 1929b:11). *Osage*: Hominy (OSU). *Pawnee*: 2 mi. E and 3 mi. N Mannford, Creek County (FWCM). *Payne*: [Stillwater, Lake Carl Blackwell, and Yost Lake] (Moore and Rigney, 1942:79). *Pittsburg*: Lake McAlester (Laughlin, 1959:83). *Tulsa*: 2 mi. S Alsuma (Burt, 1935:333); Tulsa (CM, UI).

Regina rigida sinicola (Huheey)

Western Glossy Water Snake

Recognition.—Shiny, brownish or black snakes having obscure dark stripes on back and sides in some specimens; lateral pale stripe confined to first dorsal scale row; belly with two rows of large black spots simulating stripes that converge to single line on neck and under tail; dorsal scales keeled in 19 rows at midbody; anal plate divided.

Distribution.—Southeastern Oklahoma; known only from Latimer, Pittsburg, Pushmataha, and McCurtain counties (map, Fig. 105).

280

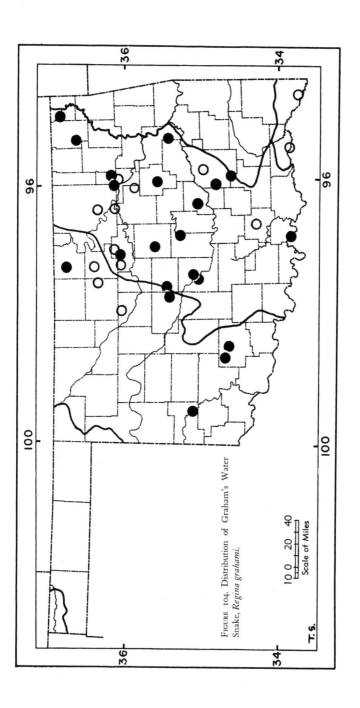

FIGURE 104. Distribution of Graham's Water Snake, *Regina grahami.*

T. S.

Scale of Miles
10 0 20 40

Remarks.—Associated with the biota of the Coastal Plain, glossy water snakes occur to the north in the Ouachita Mountains in lowland habitats along streams. An examination of field notes on the specimen reported by Ortenburger (1927a:97) from Choctaw County (OU 1735) indicates that the snake was taken along the Kiamichi River in Pushmataha County. The snake from Grassy Lake, McCurtain County, was found under a board along the lake shore. See Huheey (1959:309).

Specimens examined (OU except as indicated).—*Latimer*: Wilburton. *McCurtain*: Grassy Lake, 5.5 mi. SE Tom (ECSC). *Pittsburg*: Elm Creek, SE Blanco (ECSC). *Pushmataha*: 4 mi. E Tuskahoma.

Additional records.—*McCurtain*: Little River S Broken Bow (Clarence J. McCoy, Jr., personal communication; one specimen taken in the spring of 1957 in the possession of Robert M. Sutton, U.S. Fish and Wildlife Service, Oklahoma City). *Pushmataha*: 5 mi. E Nashoba (Harold E. Laughlin, personal communication).

Rhinocheilus lecontei tesselatus Garman

Texas Long-nosed Snake

Recognition.—Red, black, and yellow snakes having black middorsal blotches with narrow yellow borders, separated by red interspaces; sides of body having black speckling in red areas and yellow speckling in wider black blotches; snout somewhat pointed, rostral enlarged; belly usually unmarked, or with scattered black marks at sides; most subcaudals in single row; dorsal scales smooth in 23 rows at midbody; anal plate single.

Distribution.—Western Oklahoma;   known as far east as Alfalfa, Blaine, and Comanche counties (map, Fig. 106).

Remarks.—Long-nosed snakes occur in sparsely vegetated places of the Grassland in hilly or flat, sandy or slightly rocky

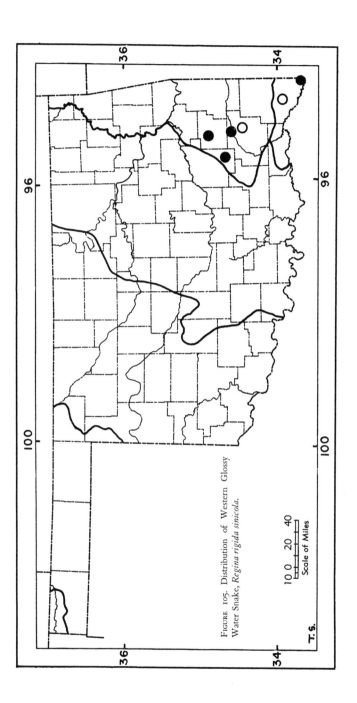

FIGURE 105. Distribution of Western Glossy
Water Snake, *Regina rigida sinicola.*

terrain, and seem to be limited eastward by wooded or dense grassy areas of the Oak-Woodland. The few records of occurrence doubtless reflect the burrowing ability and nocturnal habit of the species, although one specimen was found in early morning.

See Ortenburger and Bird (1933:61) and Ortenburger and Freeman (1930:184–185).

Specimens examined (OU except as indicated).—*Alfalfa*: 10 mi. E Cherokee; Salt Plains Wildlife Refuge (NWSC). *Beaver*: 12 mi. E Forgan. *Comanche*: Sterling; 6 mi. S and 1 mi. E Sterling. *Custer*: 6 mi. NW Custer City. *Greer*: 4 mi. W Mangum (FMNH). *Harmon*: 0.5 mi. S and 1.5 mi. W Hollis; 7 mi. SW Hollis. *Harper*: near Gate, Beaver County; 1 mi. W Speermoore. *Jackson*: 3.5 mi. W Duke. *Woods*: 12 mi. W Alva (KU). *Woodward*: SE edge Fort Supply.

Additional records.—*Blaine*: Canton Reservoir (OSU). *Cimarron*: 8 mi. SW Boise City (ECSC); between Boise City and Kenton (CCC). *Dewey*: 10 mi. E Vici (McCoy, 1960a:43). *Greer*: 2 mi. W and 3 mi. S Reed (KKA). *Harmon*: 3 mi. W Hollis (UA); 5 mi. N Hollis (OSU); several from 3 to 6 mi. S Hollis (FWCM). *Harper*: 5–6 mi. W May (OSU). *Jackson*: 8.5 mi. W and 2.5 mi. N Altus (ECSC). *Woodward*: 2 mi. W Woodward, and 4 mi. E Woodward (OSU). *Woods*: 10 mi. NW Alva (McCracken, 1966:20).

Sistrurus catenatus tergeminus (Say)

Western Massasauga

Recognition.—Poisonous small rattlesnakes (rarely more than 30 inches in length) having facial pit between eye and nostril, and head wider than neck; top of head covered with large scales, only one large scale between large supraocular scales; grayish brown with brown middorsal blotches and smaller ones on sides; belly pale with dark, irregular smudges

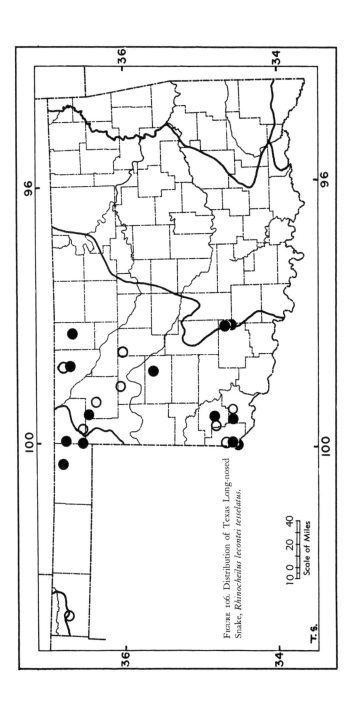

FIGURE 106. Distribution of Texas Long-nosed Snake, *Rhinocheilus leconteí tessellatus.*

and mottling; most subcaudals undivided; upper preocular large, touching nasal; dorsal scales keeled in 25 (rarely 23) rows at midbody; anal plate single.

Distribution.—Western Oklahoma; known as far east as Osage and Cleveland counties (map, Fig. 107).

Remarks.—The western massasauga is apparently largely confined to the Grassland. The extensive wooded areas to the east in the Oak-Woodland and Interior Highlands presumably limit the eastern dispersal of the species, whereas the High Plains probably is a barrier to the west. The panhandle presumably is occupied by the Desert Massasauga, *Sistrurus catenatus edwardsi* (see Gloyd, 1955, and Knopf and Tinkle, 1961:128), which is distinguished from *S. c. tergeminus* in having a paler dorsal ground color, a mostly whitish unmarked belly, and 23 dorsal scale rows at midbody.

Individuals have been taken in flat, short-grass areas (Kiowa County), on rocky hillsides (Comanche County, Fig. 12), and from limestone outcroppings in a small prairie (Osage County). Massasaugas are not uncommon during light rains at night on highways in April and May (Harper County and parts of adjacent Texas). A snake from Kiowa County ate a collared lizard.

See Gloyd (1940:50), Klauber (1956, I:611), Ortenburger and Bird (1933:61), Van Vleet (1902:173).

Specimens examined (OU except as indicated).—*Alfalfa*: 4 mi. E Cherokee; N Jet (NWSC). *Beaver*: 6 mi. W Rosston, Harper County. *Blaine*: Canton Reservoir. *Cleveland*: 9 mi. E Norman. *Comanche*: 8 mi. N Cache; Wichita Mts. Wildlife Refuge. *Custer*: Weatherford. *Dewey*: near Leedey (ECSC). *Harper*: 1 mi. W Rosston; 6 mi. SE Englewood, Kansas. *Kay*: 12 and 14 mi. E Newkirk (KU). *Kiowa*: 10 mi. NW Meers, Comanche County. *Osage*: 13 mi. W Pawhuska. *Woods*: 8 mi. S Alva (NWSC); near Freedom (ECSC).

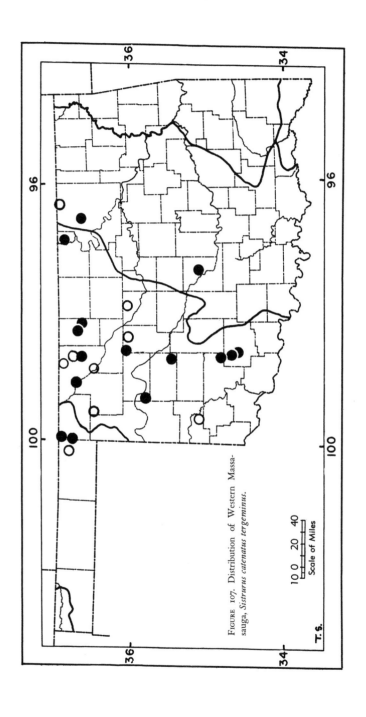

FIGURE 107. Distribution of Western Massasauga, *Sistrurus catenatus tergeminus*.

Scale of Miles

10 0 20 40

T. S.

Additional records.—*Beaver*: Buckshot Arroyo [near Knowles] (Woodburne, 1956:125). *Beckham*: 10 mi. S Sayre (ECSC). *Blaine*: 6 mi. W Okeene (Carter, 1966:35). *Cleveland*: W Norman (Van Vleet, 1902:173). *Kingfisher*: Hennessey (Cope, 1894:387). *Osage*: 13 mi. W and 3 mi. N Pawhuska (OSU); 26 mi. N Pawhuska (AMNH). *Woods*: Alva (Gloyd, 1940:42); 1.5 mi. S Waynoka, and 11.5 mi. N and 6 mi. W Alva (McCracken, 1966:28). *Woodward*: 2 mi. S Fort Supply (McCoy, 1960a:43). *County unknown*: Verdigris River (Gloyd, 1940:42); "Neosho river, Creek country" (Hallowell, 1854:147).

Sistrurus miliarius streckeri Gloyd

Western Pigmy Rattlesnake

Recognition.—Poisonous small rattlesnakes (rarely more than two feet in length) having facial pit between eye and nostril, and head wider than neck; top of head covered with large scales; only one large scale between supraoculars; gray with brown black middorsal blotches and smaller ones on sides; usually red brown middorsal stripe; belly mottled; upper preocular small, not touching nasal; most subcaudals undivided; dorsal scales keeled, usually in 21 rows at midbody; anal plate single.

Distribution.—Eastern Oklahoma; known as far west as Caddo County (map, Fig. 108).

Remarks.—Most records of occurrence suggest a preference for the Oak-Woodland; the species is probably more abundant in the Ozark and Ouachita mountains than available records indicate. The record of *Sistrurus catenatus edwardsi* from Sans Bois Creek, Haskell County (Ortenburger, 1925:87, USNM 491), is based on a specimen of *miliarius* (Gloyd, 1940: 73).

See Bonn and McCarley (1953:471), Carpenter (1956:43; 1960b), Mahaffey (1954).

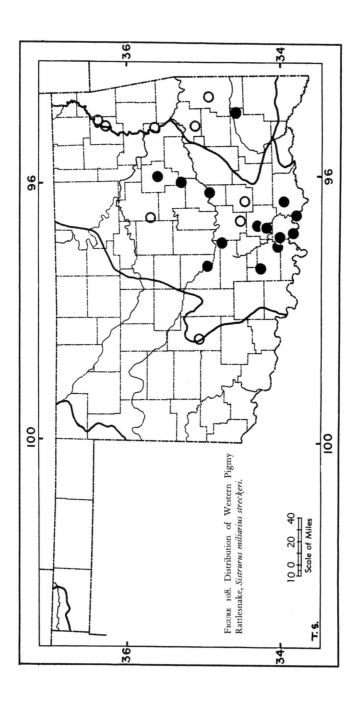

FIGURE 108. Distribution of Western Pigmy Rattlesnake, *Sistrurus miliarius streckeri*.

Specimens examined (OU except as indicated).—*Bryan*: 300 yards below Denison Dam; near Durant (presented to Harold A. Dundee by E. B. Kilpatrick). *Carter*: 9 mi. N and 11 mi. W Ardmore (ECSC); 7 mi. S and 2 mi. E Ardmore (FMNH). *Cleveland*: South Lake, Lexington Game Management Area. *Garvin*: 3 mi. N Stratford (ECSC). *Hughes*: 5 mi. NE Calvin along Canadian River (SESC). *Johnston*: Reagan; Randolph Bottoms, 4 mi. E Russet. *Marshall*: near McMillan; 1 mi. W Willis; 1 mi. NNW Willis. *Okfuskee*: 8 mi. E Weleetka (ECSC). *Okmulgee*: no data. *Pushmataha*: 7 mi. NNW Honobia.

Additional records (Gloyd, 1940:73, except as indicated).— *Bryan*: 5 mi. SW Colbert (TNHC). *Caddo*: Fort Cobb. *Coal*: 11 mi. SE Tupelo (ECSC). *Creek*: near Milfay (ECSC). *Haskell*: Sans Bois Creek. *LeFlore*: Wister. *Mayes*: [near Spavinaw] (McCoy, 1960a: 43); fish hatchery, Salina (OSU). *Muskogee*: Braggs (McCoy, 1960a:43). *Okmulgee*: Okmulgee. *Pontotoc*: S Fittstown (Carter, 1966:36).

Sonora episcopa episcopa (Kennicott)

Great Plains Ground Snake

Recognition.—Plain, pale brownish, sometimes reddish orange snakes of small size (rarely more than 1.5 feet in length), occasionally having pattern of one to several brownish black crossbands; most body scales often well defined, each having dark anterior borders and often small dot at apex; belly white to pale yellow, usually unmarked but with smudges posteriorly and under tail in some specimens; six or seven supralabials; loreal usually present, occasionally absent; two or three postoculars; dorsal scales smooth in 15 rows throughout length of body; anal plate divided.

Distribution.—Throughout the state (map, Fig. 109).

Remarks.—Ground snakes are secretive, burrowing, often in association with flat-headed snakes (*Tantilla*), and commonly

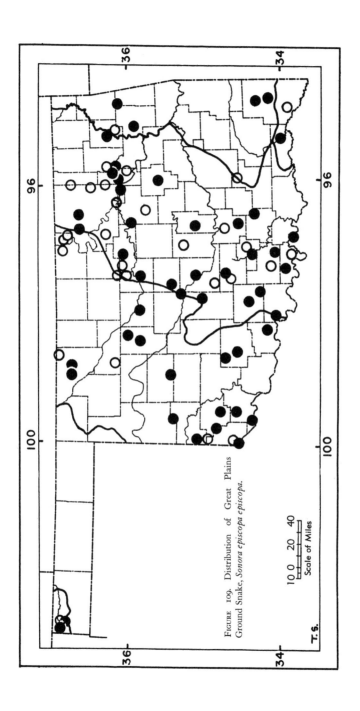

FIGURE 109. Distribution of Great Plains
Ground Snake, *Sonora episcopa episcopa.*

Scale of Miles
10 0 20 40

T. S.

found under small rocks on grassy or partly wooded hillsides; individuals seem most abundant in early spring after rains. Ground snakes are most frequent in the Oak-Woodland, and least abundant in the Interior Highlands near the eastern limit of range for the species. The only red orange snakes seen by me are from the Mesa de Maya in Cimarron County. A collared lizard from Comanche County ate a snake of this species. See account of *Lampropeltis triangulum*.

See Carpenter (1956:43; 1958b:115), Carter and Cox (1968), Dundee (1950a:29), Kassing (1961), Force (1930:34), Moore and Rigney (1942:79), Ortenburger (1923), Webb and Ortenburger (1955:90).

Specimens examined (OU except as indicated).—*Adair*: 5 mi. S Kansas, Delaware County. *Beckham*: 2 mi. W and 5.5 mi. S Erick. *Blaine*: 8 mi. SW Okeene; 6 mi. N Watonga; Roman Nose State Park. *Canadian*: 3 mi. SE Mustang. *Carter*: Ardmore; 5–6 mi. SE Ardmore; 6 mi. S and 2 mi. W Ardmore. *Cherokee*: 2 mi. E Hulbert. *Choctaw*: Sawyer; 4–5 mi. W Fort Towson. *Cimarron*: Kenton; 6.9 mi. E Kenton (TTC); Black Mesa State Park (ECSC). *Cleveland*: 4 mi. E Norman; 3 mi. NE Norman. *Comanche*: 4 mi. N Cache; Wichita Mts. Wildlife Refuge. *Cotton*: 1 mi. S Temple City Lake. *Creek*: Drumright. *Custer*: 3.5 mi. S Clinton (ECSC). *Garvin*: Maysville. *Grady*: between Blanchard, McClain County, and Chickasha. *Greer*: 3 mi. N Mangum; 2.5 mi. S Mangum (KU). *Harmon*: NW Reed, Greer County; 7 mi. SW Hollis; 6 mi. S Hollis. *Jackson*: 4 mi. SE El Dorado; 3 mi. N Duke; 6 mi. SE Duke (TTC). *Jefferson*: 4.5 mi. W Waurika. *Johnston*: 3 mi. W Bromide. *Kingfisher*: no data. *Logan*: Guthrie; 5 mi. NW Guthrie. *Love*: 4 mi. E and 3 mi. S Oswalt. *Marshall*: 1 mi. E Powell; UOBS; Shay. *Mayes*: 6 mi. SE Pryor. *McCurtain*: 9 mi. N Beavers Bend State Park; 24 mi. N Broken Bow. *Murray*: Arbuckle Mts. *Oklahoma*: Oklahoma City. *Okmulgee*: no data. *Osage*: 13 mi. W Pawhuska; 2 mi. E Burbank. *Payne*: Stillwater (KU). *Pontotoc*: 1.5 mi. W Fittstown. *Roger Mills*: 1 mi. N Berlin. *Rogers*: 3 mi. W Catoosa; 2 mi. NE Catoosa. *Seminole*: Bowlegs. *Stephens*: Loco; 10 mi. E

Duncan. *Tulsa*: 2 mi. S Sand Springs; 15 mi. NE Tulsa; 5–6 mi. W Tulsa. *Woods*: 12 mi. W Alva (KU); 1.5 mi. E Tegarden.

Additional records.—Atoka: Limestone Gap (HAD). *Carter*: 10 mi. W Ardmore (KU). *Cimarron*: S Graham, about 5 mi. E Kenton on Cimarron River (OSU). *Creek*: 2 mi. W Bristow (Burt, 1935:332). *Garvin*: Table Top Mts., 7.5 mi. NW Elmore City (SESC). *Harmon*: Hollis (FWCM); 1 mi. N Elm Fork of Red River bridge on State Highway 30 (FMNH). *Kay*: 4 mi. W Lyman, Osage County (Burt, 1935:332); Newkirk (UI); 6 mi. NE Newkirk (FMNH); 13 mi. E Newkirk (KU). *Logan*: 1 mi. N Mulhall (Burt, 1935:332); 2 mi. N Mulhall (Burt and Hoyle, 1935:211). *Love*: 3 mi. N Marietta (FMNH). *Major*: 18 mi. E Fairview (UMMZ). *Mayes*: Locust Grove (USNM). *McClain*: Payne (UMMZ). *McCurtain*: 2 mi. E Garvin (UMMZ). *Murray*: Sulphur (USNM). *Noble*: 3 mi. N Orlando, Logan County (Burt and Hoyle, 1935:211). *Okmulgee*: W Okmulgee (USNM). *Osage*: W Skiatook, Tulsa County (USNM); 2 mi. SE Avant (Burt and Hoyle, 1935:211); 4 mi. W Pawhuska (Burt, 1935:332); 3 mi. W Bartlesville, Washington County (McCoy, 1960a:43). *Pontotoc*: Ada (USNM). *Pawnee*: Keystone (USNM); 2 mi. N Pawnee, and 2 mi. SE Pawnee (Burt, 1935:332). *Payne*: several within 5 mi. radius Stillwater, 7 mi. W and 3 mi. S Stillwater, and Lake Carl Blackwell (OSU). *Pottawatomie*: within 12 mi. radius Shawnee (Webster, 1936:21). *Rogers*: 6 mi. W Claremore (Burt and Hoyle, 1935:211); 1 mi. W Catoosa (UI). *Tulsa*: Tulsa and vicinity (CM, KU, UMMZ, USNM); 5 mi. SE Tulsa (CM); Turley (KU); 1 mi. S Sand Springs (TNHC); 4 mi. SW Sand Springs (AMNH); near Broken Arrow, Limestone, and Lost City (USNM); Garnett (UMMZ, USNM). *Washington*: Bartlesville (AMNH). *Woods*: 18 mi. N and 3 mi. W Alva (McCracken, 1966:22).

Storeria dekayi (Holbrook)

Brown Snakes

Recognition.—Small brownish, gray, or red brown snakes (rarely more than 15 inches in length) having pale middorsal stripe; dorsum with dark crossbars or two longitudinal rows of dark dots on back; two dark blotches on neck; belly whitish, unmarked except for occasional dark peppering laterally; loreal absent; one preocular contacting nasal; young having pale band across neck; dorsal scales keeled in 17 rows throughout length of body; anal plate divided.

Distribution.—Eastern Oklahoma; known as far west as Woodward and Comanche counties; two subspecies (map, Fig. 110).

Remarks.—Trapido (1944) recognized the following two subspecies of *Storeria dekayi* (and intergradation between them) in Oklahoma:

S. d. texana Trapido, Texas Brown Snake.—Two parallel rows of small dark spots flanking pale middorsal stripe; large dark spot under eye; no vertical dark line or bar on anterior temporal.
S. d. wrightorum Trapido, Midland Brown Snake.—Short dark crossbars on back; vertical dark line on anterior temporal.

Trapido (1944) recorded *texana* as far east as Adair, Sequoyah, LeFlore, and McCurtain counties, and *wrightorum* as far west as "Indian Territory, Neutral Strip" (see Fig. 3). He recorded both subspecies from Bryan and McCurtain counties; *texana* and intergrades from Cleveland, Osage, Murray, Pottawatomie, Okmulgee, and Latimer counties; and intergrades and both subspecies from LeFlore and Tulsa counties. Intergradation seems to occur over a broad geographic area, generally the eastern half of Oklahoma, and I have not attempted to indicate intergradation on the distribution map. My subjective impression is that *wrightorum* is associated mostly with the Interior Highlands and that *texana* occurs in the rest of the state. Reports of the species in the Texas panhandle (Tinkle and Knopf, 1964:45) and in Colorado (Maslin, 1959:74) suggest the occur-

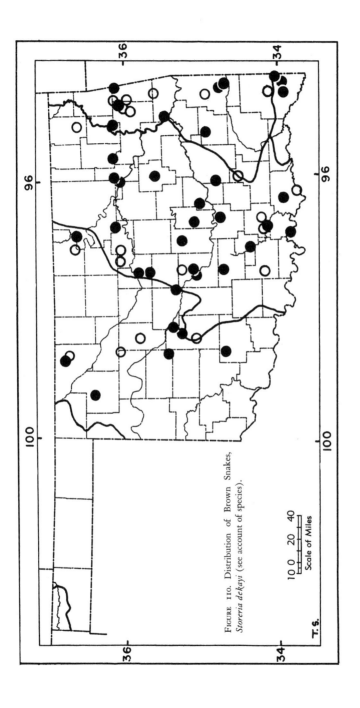

FIGURE 110. Distribution of Brown Snakes, *Storeria dekayi* (see account of species).

Scale of Miles
10 0   20   40

T. S.

rence of brown snakes in suitable mesic habitats in the western-most counties of Oklahoma.

Brown snakes are somewhat secretive, inhabiting wooded or shrubby areas where they may be found under rocks, logs, and other cover, but individuals forage in late afternoon or at dusk. Reproductive data are no more precise than: seven young were born on July 31 (Cleveland County); a female containing 12 embryos was found on July 25 (McCurtain County) and another containing 11 on July 4 (Sequoyah County).

See Carpenter (1956:43; 1958b:113; 1959c:34), Carter and Cox (1968), Ciochetti (1959), Force (1925a:27; 1925b:83), McCoy (1961c), Trowbridge (1937:298).

Specimens examined (OU except as indicated).—*Adair*: 4 mi. NW Watts. *Bryan*: near Durant. *Caddo*: between Hinton and Binger. *Canadian*: near Wheatland, Oklahoma County; Devils Canyon. *Cherokee*: 2 mi. S Scraper. *Cleveland*: several within 7 mi. radius Norman. *Comanche*: Wichita Mts. Wildlife Refuge. *Custer*: 2 mi. E and 1 mi. S Weatherford (SWSC). *Garvin*: Maysville. *Hughes*: Holdenville (ECSC). *Johnston*: 6 mi. SW Tishomingo (ECSC). *Latimer*: several within 9 mi. radius Wilburton. *LeFlore*: 1.5 mi. E Zoe; near Page. *Logan*: Guthrie; 5 mi. N Edmond, Oklahoma County. *Marshall*: UOBS. *Mayes*: 2.7 mi. N Locust Grove; 4 mi. S Locust Grove. *McClain*: 5 mi. S Norman, Cleveland County. *McCurtain*: 10 and 14 mi. SE Broken Bow; 14 mi. E Broken Bow; 6 mi. N Idabel. *Murray*: Price's and Turner falls. *Okmulgee*: Okmulgee. *Osage*: 10 mi. E Ponca City, Kay County. *Pawnee*: near Quay. *Pittsburg*: 5 mi. E and 1 mi. S Stuart, Hughes County (ECSC). *Pontotoc*: 7 mi. NE Ada (ECSC). *Pottawatomie*: Shawnee. *Rogers*: 6 mi. E Catoosa. *Seminole*: Bowlegs. *Sequoyah*: 3 mi. NE Gore. *Tulsa*: Tulsa; Red Fork. *Woods*: 8 and 11 mi. NW Alva (ECSC). *Woodward*: Boiling Springs State Park.

Additional records.—*Adair*: [5 mi. S] vicinity of Kansas, Delaware County (Trapido, 1944:68); Tyner Creek, near Proctor (OSU, KU). *Atoka*: Lake Atoka, 12 mi. S and 1 mi. W Kiowa, Pittsburg County (ECSC). *Blaine*: no data (CCC). *Bryan*: [3 mi. SE Yuba]

(Trapido, 1944:63). *Caddo*: Fort Cobb (Trapido, 1944:68); Kiwanis Canyon (Carpenter, 1958a:73). *Carter*: 2 mi. N and 0.5 mi. E Healdton (ECSC). *Cherokee*: Tahlequah (McCoy, 1960a:42); Hanging Rock (UI). *Cleveland*: 7 mi. E Moore (OU). *Craig*: Vinita (Trapido, 1944:69). *Dewey*: Canton Reservoir (CCC). *Johnston*: 5 mi. NW Tishomingo (SESC); 4 mi. N Milburn (Carpenter, 1955a:41). *Kay*: Arkansas River near Ponca City (Trapido, 1944:69); Ponca City (McCoy, 1960a:42). *LeFlore*: Wister (Trapido, 1944:63, 69). *McCurtain*: 4.8 mi. N Beavers Bend State Park (OU); between Idabel and Broken Bow (TNHC). *Payne*: [several within 4 mi. radius] Stillwater (Trapido, 1944:69); Lake Carl Blackwell (KKA). *Sequoyah*: 0.5 mi. S Adair-Sequoyah county line (OU). *Woods*: several vicinity Alva (McCracken, 1966:24).

Storeria occipitomaculata occipitomaculata (Storer)
Northern Red-bellied Snake

Recognition.—Small, dark brownish or gray snakes (rarely more than 15 inches in length), usually having pale middorsal stripe; pale lateral stripe on second scale row; three pale spots often on neck; loreal absent; usually two preoculars touching nasal; belly mostly red (in life) with lateral ends of ventral scales heavily pigmented; dorsal scales keeled in 15 rows throughout length of body; anal plate divided.

Distribution.—Eastern Oklahoma; known as far west as Tulsa County (map, Fig. 111).

Remarks.—Except for Dundee's comments (1948), data for Oklahoma specimens are lacking. The species seems to be limited mostly to the Interior Highlands.

Specimens examined.—*Adair*: 0.5 mi. E and 1 mi. N Proctor (UMMZ). *Cherokee*: 5 mi. N and 3 mi. E Tahlequah (UMMZ). *Latimer*: 2.5 mi. N Wilburton (OU); Robbers Cave State Park (NWSC). *Mayes*: 5 mi. N Locust Grove, and near Lower Spavinaw Lake (OU). *McCurtain*: State Game Refuge (OU). *Pushmataha*: near Nashoba (OU). *Tulsa*: Tulsa (UMMZ).

Additional records.—Cherokee: Camp Muskogee (McCoy, 1960a: 42). *Delaware*: 1.7 mi. W Flint (AMNH).

Tantilla gracilis Baird and Girard

Flat-headed Snake

Recognition.—Plain pale brown snakes less than ten inches long; head slightly darker brown than body, usually having sharp line of demarcation on cheek between dark head cap and pale side of head; belly whitish, but having pink midventral area in life; loreal absent, with nasal pointed posteriorly; six supralabials; one postocular; dorsal scales smooth in 15 rows throughout length of body; anal plate divided.

Distribution.—Eastern Oklahoma; known as far west as Kay, Blaine, Caddo, and Comanche counties (map, Fig. 112).

Remarks.—Records of the species in the Texas panhandle (P. W. Smith, 1956; Tinkle and Knopf, 1964:45) indicate either that populations of this species are relatively isolated, like those of *Storeria dekayi*, *Thamnophis sirtalis*, and *Tropidoclonion lineatum*, or that flat-headed snakes occur farther to the west in Oklahoma than is now known.

Tantilla gracilis, seemingly best adapted to loose soils of the Interior Highlands and Oak-Woodland, extends westward into the Grassland. Individuals are secretive and burrow, and are most abundantly found in early spring in open or wooded, flat or hilly terrain, under cover of trash, logs, or usually small (limestone) rocks. See account of *Lampropeltis triangulum*.

See Carpenter (1956:43; 1958b:115), Dundee and Burger (1948), Force (1930:36; 1935:646), Kassing (1961:185, 187, 188); Kirn, Burger, and Smith (1949), Smith and Leonard (1934:195).

Specimens examined (OU except as indicated).—*Adair*: 3 mi. E Proctor; 4 mi. N Stilwell; 3 mi. S Kansas, Delaware County. *Atoka*: 15 mi. SE Atoka. *Blaine*: 6 mi. W Okeene. *Bryan*: no data. *Carter*:

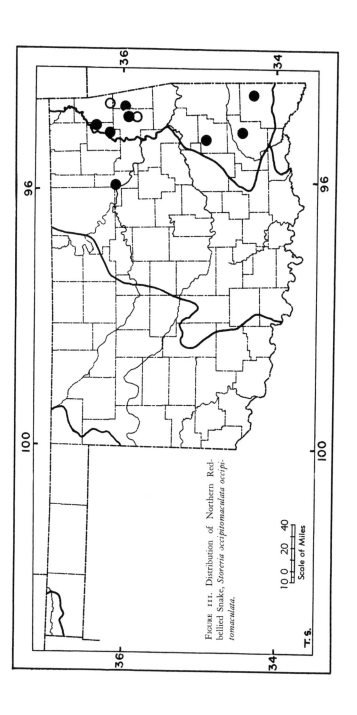

FIGURE III. Distribution of Northern Red-bellied Snake, *Storeria occipitomaculata occipitomaculata*.

T. S.

10 0   20   40

Scale of Miles

Ardmore; 6 mi. SW Ardmore; 5 mi. SE Ardmore. *Cherokee*: Camp Egan; 4 mi. N and 5 mi. E Tahlequah (KU); 2 mi. E Welling; 5 mi. W Welling; 2 mi. S Scraper; 2 mi. E Hulbert. *Cleveland*: 4, 7, and 9 mi. E Norman; 2 mi. N Norman; 8 mi. NE Norman; 3–4 mi. S Norman; 9 mi. E Lexington. *Comanche*: 3 mi. E Sterling; Wichita Mts. Wildlife Refuge. *Creek*: Drumright (KU). *Garvin*: Maysville. *Hughes*: no data. *Latimer*: Lutie; Wilburton; 2 mi. N Wilburton; 8 mi. NW Wilburton; 25.3 mi. N Clayton, Pushmataha County (TTC). *LeFlore*: Stapp; 18 mi. SW Wister. *Logan*: Guthrie; 5 mi. NW Guthrie. *Marshall*: UOBS; 1 mi. E Powell; 8 mi. W Kingston; Shay. *McClain*: 9 mi. SW Norman, Cleveland County. *McCurtain*: Idabel. *Murray*: Turner Falls; Dougherty; Platt National Park (KU). *Nowata*: Coody's Bluff. *Oklahoma*: 5 mi. NE Oklahoma City. *Okmulgee*: Okmulgee. *Osage*: 13 mi. W Pawhuska; 2 mi. E Barnsdall; NW Tulsa, Tulsa County. *Ottawa*: 6 mi. E Miami (KU); several within 2.5 mi. radius Peoria (KU); within 4 mi. radius Quapaw (KU). *Pawnee*: near Quay; 0.5 mi. N Hallet. *Payne*: near Drumright, Creek County (KU); Stillwater; near Lake Carl Blackwell. *Pottawatomie*: Shawnee; 5 mi. W Shawnee; 2 mi. NE Shawnee; St. Louis. *Pushmataha*: near Nashoba; 3 mi. NE Cloudy; 0.5 mi. S Clayton (TTC). *Rogers*: 2 mi. NE Catoosa; 8 mi. E Catoosa. *Seminole*: Bowlegs. *Stephens*: 10 mi. E Duncan. *Tulsa*: Tulsa; 2 mi. SW Tulsa (KU); 9 mi. SE Tulsa; 5 and 7–8 mi. SW Tulsa; 2 mi. S Sand Springs; E Bixby. *Wagoner*: 2 mi. S Catoosa, and 6 mi. SE Catoosa, Rogers County; 2 mi. S Okay (KU).

Additional records.—Adair: 3 mi. S Bunch (KU); 4 mi. W Stilwell (UI). *Atoka*: Limestone Gap (Stone, 1903:542). *Caddo*: Kiwanis Canyon (OU); Devils Canyon (OSU); Fort Cobb (Cope, 1900:1112; Kirn, Burger and Smith, 1949:243). *Canadian*: Methodist [Devils] Canyon (Carter, 1966:35). *Cherokee*: Camp Muskogee (OSU); near Barber, and 4 mi. SE Cookson (KU). *Choctaw*: 7 mi. W Fort Towson (FMNH). *Comanche*: Fort Sill (AMNH). *Craig*: 4 mi. SW Whiteoak (Burt and Hoyle, 1935:215). *Creek*: 2 mi. W Bristow, 1 mi. NW Milfay, 2 mi. E Sapulpa, 4 mi. SW Sapulpa, and 1 mi. SW Oakhurst, Tulsa County (Burt, 1935:336). *Grady*: near Minco (Carpenter, 1958a:74). *Hughes*: 10 mi. E We-

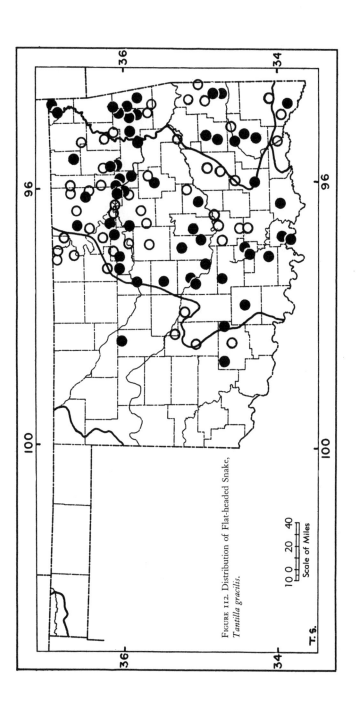

FIGURE 112. Distribution of Flat-headed Snake, *Tantilla gracilis*.

tumka (UMMZ). *Johnston*: 2 mi. W Connerville (ECSC). *Kay*: 3 mi. NE Ponca City (OSU); 13 mi. E Newkirk (KU); 4 mi. W Lyman, Osage County (Burt, 1935:336); 6 mi. SE Chilocco, and 6 mi. NE Newkirk (Burt and Hoyle, 1935:215). *LeFlore*: Wister, and Sugarloaf Mt. (Stone, 1903:542); Panama (KU). *Lincoln*: 3 mi. N Chandler (Burt, 1935:336). *Mayes*: 6 mi. SE Pryor (KU); Locust Grove (USNM); 5 mi. SW Locust Grove (TNHC). *Mc-Curtain*: 25 mi. W Broken Bow (OU); 2 mi. E Garvin (UMMZ); Beavers Bend State Park (OU, OSU, FWCM). *Murray*: 5 mi. S and 2 mi. W Davis (FWCM). *Muskogee*: 3 mi. S and 3 mi. W Porum (HAD). *Noble*: 6 mi. E Perry (McCoy, 1960a:43). *Okmulgee*: Bald Hill (FMNH). *Osage*: 13 mi. SE Fairfax (UMMZ); 2 mi. N Sand Springs, and 2 mi. NW Tulsa, Tulsa County (TNHC); 2 mi. SE Avant, 4 mi. W Pawhuska, and 7 mi. W Bartlesville, Washington County (Burt and Hoyle, 1935:215). *Pawnee*: 2 mi. N Pawnee and 2 mi. SE Pawnee (Burt, 1935:336); 2 mi. E and 3 mi. N Mannford, Creek County (FWCM). *Payne*: 4 mi. W Quay (Burt, 1935:336); 1 mi. NE Ripley (UMMZ); several within 7 mi. radius Stillwater, 2 mi. W Yale, and 1 mi. N and 1 mi. W Yost Lake (OSU). *Pittsburg*: McAlester (UI); 18 mi. S McAlester (Stone, 1903:542). *Pontotoc*: 4 mi. W Allen, 5 mi. S Fittstown, 7 mi. NE Ada, and 10 mi. W Ada (ECSC). *Pushmataha*: 18 mi. SSE Talihina, LeFlore County (TCWC). *Rogers*: 6 mi. W Claremore (Burt and Hoyle, 1935: 215); 6 mi. E Catoosa (Dundee and Burger, 1948); 1 mi. W Catoosa (UI); 12 mi. E Tulsa, Tulsa County (CM); 2 mi. NE Garnett, Tulsa County (UMMZ); Tulsa Fin and Feather Club (OSU). *Tulsa*: near Keystone, Payne County, and Skiatook (USNM); Red Fork, Lost City, and several within vicinity Tulsa (FMNH); 1 mi. S Sand Springs (TNHC); Turley (KU). *Washington*: 2 mi. S Bartlesville (AMNH).

Tantilla nigriceps Kennicott

Black-headed Snakes

Recognition.—Pale brown snakes usually less than 15 inches long, having black head cap usually pointed behind and sharply demarcated from body color; broad midventral pink area (in life) lacking on underside of head; loreal absent with nasal pointed posteriorly; seven supralabials; two postoculars; dorsal scales smooth in 15 rows throughout length of body; anal plate divided.

Distribution.—Western Oklahoma; known as far east as Woods, Custer, and Comanche counties; two subspecies (map, Fig. 113).

Remarks.—The two subspecies of *Tantilla nigriceps* are distinguished by the number of ventral scales. Ventrals are fewer in *fumiceps* than *nigriceps*, and males have fewer ventrals than females (Blanchard, 1938; Smith, 1942).

T. n. nigriceps Kennicott, Plains Black-headed Snake.—Ventrals usually more than 150.
T. n. fumiceps (Cope), Texas Black-headed Snake.—Ventrals usually fewer than 150.

Intergradation presumably occurs in western Oklahoma (see discussion of southwestern filter barrier, page 49), with *nigriceps* to the north and *fumiceps* to the south. The extent and limits of the intergrading area are uncertain pending further study, especially of specimens from northwestern Oklahoma. Most specimens are from the southwest corner of the state, where the population is most like *fumiceps*; to judge from the average ventral count in females, however, southwestern Oklahoma seems to be mostly an intergrading area. Of 17 specimens from southwestern Oklahoma (south of Custer County), ventral counts average 141.5, ranging from 131 to 155; only two females have counts exceeding 150 (152 and 155), but they are from the same locality (Jackson County) as three females with counts of 144, 147 and 147. Ventrals in 11 males average 137.3 (131–142), and in six females 149.2 (144–155). Caudals average 48.1 (39–57) in 17 specimens—51.3 (45–57) in 11 males, and 42.2 (39–45) in six females. Of these 17 specimens, the largest female measures 247 mm in body length (tail incomplete), whereas the largest male is 189 mm (tail, 49 mm). Of 20 specimens from southwestern Oklahoma, three (including two of ten from Jackson County) have the mental touching the first pair of genials. The configuration of the posterior edge of the black head cap is variable; it may form an acute angle three or four scale-lengths long, or form a "rounded," obtuse angle (nearly straight in some specimens) two scale-lengths behind the parietals, or only the first two or three scales of the middorsal row may be darkened.

Black-headed snakes occur in the Grassland and High Plains, and are the western counterparts of *Tantilla gracilis* in eastern Oklahoma. Donald Tinkle and I collected ten individuals in less than 30 minutes underneath small flat rocks on a grassy hillside on an overcast afternoon with intermittent light rain (May 11, 1957, Jackson County); one of the snakes had eaten a centipede. The specimen from Tillman County was found in an overgrazed pasture beneath a dried cow dropping.

Reports of this species from Payne County (Smith and Leonard, 1934:195, Moore and Rigney, 1942:80) refer to two specimens of *Tantilla atriceps* (see page 60).

Specimens examined (OU except as indicated).—*Beckham*: 4 mi. SE Erick. *Comanche*: Wichita Mts. Wildlife Refuge. *Custer*: Weatherford (SWSC). *Dewey*: Seiling (FMNH). *Greer*: 3 mi. S Mangum. *Harmon*: 6 mi. S Hollis; NW Reed, Greer County. *Jackson*: 6 mi. SE Duke (TTC). *Kiowa*: Cooperton. *Texas*: Goodwell. *Tillman*: no data. *Woods*: Alva (KU); 18 mi. W and 5 mi. N Alva (ECSC).

Additional records.—*Cimarron*: 14 mi. E Kenton (ECSC). *Harmon*: 3 mi. W and 5 mi. S Hollis (FMNH). *Jackson*: 8.5 mi. W and 2.5 mi. N Altus (ECSC). *Kiowa*: 9 mi. S Lone Wolf and 2 mi. S Lugert (OSU).

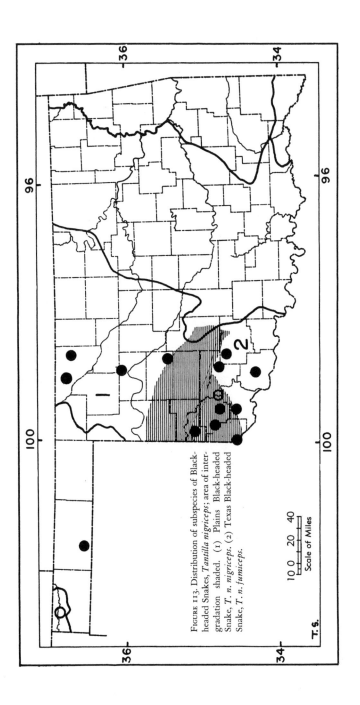

FIGURE 113. Distribution of subspecies of Black-headed Snakes, *Tantilla nigriceps*; area of inter-gradation shaded. (1) Plains Black-headed Snake, *T. n. nigriceps.* (2) Texas Black-headed Snake, *T. n. fumiceps.*

Thamnophis elegans vagrans (Baird and Girard)
Wandering Garter Snake

Recognition.—Dark, mostly uniform gray or brownish snakes, but having ill-defined, pale, longitudinal stripes and indistinct, blackish marks between middorsal and lateral stripes; pale lateral stripe on second and third rows of dorsal scales anteriorly; belly dusky gray with broad midventral blackish area; dorsal scales keeled in 21 rows at midbody; anal plate single.

Distribution.—Known only from the northwestern corner of Cimarron County in the panhandle.

Remarks.—The species is limited to the Mesa de Maya on the High Plains. Individuals have been found along slow-moving creeks and streams, near temporary and artificial ponds, and under rocks on hillsides. See Ortenburger and Freeman (1930: 185–186), and account of *Thamnophis radix haydeni*.

Specimens examined.—*Cimarron*: Black Mesa, 3 mi. N Kenton (OU); 4 mi. NW Kenton (OU); 2 mi. W Kenton (TTC).

Additional record.—*Cimarron*: 0.5 mi. SE State Monument (Fitch, 1940:25).

Thamnophis marcianus (Baird and Girard)
Checkered Garter Snakes

Recognition.—Striped snakes having predominant checkerboard pattern of alternating blackish spots; pale middorsal stripe narrow, mostly confined to the vertebral scale row; pale lateral stripe on third dorsal scale row anteriorly; well-defined, pale, curved mark behind angle of jaw followed by black blotch; belly without markings except for small black marks laterally on ends of ventrals; dorsal scales keeled in 21 rows at midbody; anal plate single.

Distribution.—Western Oklahoma; known as far east as Garfield, Logan, Oklahoma, Stephens, and Jefferson counties; two subspecies (map, Fig. 114).

Remarks.—Mittleman (1949) recognized two subspecies of *Thamnophis marcianus* in Oklahoma, distinguishing them principally by the number of ventral scales (155 or fewer in the eastern checkered garter snake, *T. m. marcianus*, and 156 or more in the western checkered garter snake, *T. m. nigrolateris*). On the basis of the number of ventrals and caudals, and the combined number of ventral and caudal scales (Mittleman, 1949), the checkered garter snakes in Oklahoma are considered to be predominantly *nigrolateris*, those from the southwestern part of the state tending toward *marcianus*. Although ventral scales have not been counted on all known Oklahoma specimens, all counts of 155 or fewer (*marcianus*) are for snakes found in southwestern Oklahoma, except for two specimens from Harper (152) and Blaine (155) counties. However, of 18 males and females from southwestern Oklahoma (Comanche, Kiowa, Jackson, Harmon, and Beckham counties), ventrals average 157.6, with extremes of 148 and 165, thus tending toward *nigrolateris*. The region of intergradation seems to be widespread in most of western Oklahoma and difficult to delineate, and I have not attempted to indicate intergradation on the distribution map. Stebbins (1966:173, Map 154) did not recognize the existence of two subspecies.

Checkered garter snakes occur in the High Plains and Grassland, frequenting mesic habitats along rivers and small streams and by ponds, but they have also been found foraging overland in places where no water was in sight. A half-grown snake captured on a rainy night about 1:00 a.m. among calling individuals of *Bufo cognatus* and *Scaphiopus bombifrons*, regurgitated a small spadefoot toad (Texas County). A female, approximately

495 mm in body length, contained ten embryos on June 28 (Texas County). See account of *Thamnophis radix*.

See McCoy (1961d), Ortenburger and Freeman (1930:185), Webb and Ortenburger (1955:91), Van Vleet (1902:172).

Specimens examined (OU except as indicated).—*Alfalfa*: Great Salt Plain Reservoir Dam. *Beaver*: vicinity Gate. *Beckham*: 8 mi. SW Carter. *Blaine*: 6 mi. N Watonga. *Canadian*: near Okarche. *Comanche*: 12 mi. S Lawton; Wichita Mts. Wildlife Refuge. *Cotton*: 14 mi. E Devol. *Garfield*: 2 mi. E and 3 mi. N Garber. *Harmon*: 3 mi. E Vinson; 0.5 mi. W McQueen; 1 mi. W junction State Highway 30 and Elm Fork of Red River. *Harper*: vicinity Gate, Beaver County. *Jackson*: near Altus; 7 mi. E El Dorado. *Kiowa*: Roosevelt; 3 mi. S Cooperton; Cooperton; 5 mi. W Gotebo. *Oklahoma*: SW Oklahoma City. *Stephens*: Duncan. *Texas*: 2 mi. SW Guymon (RGW); 6 mi. W Texas-Beaver county line; 4 mi. E and 7 mi. S Guymon. *Woods*: 2 mi. E Waynoka (RGW).

Additional records.—*Comanche*: 5 and 7 mi. N Cache, and 5 mi. NE Cache (Mittleman, 1949:244). *Cotton*: 6 mi. E Randlett (CCC). *Garfield*: Enid (McCoy, 1961d); 10 mi. E Enid (CCC). *Greer*: 1 mi. N and 3 mi. W Mangum (McCoy, 1960a:42). *Harmon*: 3 mi. W Hollis (UA); several within 6 mi. radius Hollis (FWCM). *Jefferson*: Waurika area (MU). *Kiowa*: 2.2 mi. W Hobart (OSU). *Logan*: 21 mi. E Hennessey, Kingfisher County (McCoy, 1961d). *Tillman*: vicinity Slough Creek, E Hollister (Mittleman, 1949:243). *Woods*: Alva (Mittleman, 1949:247); 2 mi. S Capron, and several vicinity Alva (McCracken, 1966:24); Whitehorse Springs (Ruthven, 1908:62). *Woodward*: 2 mi. N Alabaster Caverns State Park (McCoy, 1960a:42); Fort Supply (Cope, 1894:387; Ruthven, 1908:62).

Thamnophis proximus proximus (Say)

Western Ribbon Snake

Recognition.—Prominently striped, slender snakes; usually uniform black, or brownish, between pale longitudinal stripes; pale lateral stripe on dorsal scale rows three and four anteriorly; whitish supralabials usually eight, lacking dark marks on su-

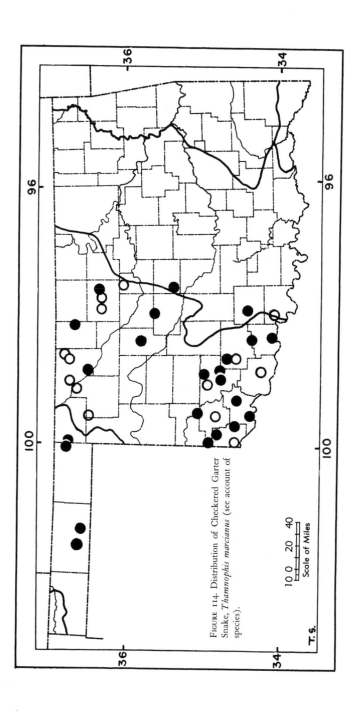

FIGURE 114. Distribution of Checkered Garter Snake, *Thamnophis marcianus* (see account of species).

Scale of Miles

10 0 20 40

T. S.

tures, and contrasting with dark top of head; vertical pale bar on preocular; complete tail long, one fourth to one third total length of snake; belly whitish to pale yellow green, lacking dark marks; dorsal scales keeled in 19 rows at midbody; anal plate single.

Distribution.—Throughout the state (map, Fig. 115).

Remarks.—Ribbon snakes in extreme western Oklahoma are representative of an intergradient population between *T. p. proximus* and *T. p. diabolicus* (Rossman, 1963:132; 110, Fig. 2). *Thamnophis p. diabolicus* differs from *T. p. proximus* in having an olive gray to brown ground color (black in *proximus*) and a dark ventrolateral stripe encroaching on edges of ventrals (not including edges of ventrals in *proximus*). Probably the subspecies intergrade in the western part of the Grassland, with *diabolicus* inhabiting the High Plains and *proximus* the rest of the state to the east. The only specimen from the panhandle (Texas County, OU 4721) is brown. The relationships of the two subspecies in western Oklahoma are uncertain.

Ribbon snakes, less abundant in western than in eastern Oklahoma, are frequently observed about sloughs and streams, but have been found some distance from water in vegetated places. The westernmost specimen was taken along Coldwater Creek, a tributary of Beaver River. On the sandy, weedy bank of Dog Creek (Woods County) six snakes were found by locating the protesting calls of ranid frogs being eaten.

See Bonn and McCarley (1953:470), Burt and Hoyle (1935: 214), Carpenter (1956:43; 1958b:113–114; 1959c:34), Carter and Cox (1968), Force (1930:36), Rossman (1963:114), Sturgis (1939:20), Trowbridge (1937:298), Ortenburger and Freeman (1930:186).

Specimens examined (OU except as indicated).—*Adair*: Proctor. *Alfalfa*: 6 mi. N and 10 mi. E Cherokee. *Beckham*: 5 mi. S Carter.

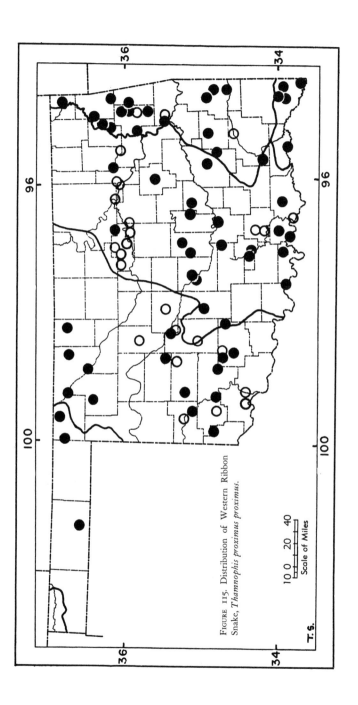

FIGURE 115. Distribution of Western Ribbon Snake, *Thamnophis proximus proximus*.

Bryan: no data. *Caddo*: Kiwanis Park (SWSC). *Cherokee*: Mc-Spadden Falls; 2 mi. SW Cookson; 4 mi. SE Ellerville; 4 mi. N Fort Gibson, Muskogee County; 1 and 5 mi. S Scraper; 3 mi. N Scraper. *Choctaw*: 2 mi. SW Grant; Red River Fisheries. *Cleveland*: 2–4 mi. S Norman. *Comanche*: 3 mi. E Sterling; 5 mi. N Cache; Wichita Mts. Wildlife Refuge. *Custer*: Weatherford (SWSC). *Delaware*: 0.5 mi. SW Flint; Dripping Springs; Chloeta. *Garvin*: Stratford, and 2 mi. N Stratford (ECSC). *Grady*: Chickasha. *Harmon*: 3 mi. E Vinson. *Harper*: near Gate, Beaver County; 8 mi. N Buffalo. *Hughes*: 2 mi. N Yeager. *Jefferson*: near Petersburg. *Kiowa*: Cooperton; Quartz Mt. State Park. *Latimer*: Wilburton; 6 mi. S Wilburton; 5.5 mi. E Wilburton. *LeFlore*: Wister; 17 mi. SW Wister; 6 mi. SW Page. *Love*: 8 mi. N Marietta. *Marshall*: UOBS; Madill Lake. *Mayes*: 4 mi. S Spavinaw; 4 mi. N Locust Grove. *McClain*: 4 mi. SW Norman, Cleveland County. *McCurtain*: 4 mi. NW Broken Bow; 13–15 mi. SE Broken Bow; SE corner of county; 6 mi. NE Idabel. *Murray*: Dougherty; Price's and Turner falls. *Okmulgee*: Okmulgee. *Ottawa*: 3 mi. E Wyandotte. *Pawnee*: near Quay. *Pittsburg*: 3 mi. E McAlester (ECSC); near Haileyville. *Pontotoc*: 7 mi. NE Ada (ECSC). *Pottawatomie*: Shawnee; 3 mi. E Shawnee; Lake Tecumseh; 9 mi. W Tecumseh. *Pushmataha*: 4 mi. W Antlers (ECSC). *Rogers*: 1 mi. W Catoosa. *Seminole*: 3 mi. N Wewoka (ECSC). *Sequoyah*: 2 mi. NE Gore. *Texas*: 8 mi. SE Guymon. *Washita*: in western part of county between Carter, Beckham County, and Cordell. *Woods*: 2 mi. W Edith; 2 mi. W and 1 mi. S Waynoka; W Alva (NWSC). *Woodward*: 3.5 mi. WNW Woodward.

Additional records.—Beckham: 1 mi. S Sayre, and 4 mi. W Sayre (Burt, 1935:335); 4 mi. SW Sayre (Burt and Hoyle, 1935:214). *Blaine*: no data (CCC). *Bryan*: 5 mi. SW Colbert (SESC). *Caddo*: Fort Cobb (Yarrow, 1882:114; Ortenburger, 1925:87). *Canadian*: El Reno (FMNH); Devils Canyon (Carpenter, 1958a:73). *Cherokee*: Camp Muskogee (OSU); 4 mi. W and 5.4 mi. SE Scraper (UMMZ). *Comanche*: "Mayers" (= Meers, USNM). *Creek*: Drumright (Smith and Leonard, 1934:195). *Custer*: 5 mi. NE Weatherford (SWSC). *Greer*: 4 mi. SE Mangum (Burt and Hoyle,

1935:214). *Jackson*: 11.5 mi. S and 2 mi. E Altus (ECSC). *Johnston*: Tishomingo (OSU); 3 mi. N Tishomingo (Carpenter, 1955a:41); Reagan (CCC); 0.5 mi. W Tishomingo (TCWC). *Mayes*: Spavinaw (OSU); near Lower Spavinaw Lake (OU). *McCurtain*: mouth Mountain Fork River (OSU); Idabel (UMMZ); 2 mi. SW Tom (UI). *Murray*: Camp Classen (OSU). *Osage*: 15 mi. W Tulsa, Tulsa County (TNHC). *Payne*: Cushing (UMMZ); Stillwater (UMMZ, OSU, MCZ); Lake Carl Blackwell (OSU); 1 mi. S and 1 mi. E Mehan, and Yost Lake (FWCM). *Pittsburg*: 2.5 mi. NE Krebs (UMMZ). *Pushmataha*: 3 mi. E Tuskahoma (FMNH). *Rogers*: 5 mi. S Inola (UMMZ); Tulsa Fin and Feather Club (OSU). *Sequoyah*: Swimmers Creek, 10 mi. E Gore (OSU). *Tillman*: Tillman-Jackson county line (USNM). *Tulsa*: Tulsa (AMNH); Mohawk Park, and Garnett (UMMZ); Red Fork (UMMZ, UI). *Washita*: 2 mi. N and 2 mi. W Corn (SWSC).

Thamnophis radix haydeni (Kennicott)

Western Plains Garter Snake

Recognition.—Striped snakes having alternating rows of blackish spots between pale longitudinal stripes; middorsal stripe wide, involving one complete row and half of each adjacent row; lateral stripe on third and fourth scale rows anteriorly; supralabials usually seven; belly having rather large black spots along sides; dorsal scales keeled in 21 rows at midbody; anal plate single.

Distribution.—Known only from the panhandle of Oklahoma (map, Fig. 116).

Remarks.—*Thamnophis radix* is confined to the Mesa de Maya and High Plains. Individuals of *radix* are reported to have been found among small rocks along a wet, sandy stretch of river bed, in a clump of tall sedges, and in a dry tumbleweed about 20 feet from water. In the summer of 1926 Beryl Freeman collected 21 individuals of *radix* and four of *T. elegans vagrans*

313

northwest of Kenton, Cimarron County, in and around a shallow, artificial pond that was edged with sunflowers, grasses, and other herbs; the snakes were feeding on tadpoles of *Scaphiopus*; one female *radix* had eaten 16.

Smith's remarks about hybridization of *T. radix* and *T. marcianus* in southwestern Kansas (1946:99), supplement those made by Ruthven (1908:69) and Smith (1949:287) about Oklahoma specimens having characteristics of both species. A specimen from Alfalfa County (OU 28831), identified as *radix* by Carpenter (1958a:73), is herein referred to the species *marcianus*. The reports of *radix* from Grady (Ortenburger and Freeman, 1930:186) and Pottawatomie (Webster, 1936:21) counties are presumably based on other kinds of snakes.

Specimens examined (all OU).—*Cimarron*: Black Mesa, 3–4 mi. N Kenton; 4 mi. NW Kenton; 6 mi. SE Kenton. *Texas*: 8 mi. SE Guymon.

Additional records.—*Beaver*: no data (Marr, 1944:487). *Cimarron*: 0.5 mi. SE State Monument (Smith, 1949:292); 6 mi. N Kenton (OSU).

Thamnophis sirtalis parietalis (Say)

Red-sided Garter Snake

Recognition.—Dark, striped snakes, having obscure blotched pattern; middorsal stripe prominent, pale yellow to red; lateral stripes on second and third scale rows anteriorly; reddish skin often between scales on sides; usually seven upper labials; dark spots on lateral ends of ventrals; dorsal scales keeled in 19 rows at midbody; anal plate single.

Distribution.—Eastern Oklahoma; known as far west as Woodward and Cotton counties (map, Fig. 117).

Remarks.—*Thamnophis sirtalis* occurs sparingly in the Grass-

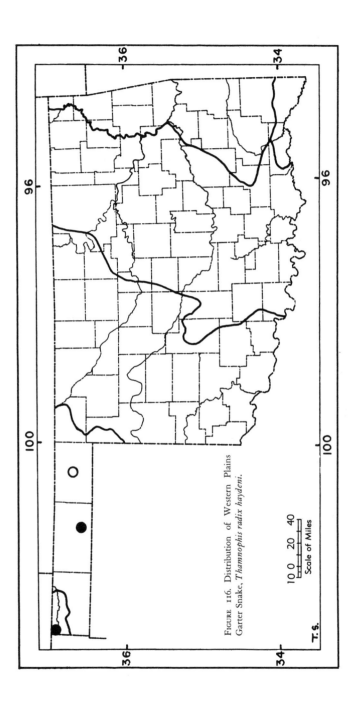

FIGURE 116. Distribution of Western Plains
Garter Snake, *Thamnophis radix haydeni.*

land. Red-sided garter snakes, less frequently observed than ribbon snakes, can be expected in most riparian habitats, but have been found in wooded or shrubby areas away from water. A female contained 34 embryos on July 19 (Johnston County).

It is expected that the Texas garter snake, *T. sirtalis annectens* (if it is distinguishable from *parietalis*), will be found in Oklahoma because disjunct populations from Meade County State Park, Kansas, and the Texas panhandle represent that subspecies according to Fitch and Maslin (1961:295–296). The subspecies *annectens* differs from *parietalis* (Brown, 1950:203) in that the pale lateral stripe involves the fourth dorsal scale row (instead of only the second and third), the middorsal stripe is orangish (instead of yellow), the upper row of dark blotches forms a distinct, alternating series (instead of being indistinct and fused into a broad black stripe), and the skin is not reddish on sides. At this time, however, the status of *annectens* in Oklahoma is uncertain, and all *Thamnophis sirtalis* are referred to *parietalis*. Stebbins (1966: 166, Map 157) did not recognize *annectens*. The wide middorsal stripe of live Oklahoma specimens varies from yellowish through orange to red, and most have reddish skin between the scales on the sides of the body; the pale lateral stripes are predominantly on the second and third scale rows. The Red River may serve as a partial barrier to the northward dispersal of *annectens* into Oklahoma. Possible intergradation of the red-sided garter snake with the eastern garter snake, *Thamnophis sirtalis sirtalis*, should be investigated in eastern Oklahoma.

See Carpenter (1956:43; 1958b:114; 1959c:34), Carter and Cox (1968), Force (1925a:27; 1925b:83; 1930:36), Trowbridge (1937: 298).

Specimens examined (OU except as indicated).—*Adair*: 4 mi. NW Watts. *Alfalfa*: 6.7 mi. E and 4.9 mi. S Byron (KU); 7 mi. E Ingersoll. *Bryan*: no data. *Canadian*: Mustang; Devils Canyon. *Carter*: Ardmore. *Cleveland*: several within 4 mi. radius Norman;

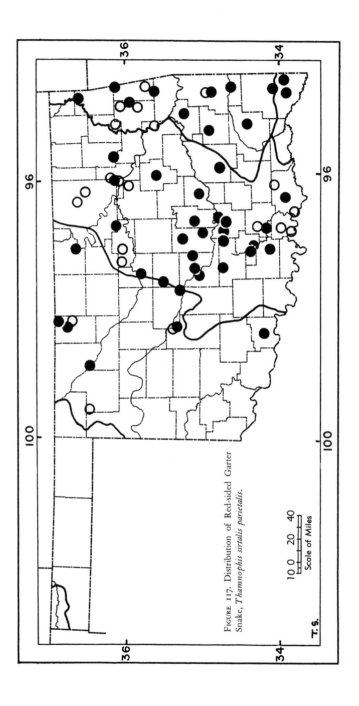

FIGURE 117. Distribution of Red-sided Garter Snake, *Thamnophis sirtalis parietalis*.

Scale of Miles

10 0 20 40

T. S.

7 and 17 mi. E Norman. *Cherokee*: 1.5 mi. NE Eldon. *Cotton*: no data. *Delaware*: 6 mi. NE Grove. *Garvin*: 3 mi. S Stratford (ECSC); Maysville. *Haskell*: 13 mi. E Stigler. *Hughes*: no data. *Johnston*: 3 mi. E Ravia. *Kay*: Ponca City. *Latimer*: Robbers Cave State Park (NWSC); 2 and 8 mi. NW Wilburton. *LeFlore*: 6.5 mi. W Heavener; 5 mi. E Big Cedar. *Logan*: Guthrie. *McClain*: 8 mi. SW Norman, Cleveland County. *McCurtain*: Beavers Bend State Park; 2 mi. N Broken Bow; 15 mi. SE Broken Bow; 6 mi. N Idabel. *Murray*: Dougherty; 4 mi. S Davis. *Oklahoma*: Lake Hefner. *Okmulgee*: Okmulgee. *Osage*: NW edge Tulsa, Tulsa County. *Pawnee*: near Quay. *Pittsburg*: 12 mi. SW McAlester (ECSC). *Pontotoc*: 2 mi. S Ada, 7 mi. NE Ada, and 10 mi. W Ada (ECSC). *Pottawatomie*: Shawnee; St. Louis. *Pushmataha*: near Nashoba. *Rogers*: 8 mi. E Catoosa. *Seminole*: Bowlegs. *Sequoyah*: 0.5 mi. S Adair County line on U.S. Highway 59. *Woods*: 2 mi. W and 1 mi. S Waynoka.

Additional records.—*Adair*: 5 mi. SE Stilwell (UI); Tyner Creek near Proctor (OSU). *Alfalfa*: 5 mi. N Vining (OSU). *Bryan*: 6 mi. E Caddo, and 5 mi. SW Colbert (SESC). *Caddo*: Kiwanis Canyon (Carpenter, 1958a:73). *Cherokee*: Camp Muskogee, and 8 mi. E Tahlequah (OSU); Scraper (UMMZ). *Creek*: Sapulpa (Ortenburger, 1927a:98). *Johnston*: Ballard Park [near Reagan] (Carpenter, 1956:43; 1958a:73). *LeFlore*: Wister (CM). *Marshall*: 1 mi. E Powell, 2 mi. W Willis, and 3 mi. SW Madill (Carpenter, 1956:43); 5 mi. N Willis (Carpenter, 1958a:73). *Mayes*: 5 mi. SW Locust Grove (TNHC). *Murray*: Arbuckle Mts. (Ortenburger, 1926b: 146). *Muskogee*: Braggs (McCoy, 1960a:42). *Osage*: Pawhuska (UMMZ); 1 mi. S Tallant (TNHC). *Payne*: Stillwater, and Lake Carl Blackwell (OSU). *Tulsa*: Tulsa (AMNH, UI); 2 mi. N Turley (TNHC); Red Fork (UI, UMMZ). *Woodward*: Fort Supply (USNM).

Tropidoclonion lineatum annectens Ramsey

Central Lined Snake

Recognition.—Small, striped, brownish snakes (rarely more than 1.5 feet long) having buffy middorsal and whitish lateral stripes flanked by black spots; pale lateral stripe on second and third dorsal scale rows; five or six supralabials; double row of large, black, halfmoon-shaped spots in yellow (in life) mid-ventral area on belly; dorsal scales keeled in 17 (rarely 19) rows at midbody; anal plate single.

Distribution.—Central Oklahoma; known as far east as Cherokee and Bryan counties, and as far west as Kay, Kingfisher, Comanche, and Cotton counties; an isolated record in Cimarron County (map, Fig. 118).

Remarks.—Lined snakes occur mostly in the Oak-Woodland. The habitat and habits of *Tropidoclonion* generally correspond to those of other small secretive and burrowing species, especially *Diadophis*. Lined snakes seem to be especially tolerable of urban areas. Westward, the species occurs in mesic habitats along rivers and streams.

Blair (1950c) reported *Tropidoclonion lineatum* from the floodplain of the Cimarron River north of Kenton in the northwestern corner of Cimarron County, but unfortunately no specimens were preserved (Ramsey, 1953:8). The disjunct population in Colorado is referred to the subspecies *lineatum* (nearest records to Oklahoma from Otero [Maslin, 1950:93] and Bent [Smith, Maslin, and Brown, 1965:29] counties), whereas the lined snakes in Mora and San Miguel counties, New Mexico, previously referred to *lineatum*, were recently described as *T. l. mertensi* by Smith (1965:3). Tinkle and Knopf (1964:46) reported lined snakes from the northern part of the Texas panhandle (nearest records to Oklahoma from east of Stratford, Sherman County) that seemed intermediate between *T. l. annectens* and the Texas lined snake, *T. l. texanum*. The subspecific status of lined snakes from Cimarron County is therefore questionable.

See Blair (1961), Blanchard and Force (1930), Bonn and McCarley (1953:470), Carpenter (1956:43), Force (1925a:27;

1925b:83; 1930:32, 36; 1931; 1936b), Force and Schmerchel (1933), Kassing (1961:187), McCoy (1961c), Smith and Smith (1962:2).

Specimens examined (OU except as indicated).—*Bryan*: no data. *Carter*: 5 mi. SE Ardmore. *Comanche*: Wichita Mts. Wildlife Refuge. *Cotton*: near Temple, east of Cache Creek. *Hughes*: 2 mi. N Yeager. *Kay*: Ponca City. *Marshall*: 9 mi. N Willis. *Muskogee*: near Muskogee (KU). *Noble*: Otoe Indian Reservation. *Oklahoma*: Oklahoma City. *Okmulgee*: Okmulgee. *Osage*: 13 mi. W Pawhuska; Osage Hills State Park. *Pawnee*: near Quay. *Pontotoc*: Ada (ECSC). *Pottawatomie*: Shawnee. *Rogers*: 3 mi. W Catoosa. *Seminole*: Wewoka (ECSC). *Tulsa*: Tulsa.

Additional records.—*Bryan*: below Denison Dam (Bonn and McCarley, 1953:470). *Cherokee*: Camp Muskogee (McCoy, 1960a: 42). *Cleveland*: 4 mi. SE Norman (OU). *Garvin*: ¼ mi. E Stratford (ECSC). *Johnston*: Tishomingo (ECSC). *Kay*: 13 mi. NE Newkirk (Ramsey, 1953:21); 6 mi. NE Newkirk, and 6 mi. SE Chilocco (Burt and Hoyle, 1935:213). *Kingfisher*: Hennessey (Cope, 1894:387). *Logan*: Williamson (Ramsey, 1953:21; not found, possibly because of a transcription error of the collector, W. E. Williamson, who obtained some OSU specimens in Noble County). *Noble*: 5–6 mi. E Perry (Ramsey, 1953:21). *Osage*: Hominy (Ramsey, 1953:21). *Pawnee*: 2 mi. SE Pawnee (Burt, 1935:334). *Payne*: Stillwater, and 4 mi. S Stillwater (Ramsey, 1953:21); several within 7 mi. radius Stillwater (OSU). *Tulsa*: 5 mi. SE Tulsa (CM).

Virginia striatula (Linnaeus)

Rough Earth Snake

Recognition.—Small grayish or pale brown, unmarked snakes (usually not more than one foot in length) having a slightly tapered head; belly whitish, unmarked; preocular lacking, loreal elongate touching eye; one postocular; internasals fused into single plate; five supralabials; dorsal scales keeled in 17 rows at

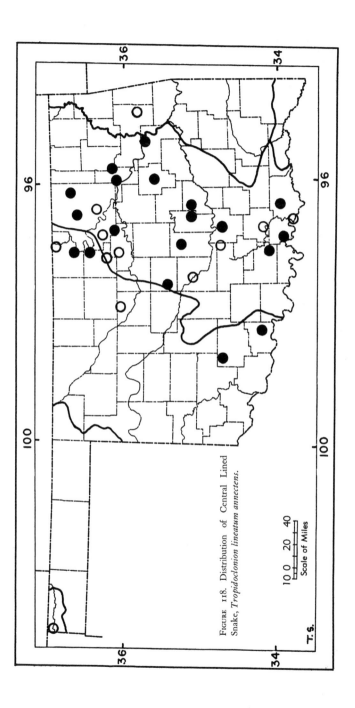

FIGURE 118. Distribution of Central Lined Snake, *Tropidoclonion lineatum annectens.*

Scale of Miles
10 0 20 40

T. S.

midbody; anal plate divided. Young usually having white marks on parietals.

Distribution.—Eastern Oklahoma; known as far west as Payne, Cleveland, Garvin, and Love counties (map, Fig. 119).

Remarks.—Rough earth snakes occur in the Interior Highlands and Oak-Woodland. Individuals are secretive and burrow, and are found under logs or rocks, usually on wooded and grass-herb covered hillsides; one was found foraging on a dirt road at dusk. A female approximately 200 mm in body length contained seven well-developed embryos on July 24 (Bryan County); another female about 195 mm in body length deposited six young on August 5 (Marshall County). Of 49 specimens, all have five supralabials, one postocular, and fused internasals (irregular sutures in two).

See Blanchard (1924b:83), Bonn and McCarley (1953:470), Burt (1935:334), Burt and Hoyle (1935:212), Carpenter (1956: 43; 1958b:114), Carter and Cox (1968), Force (1930:36), Moore and Rigney (1942:79), Schmidt (1919:72), Smith (1956:286, illus.).

Specimens examined (OU except as indicated).—*Atoka*: Stringtown Refuge. *Bryan*: 5 mi. SW Colbert. *Carter*: 5 mi. SE Ardmore; 6 mi. S Ardmore. *Cherokee*: 2 mi. E Hulbert. *Cleveland*: Lexington Game Area. *Latimer*: 2 mi. N Wilburton. *Love*: 4 mi. E and 3 mi. S Oswalt. *Marshall*: 1 and 2 mi. E Willis. *McCurtain*: 6 mi. N Idabel; 5 mi. NE Idabel; Beavers Bend State Park; 1 mi. S Bethel. *Murray*: Arbuckle Mts. *Okmulgee*: Okmulgee. *Pottawatomie*: 1 mi. S Tecumseh. *Pushmataha*: near Nashoba; 0.5 mi. S Clayton (TTC). *Rogers*: 8 mi. E Catoosa; 2 mi. NE Catoosa. *Sequoyah*: 15.5 mi. N Sallisaw. *Tulsa*: Red Fork; 5 mi. SW Tulsa; near Bixby. *Wagoner*: 6 mi. SE Catoosa, Rogers County.

Additional records.—*Adair*: Stilwell (Ortenburger, 1925:86). *Bryan*: Caddo Gap (UI). *Cherokee*: 14 mi. NNE Tahlequah (UMMZ); 4 mi. SE Cookson (KU). *Creek*: Drumright (USNM);

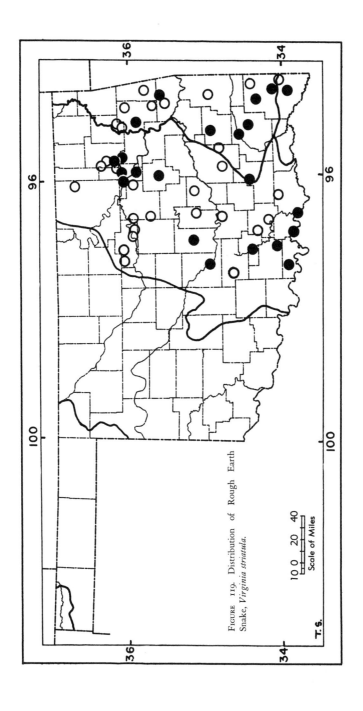

FIGURE 119. Distribution of Rough Earth
Snake, *Virginia striatula*.

Scale of Miles

10 0 20 40

1 mi. NW Milfay (Burt, 1935:334); Sapulpa (Schmidt, 1919:72). *Garvin*: Table Top Mts., 7.5 mi. NW Elmore City (ECSC). *Hughes*: 5 mi. SE Wetumka (ECSC). *Johnston*: 4 mi. S Mill Creek (ECSC); 2.5 mi. E Tishomingo (ECSC). *LeFlore*: Wister (CM). *Marshall*: 4.5 mi. N UOBS (OU). *Mayes*: Cedar Crest Lake (McCoy, 1960a:42); 4 mi. S Locust Grove (INHS). *McCurtain*: 4 mi. SE Smithville (OSU); 1 mi. N Idabel (TCWC); 3 mi. E Eagletown (UI). *Murray*: Camp Classen (OSU, SESC). *Osage*: 7 mi. W Bartlesville, Washington County (Burt and Hoyle, 1935:212). *Payne*: several within 4 mi. radius Stillwater, 7 mi. W and 3 mi. S Stillwater, and Lake Carl Blackwell (OSU); Cushing (KKA); near Ripley (Moore and Rigney, 1942:79); 1–2 mi. NE Ripley (UA, UMMZ). *Pittsburg*: Hartshorne (McCoy, 1960a:42); 11 mi. S McAlester (UI). *Pontotoc*: 7 mi. NE Ada (Carter, 1966:35). *Rogers*: Caney River, 0.1 mi. E on U.S. Highway 169 (FWCM); 7 mi. W Claremore (USNM); 6 mi. E Catoosa (Dundee and Burger, 1948). *Seminole*: 3 mi. S and 5 mi. W Wewoka, and 3 mi. N and 1 mi. E Wewoka (ECSC). *Sequoyah*: 3.1 mi. S Marble City (UA). *Tulsa*: Tulsa (FWCM, TNHC); 4 mi. S Tulsa (TNHC); Lost City (CM); Garnett (USNM). *Wagoner*: 4 mi. S Catoosa, Rogers County (KU).

Virginia valeriae elegans (Kennicott)
Western Earth Snake

Recognition.—Small gray or red brown snakes (usually not more than one foot in length), unmarked or having pale middorsal streak flanked by series of dark flecks; belly whitish without markings; preocular lacking, loreal elongate touching eye; usually two or three (rarely one) postoculars; two internasals; six supralabials; dorsal scales smooth or faintly keeled posteriorly in 17 rows at midbody; anal plate divided.

Distribution.—Eastern Oklahoma; known as far west as Payne and Carter counties (map, Fig. 120).

Remarks.—Western earth snakes closely resemble the rough earth snakes; both species have been taken at the same places and

324

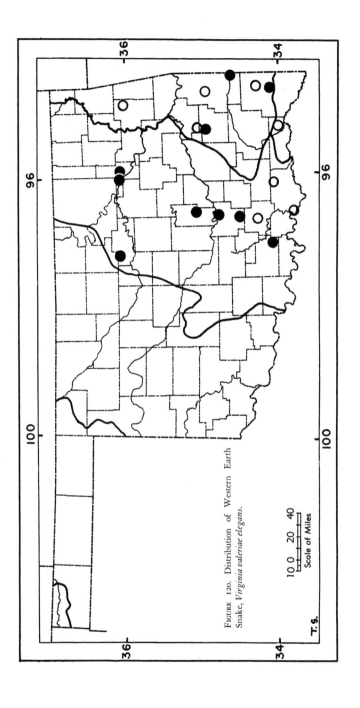

FIGURE 120. Distribution of Western Earth Snake, *Virginia valeriae elegans*.

10 0 20 40
Scale of Miles

T. S.

seem to have similar habits in corresponding habitats, but *valeriae* seems to be less abundant than *striatula*. The individual from Carter County was found in a pile of leaves on a rocky, wooded hillside. See Force (1930:35).

Specimens examined (OU except as indicated).—*Carter*: 6 mi. SE Ardmore. *Latimer*: Robbers Cave State Park (NWSC). *LeFlore*: 13 mi. E Big Cedar; just west of Oklahoma-Arkansas state line on U.S. Highway 63. *McCurtain*: near Beavers Bend State Park. *Payne*: near Lake Carl Blackwell (ECSC). *Pontotoc*: 8 mi. NE Ada, and 5 mi. S Fittstown (ECSC). *Seminole*: 3 mi. S and 5 mi. W Wewoka (ECSC). *Tulsa*: Red Fork; 5 mi. SW Tulsa; 9 mi. SE Tulsa.

Additional records.—*Bryan*: below Denison Dam (CCC); 10 mi. N Bokchito (Laughlin, 1964:62). *Cherokee*: Hanging Rock (UI); 0.25 mi. N Hanging Rock (McCoy, 1960a:42). *Choctaw*: Fort Towson (Blanchard, 1923:355). *Haskell*: 4 mi. S and 3 mi. E Quinton, Pittsburg County (HAD). *Johnston*: no data (CCC). *LeFlore*: Wister (CM). *McCurtain*: McCurtain Game Preserve (Carter, 1966:35). *Tulsa*: Tulsa (OSU, CM); Limestone (USNM).

Type Specimens and
Type Localities of
Reptiles in Oklahoma

Because some relevant information concerning type specimens (briefly, "types") and type localities of reptiles in Oklahoma seems inappropriate under the accounts of species, it is included here with a list of all name combinations that are based on types from Oklahoma.

In the Check List of North American Amphibians and Reptiles prepared by Schmidt (1953), two incorrect restrictions of indefinite type localities in Oklahoma are: *Agama cornuta* (= *Phrynosoma cornutum*), "Fort Towson, Indian Territory [Choctaw County, Oklahoma]"—see Smith and Taylor (1950: 358; although no objective evidence is available, their restriction to Fort Riley, Kansas, is the most accurate); and, *Scotophis emoryi* (= *Elaphe guttata emoryi*), "Howard Springs, Ellis County, Oklahoma"—see Dowling (1951:43).

Some Oklahoma specimens that were originally part of a type series have been subsequently referred to taxa different from those originally proposed. The original name combinations were:

Pseudemys texana Baur.—Baur (1893:224) referred a turtle from "near Old Fort Cobb, I.T. [Caddo County, Oklahoma]" to his new species, *Pseudemys texana*. According to Stejneger (1938:173), the soft parts of this turtle are cataloged as USNM 7173, and the dry shell as ANSP 247. Edmond V. Malnate (personal communication) informed me of a notation (initialed E. R. Dunn, 1940) in the ANSP catalog to the effect that number 247 was sent "back to USNM." Cochran (1961:234) listed

USNM 7173 as a probable paratype of *texana*. But the turtle from Fort Cobb, now known as *Pseudemys floridana hoyi*, was shown to be distinct from *texana* by Stejneger (1938) and Carr (1938:108, footnote).

Arizona elegans Kennicott.—One (USNM 4266) of the two syntypes that formed the basis of Kennicott's description (in Baird, 1859:18–19) of *Arizona elegans*, was illustrated by Cope (1900:863, fig. 201, mistakenly captioned as USNM 4276), and was from "Between Arkansas and Cimarron," a locality considered to be in Oklahoma by Blanchard (1924a:table) and Cochran (1961:158), and presumably so by Klauber, who assigned USNM 4266 to his new subspecies *Arizona elegans blanchardi* (1946:319).

Ophibolus doliata syspilus Cope.—Two specimens (both USNM 1846) from "Fort Towson, Ark. [Choctaw County, Oklahoma]" were assigned by Cope (1889:385) to his new subspecies, *Ophibolus doliata syspilus*, and listed as paratypes of *syspila* by Cochran (1961:203). Blanchard (1921:177, table), however, considered USNM 1846 as representative of *Lampropeltis triangulum amaura*.

Name combinations that are junior synonyms and based on types that were collected in Oklahoma are:

Terrapene ornata var. *cimarronensis Cragin* (= *Terrapene ornata ornata*, Schmidt, 1953:95).—Cragin (1894:37) named a box turtle *Terrapene ornata* var. *cimarronensis* "for what appears to be merely a color variety of *T. ornata* in which the ordinarily yellow parts on the limbs and necks are replaced by bright red." The indefinite type locality—" 'Red beds' country of the Cimarron basin" perhaps is in Oklahoma.

Caudisona lecontei Hallowell (= *Crotalus viridis viridis*, Baird and Girard, 1853:8; Klauber, 1956, I:45).—Hallowell

(1852:180) described *Caudisona lecontei* from the "Cross Timbers," which, according to Stejneger in Amaral (1929:87), "is
located along the North Fork of the Canadian River . . . about
36° N. Lat. and 98° 30' W Long."; those readings of latitude
and longitude place the "Cross Timbers" near Canton Reservoir
in Blaine County. The holotype (USNM 4233), obtained by
Dr. Samuel W. Woodhouse and illustrated by Hallowell (1854:
Pl. 18), presumably has been lost.

Bascanium flagelliforme bicinctum Yarrow (= *Masticophis
flagellum testaceus*, Ortenburger, 1928c:93).—A young coachwhip (USNM 11814) from "Old Fort Cobb, Tex. [Caddo
County, Oklahoma]" was named *Bascanium flagelliforme
bicinctum* by Yarrow (1883:153).

Ophibolus evansii Kennicott (= *Lampropeltis calligaster
calligaster*, Blanchard, 1921:116).—Kennicott (1859:99) described *Ophibolus evansii* on the basis of four syntypes. One of
these, USNM 1702, was obtained by Heinrich B. Möllhausen
(artist-topographer with Lieut. Whipple's Pacific Railroad Survey
field party in July, 1853) from the Canadian River, Arkansas
(Yarrow, 1882:94; Cope, 1900:906); the locality was later
amended to Canadian River, Indian Territory (Blanchard,
1921:125; Cochran, 1961:203).

Psammophis flavi-gularis Hallowell (= *Masticophis flagellum testaceus*, Smith, Maslin, and Brown, 1965:25).—The type
locality of *Psammophis flavi-gularis* as given in the original
description (Hallowell, 1852:179) is "in the sandy region reach-
ing from the frontiers of Texas to the Creek Territory, and
designated by a strip of timber extending across it." Later,
Hallowell (1854:132) referred to the locality as "Cross Timbers,
near Creek boundary, . . . " and illustrated one of the two specimens (1854:Pl. XI). Cope (1861:561) listed two specimens as
D[rymobius] testaceus from "Cross-Timbers, Ind. Ter'y."

329

Ortenburger (1928c:92) listed the type (lectotype), obtained by Dr. Samuel W. Woodhouse, as ANSP 5388 from "Cross Timbers, Indian Territory [Oklahoma]." Smith and Taylor (1950:360), without supporting evidence, restricted the type locality to Maysville, Garvin County, Oklahoma.

As has been explained on page 10, the Cross Timbers as applied to specimens obtained by Woodhouse is most likely a locality somewhere along or close to the northern boundary of the Creek Nation (from Payne County west along southern border of Garfield and Major counties; see Fig. 1). Pending further evidence, the type locality of *flavigularis* would seem more appropriately restricted to the vicinity of Canton Reservoir, Blaine County, the same restricted type locality for *Caudisona lecontei* (= *Crotalus v. virdis*), the type of which was collected under the same circumstances.

Scotophis laetus Baird and Girard (= *Elaphe obsoleta obsoleta*, Dowling, 1951).—The holotype of *Scotophis laetus*, presumably lost, was taken by Marcy and McClellan's exploration of the Red River, which included southwestern Oklahoma and the eastern part of the Texas panhandle. The indefinite type locality, "Red River, Ark.," may be in Oklahoma.

Tontilla kirnia Blanchard (= *Tantilla nigriceps fumiceps*, Smith, 1941).—In the type description of *Tantilla kirnia*, Blanchard (1938:373) designated OU 13117 from Comanche County, Oklahoma, as a paratype.

Types (holotypes, paratypes, lectotypes, or syntypes) of currently recognized taxa that were found in Oklahoma include the following:

Agama collaris Say (= *Crotaphytus collaris collaris*).—The holotype of *Agama collaris*, obtained by Long's expedition to the Rocky Mountains, was deposited in Peale's Philadelphia

Museum and has since been lost (see page 9). The holotype was obtained by Captain John R. Bell's detachment on Tuesday, September 5, 1820, near Colonel Hugh Glenn's Trading Post on the east bank of the Verdigris River, about two miles above its confluence with the Arkansas River. The type locality is in Wagoner County about four miles east-northeast of Fort Gibson, Muskogee County, near the Muskogee-Wagoner county line.

Holbrookia maculata perspicua Axtell.—In describing this subspecies, Axtell (1956:166) designated OU 10953 from two and one-half miles northeast Norman, Cleveland County, as the holotype. According to Cochran (1961:117) USNM 44981 from "Mayers" (= Meers), Comanche County, is a paratype.

Sceloporus consobrinus Baird and Girard (= *Sceloporus undulatus consobrinus*).—Smith (1938:10) considered the type locality to be the Red River, Beckham County, Oklahoma, having amended the type locality of Roger Mills County as given by Stejneger and Barbour (1933:11). The type locality as given by Stejneger and Barbour (1943:82)—"Beckham County, Oklahoma, near confluence of North Fork of the Red River and Suydam Creek"—seems to be essentially correct. But there is no longer a tributary of the North Fork of the Red River in Beckham County known as Suydam Creek.

The holotype, which has been destroyed (Jones, 1926:1, 3), was described and illustrated by Baird and Girard (1854:208, Pl. X, figs. 5–12), and obtained on June 6, 1852, between latitudes of 35° 15' 43" (June 4) and 35° 24' 50" (June 8) near the junction of "a large creek flowing into Red River, which, . . . I have called 'Suydam creek.' It is thirty feet wide; the water clear, but slightly brackish, and flows rapidly over a sandy bed between abrupt clay banks, which are fringed with cotton-wood trees" (page 25 of itinerary of Marcy and McClellan; see Baird and Girard, 1854).

Judging from a folded map (included with another map as a separate volume accompanying the text) showing the itinerary of Marcy and McClellan and the geographic position of place names mentioned in the text, Suydam Creek is the same as the present-day Timber Creek. Timber Creek (no signpost; second bridge east of Sayre; Deep Creek bridge is the first) intersects State Highway 152 3.8 miles east of Sayre (from junction of U.S. 66 and State Highway 152 in Sayre). Long-time residents in Sayre had never heard of a Suydam Creek. The type locality of *Sceloporus consobrinus* is herein amended to about four miles east-southeast of Sayre, near or at the confluence of Timber Creek and the North Fork of the Red River, Beckham County, Oklahoma.

Tropidonotus transversus Hallowell (= *Natrix erythrogaster transversa*).—In the original description of *Tropidonotus transversus*, Hallowell (1852:177) gave the type locality as "Creek boundary, found near the banks of the Arkansas and its tributaries." Later, Hallowell mentioned two specimens from the Creek country and illustrated one of them (1854:147, Pl. XVI). Cope (1900:975) referred to USNM 1316 as a type that was collected (seemingly incorrectly) in 1858 and received from Wurdeman. The holotype is ANSP 5044 (Conant, 1969:26–27). Smith and Taylor (1950:360) restricted the type locality to Tulsa, Tulsa County, whereas Cochran (1961:223), listing USNM 1316 as a cotype and crediting the specimen to Woodhouse, designated the type locality as near Keystone (in Pawnee County), Tulsa County, Oklahoma.

Tropidonotus rhombifer Hallowell (= *Natrix rhombifera rhombifera*).—The type locality of *Tropidonotus rhombifer* as given in the original description (Hallowell, 1852:177) was "Arkansas river and its tributaries, near the northern boundary of the Creek Nation." Two specimens from the Creek country were available to Hallowell, and he later illustrated one of them

(1854:147, Pl. XV). The type locality was, for some reason, incorrectly restricted to Fort Smith, Arkansas, by Schmidt (1953:61), after Smith and Taylor (1950:360) had restricted it to Tulsa, Tulsa County. Cochran (1961:223) placed the type locality near Keystone (Pawnee County), Tulsa County, and listed USNM 7253 as a cotype received from Woodhouse. The holotype is ANSP 5047 (Conant, 1969:55–56). The two types of *Tropidonotus rhombifer* and those of *T. transversus* were collected by Samuel W. Woodhouse, in the course of surveying the northern border of the Creek Nation in 1849 or 1850 (p. 10). The type locality for both species is that part of the Arkansas River that coincides with the northern border of the Creek Nation for a distance of about seventeen miles along the Osage-Tulsa county line between Keystone and Tulsa.

Storeria dekayi texana Trapido.—Two specimens credited to Edward Palmer, USNM 11820 and 11823, from Fort Cobb, Caddo County, Oklahoma, are listed as paratypes by Cochran (1961:214).

Eutaenia marciana Baird and Girard (= *Thamnophis marcianus marcianus*).—The type locality of *Eutaenia marciana* was discussed by Mittleman (1949:242–243) and restricted to the vicinity of Slough Creek, east of Hollister, Tillman County, Oklahoma. The lectotype, USNM 844 (one of ten syntypes), was to my knowledge first designated as the type by Yarrow (1882:118).

Tropidoclonion lineatum annectens Ramsey.—Ramsey (1953) recognized geographic variation in *Tropidoclonion lineatum* and designated KU 30005 from Tulsa, Tulsa County, Oklahoma, as the holotype of *T. l. annectens*; KU 30006–11, from the same locality, were listed as paratypes.

Glossary

ABDOMINALS.—Paired shields of the turtle plastron, between the femoral and pectoral shields (Figs. 15, right; 18); in the genera *Chelydra* and *Macroclemys*, the abdominal shield forms the main element of the bridge (Fig. 17, left).

ANAL PLATE.—In snakes, the large scale which either covers or is located just in front of the anus and separates the ventral scales of the body from the caudal scales of the tail (Fig. 31E); may be single or divided into two parts; counts of ventrals or caudals exclude the anal plate.

ANTERIOR.—Pertaining to the front or head end of the body.

ANTERIOR SUPRALABIAL.—In the snake genus *Leptotyphlops*, a single or paired scale touching the edge of the upper lip and immediately in front of the scale (ocular) surrounding the eye (Fig. 95).

AZYGOUS SCALE.—An unpaired scale; in the hognose snake *Heterodon platyrhinos*, a narrow median scale on top of the head just behind the enlarged rostral (Fig. 45, lower left).

BRIDGE.—The bony connection on either side between the upper and lower halves of the turtle shell (Figs. 15, right; 17, left).

CARAPACE.—The top half of the turtle shell (Fig. 15, left).

CAUDALS.—Scales on the tail; used interchangeably with subcaudals and designating the widened scales on the undersurface of the tail, whether entire (Fig. 38) or divided (Fig. 39). Counts of caudals or subcaudals exclude the anal plate, but include the cornified tip at the end of the tail; the anteriormost caudal is the first scale continuous midventrally (caudals single) or the first pair of scales that touch midventrally (caudals divided).

COMPRESSED.—Flattened sideways or laterally.

COSTALS.—The two rows of shields of the turtle carapace, on either side of the single medial row of vertebrals (Fig. 15, left).

COTYPE.—A term formerly used for syntype.

334

Depressed.—Flattened from top to bottom or dorsoventrally.

Dorsal, Dorsum.—Pertaining to the back or upper surface.

Dorsal scales.—In lizards, the scales on the back, counted in a straight line along the middle of the back from the posteriormost enlarged scales on top of the head (excluding nuchal scales in *Eumeces,* Fig. 22, left) to a point even with the rear margin of the hind legs when the legs are held at right angles to the body; in snakes, all the small scales on the body counted diagonally from their contact with the enlarged ventral scales on one side to the ventral scales on the other side (Fig. 31D).

Dorsolateral.—Situated on or along the sides of the back.

Facial pit.—A roundish cavity on each side of the head, between nostril and eye (Fig. 33, upper right).

Femorals.—The paired shields of the turtle plastron, just in front of the anals (Figs. 15, right; 17, left; 18).

Femoral pores.—A series of small pits or pores on the undersurface of the thighs; counts of femoral pores refer to the number occurring on one leg only (Figs. 21, 28, 29, ventral surface of leg).

Frontal.—The large scale on the middle of the top of the head, between the eyes (Figs. 31B; 22, left).

Frontonasal.—In lizards of the genera *Eumeces* and *Lygosoma,* a single scale on top of the head, just in front of the prefrontals (Fig. 22, left).

Genials.—Same as chin shields (Fig. 31C); most snakes have two (anterior and posterior) pairs of chin shields.

Gular.—Pertaining to the throat; in turtles, the most anterior shield of the plastron, which may be paired, single, or absent (Figs. 15, right; 17, left; 18).

Holotype.—The single specimen designated or indicated as the "type-specimen" of a nominal species-group taxon at the time of the original publication.

Immaculate.—No markings or pattern.

Infralabials.—Lower labials, the enlarged scales bordering the lower lip; counts of infralabials exclude the anteriormost mental (Figs. 31A, C; 22, right).

Internasals.—In snakes, two scales (fused into one scale in some cases, Fig. 41, left) on top of the snout, just behind the rostral and between the nasals (Figs. 41, right; 31A, B).

KEEL.—Raised, longitudinal ridge on the scales of lizards (Fig. 30, upper right) or snakes (Fig. 37, left); in turtles, one or more longitudinal ridges on the carapace.

LABIAL.—Referring to the lips, or scales on lips; see infralabials and supralabials.

LATERAL.—Pertaining to the right or left side.

LECTOTYPE.—One of two or more syntypes so designated after the original publication of a species-group name.

LONGITUDINAL.—Lengthwise, extending the length of the body.

LOREAL.—Region or scales between eye and nostril on the side of the head; in snakes, usually one scale between the preocular(s) and nasal scale (Figs. 31A; 42, lower right); if only one scale that is longer than high is between the nasal and orbit, it is regarded as a loreal (Fig. 43)—if that one scale is higher than long, it is a preocular, and a loreal is absent (Figs. 40, 44); see nasal.

MANDIBULAR SYMPHYSIS.—The firm anterior juncture of the two halves of the lower jaw.

MARGINALS. The small shields around the edge of the carapace, except the anteriormost nuchal (Fig. 15).

MEDIAL, MEDIAN.—In the middle.

MELANISTIC.—Black or nearly black.

MENTAL.—Unpaired scale at the tip of the lower jaw, bordering the lower lip, in lizards (Fig. 22, right) and snakes (Fig. 31C).

MIDDORSAL.—Situated on or along the middle of the back.

MIDVENTRAL.—Situated on or along the middle of the belly.

NASAL.—The scale surrounding the nostril (Figs. 22, right; 31A); the posterior half of a divided nasal scale may touch the preocular(s) and be mistaken for a loreal (Figs. 40, 44, 47).

NUCHAL.—An unpaired scute of the carapace in turtles (Fig. 15, left), or a pair (or two pairs) of enlarged dorsal scales on the neck just posterior to the enlarged dorsal scales of the head in the genus *Eumeces* (Fig. 22, left).

ORBIT.—The space or bony cavity containing the eye.

PARATYPE.—Every specimen in a type-series, other than the holotype.

PARIETAL.—Large paired scales on the top and at the rear of the head in lizards (Fig. 22, left), and snakes (Fig. 31A, B).

PECTORALS.—Paired shields of the turtle plastron, between the humerals and abdominals (Figs. 15, right; 17, left; 18).

PLASTRON.—The bottom half of the turtle shell (Figs. 15, right; 17, left; 18).

POSTERIOR.—Pertaining to the hind or tail end of the body.

POSTANTEBRACHIAL SCALES.—Scales on the posterior surface of the forelimbs; an enlarged patch of scales in the whiptail lizard, *Cnemidophorus gularis* (Fig. 21, lower left).

POSTLABIALS.—In lizards of the genus *Eumeces*, usually one or two scales just behind the last supralabial and in front of the ear opening (Fig. 22, right).

POSTMENTAL.—One or two chin scales, wider than long, just behind the mental (Fig. 25).

POSTNASAL.—In lizards, a small scale on the side of the head, just behind the nasal (Fig. 22, right).

POSTOCULAR.—The region behind the eye; one or more scales bordering the hind rim of the orbit (Fig. 31A).

PREFRONTALS.—Usually two scales on top of the head, immediately in front of the frontal (Figs. 31A, B; 22, left).

PREOCULARS.—One or two scales bordering the front rim of the orbit (Figs. 22, right; 31A); in snakes, if the only scale between the eye and the nasal is higher than long, it is regarded as a preocular (Figs. 40, 44); see loreal and nasal.

ROSTRAL.—The scale at the tip of the snout, bordering the upper lip (Figs. 22, 31A); enlarged and/or upturned in some species.

SCUTE.—A large scale, sometimes referring to one of the ventral scales in snakes; used interchangeably with the term "shield" for the large scales on the turtle shell.

SEPTAL RIDGE.—A whitish ridge projecting from each side of the nasal septum in the spiny softshell turtle, *Trionyx spiniferus* (Fig. 16, left).

SHIELD.—Same as scute.

SNOUT-VENT LENGTH.—Length of body, measured in a straight line from the tip of the snout to the anterior lip of the anus.

337

Subcaudals.—Same as caudals.

Suboculars.—One or more scales immediately under the eye, between the eye and supralabials (Fig. 36, left).

Supralabials.—Upper labials, the scales bordering the upper lip (Figs. 22, right; 31A), usually enlarged in snakes; counts of supralabials exclude the anteriormost rostral.

Supramarginals.—In the turtle genus *Macroclemys*, the small shields of the carapace, above the bridge and between the marginals and costals (Fig. 17, right).

Supranasals.—In lizards of the genus *Eumeces*, the paired scales between the nasals and just behind the rostral (Fig. 22, left), in the same position as the internasals in snakes.

Supraoculars.—One or more scales on top of the head, immediately above the eye (Figs. 22, left; 31A, B).

Suture.—The common border between two scales or scutes; for example, the interfemoral suture is the common medial border between the two femorals.

Synonyms.—Two (or more) zoological names for the same taxon; the oldest name, which is the acceptable name, is the senior synonym, whereas the other name(s) is the junior synonym.

Syntype.—Every specimen in a type-series in which no holotype has been designated.

Taxa (plural of taxon).—Groups of animals with zoological names; e.g., Reptilia, Iguanidae, *Sceloporus*, *Sceloporus undulatus*.

Thigh.—The part of the leg between the knee and the body.

Transverse.—Crosswise, extending across the body.

Type locality.—The locality at which a holotype or type-series was collected.

Uniform.—No markings or pattern, all one color.

Ventral, Venter.—Pertaining to the belly or under surface.

Ventral scales, Ventrals.—In snakes, the transversely widened scales covering the belly (Fig. 31E). Ventral counts exclude the anal plate, but there are two methods of determining the anteriormost ventral—the Blanchard system, in which all transversely widened scales are counted (Fig. 31C), and the Dowling system, in which only those scales that touch the first row of dorsal scales on each side of the body are counted; ventral counts using the more arbitrary Blanchard system include about two more scales than the more precise Dowling system.

Ventrolateral.—Situated on or along the sides of the belly.

Vertebral.—Pertaining to the middle of the back; in turtles, the single medial row of scutes of the carapace, excluding the small anteriormost nuchal (Fig. 15, left).

References

Adler, K. K. 1958. List of the specimens of Chelonia and Crocodilia preserved in the author's private collection. Spec. Publ. Ohio Herp. Soc., No. 2, pp. 8–21.

Allen, R., L. G. Gumbreck, and M. R. Shetlar. 1960. Some preliminary studies of "stress" in the western diamondback rattlesnake (*Crotalus atrox*). Proc. Oklahoma Acad. Sci. (for 1959), 40:19–21.

Anderson, P. 1942. New record for *Salvadora lineata*. Copeia, No. 2, p. 127.

———. 1965. The reptiles of Missouri. Univ. Missouri Press, Columbia, Missouri, pp. xxiii + 330.

Amaral, A. do. 1929. Studies of Nearctic Ophidia V. On *Crotalus confluentus* Say, 1823, and its allied forms. Bull. Antivenin Inst. Amer., 2(4):86–97.

Anonymous. 1946. Deep Fork rattler. Oklahoma Game and Fish News, 2(10):10, illus.

———. 1950a. Traps turtles to improve Lawtonka fishing. *Ibid.*, 6(7–8):10, illus.

———. 1950b. Season's first big snapper. *Ibid.*, 6(7–8):22, illus.

———. 1951. [photograph and caption]. *Ibid.*, 7(5):12.

———. 1952a. 300 years old? *Ibid.*, 8(9):6, illus.

———. 1952b. Dramatic dining. *Ibid.*, 8(11):20, illus.

———. 1954a. Rattlesnake roundup. *Ibid.*, 10(4):5, illus.

———. 1954b. Happy bow hunters. *Ibid.*, 10(12):8, illus.

———. 1954c. Rattlesnakes protected? *Ibid.*, 10(7–8):17.

———. 1955a. Big one that didn't get away. *Ibid.*, 11(4):15, illus.

———. 1955b. Huge snapping turtle greates [*sic*] interest. *Ibid.*, 11(11):10, illus.

———. 1955c. Turtles removed. *Ibid.*, 11(11):14.

———. 1956a. Snakey fishing story. *Ibid.*, 12(4):4, illus.

———. 1956b. Rare specimen. *Ibid.*, 12(6):15, illus.

——. 1956c. Season's largest turtle? *Ibid.*, 12(7):10.

——. 1957. Jackson County rattlers. *Ibid.*, 13(5):14, illus.

——. 1958. With the men in the field. Oklahoma Wildlife, 14(9):9, illus.

——. 1959a. [photograph and caption]. *Ibid.*, 15(5):15.

——. 1959b. [photograph and caption]. *Ibid.*, 15(6):17.

——. 1959c. Boa off range. *Ibid.*, 15(7–8):3.

——. 1959d. [photograph and caption]. *Ibid.*, 15(7–8):17.

——. 1959e. Sportsmen's ABC's. *Ibid.*, 15(12):10, illus.

——. 1960a. Snake bounty hunters. *Ibid.*, 16(6):20, illus.

——. 1960b. Wildlife lessons. *Ibid.*, 16(9):13, illus.

——. 1960c. Turtle comeback. *Ibid.*, 16(9):19, illus.

——. 1960d. [photograph and caption]. *Ibid.*, 16(9):20.

——. 1961. [photograph and caption]. *Ibid.*, 17(12):19.

——. 1962. Tourist turtle. *Ibid.*, 18(3):22.

Auffenberg, W. 1955. A reconsideration of the racer, *Coluber constrictor*, in eastern United States. Tulane Stud. Zool., 2(6):89–155.

Axtell, R. W. 1956. A solution to the long neglected *Holbrookia lacerata* problem, and the description of two new subspecies of *Holbrookia*. Bull. Chicago Acad. Sci., 10(11):163–179.

Baird, S. F. 1859. Reptiles of the boundary, (Vol. 2, pt. 2, pp. 1–35, pls. 1–41). In W. H. Emory, Report on the United States and Mexican Boundary Survey made under the direction of the Secretary of the Interior, U.S. 34th Congress, 1st Session, Exec. Document 108, Washington, pp. 62+32+35+11, pls. 27+25+35+41.

——, and C. Girard. 1853. Catalogue of North American reptiles in the museum of the Smithsonian Institution. Part I.—Serpents. [Publ. Smithsonian Inst.] pp. xvi + 172.

——, and ——. 1854. Appendix F.—Reptiles (serpents and batrachians, pp. 188–215, pls. I–XI). In R. B. Marcy and G. B. McClellan, Exploration of the Red River of Louisiana, in the year 1852: Senate Exec. Document, 33rd Congress, 1st Session [Volume I], Washington, pp. xv + 286, illus. (first printed 1853 as Senate Exec. Document 54, 32nd Congress, 2nd Session, Washington, with changes in pagination). Two folded maps accompany Marcy and McClellan's report [Volume II].

Baur, G. 1893. Notes on the classification and taxonomy of the Testudinata IV. The species of the genus *Pseudemys*. Proc. Amer. Philos. Soc., 31:221–225.

Blair, A. P. 1950a. Notes on two anguid lizards. Copeia, No. 1, p. 57.

––––––. 1950b. The alligator in Oklahoma. *Ibid.*, No. 1, p. 57.

––––––. 1950c. Some cold-blooded vertebrates of the Oklahoma panhandle. *Ibid.*, No. 3, p. 234.

––––––. 1961. Notes on *Ophisaurus attenuatus attenuatus* (Anguidae). Southwestern Nat., 6(3–4):201.

––––––, and H. L. Lindsay, Jr. 1961. *Hyla avivoca* (Hylidae) in Oklahoma. *Ibid.*, 6(3–4):202.

Blair, W. F. 1938. Ecological relationships of the mammals of the Bird Creek region, northwestern Oklahoma. Amer. Midland Nat., 20(3):473–526.

––––––. 1939. Faunal relationships and geographic distribution of mammals in Oklahoma. *Ibid.*, 22(1):85–133.

––––––, and A. P. Blair. 1941. Food habits of the collared lizard in northeastern Oklahoma. *Ibid.*, 26(1):230–232.

––––––, and T. H. Hubbell. 1938. The biotic districts of Oklahoma. *Ibid.*, 20(2):425–454.

Blanchard, F. N. 1921. A revision of the king snakes: genus *Lampropeltis*. Bull. U.S. Nat. Mus., No. 114, pp. vi + 260.

––––––. 1923. The snakes of the genus *Virginia*. Papers Michigan Acad. Sci. Arts Letters, 3:343–365.

––––––. 1924a. A new snake of the genus *Arizona*. Occas. Papers Mus. Zool. Univ. Michigan, No. 150, pp. 1–3.

––––––. 1924b. The status of *Amphiardis inornatus* (Garman). Copeia, No. 134, pp. 83–85.

––––––. 1932. A clutch of eggs of the speckled king snake, *Lampropeltis getulus holbrooki* (Stejneger). *Ibid.*, No. 2, p. 98.

––––––. 1938. Snakes of the genus *Tantilla* in the United States. Zool. Ser. Field Mus. Nat. Hist., 20(28):369–376.

––––––. 1942. The ring-neck snakes, genus *Diadophis*. Bull. Chicago Acad. Sci., 7(1):1–144.

––––––, and E. R. Force. 1930. The age of attainment of sexual maturity in the lined snake, *Tropidoclonion lineatum* (Hallowell). Bull. Antivenin Inst. Amer., 3(4):96–98.

Bogert, C. M. 1939. A study of the genus *Salvadora*, the patch-nosed snakes. Publ. Univ. California Los Angeles Biol. Sci., 1(10): 177–236.

———, and V. D. Roth. 1966. Ritualistic combat of male gopher snakes, *Pituophis melanoleucus affinis* (Reptilia, Colubridae). Amer. Mus. Novitates, No. 2245, pp. 1–27.

Bonn, E. W., and W. H. McCarley. 1953. The amphibians and reptiles of the Lake Texoma area. Texas J. Sci., 5(4):465–471.

Boyer, D. R. 1957. Sexual dimorphism in a population of the western diamond-backed rattlesnake. Herpetologica, 13:213–217.

Bragg, A. N. 1948. The canebrake rattler in Oklahoma. Proc. Oklahoma Acad. Sci. (for 1947), 28:36–37.

———, et al. 1950. Researches on the Amphibia of Oklahoma. Univ. Oklahoma Press, Norman, Oklahoma, pp. 1–154.

———, and W. N. Bragg. 1957. The southern painted turtle in Oklahoma. Copeia, No. 4, pp. 307–308.

Branson, E. B. 1904. Snakes of Kansas. Kansas Univ. Sci. Bull., 2(13):353–430.

Breckenridge, W. J. 1944. Reptiles and amphibians of Minnesota. Univ. Minnesota Press, Minneapolis, pp. xiii + 202.

Brown, B. C. 1950. An annotated check list of the reptiles and amphibians of Texas. Baylor Univ. Stud., Baylor Univ. Press, Waco, Texas, pp. xii + 259.

Bruner, W. E. 1931. The vegetation of Oklahoma. Ecol. Monogr., 1(2):99–188.

Buck, P., and R. W. Kelting. 1962. A survey of the tall-grass prairie in northeastern Oklahoma. Southwestern Nat., 7(3–4):163–175.

Burger, W. L., Jr. 1947. A taxonomic and statistical study of the keeled green snake, *Opheodrys aestivus*. Bull. Ecol. Soc. Amer., 28(5):54 (abstract).

———. 1948. *Farancia abacura reinwardtii* in Oklahoma. Copeia, No. 2, p. 133.

———. P. W. Smith, and H. M. Smith. 1949. Notable records of reptiles and amphibians in Oklahoma, Arkansas and Texas. J. Tennessee Acad. Sci., 24(2):130–134.

Burt, C. E. 1928a. A key to the species of lizards definitely reported from Kansas. Bristow Enterprise Press (privately printed), pp. 1–2.

343

————. 1928b. The synonomy [*sic*], variation, and distribution of the collared lizard, *Crotaphytus collaris* (Say). Occas. Papers Mus. Zool. Univ. Michigan, No. 196, pp. 1–19.

————. 1931a. A report on some amphibians and reptiles from Kansas, Nebraska, and Oklahoma. Proc. Biol. Soc. Washington, No. 44, pp. 11–16.

————. 1931b. A study of the teiid lizards of the genus *Cnemidophorus* with special reference to their phylogenetic relationships. Bull. U.S. Nat. Mus., No. 154, pp. viii+286.

————. 1935. Further records of the ecology and distribution of amphibians and reptiles in the middle west. Amer. Midland Nat., 16(3):311–336.

————, and M. D. Burt. 1929a. Field notes and locality records on a collection of amphibians and reptiles chiefly from the western half of the United States. II. Reptiles. J. Washington Acad. Sci., 19:448–460.

————, and ————. 1929b. A collection of amphibians and reptiles from the Mississippi Valley, with field observations. Amer. Mus. Novitates, No. 381, pp. 1–14.

————, and W. L. Hoyle. 1935. Additional records of the reptiles of the central prairie region of the United States. Trans. Kansas Acad. Sci. (for 1934), 37:193–216.

Cagle, F. R. 1953. Two new subspecies of *Graptemys pseudogeographica*. Occas. Papers Mus. Zool. Univ. Michigan, No. 546, pp. 1–17.

————. 1954. Two new species of the genus *Graptemys*. Tulane Stud. Zool., 1(11):167–186.

Cahn, A. H. 1937. The turtles of Illinois. Illinois Biol. Monogr., 16(1–2):1–218.

Carpenter, C. C. 1955a. Records of distribution for amphibians and reptiles of Oklahoma. Proc. Oklahoma Acad. Sci. (for 1954), 35:39–41.

————. 1955b. An unusually large diamond-backed water snake (*Natrix rhombifera*) from Buncombe Creek, Lake Texoma. *Ibid.*, 35:42.

————. 1955c. Sounding turtles: a field locating technique. Herpetologica, 11:120.

————. 1956. The amphibians and reptiles of the University of Oklahoma Biological Station area in south central Oklahoma. Proc. Oklahoma Acad. Sci. (for 1955), 36:39–46.

————. 1957a. Carapace pits in the three-toed box turtle, *Terrapene carolina triunguis* (Chelonia-Emydidae). Southwestern Nat. (for 1956), 1(2):83–86.

————. 1957b. An albino speckled king snake. Herpetologica, 13:78.

————. 1957c. Hibernation, hibernacula and associated behavior of the three-toed box turtle (*Terrapene carolina triunguis*). Copeia, No. 4, pp. 278–282.

————. 1958a. Additional distribution records for Oklahoma reptiles. Proc. Oklahoma Acad. Sci. (for 1957), 38:71–74.

————. 1958b. Reproduction, young, eggs and food of Oklahoma snakes. Herpetologica, 14:113–115.

————. 1958c. An unusual Ouachita map turtle. *Ibid.*, 14:116.

————. 1959a. A population of the six-lined racerunner (*Cnemidophorus sexlineatus*). *Ibid.*, 15:81–86.

————. 1959b. A population of *Sceloporus undulatus consobrinus* in south-central Oklahoma. Southwestern Nat., 4(2):110–111.

————. 1959c. Reptiles and amphibians of the Oliver Wildlife Preserve. Proc. Oklahoma Acad. Sci. (for 1956), 37:33–34.

————. 1960a. Aggressive behavior and social dominance in the six-lined racerunner (*Cnemidophorus sexlineatus*). Animal Behaviour, 8(1–2):61–66.

————. 1960b. A large brood of western pigmy rattlesnakes. Herpetologica, 16:142–143.

————. 1960c. Reproduction in Oklahoma *Sceloporus* and *Cnemidophorus*. *Ibid.*, 16:175–182.

————. 1961. Temperature relationships of two Oklahoma lizards. Proc. Oklahoma Acad. Sci. (for 1960), 41:72–77.

————. 1962. Patterns of behavior in two Oklahoma lizards. Amer. Midland Nat., 67(1):132–151.

————, et al. 1961. A *Uta* invasion of Oklahoma. Southwestern Nat., 6(3–4):192–193.

Carr, A. F., Jr. 1938. A new subspecies of *Pseudemys floridana*, with notes on the *floridana* complex. Copeia, No. 3, pp. 105–109.

————. 1949. The identity of *Malacoclemmys kohnii* Baur. Herpetologica, 5:9–10.

————. 1952. Handbook of turtles. The turtles of the United States, Canada, and Baja California. Comstock Publ. Assoc., Cornell Univ. Press, Ithaca, New York, pp. xv + 542.

Carter, W. A. 1966. Distribution records for Oklahoma reptiles. Proc. Oklahoma Acad. Sci. (for 1965), 46:33–36.

————, and R. Cox. 1968. Amphibians and reptiles known from Pontotoc County, Oklahoma. *Ibid.* (for 1966), 47:66–71.

Chenoweth, W. L. 1948. Birth and behavior of young copperheads. Herpetologica, 4:162.

Ciochetti, E. H. 1959. Ophidian notes. *Ibid.*, 15:222.

Cochran, D. M. 1961. Type specimens of reptiles and amphibians in the United States National Museum. Bull. U.S. Nat. Mus., No. 220, pp. xv+291.

Committee on Herpetological Common Names. 1956. Common names for North American amphibians and reptiles. Copeia, No. 3, pp. 172–185.

Conant, R. 1942. Notes on the young of three recently described snakes, with comments upon their relationships. Bull. Chicago Acad. Sci., 6(10):193–200.

————. 1949. Two new races of *Natrix erythrogaster*. Copeia, No. 1, pp. 1–15.

————. 1958. A field guide to reptiles and amphibians of eastern North America. Houghton Mifflin Co., Boston, pp. xv + 366.

————. 1960. The queen snake, *Natrix septemvittata*, in the Interior Highlands of Arkansas and Missouri, with comments upon similar disjunct distributions. Proc. Acad. Nat. Sci. Philadelphia, 112(2):25–40.

————. 1963. Evidence for the specific status of the water snake *Natrix fasciata*. Amer. Mus. Novitates, No. 2122, pp. 1–38.

————. 1969. A review of the water snakes of the genus *Natrix* in Mexico. Bull. Amer. Mus. Nat. Hist., 142:1–140, 22 pls.

————, and C. J. Goin. 1948. A new subspecies of soft-shelled turtle from the central United States, with comments on the application of the name *Amyda*. Occas. Papers Mus. Zool. Univ. Michigan, No. 510, pp. 1–19.

Cope, E. D. 1861. Catalogue of the Colubridae in the museum of the Academy of Natural Sciences of Philadelphia. Part 3. Proc. Acad. Nat. Sci. Philadelphia, [12]:553–566.

——. 1889. On the snakes of Florida. Proc. U.S. Nat. Mus. (for 1888), 11:381–394.

——. 1894. On the Batrachia and Reptilia of the plains at latitude 36° 36'. Proc. Acad. Nat. Sci. Philadelphia (for 1893), [45]:386–387.

——. 1900.The crocodilians, lizards, and snakes of North America. Report U.S. Nat. Mus. for 1898, pp. 153–1270.

Coulter, M. W. 1957. Predation by snapping turtles upon aquatic birds in Maine marshes. J. Wildlife Manag., 21(1):17–21.

Cragin, F. W. 1894. Herpetological notes from Kansas and Texas. Colorado College Stud., 5th Ann. Publ., pp. 37–39.

Cross, F. B., and G. A. Moore. 1952. The fishes of the Poteau River, Oklahoma and Arkansas. Amer. Midland Nat., 47(2):396–412.

Curd, M. R. 1950. The salamander *Amphiuma tridactylum* in Oklahoma. Copeia, No. 4, p. 324.

Day, D. 1962. Pet turtles. Oklahoma Wildlife, 18(5):21.

Dellinger, S. C., and J. D. Black. 1938. Herpetology of Arkansas. Part I. The reptiles. Occas. Papers Univ. Arkansas Mus., 1:1–47.

Diener, R. A. 1957. An ecological study of the plain-bellied water snake. Herpetologica, 13:203–211.

——. 1961. Notes on a bite of the broad-banded copperhead, *Ancistrodon contortrix laticinctus* Gloyd and Conant. *Ibid.*, 17:143–144.

Dixon, J. R. 1965. A taxonomic reevaluation of the night snake *Hypsiglena ochrorhyncha* and relatives. Southwestern Nat., 10(2):125–131.

Dowling, H. G. 1951. A taxonomic study of the ratsnakes, genus *Elaphe* Fitzinger. I. The status of the name *Scotophis laetus* Baird and Girard 1853. Copeia, No. 1, pp. 39–44.

——. 1956. Geographic relations of Ozarkian amphibians and reptiles. Southwestern Nat., 1(4):174–189.

——. 1957. A review of the amphibians and reptiles of Arkansas. Occas. Papers Univ. Arkansas Mus., No. 3, pp. 1–51.

————. 1958. Pleistocene snakes of the Ozark Plateau. Amer. Mus. Novitates, No. 1882, pp. 1–9.

————. 1959. Classification of the Serpentes: A critical review. Copeia, No. 1, pp. 38–52.

Duck, L. G., and J. B. Fletcher. 1943a. A survey of the game and furbearing animals of Oklahoma. Oklahoma Game and Fish Commission, State Bull. 3, Oklahoma City, Oklahoma, pp. 1–144.

————, and ————. 1943b. A game type map of Oklahoma. Oklahoma Game and Fish Department, Oklahoma City, Oklahoma.

Dundee, H. A. 1948. *Storeria occipitomaculata* in Oklahoma. Copeia, No. 3, p. 216.

————. 1950a. Additional records of *Hypsiglena* from Oklahoma, with notes on the behavior and the eggs. Herpetologica, 6:28–30.

————. 1950b. The type locality of *Elaphe l. laeta. Ibid.*, 6:55.

————. 1950c. *Kinosternon subrubrum hippocrepis* (Gray) in Oklahoma. *Ibid.*, 6:138–139.

————, and W. L. Burger, Jr. 1948. A denning aggregation of the western cottonmouth. Nat. Hist. Misc., No. 21, pp. 1–2.

Edgren, R. A. 1952a. Biogeographical and behavioral considerations of the snakes of the genus *Heterodon*. Doctoral dissertation, Northwestern University, Evanston, Illinois, 232 pp., unpublished.

————. 1952b. A synopsis of the snakes of the genus *Heterodon*, with the diagnosis of a new race of *Heterodon nasicus* Baird and Girard. Nat. Hist. Misc., No. 112, pp. 1–4.

————. 1957. Melanism in hog-nosed snakes. Herpetologica, 13: 131–135.

————. 1961. A simplified method for analysis of clines; geographic variation in the hognose snake *Heterodon platyrhinos* Latreille. Copeia, No. 2, pp. 125–132.

Etheridge, R. 1960. The slender glass lizard, *Ophisaurus attenuatus*, from the Pleistocene (Illinoian glacial) of Oklahoma. *Ibid.*, No. 1, pp. 46–47.

Faxon, W. 1915. Relics of Peale's Museum. Bull. Mus. Comp. Zool., 59(3):117–148.

Fitch, H. S. 1940. A biogeographical study of the *ordinoides* artenkreis of garter snakes (genus *Thamnophis*). Univ. California Publ. Zool., 44(1):1–150.

———. 1954. Life history and ecology of the five-lined skink, *Eumeces fasciatus*. Univ. Kansas Publ. Mus. Nat. Hist., 8(1):1–156.

———. 1955. Habits and adaptations of the Great Plains skink (*Eumeces obsoletus*). Ecol. Monogr., 25:59–83.

———. 1960. Autecology of the copperhead. Univ. Kansas Publ. Mus. Nat. Hist., 13(4):85–288.

———. and H. W. Greene. 1965. Breeding cycle in the ground skink, *Lygosoma laterale*. *Ibid.*, 15(11):565–575.

———. and T. P. Maslin. 1961. Occurrence of the garter snake, *Thamnophis sirtalis* in the Great Plains and Rocky Mountains. *Ibid.*, 13(5):289–308.

Force, E. R. 1925a. Notes on reptiles and amphibians of Okmulgee County, Oklahoma. Copeia, No. 141, pp. 25–27.

———. 1925b. Notes on reptiles and amphibians of Okmulgee County, Oklahoma. Proc. Oklahoma Acad. Sci., 5:80–83 (slight modification of Force, 1925a).

———. 1928. A preliminary check list of amphibians and reptiles of Tulsa County, Oklahoma. *Ibid.*, 8:78–79.

———. 1930. The amphibians and reptiles of Tulsa County, Oklahoma, and vicinity. Copeia, No. 2, pp. 25–39.

———. 1931. Habits and birth of young of the lined snake, *Tropidoclonion lineatum* (Hallowell). *Ibid.*, No. 2, pp. 51–53.

———. 1935. A local study of the opisthoglyph snake *Tantilla gracilis* Baird and Girard. Papers Michigan Acad. Sci. Arts Letters (for 1934), 20:645–659.

———. 1936a. Notes on the blind snake, *Leptotyphlops dulcis* (Baird and Girard) in northeastern Oklahoma. Proc. Oklahoma Acad. Sci. (for 1935), 16:24–26.

———. 1936b. The relation of the knobbed anal keels to age and sex in the lined snake *Tropidoclonion lineatum* (Hallowell). Papers Michigan Acad. Sci. Arts Letters, 21:613–617.

———, and N. L. Schmerchel. 1933. Sexual differentiation in the tail length of the lined snake *Tropidoclonion lineatum* (Hallowell). The Biologist, 14(2):70–72.

Foreman, C. T. 1947. The cross timbers. The Star Printery, Muskogee, Oklahoma, pp. 123 [+ 8].

Gehlbach, F. B. 1956. Annotated records of southwestern amphibians and reptiles. Trans. Kansas Acad. Sci., 59(3):364–372.

Glass, B. P. 1949. Records of *Macrochelys temminckii* in Oklahoma. Copeia, No. 2, pp. 138–141.

————, and H. A. Dundee. 1950. *Cnemidophorus tesselatus* (Say) in Oklahoma. Herpetologica, 6:30.

Gloyd, H. K. 1940. The rattlesnakes, genera *Sistrurus* and *Crotalus*. Spec. Publ. Chicago Acad. Sci., No. 4, pp. iii + 266.

————. 1955. A review of the massasaugas, *Sistrurus catenatus*, of the southwestern United States (Serpentes: Crotalidae). Bull. Chicago Acad. Sci., 10(6):83–98.

————. 1969. Two additional subspecies of North American crotalid snakes, genus *Agkistrodon*. Proc. Biol. Soc. Washington, 82:219–232.

————, and R. Conant. 1934. The broad-banded copperhead: a new subspecies of *Agkistrodon mokasen*. Occas. Papers Mus. Zool. Univ. Michigan, No. 283, pp. 1–5.

————, and ————. 1938. The subspecies of the copperhead, *Agkistrodon mokasen* Beauvois. Bull. Chicago Acad. Sci., 5(7): 163–166.

————, and ————. 1943. A synopsis of the American forms of *Agkistrodon* (copperheads and moccasins). Bull. Chicago Acad. Sci., 7(2):147–170.

Gould, C. N. 1933. Oklahoma place names. Oklahoma Univ. Press, Norman, Oklahoma, 146 pp.

Grobman, A. B. 1941. A contribution to the knowledge of variation in *Opheodrys vernalis* (Harlan), with the description of a new subspecies. Misc. Publ. Mus. Zool. Univ. Michigan, No. 50, pp. 1–38.

Hallowell, E. 1852. Descriptions of new species of reptiles inhabiting North America. Proc. Acad. Nat. Sci. Philadelphia, 6(5):177–182.

————. 1854. Reptiles (pp. 106–147, pls. 1–10, XI–XIII, 13, XIV–XVIII, 20). In L. Sitgreaves, Report of an expedition down the Zuni and Colorado rivers in 1851. U.S. 33rd Congress, 1st Session, Senate Exec. Document, Washington, 198 pp.

———. 1857. Notice of a collection of reptiles from Kansas and Nebraska, presented to the Academy of Natural Sciences, by Dr. Hammond, U.S.A. Proc. Acad. Nat. Sci. Philadelphia, 8(5):238–253.

Harney, L. 1955. Notes on the food habits of three common lizards of southern Oklahoma. Proc. Oklahoma Acad. Sci. (for 1953), 34:85–86.

Harwood, P. D. 1931. Some parasites of Oklahoma turtles. J. Parasit., 18(2):98–101.

Hibbard, C. W. 1960. An interpretation of Pliocene and Pleistocene climates in North America. Michigan Acad. Sci. Arts Letters, 62nd Ann. Report (for 1959–1960), pp. 5–30.

———. 1963. The presence of *Macroclemys* and *Chelydra* in the Rexroad fauna from the Upper Pliocene of Kansas. Copeia, No. 4, pp. 708–709.

Hughes, W. 1947. Rattlesnake roundup. Oklahoma Game and Fish News, 3(5):4–5, 16.

———. 1950. Exit-rattlers. *Ibid.*, 6(5):12–13.

———. 1954. Hallowe'en spookface on the cover. *Ibid.*, 10(10):10.

Huheey, J. E. 1959. Distribution and variation in the glossy snake, *Natrix rigida* (Say). Copeia, No. 4, pp. 303–311.

Hurter, J., and J. K. Strecker. 1909. Amphibians and reptiles of Arkansas. Trans. Acad. Sci. St. Louis, 18(2):11–27.

James, E. 1823. Account of an expedition from Pittsburgh to the Rocky Mountains, performed in the years 1819 and '20. H. C. Carey and I. Lea, Philadelphia, Vol. 2, pp. 442 + XCVIII.

Jenni, B. 1954. Two tails odd but not a freak. Oklahoma Fish and Game News, 10(9):11.

———. 1955. Wake up! It's 58° Fahrenheit. *Ibid.*, 11(4):10.

———. 1958. Look Out! Rattler! Oklahoma Wildlife, 14(4):9, illus.

———. 1966. Combat dance of the male rattlesnake rarely seen by man! Outdoor Oklahoma, 22(5):6–7.

Jones, J. P. 1926. The proper name for *Sceloporus consobrinus* Baird and Girard. Occas. Papers Univ. Michigan Mus. Zool., No. 172, pp. 1–3.

Kassing, E. F. 1961. A life history study of the Great Plains ground snake, *Sonora episcopa episcopa* (Kennicott). Texas J. Sci., 13(2): 185–203.

Kessler, E. 1966. A storm's incalculable energy. Nat. Hist., 75(4): 12–17.

Kennicott, R. 1859. Notes on *Coluber calligaster* of Say, and a description of new species of serpents in the collection of the Northwestern University of Evanston, Illinois. Proc. Acad. Nat. Sci. Philadelphia, [11]:98–100.

Kern, G. W. 1956. A shrew eaten by a king snake, *Lampropeltis calligaster* (Harlan). Herpetologica, 12:135.

Kinsey, A. 1952. The snake with a noisy tail. Oklahoma Game and Fish News, 8(6):8–10.

———. 1956. Cottonmouths crawl at night. *Ibid.*, 12(9):4.

Kirn, A. J., W. L. Burger, Jr., and H. M. Smith. 1949. The subspecies of *Tantilla gracilis*. Amer. Midland Nat., 42(1):238–251.

Klau, H. H., and P. R. David. 1952. The bimodality of length distribution in *Heterodon p. platyrhinos* L. and its relation to the season in which the specimens were collected. *Ibid.*, 47(2):364–371.

Klauber, L. M. 1930. Differential characteristics of southwestern rattlesnakes allied to *Crotalus atrox*. Bull. Zool. Soc. San Diego, 6:1–72.

———. 1940. The worm snakes of the genus *Leptotyphlops* in the United States and northern Mexico. Trans. San Diego Soc. Nat. Hist., 9(18):87–162.

———. 1946. The glossy snake, *Arizona*, with descriptions of new subspecies. *Ibid.*, 10(17):311–398.

———. 1956. Rattlesnakes. Their habits, life histories, and influence on mankind. Volumes I and II. Univ. California Press, Berkeley, California, 1476 pp.

Knopf, G. N., and D. W. Tinkle. 1961. The distribution and habits of *Sistrurus catenatus* in northeast Texas. Herpetologica, 17:126–131.

Kolb, D. W. 1946. Snake story. Oklahoma Game and Fish News, 2(10):22.

Kuntz, R. E. 1940. *Hypsiglena ochrorhynchus* in Oklahoma. Copeia, No. 2, p. 136.

Lagler, K. F. 1943. Food habits and economic relations of the turtles of Michigan with especial reference to fish management. Amer. Midland Nat., 29(2):257–312.

———. 1945. Economic relations and utilization of turtles. Invest. Indiana Lakes Streams, 3(2):139–165.

Lane, H. H. 1909. *Alligator mississippiensis* in Oklahoma. Science, N. S., 30(782):923–924.

Laughlin, H. E. 1959. Stomach contents of some aquatic snakes from Lake McAlester, Pittsburgh [*sic*] County, Oklahoma. Texas J. Sci., 11(1):83–85.

———. 1964. Some distributional records of amphibians and reptiles from southeastern Oklahoma. Proc. Oklahoma Acad. Sci. (for 1963), 44:61–63.

Legler, J. M. 1960. Natural history of the ornate box turtle, *Terrapene ornata ornata* Agassiz. Univ. Kansas Publ. Mus. Nat. Hist., 11(10):527–669.

Little, E. L., Jr. 1939. The vegetation of the Caddo County Canyons, Oklahoma. Ecology, 20(1):1–10.

Lowe, C. H., Jr. 1966. The prairie lined racerunner. J. Arizona Acad. Sci., 4(1):44–45.

Mahaffey, J. 1954. Snakes alive! Oklahoma Game and Fish News, 10(9):10–11.

Mahmoud, I. Y. 1967. Courtship behavior and sexual maturity in four species of kinosternid turtles. Copeia, No. 2, pp. 314–319.

———. 1969. Comparative ecology of the kinosternid turtles of Oklahoma. Southwestern Nat., 14(1):31–66.

Marr, J. C. 1944. Notes on amphibians and reptiles from the central United States. Amer. Midland Nat., 32(2):478–490.

Maslin, T. P. 1950. Herpetological notes and records from Colorado. Herpetologica, 6:89–95.

———. 1953. The status of the whipsnake *Masticophis flagellum* (Shaw) in Colorado. *Ibid.*, 9:193–200.

———. 1956. *Sceloporus undulatus erythrocheilus* ssp. nov. (Reptilia, Iguanidae) from Colorado. *Ibid.*, 12(4):291–294.

———. 1959. An annotated check list of the amphibians and reptiles of Colorado. Univ. Colorado Stud. Ser. Biol., No. 6, pp. vi + 98.

McConkey, E. H. 1954. A systematic study of the North American lizards of the genus *Ophisaurus*. Amer. Midland Nat., 51(1): 133–171.

McCoy, C. J., Jr. 1958. Daily activity of some Oklahoma lizards. Ohio Herpetol. Soc. Trimonthly Rep., 1(3):12 (reprinted January 1, 1961).

————. 1960a. New county records and range extensions for Oklahoma reptiles. Proc. Oklahoma Acad. Sci. (for 1959), 40:41–43.

————. 1960b. Systematics and variation of *Sceloporus undulatus* in Oklahoma. Dissertation for degree of Master of Science, Oklahoma State University, 55 pp.

————. 1960c. An unusually large aggregation of *Leptotyphlops*. Copeia, No. 4, p. 368.

————. 1961a. Distribution of the subspecies of *Sceloporus undulatus* (Reptilia: Iguanidae) in Oklahoma. Southwestern Nat., 6(2):79–85.

————. 1961b. Birth season and young of *Crotalus scutulatus* and *Agkistrodon contortrix laticinctus*. Herpetologica, 17:140.

————. 1961c. A technique for collecting in urban areas. J. Ohio Herp. Soc., 3(1):4.

————. 1961d. *Thamnophis marcianus* in central Oklahoma. *Ibid.*, 3(2):23–24.

————. 1968. The development of melanism in an Oklahoma population of *Chrysemys scripta elegans* (Reptilia: Testudinidae). Proc. Oklahoma Acad. Sci. (for 1966), 47:84–87.

McCracken, W. A. 1966. The reptiles of Woods County, Oklahoma. Dissertation for degree of Master of Science, Oklahoma State University, 34 pp., unpublished.

McMullen, D. B. 1940. Cutaneous myiasis in a box turtle. Proc. Oklahoma Acad. Sci. (for 1939), 20:23–25.

Milstead, W. W. 1967. Fossil box turtles (*Terrapene*) from central North America, and box turtles of eastern Mexico. Copeia, No. 1, pp. 168–179.

————. 1969. Studies on the evolution of box turtles (genus *Terrapene*). Bull. Florida State Mus. Biol. Sci., 14(1):1–113.

Mittleman, M. B. 1949. Geographic variation in Marcy's garter snake, *Thamnophis marcianus* (Baird and Girard). Bull. Chicago Acad. Sci., 8(10):235–249.

Moore, G. A., and C. C. Rigney. 1942. Notes on the herpetology of Payne County, Oklahoma. Proc. Oklahoma Acad. Sci. (for 1941), 22:77–80.

Morris, J. W., and E. C. McReynolds. 1965. Historical atlas of Oklahoma. Univ. Oklahoma Press, Norman, Oklahoma, pp. V–VII + 70 + IX–XXX.

Moss, D. 1955. The effect of the slider turtle *"Pseudemys Scripta Scripta"* (Schoepff) on the production of fish in farm ponds. Proc. Southeastern Assoc. Game Fish Commissioners Meeting, Daytona Beach, Florida, October 2–5, 1955, pp. 97–100.

Ortenburger, A. I. 1923. The status of *Sonora semiannulata* and *Sonora episcopa*. Copeia, No. 120, pp. 79–81.

———. 1925. A preliminary list of the snakes of Oklahoma. Proc. Oklahoma Acad. Sci., 5:83–87.

———. 1926a. Reptiles and amphibians collected in the Wichita Mts., Comanche County, Oklahoma. Copeia, No. 155, pp. 137–138.

———. 1926b. Reptiles and amphibians collected in the Arbuckle Mts., Murray County, Oklahoma. *Ibid.*, No. 156, pp. 145–146.

———. 1927a. A report on the amphibians and reptiles of Oklahoma. Proc. Oklahoma Acad. Sci. (for 1926), 6:89–100.

———. 1927b. A key to the snakes of Oklahoma. *Ibid.*, 6:197–218.

———. 1927c. A list of reptiles and amphibians from the Oklahoma panhandle. Copeia, No. 163, pp. 46–48.

———. 1928a. Plant collections representative of some typical communities of western Oklahoma. Proc. Oklahoma Acad. Sci., 8:49–52.

———. 1928b. Plant collections representative of some typical communities of eastern Oklahoma. *Ibid.*, 8:53–67.

———. 1928c. The whip snakes and racers: genera *Masticophis* and *Coluber*. Mem. Univ. Michigan Mus., 1:xvii + 247.

———. 1929a. Reptiles and amphibians from southeastern Oklahoma and southwestern Arkansas. Copeia, No. 170, pp. 8–12.

———. 1929b. Reptiles and amphibians from northeastern Oklahoma. *Ibid.*, No. 170, pp. 26–28.

———. 1930a. Reptiles and amphibians from Pawnee County, Oklahoma. *Ibid.*, No. 173, pp. 94–95.

———. 1930b. A key to the lizards and snakes of Oklahoma. Publ. Univ. Oklahoma Biol. Surv., 2(4):209–239.

———, and R. D. Bird. 1933. The ecology of the western Oklahoma salt plains. *Ibid.*, 5(3):49–64.

———, and B. Freeman. 1930. Notes on some reptiles and amphibians from western Oklahoma. *Ibid.*, 2(4):175–188.

Penfound, W. T. 1962. The savannah concept in Oklahoma. Ecology, 43(4):774–775.

Peters, J. A. 1951. Studies on the lizard *Holbrookia texana* (Troschel) with descriptions of two new subspecies. Occas. Papers Mus. Zool. Univ. Michigan, No. 537, pp. 1–20.

Preston, J. R., and W. L. Pratt, Jr. 1962. An eastward range extension of *Uta stansburiana stejnegeri*. Herpetologica, 18:53.

Ramsey, L. W. 1951. New localities for several Texas snakes. *Ibid.*, 7:176.

———. 1953. The lined snake, *Tropidoclonion lineatum* (Hallowell). *Ibid.*, 9:7–24.

Raun, G. G. 1965. A guide to Texas snakes. Mus. Notes No. 9, Texas Memorial Mus., 85 pp.

Reeve, W. L. 1952. Taxonomy and distribution of the horned lizards genus *Phrynosoma*. Univ. Kansas Sci. Bull., 34(14):817–960.

Rice, E. L., and W. T. Penfound. 1959. The upland forests of Oklahoma. Ecology, 40(4):593–608.

Rossman, D. A. 1963. The colubrid snake genus *Thamnophis*: A revision of the *sauritus* group. Bull. Florida St. Mus. Biol. Sci., 7(3):99–178.

Ruthven, A. G. 1908. Variations and genetic relationships of the garter-snakes. Bull. U.S. Nat. Mus., No. 61, pp. xii + 201.

Schmidt, K. P. 1919. Rediscovery of *Amphiardis inornatus* (Garman), with notes on other specimens from Oklahoma. Copeia, No. 73, pp. 71–73.

———. 1953. A check list of North American amphibians and reptiles. Sixth ed., Amer. Soc. Ichth. Herp., Univ. Chicago Press, pp. viii + 280.

Schwartz, A. 1956. Geographic variation in the chicken turtle. Fieldiana Zoology, 34(41):461–503.

Self, J. T. 1938. Note on the food habits of *Chelydra serpentina.* Copeia, No. 4, p. 200.

Shirk, G. H. 1965. Oklahoma place names. Univ. Oklahoma Press, Norman, Oklahoma, pp. xv + 233.

Sisk, M. E., and C. J. McCoy, Jr. 1964. Stomach contents of *Natrix r. rhombifera* (Reptilia: Serpentes) from an Oklahoma lake. Proc. Oklahoma Acad. Sci. (for 1963), 44:68–71.

Smith, C. C., and G. Acker. 1940. A collection of reptiles from Logan County, Oklahoma. *Ibid.* (for 1939), 20:65.

Smith, A. G. 1949. The subspecies of the plains garter snake, *Thamnophis radix.* Bull. Chicago Acad. Sci., 8(14):285–300.

Smith, H. M. 1938. Remarks on the status of the subspecies of *Sceloporus undulatus,* with descriptions of new species and subspecies of the *undulatus* group. Occas. Papers Univ. Michigan Mus. Zool., No. 387, pp. 1–17.

———. 1941. Synonymy of *Tantilla nigriceps fumiceps* Cope. Copeia, No. 2, p. 112.

———. 1942. A resumé of Mexican snakes of the genus *Tantilla.* Zoologica, 27(7):33–42.

———. 1944. Snakes of the Hoogstraal expeditions to northern Mexico. Zool. Ser. Field Mus. Nat. Hist., 29(8):135–152.

———. 1946. Hybridization between two species of garter snakes. Univ. Kansas Publ. Mus. Nat. Hist., 1(14):97–100.

———. 1950. Handbook of amphibians and reptiles of Kansas. Misc. Publ. Mus. Nat. Hist. Univ. Kansas, No. 2, pp. 1–336.

———. 1956. Handbook of amphibians and reptiles of Kansas. *Ibid.,* second ed., No. 9, pp. 1–356.

———. 1965. Two new colubrid snakes from the United States and Mexico. J. Ohio Herp. Soc., 5(1):1–4.

———, and A. B. Leonard. 1934. Distributional records of reptiles and amphibians in Oklahoma. Amer. Midland Nat., 15(2):190–196.

———, T. P. Maslin, and R. L. Brown. 1965. Summary of the distribution of the herpetofauna of Colorado. A supplement to an annotated check list of the amphibians and reptiles of Colorado. Univ. Colorado Stud. Ser. Biol., No. 15, pp. 1–52.

———, and O. Sanders. 1952. Distributional data on Texas amphibians and reptiles. Texas J. Sci., 4(2):204–219.

———, and J. L. Slater. 1949. The southern races of *Eumeces septentrionalis* (Baird). Trans. Kansas Acad. Sci., 52(4):438–448.

———, and E. H. Taylor. 1950. Type localities of Mexican reptiles and amphibians. Univ. Kansas Sci. Bull., 33(8):313–380.

Smith, P. W. 1956. Extension of known range of the flatheaded snake. Herpetologica, 12:327.

———. 1961. The amphibians and reptiles of Illinois. Bull. Illinois Nat. Hist. Surv., No. 28 (art. 1), pp. 1–298.

———, and H. M. Smith. 1952. Geographic variation in the lizard *Eumeces anthracinus*. Univ. Kansas Sci. Bull., 34:679–694.

———, and ———. 1962. The systematic and biogeographic status of two Illinois snakes. Occas. Papers Adams Center Ecol. Stud., No. 5, pp. 1–10.

Snider, L. C. 1917. Geography of Oklahoma. Bull. Oklahoma Geol. Surv., 27:1–325.

Stebbins, R. C. 1954. Amphibians and reptiles of western North America. McGraw-Hill Book Co., Inc., New York, pp. xxii + 528.

———. 1966. A field guide to western reptiles and amphibians. Houghton Mifflin Co., Boston, pp. xiv + 279.

Stejneger, L. 1890. Annotated list of reptiles and batrachians collected by Dr. C. Hart Merriam and Vernon Bailey on the San Francisco Mountain Plateau and desert of the Little Colorado, Arizona, with descriptions of new species. North Amer. Fauna, 3(pt. 5):103–118.

———. 1938. Restitution of the name *Ptychemys hoyi* Agassiz for a western river tortoise. Proc. Biol. Soc. Washington, No. 51, pp. 173–176.

———, and T. Barbour. 1933. A check list of North American amphibians and reptiles. Third ed., Harvard Univ. Press, Cambridge, Massachusetts, pp. xiv + 185.

———, and ———. 1943. A check list of North American amphibians and reptiles. Fifth ed., Bull. Mus. Comp. Zool., 93(1): xix + 260.

Stone, W. 1903. A collection of reptiles and batrachians from Arkansas, Indian Territory and western Texas. Proc. Acad. Nat. Sci. Philadelphia, 55:538–542.

Story, J. H. 1958. Senior citizen likes rattlesnake hunting. Oklahoma Wildlife, 14(9):20.

Stull, O. G. 1940. Variations and relationships in the snakes of the genus *Pituophis*. Bull. U.S. Nat. Mus., No. 175, pp. i + 225.

Sturgis, R. S. 1939. The Wichita Mountains Wildlife Refuge. Chicago Nat., 2(1):9–20.

Tanner, W. W., and R. B. Loomis. 1957. A taxonomic and distributional study of the western subspecies of the milk snake, *Lampropeltis doliata*. Trans. Kansas Acad. Sci., 60(1):12–42.

Taylor, E. H. 1932. *Eumeces laticeps*: A neglected species of skink. Univ. Kansas Sci. Bull., 20(14):263–271.

———. 1936. A taxonomic study of the cosmopolitan scincoid lizards of the genus *Eumeces* with an account of the distribution and relationships of its species. *Ibid*. (for 1935), 36(14):1–643.

———. 1937. Notes and comments on certain American and Mexican snakes of the genus *Tantilla* with descriptions of new species. Trans. Kansas Acad. Sci. (for 1936), 39:335–348.

———. 1938. Notes on the herpetological fauna of the Mexican state of Sinaloa. Univ. Kansas Sci. Bull. (for 1936), 24(20): 505–537.

Taylor, R. J., and H. Laughlin. 1964. Additions to the herpetofauna of Bryan County, Oklahoma. Southwestern Nat., 9(1):41–43.

Taylor, W. E. 1895. The box tortoises of North America. Proc. U.S. Nat. Mus., 17(1019):573–588.

Tinkle, D. W., and G. N. Knopf. 1964. Biologically significant distribution records for amphibians and reptiles in northwest Texas. Herpetologica, 20:42–47.

Thoburn, J. B. 1916. A standard history of Oklahoma. Volumes I and II. Amer. Historical Soc., Chicago and New York, pp. lvi + 448; viii + 449–947.

Trapido, H. 1944. The snakes of the genus *Storeria*. Amer. Midland Nat., 31(1):1–84.

Trowbridge, A. H. 1937. Ecological observations on amphibians and reptiles collected in southeastern Oklahoma during the summer of 1934. Amer. Midland Nat., 18(2):285–303.

Twente, J. W., Jr. 1955. Aspects of a population study of cavern-dwelling bats. J. Mamm., 36(3):379–390.

Van Denburgh, J. 1924. Notes on the herpetology of New Mexico, with a list of species known from that state. Proc. California Acad. Sci., Fourth Ser., 13(12):189–230.

Vanderpol, Mrs. Bert. 1955. Horned toads. Oklahoma Game and Fish News, 11(6):inside back cover.

Van Vleet, A. H. 1902. Snakes of Oklahoma. Terr. Oklahoma Dep't Geol. Nat. Hist., Second Bienn. Rep. (for 1901–1902), pp. 167–173.

Weaver, W. G., Jr., and F. L. Rose. 1967. Systematics, fossil history, and evolution of the genus *Chrysemys*. Tulane Stud. Zool., 14(2): 63–73.

Webb, R. G. 1950. Range extension of the chicken turtle in Oklahoma. Herpetologica, 6:137–138.

————. 1956. Size at sexual maturity in the male softshell turtle, *Trionyx ferox emoryi*. Copeia, No. 2:121–122.

————. 1961. Observations on the life histories of turtles (genus *Pseudemys* and *Graptemys*) in Lake Texoma, Oklahoma. Amer. Midland Nat., 65(1):193–214.

————. 1962. North American Recent soft-shelled turtles (Family Trionychidae). Univ. Kansas Publ. Mus. Nat. Hist., 13(10): 429–611.

————, and A. I. Ortenburger. 1955. Reptiles of the Wichita Mountains Wildlife Refuge, Comanche County, Oklahoma. Proc. Oklahoma Acad. Sci. (for 1953), 34:87–92.

Webster, E. B. 1936. A preliminary list of the reptiles and amphibians of Pottawatomie County, Oklahoma, near Shawnee. *Ibid.*, 16:20–22.

Werler, J. E. 1964. Poisonous snakes of Texas and first aid treatment of their bites. Texas Parks and Wildlife Dept. Bull., No. 31, Austin, Texas, 62 pp.

Wickham, M. M. 1922a. Notes on the migration of *Macrochelys lacertina*. Proc. Oklahoma Acad. Sci., 2:20–22.

———. 1922b. Further notes on the migration of *Terrapene carolina* in Oklahoma. *Ibid.*, 2:22.

Wiedeman, V. E., and W. T. Penfound. 1960. A preliminary study of the shinnery in Oklahoma. Southwestern Nat., 5(3):117–122.

Williams, K. L., B. C. Brown, and L. D. Wilson. 1966. A new subspecies of the colubrid snake *Cemophora coccinea* (Blumenbach) from southern Texas. Texas J. Sci., 18(1):85–88.

———, and L. D. Wilson. 1967. A review of the colubrid snake genus *Cemophora* Cope. Tulane Stud. Zool., 13(4):103–124.

Woodburne, M. O. 1956. Notes on the snake *Sistrurus catenatus tergeminus* in southwestern Kansas and northwestern Oklahoma. Copeia, No. 2, pp. 125–126.

———. 1959. A fossil alligator from the Lower Pliocene of Oklahoma and its climatic significance. Papers Michigan Acad. Sci. Arts Letters (for 1958), 44:47–51.

Wright, A. H., and A. A. Wright. 1952. List of the snakes of the United States and Canada by states and provinces. Amer. Midland Nat., 48(3):574–603.

———, and ———. 1957. Handbook of snakes of the United States and Canada. Volume II. Comstock Publ. Assoc., Cornell Univ. Press, pp. ix + 565–1105.

Wyatt, F. S., and G. Rainey. 1919. Brief history of Oklahoma. Webb Publ. Co., Oklahoma City, Oklahoma, 135 pp.

Yarrow, H. C. 1882. Check list of North American Reptilia and Batrachia, with catalog of specimens in U.S. National Museum. Bull. U.S. Nat. Mus., No. 24, pp. [v +] 249.

———. 1883. Description of new species of reptiles in the United States National Museum. Proc. U.S. Nat. Mus., 6:152–154.

Index

365